Britain's Economic Performance

RICHARD E. CAVES AND LAWRENCE B. KRAUSE
Editors

Britain's Economic Performance

RUDIGER DORNBUSCH AND STANLEY FISCHER

DAVID C. SMITH

RICHARD E. CAVES

JOSEPH A. PECHMAN

MARSHALL E. BLUME

HENDRIK S. HOUTHAKKER

THE BROOKINGS INSTITUTION
Washington, D.C.

Library of Congress Cataloging in Publication Data:

Main entry under title:

Britain's economic performance.

    Includes bibliographical references and index.
    1. Great Britain—Economic policy—1945–
—Addresses, essays, lectures.   I. Caves, Richard E.
II. Krause, Lawrence B
HC256.6.B7298   338.941   79-3773
ISBN 0-8157-1320-7
ISBN 0-8157-1319-3 (pbk.)

1 2 3 4 5 6 7 8 9

THE BROOKINGS INSTITUTION is an independent organization devoted to nonpartisan research, education, and publication in economics, government, foreign policy, and the social sciences generally. Its principal purposes are to aid in the development of sound public policies and to promote public understanding of issues of national importance.

The Institution was founded on December 8, 1927, to merge the activities of the Institute for Government Research, founded in 1916, the Institute of Economics, founded in 1922, and the Robert Brookings Graduate School of Economics and Government, founded in 1924.

The Board of Trustees is responsible for the general administration of the Institution, while the immediate direction of the policies, program, and staff is vested in the President, assisted by an advisory committee of the officers and staff. The by-laws of the Institution state: "It is the function of the Trustees to make possible the conduct of scientific research, and publication, under the most favorable conditions, and to safeguard the independence of the research staff in the pursuit of their studies and in the publication of the results of such studies. It is not a part of their function to determine, control, or influence the conduct of particular investigations or the conclusions reached."

The President bears final responsibility for the decision to publish a manuscript as a Brookings book. In reaching his judgment on the competence, accuracy, and objectivity of each study, the President is advised by the director of the appropriate research program and weighs the views of a panel of expert outside readers who report to him in confidence on the quality of the work. Publication of a work signifies that it is deemed a competent treatment worthy of public consideration but does not imply endorsement of conclusions or recommendations.

The Institution maintains its position of neutrality on issues of public policy in order to safeguard the intellectual freedom of the staff. Hence interpretations or conclusions in Brookings publications should be understood to be solely those of the authors and should not be attributed to the Institution, to its trustees, officers, or other staff members, or to the organizations that support its research.

Foreword

IN THE LATE 1960s a team of American and Canadian economists organized by the Brookings Institution surveyed the structural and policy issues affecting the performance of the British economy. Their findings appeared in *Britain's Economic Prospects,* a Brookings book by Richard E. Caves and associates that was published in 1968.

In the late 1970s, Britain faced economic problems that were somewhat similar to those of the 1960s, yet different in several ways. North Sea oil and gas had begun to flow, and balance-of-payments constraints had been eased by the advent of flexible exchange rates. But labor relations had worsened, the inflation rate had risen, and Britain's rate of economic growth had fallen further behind those of other European countries. At the same time the U.S. economy had begun to show symptoms of the British disease: terms of trade declined, productivity grew more slowly, and macroeconomic policy failed to meet its objectives. Some observers detected in the dialogue over U.S. policy a yearning for scapegoats long familiar to many Britons.

For these reasons it seemed desirable to prepare a sequel to *Britain's Economic Prospects,* and in 1978 another team of American and Canadian economists headed by Richard E. Caves and Lawrence B. Krause was formed to undertake the primary research. In contrast to the earlier project, a narrower range of topics was selected, and British critics were brought in at the outset rather than left to fire their volleys after the Brookings book appeared. Caves and Krause organized the volume, selected topics, and chose authors with the aid of much good advice secured in both Britain and America. The resulting papers became the subject of a conference held in May 1979 at Ditchley Park, England; the conference participants (listed on pp. 381–82) included the discussants whose formal comments appear in this volume and a group of distinguished observers of the British economy. After the conference, the North American authors were allowed time for a final revision of their drafts and some second thoughts on their conclusions before the volume went to press.

The project benefited greatly from the cooperation of the National Institute of Economic and Social Research in London and its director, Mr. G. D. N. Worswick. The Institute organized the conference at Ditchley Park, provided a base of operations, and made it possible for the North American investigators working in England to meet and talk with British economists, government officials, and others in Britain who responded to queries with the traditional—and admirable—British patience and generosity. The project was made possible by grants from the George Soros Charitable Trust to the Brookings Institution and from the German Marshall Fund to the National Institute of Economic and Social Research.

The manuscript was edited by Caroline Lalire. The risk of factual error was minimized by the work of Judith L. Cameron, Ellen W. Smith, and Clifford A. Wright. The index was prepared by Diana Regenthal.

The views expressed in this book are those of its contributors and should not be ascribed to the other staff members, officers, or trustees of the Brookings Institution, to the National Institute of Economic and Social Research, to the George Soros Charitable Trust, or to the German Marshall Fund.

BRUCE K. MAC LAURY
President

June 1980
Washington, D.C.

Contents

Tables

Contents

Figures

Britain's Economic
Performance

RICHARD E. CAVES AND LAWRENCE B. KRAUSE

Introduction and Summary

MORE THAN a decade has passed since the Brookings Institution published the book by Richard E. Caves and Associates entitled *Britain's Economic Prospects* (April 1968). Attention was drawn to Britain at that time because the economy was perceived to be underperforming. But at the outset of that book it was noted that "Britain's economic performance since World War II outstrips any earlier period in the past half century."[1] Thus, measured by Britain's own economic history, the postwar record through 1967 was one of success, not failure.

It was only when one compared Britain to other European industrial countries and Japan, which had accomplished economic miracles, that the U.K. performance appeared inadequate. As seen in table 1, the U.K. growth rate of gross domestic product (GDP) between 1957 and 1967 was only 65 percent of the average rate for member states of the Organisation for Economic Co-operation and Development (OECD). It was below that of the slow-growing United States, only about one-half of the growth rate of France and West Germany, and less than one-third of that of Japan. Still, in 1967 the per capita GDP of Britain trailed only that of the United States; it was about the same as those of France and Germany and decidedly higher than that of Japan (table 2).[2] Observers were dissatisfied with Britain's economic performance, therefore, because they

1. Page 3. A similar statement appears on page 231.
2. Absolute comparisons of standards of living are fraught with statistical and analytical difficulties. The British standard of living might well have been much higher. Thus only rough orders of magnitude are implied for a single-year comparison as well as for changes over time. Alternative measures are shown in table 3.

saw the United Kingdom underperforming other countries more or less similarly situated and believed that the United Kingdom could more nearly match their accomplishments.

The Period 1967–78

How well has Britain achieved its macroeconomic goals of economic growth, price stability, and balance-of-payments equilibrium since 1967? With respect to economic growth the record is far from distinguished: Britain did not rise in the international growth rankings. All OECD countries grew more slowly on average during the 1967–78 period than in 1957–67 (table 1), but Britain's growth rate declined a bit more and reached only 60 percent of the OECD average. And Britain's growth no longer compared so favorably with its own previous growth.

Interestingly enough, during the first part of the 1967–68 period the United Kingdom showed no evidence of a deteriorating growth performance. In fact Britain grew a bit faster annually from 1967 through 1973 than it had in 1957–67 and reached 70 percent of the OECD average. During this period the United States was the only major industrial country evidencing some slowing of growth. Subsequently the story is different. Although every OECD country had a difficult time from 1973 through 1978, Britain's experience worsened in that its growth was 1.1 percent a year, only 45 percent of the average of 2.5 percent for all OECD countries.

Comparisons of levels of GDP per capita measured at current exchange rates also came out less favorable to Britain in 1978 than in 1967 (table 2). Britain's per capita GDP in 1978 was decidedly less than that of West Germany, which had apparently moved ahead of the United States. Britain had also been overtaken by France and Japan and indeed looked poor beside the OECD countries taken as a whole.

The comparisons in table 2 depend on market exchange rates, which are known to deviate from purchasing-power equivalents—the conversion factors needed to compare real products per capita of different countries. These purchasing-power measures and the resulting estimates of real GDP per capita are shown in table 3. The data are indexes of real GDP per capita relative to the United States for the years 1967 and 1975. The differences from the United States in levels of income vary from those indicated in table 2, but the rank ordering of countries does not vary much.

Table 1. *Average Annual Growth Rates of Gross Domestic Product or Gross National Product for the United Kingdom, Four Other Industrial Countries, and OECD Countries as a Whole, Selected Periods, 1957–78*

Percent

	Main periods		Subperiods	
Country	1957–67	1967–78	1967–73	1973–78
United Kingdom[a]	3.1	2.3	3.4	1.1
United States[b]	4.1	3.0	3.5	2.4
Japan[b]	10.4	7.2	10.2	3.7
France[a]	5.6	4.4	5.6	2.9
West Germany[b]	5.5	3.8	5.3	2.0
All OECD countries	4.8[c]	3.8[d]	4.8[d]	2.5[d]

Sources: Organisation for Economic Co-operation and Development, *Main Economic Indicators* (Paris: OECD, various issues); and *OECD Economic Outlook* (Paris: OECD, July 1979).

a. GDP.
b. GNP.
c. Based on 1970 GNP or GDP weights and exchange rates.
d. Based on 1977 GNP or GDP weights and exchange rates.

Table 2. *Per Capita GDP of the United Kingdom, Four Other Industrial Countries, and OECD Countries as a Whole, 1967 and 1978*

Current U.S. dollars at current exchange rates

Country	1967	Country	1978
United States	4,040	West Germany	10,347
All OECD countries	2,290	United States	9,588
France	2,190	France	8,760
West Germany	2,030	Japan	8,386
United Kingdom	1,980	All OECD countries	7,683
Japan	1,150	United Kingdom	5,496

Source: OECD, *Main Economic Indicators* (various issues).

Table 3. *Indexes of Real GDP per Capita for the United Kingdom and Five Other Industrial Countries, 1967 and 1975*

United States = 100

Country	1967	Country	1975
United States	100.0	United States	100.0
West Germany	76.9	France	79.5
France	75.4	West Germany	79.2
United Kingdom	61.9	Japan	65.1
Italy	49.9	United Kingdom	62.0
Japan	48.3	Italy	47.1

Source: Irving B. Kravis, Alan Heston, and Robert Summers, *International Comparisons of Real Product and Purchasing Power* (Johns Hopkins University Press, 1978), p. 133.

In 1967 the United Kingdom's income per capita exceeded only those of Japan and Italy. By 1975 (the latest data available) the United Kingdom had been passed by Japan, though not by Italy. Between 1967 and 1975 the United Kingdom's position deteriorated substantially in relation to Japan's and moderately in relation to France's and Germany's; it remained unchanged relative to the United States' position and improved only with respect to Italy's. To the degree that economic theory gives any guidance, one would expect that those countries starting at the lowest level of per capita income would make the greatest advance. Japan did, but the performance of both Italy and the United Kingdom was disappointing by this criterion.

Britain can also take little comfort from the way it handled the problem of inflation. Up through 1967 Britain's inflation rate was fairly moderate, no greater than that of other industrial countries (except West Germany) and less than that of Japan. After 1967 all countries experienced more inflation (table 4). Until 1972 the acceleration was restrained, but Britain's inflation rate was persistently above the average of other countries and noticeably so in 1971 and 1972. After 1972 inflation accelerated swiftly, exceeding 10 percent in many countries. Britain's inflation rate outran the others, attaining about twice the average rate of OECD countries in 1975 through 1977 and much more in the other years. Some progress, however, was shown in 1978. Only Italy's performance was as bad as or worse than the United Kingdom's. There may well be significance in the fact that Italy and the United Kingdom display relatively poor economic performances with respect to both growth and inflation.

The United Kingdom did better in achieving its goal of balance-of-payments equilibrium, but with obvious costs.[3] In the 1957–67 period a balance-of-payments deficit often emerged whenever the U.K. economy began rapid growth, and efforts to quell those deficits led to stop-and-go policies to regulate demand. The deficit of $800 million in 1967 led to the devaluation of sterling in that year. As table 5 shows, the current account balance improved steadily after the 1967 devaluation (with the "J-curve" effect taken into consideration); in 1969 the balance went into surplus

---

3. Although no one concept of the balance of payments satisfactorily defines equilibrium, the current account balance comes the closest for most purposes. For a mature industrial country like the United Kingdom, equilibrium should provide for some net capital outflow unless the world economy is upset by a large OPEC current account surplus.

Table 4. *Percentage Annual Changes in Consumer Prices for the United Kingdom, Six Other Industrial Countries, and OECD Countries as a Whole, 1967–78*

Year	United Kingdom	United States	Japan	West Germany	France	Canada	Italy	All OECD countries[a]
1967	2.5	2.8	4.0	1.4	2.7	3.6	3.7	3.1
1968	4.7	4.2	5.3	2.9	4.5	4.0	1.4	4.0
1969	5.4	5.4	5.2	1.9	6.4	4.6	2.6	4.8
1970	6.4	5.9	7.7	3.4	4.8	3.3	5.0	5.6
1971	9.4	4.3	6.1	5.3	5.5	2.9	4.8	5.3
1972	7.1	3.3	4.5	5.5	6.2	4.8	5.7	4.8
1973	9.2	6.2	11.7	6.9	7.3	7.6	10.8	7.9
1974	16.0	11.0	24.5	7.0	13.7	10.8	19.1	13.4
1975	24.2	9.1	11.8	6.0	11.8	10.8	17.0	11.4
1976	16.5	5.8	9.3	4.5	9.6	7.5	16.8	8.6
1977	15.9	6.5	8.1	3.9	9.4	8.0	17.0	8.7
1978	8.3	7.7	3.8	2.6	9.1	9.0	12.1	7.9

Source: *OECD Economic Outlook* (July 1979).
a. Calculated as a weighted average of percentage changes, using private consumption weights and exchange rates.

Table 5. *Current Account Balances for the United Kingdom and Six Other Industrial Countries, 1967–78*[a]

Billions of U.S. dollars

Year	United Kingdom	United States	Japan	West Germany	France	Canada	Italy
1967	−0.8	2.6	−0.2	2.5	0.2	−0.5	1.6
1968	−0.7	0.6	1.0	3.0	−0.9	−0.1	2.6
1969	1.1	0.4	2.1	1.9	−1.5	−0.9	2.3
1970	1.8	2.3	2.0	0.9	0.1	1.1	1.1
1971	2.7	−1.4	5.8	0.8	0.5	0.4	1.9
1972	0.3	−6.0	6.6	0.8	0.3	−0.3	2.0
1973	−2.6	7.1	−0.1	4.6	−0.7	0.1	−2.7
1974	−8.6	4.9[b]	−4.7	9.9	−6.0	−1.5	−8.0
1975	−4.1	18.3	−0.7	3.5	−0.1	−4.7	−0.8
1976	−1.5	4.6	3.7	3.4	−6.1	−3.9	−2.8
1977	0.5	−14.1	10.9	4.2	−3.3	−4.0	2.5
1978	0.9	−16.0	16.5	8.7	4.1	−4.6	6.3

Source: *OECD Economic Outlook* (December 1979).
a. Includes goods, services, and all transfer payments.
b. Excludes cancellation of Indian debt (−2.0) and extraordinary grants (−0.7).

Table 6. *Unemployment Rates, Changes in Employment, and Indexes of Industrial and Manufacturing Production in the United Kingdom, 1968–78*

Year	Unemployment rate (percent)	Percentage change in employment	Index of industrial production (1975 = 100)	Index of manufacturing production (1975 = 100)
1968	2.4	−0.7	97.0	94.1
1969	2.4	−0.2	99.6	97.6
1970	2.6	−0.7	99.7	98.0
1971	3.4	−1.5	99.8	97.4
1972	3.7	0.0	102.0	100.0
1973	2.6	2.5	109.5	108.3
1974	2.6	0.6	105.1	106.5
1975	3.9	−0.4	100.0	100.0
1976	5.3	−0.7	102.0	101.4
1977	5.7	0.5	105.8	102.8
1978	5.7	0.3	109.7	103.6

Source: Central Statistical Office, *Economic Trends*, no. 309 (July 1979).

and in 1971 reached a high positive level of $2.7 billion. Subsequently the current account deteriorated, although it remained in surplus in 1972. In 1973, however, rapid growth at home and sharply rising world raw material prices provoked a current account deficit of $2.6 billion. The worst year for the British balance of payments was 1974, when, in response to the fourfold rise in petroleum prices, the deficit exceeded $8.5 billion. This deficit helped undermine confidence in sterling, and the pound declined considerably in the foreign exchange market.[4] By 1977–78 the current account regained a small surplus.

The sluggishness of British economic performance since 1973 is confirmed by certain data on the labor and produce markets. Unemployment in the United Kingdom rose from a level of about 2.6 percent in 1973–74 to 5.7 percent in 1977–78 (table 6), because the size of the work force increased but not the number of people employed. Industrial output peaked in 1973, declined for two years, and then recovered, but reached its 1973 level only in 1978. Manufacturing output (which does not include fast-rising oil production) in 1978 was still 4 percent below the peak it reached in 1973. According to a survey by the Confederation of British

4. See Rudiger Dornbusch and Stanley Fischer's paper below for details of changes in the effective exchange rate of sterling.

Industries, 40 percent of business firms reported their capacity less than fully utilized even at the 1973 cyclical peak. The proportion reporting spare capacity rose to about 80 percent at the beginning of 1976 and then declined to only 60 percent at the end of 1978.[5]

Basic Causes of Poor Performance

Many reasons have been suggested for one or another part of this deteriorating pattern of slow growth, high unemployment, and inflationary price movements in Britain. A selective survey of them provides background for the topics chosen for close study in this volume.

1. *Is there really an output gap?* It would seem obvious that when an economy has both unemployed labor and spare industrial capacity, it must have the potential for producing more than its current output and thus be suffering an output gap. Dornbusch and Fischer so conclude, and they provide estimates of the gap in their paper. But is it so obvious that there is an output gap in the United Kingdom? The question is important because the existence of such a gap would suggest the need for more stimulative demand management along well-known Keynesian lines.

To measure an output gap one must quantify the economy's potential output—not a straightforward exercise in any country, and particularly not in the United Kingdom. To an economist (although not to an engineer) the concept of usable capacity incorporates constraints related to prices. If the reservation price of all nonworking persons, for example, is substantially above the going wage rate, then the economy can be considered fully employed and incapable of producing more, unless it is shown capable of adjusting to higher wages with all the ramifications involved. The recorded rate of unemployment and the natural rate of unemployment are then equated. Some observers have placed the natural rate of unemployment in the United Kingdom between 4 percent and 7 percent of the labor force, that is, marginally below or even above the recorded rate of late 1978 and early 1979.[6]

Another way to test the existence of an output gap is to determine

5. Central Statistical Office, *Economic Trends,* no. 304 (February 1979), p. 72.

6. A figure of 1.3 million unemployed or 5.4 percent of the work force was cited as the natural rate of unemployment in *The Amex Bank Review* (New York: American Express International Banking Corporation, May 28, 1979).

whether increments of monetary demand translate themselves primarily into higher prices, as they will when an economy approaches its full economic potential. An examination of the output and price components of increments of money growth in the United Kingdom since 1968 yielded the following results. During the ten-year span, 81.5 percent of the increase in money GDP ended up, on average, as price increases. Only 71 percent of the increment of money GDP went into inflation during the years 1968–73, but the proportion soared to 92.0 percent during the years 1973–78. Thus inflation increasingly won out over real growth in the United Kingdom after 1973, putting the existence of an output gap in question.[7]

2. *Is the fight against inflation crippled by inflationary disturbances from abroad?* The fact that increases of aggregate demand translate largely into inflation might be explained by the inflation coming in from abroad. Britain imports large quantities of raw material and food. During periods when prices of internationally traded commodities are increasing rapidly, Britain's terms of trade tend to deteriorate. Between 1972 and 1974 they worsened by 30 percent.[8] This decline inflicts a significant loss of real income on a country as dependent on imports as the United Kingdom. If British trade unions are unwilling to accept a decline in real income, as is usually alleged, then they demand higher money wages to compensate themselves for the rise in import prices.[9] Thus British domestic costs are forced up by both the increased prices of imported production inputs and the domestic wage inflation. Prices rise, but output does not. This mechanism probably explains the particularly severe inflation experienced in 1974–75. If this explanation is to be general, however, one must determine why improvements in the British terms of trade, as in 1975 and 1978, did not restrain wage demands and reduce inflation. The explanation sometimes put forward is that the effect on wages works asymmetrically: unions demand compensation from British employers when import prices rise but give the employers no credit when import prices fall. If so, then the real explanation lies in the behavior of domestic labor markets rather than of import prices.

A second way that external forces might impair the performance of the

7. Calculated from data in Central Statistical Office, *Economic Trends,* no. 309 (July 1979).

8. Ibid., no. 306 (April 1979), table 44.

9. The same mechanism is at work if the currency depreciates.

domestic economy is through the balance of payments. But there has been no deteriorating trend in recent years in the current account of the balance of payments. Although Britain's share of world markets continues to decline while the share of imports in home demand rises, these shifts will not lead to a balance-of-payments problem so long as Britain's growth is slower than that of other countries. To prove that the balance of payments inhibited domestic economic performance (instead of domestic performance inhibiting the balance), one would have to show that the balance of payments was a major determinant of economic policy. Dornbusch and Fischer suggest that British monetary policy was not dominated by consideration for the balance of payments. Similarly, changes in fiscal policy can be explained by domestic factors—with the possible exception of the commitments that Britain made to the International Monetary Fund at the end of 1976, to obtain international loans.[10] Therefore the mechanism that could link the balance of payments causally to poor price performance is missing.

British observers, however, do foresee two opposite types of problems arising from the balance of payments. Because of rapid growth of North Sea oil production, some observers fear that the balance of payments will improve so markedly that sterling will be forced up in the foreign exchange markets, making British manufacturing production uncompetitive on world markets. The balance of payments would be in equilibrium, but domestic employment and growth would suffer. Thus Britain might contract the so-called Dutch disease. In his study of North Sea oil in this volume, Hendrik Houthakker indicates that the macroeconomic consequences are unlikely to be that great. Furthermore, the problem could be alleviated by capital outflows from the United Kingdom to repay debts or to make investments abroad. And it will become easier to make such investments, since the long-standing exchange controls limiting them have now been completely removed.

The opposite problem worries that group of economists known as the New Cambridge School.[11] These economists fear that the balance of payments will deteriorate in the future (presumably when oil production

10. The counterargument suggests that the shift of policy occurred at the end of 1975 and in early 1976 in response to the acceleration of inflation in the United Kingdom and had little to do with the IMF's demands. The IMF's conditions were useful to the government in countering domestic opposition to a policy of restraint.

11. Dornbusch and Fischer discuss the New Cambridge School in greater detail.

ceases to rise or begins to fall) and will keep Britain from fully utilizing domestic resources. They do not believe that the problem can be remedied through currency depreciation, because of offsetting domestic inflation. They are therefore prepared to consider a more radical remedy: generalized import protection. The deteriorating trade balance that these economists foresee occurs because of the trend rise of imports and loss of export shares, noted above. But Dornbusch and Fischer find that British elasticities of import demand are not out of line with those of other industrial countries, so that Britain's problem is not unique. Although adverse time trends do appear in equations explaining British trade, they should be interpreted not as a future certainty but as a failure of econometrics to identify some trend factors working in the past. Those factors might relate to nonprice competition or shifts in comparative advantage between Britain and nonindustrial countries. British imports and exports do respond to economic mechanisms; thus improvements in British competitiveness would cure such a problem if it developed. Dornbusch and Fischer do find that depreciation of sterling in the past has not reduced real wages for long, but the difficulty seems to lie in the domestic labor market rather than in some peculiarity of international trade. Hence the argument that Britain's economic problems have been caused by its links with the rest of the world is unconvincing.

3. *Have there been crippling mistakes in policy?* Can one attribute the disappointing economic performance of the British economy to mistakes of macroeconomic policy? This question was recently treated in great detail in an imaginative study edited by Michael Posner.[12] Four teams of researchers were set the task of reviewing two historical periods—September 1964 to July 1970 and July 1970 to mid-1977—to determine whether with hindsight one could arrive at better settings for the instruments of macroeconomic policy and to estimate with the help of econometric models what effects a better policy would have had.[13] A variety of intellectual approaches to economic management was represented. The one-man team of David Laidler employed a monetarist approach; the team of the National Institute of Economic and Social Research—M. J. C. Surrey and P. A. Ormerod—adopted a traditional Keynesian approach;

12. Michael Posner, ed., *Demand Management*, National Institute of Economic and Social Research, Economic Policy Papers 1 (London: Heinemann Educational Books, 1978). The summary chapters by Posner are particularly useful.

13. A third period looking forward to 1985 was also examined.

and the teams from the Cambridge Economic Policy Group—T. F. Cripps, M. J. Fetherston, and W. A. H. Godley—and the London Business School—R. J. Ball and T. Burns—followed different eclectic approaches. The researchers were permitted to vary macroeconomic policy instruments, including the exchange rate, monetary and fiscal policies, and incomes policy, but could change neither the microeconomic instruments used for altering industrial structure nor the external environment.

The studies reached general agreement on certain policy mistakes, such as the failure to devalue sterling sooner in the first period and the excessively high value of sterling set in the Smithsonian Agreement and the experimental tying of wages to threshold prices in the second period. The British economy could therefore have avoided some of its problems if macroeconomic policy had not been mistaken. The researchers agreed much less on optimal settings for policy instruments and the benefits that might have flowed from such settings. Simulations of radically different econometric models always turn up such differences. What is of great significance is that none of the teams was able to come up with anything approaching a miraculous path for the British economy just by varying macroeconomic policy instruments. Recognizing that constraints did come from the foreign environment and that British economic managers lacked the benefit of hindsight, we cannot convict the managers of causing the disappointing economic performance through inept setting of the macro instruments. Consequently, some other explanation for the relatively poor results must be found.

4. *Does Britain lack capacity for adjusting to external shocks?* Britain's economic performance began deteriorating in 1971 with respect to inflation, in 1973 with respect to the balance of payments, and in 1974 with respect to real growth. Why then? In this four-year period there were three seismic shocks to the world economy: the breakdown of the Bretton Woods monetary system from 1971 to 1973; the explosive rise of world prices of raw materials from 1972 to 1974; and the oil crisis in 1973–74. Very likely the deterioration in Britain's economic performance is related to these external shocks. As already noted, all industrial countries were adversely affected, but the United Kingdom more so than the others. Why? It was not just the occurrence of shocks but British reaction to them that seemed to matter.

One hypothesis is that the British economy adjusts less well than other countries to external shocks because it has less capacity for internal adjustment. The weakness arises from the microeconomic structure of the economy. One should therefore look for deficiencies in the labor market, industrial organization, the capital market, the educational system, and other aspects of society. These deficiencies could have been created by rapid growth of nonmarket expenditures that diverted resources from the productive sectors of the economy (as Bacon and Eltis suggested),[14] by excessively high marginal tax rates that discourage productive and creative activity, or by some combination of these and other factors.

A New Direction for Economic Policy

When Britain's inflation exceeded 20 percent annually for six straight quarters (from the end of 1974 to the beginning of 1976), the political basis was laid for a change in economic policy. The next step appeared to be a flight into hyperinflation, and few wanted to risk the dangers of such an experience. Thus the Labour government under Prime Minister James Callaghan and Chancellor of the Exchequer Denis Healey was forced to consider changing policy so as to give primary attention to fighting inflation. During the course of 1976 confidence in the pound continued to erode, and sterling dropped sharply in the foreign exchange market. Domestic financial markets were in turn undermined. Restoring financial stability became an absolute necessity, and late in 1976 a stabilization program was devised in conjunction with the International Monetary Fund. The program concentrated on controlling growth in the money supply (sterling M_3) and reducing government expenditures.[15] Those policies succeeded in restoring financial stability, but they did not attack the fundamental problems of the economy.

During this period controlling monetary aggregates became the central focus of monetary policy, a technique that required fairly frequent and sometimes large changes in interest rates. Besides raising interest rates to restrain the growth in the money stock, the Bank of England can force the banking system to conform to the so-called monetary corset. This instru-

14. Robert Bacon and Walter Eltis, *Britain's Economic Problem: Too Few Producers*, 2d ed. (London: Macmillan, 1978).

15. Sterling M_3 is calculated by the sum of notes and coin in public circulation, U.K. private sector sterling sight deposits (both interest- and non-interest-bearing), U.K. private sector sterling time deposits, and U.K. public sector sterling deposits.

ment quantitatively controls the growth of certain items in the balance sheets of commercial banks and thus acts to constrain their lending to the private sector.[16] Therefore, if high interest rates do not discourage private borrowing sufficiently, the monetary corset can be invoked.

When interest rate increases were anticipated, however, investors, awaiting higher yields, reduced their purchases of long-term government bonds. Thus the public sector borrowing requirement (PSBR) could not be properly financed and led directly to a rise in the monetary aggregates via the public sector deficit. In order for the Bank of England to reach the goals for the growth of monetary aggregates, it necessarily lost some of the initiative in changing interest rates to financial institutions.

Both the need to invoke the monetary corset and the forced rise in interest rates point up the close link between monetary policy and the financial aspects of fiscal policy in the United Kingdom. But under traditional U.K. budget methods, the government had no direct control over the PSBR. Government expenditures were budgeted in real terms and would rise along with inflation. To help gain some control over the PSBR, a new instrument was devised. Expenditures of government departments and other spending units (including nationalized industries) were subjected to cash limits that can bring discipline to the government's fiscal accounts, provided the limits are not changed in reaction to inflation.

This experience suggests that monetary policy as usually conceived is inadequate to manage the monetary aspects of the U.K. economy. It needs to be broadened to a more comprehensive concept of financial policy that includes the financial elements of fiscal policy as well.[17] Monetary policy may be operated so as to reach the desired growth rate of the money supply and still not achieve the policy objective of restraining liquidity in the economy. That restraint can be achieved only by a financial policy in which both monetary and fiscal policies play an appropriate role.

The first budget of Margaret Thatcher's Conservative government, brought down on June 12, 1979, signaled an even greater change in economic policy. Mrs. Thatcher had campaigned on a platform to reverse

16. The corset restricts the growth of the banks' interest-bearing eligible liabilities (IBELs). Banks are required to place with the Bank of England non-interest-bearing supplementary special deposits if the rate of increase in their IBELs exceeds the permitted rate.

17. See analyses by Gordon T. Pepper in W. Greenwell and Co., *Monetary Bulletin* (supplement to July 2, 1979, and various other issues), in which aspects of financial policy are discussed.

the direction of postwar British economic policy, and the budget reflected the platform. The policy of the new government was based on the belief that the economy would perform better if the government took a less active role in it. The specific goals were to reduce the share of economic resources absorbed by or passed through the government, to reduce the government's control over and involvement in the economy in favor of private initiative, and to improve the working of the capital and (particularly) the labor markets. The principal measures to bring these changes about included a reduction of government spending, enforced by stringent cash limits on expenditures, and a shift from direct to indirect taxation. Exchange controls on the outflow of private capital were also liberalized. The government recognized that its goals could not be reached if inflation were not overcome. Therefore monetary policy was tightened through a 2 percent rise in the rate at which the Bank of England lends to commercial banks (the MLR, or marginal lending rate) and other measures to reduce liquidity in the economy.

Whatever the long-term consequences of the Conservative program—and success was only promised in the long term—the immediate disruption to the economy could be substantial.[18] The economic prospect for the United Kingdom during 1980 may include a combination of declining real output, rising inflation, rising unemployment, a strong currency, and an unchanged balance of payments (rising contribution from the North Sea offsetting a deteriorating position in manufactures). Not all of this dismal outlook can be attributed to the new budget; partly it reflects the new external shock of a doubling of oil prices in 1979. If the short-run disturbance can be overcome, then the longer-term outlook can be improved through the supply-augmenting features of the new policy. Success, if and when it comes, will have to occur in the microeconomic foundation of the economy where the problems exist.

The Findings of the Studies

The studies that make up this volume were chosen and executed against this background of frustrated hopes for British economic policy. The book is a descendant—by no simple biological process—of *Britain's Economic*

18. For detailed analysis see London Business School Centre for Economic Forecasting, *Economic Outlook 1978–1982,* vol. 3, nos. 9 and 10 (June 1979).

Prospects. In 1968 the unique element in the United Kingdom's economic problems seemed to be its slow rate of overall economic growth. Growth then still enjoyed its status as an unalloyed blessing. The contributors to that volume were primarily concerned with locating the cause of the slow growth—in inappropriate or too-hesitant macroeconomic policies, in constraints on the adaptability or productivity of the economy, or elsewhere. Their investigations tended to put the blame for the infirmities of short-run economic policy on the tensions of pursuing an ambitious set of domestic and international objectives with an inflexible and slow-growing complement of economic resources. The present volume, more selective and sharply focused than its predecessor, is designed to illuminate the strategic factors of the British economy and economic policy from the perspective of the late 1970s. What had changed in the past decade? What had assumed greater strategic importance?

Britain's problems of macroeconomic performance, as we have shown, were similar to those of other industrial countries, only worse. High inflation coupled with high unemployment was a malady that struck the whole industrialized world, and we did not wish to study Britain's case in a way that might overstate its uniqueness. Therefore we chose to link our examination of macroeconomic policy to one particular institutional change of major importance—the adoption of a flexible (or managed floating) exchange rate. In the first paper Dornbusch and Fischer show that, flexible rate or not, the balance of international payments on current account continues to respond in the expected way to changes in competitiveness and aggregate demand in Britain and abroad. The exchange rate, however, has been a major factor in adjustment. Responding to many sorts of disturbances, both domestic and foreign, it has also imposed a subtle new learning process on British policymakers. The exchange rate helped to adjust the external value of sterling to changes in British money wages, but it seems unable to facilitate any sustained changes in the competitiveness of the real wage rate that might be needed to repair Britain's trade balance. Thus the balance in international payments was achieved through the unsatisfactory method of running the economy below full employment. The depreciation of sterling has tended to raise prices of internationally traded goods relative to purely domestic products, a fact that does tend to promote adjustment by attracting resources into traded goods industries. But even this correction might be reversed at full employment.

Some improvements in the balance of payments might be achieved if fiscal policy were tightened, since the evidence suggests that the fiscal and the balance-of-payments deficits are positively related. If economic activity could be sustained through increased industrial investment and supported by some real depreciation of sterling, Britain's unsatisfactory export performance might be reversed. However, even these changes are unlikely to restore full employment without the creation of real-wage flexibility.

Dornbusch and Fischer conclude that rising import prices have been one correlate of inflation, but a proportionally weaker force than rising money wages. British labor has taken on a linchpin role among alleged adverse influences on inflation in the short run and productivity in the long run. In the next paper David C. Smith investigates both the recent increase in trade union membership and the factors explaining the rising trend of industrial disputes. He finds that union membership rose in response to severe unanticipated changes in inflation and the associated increase in the demand for unions' collective-bargaining services. Other conditions also had their effects: changes in labor force characteristics were unfavorable, while public policy was favorable. Smith finds that the growth of unionization was in turn positively related to strike activity. And also higher and more uncertain rates of inflation directly provoke an increase in strikes. The evidence of the first two papers reveals a disturbing, vicious cycle in the cause-and-effect relations among the exchange rate, inflation, and trade union aggressiveness. Exchange rate flexibility makes real wages more variable. This uncertainty joins with greater unanticipated inflation in raising the membership of trade unions and the aggressiveness of their efforts to maintain real wages. These factors complicate the management of macroeconomic policy, and policy failures contribute further to the variability of the exchange rate and real wage.

The short-term macroeconomic problems of wage-price stability and full employment in Britain are clearly not helped by a rate of productivity growth that, despite hopeful signs earlier in the 1970s, continues to lag behind those of most other industrial countries. In the third paper Caves investigates various hypotheses about the causes of low levels of industrial productivity. His procedure is to match U.K. manufacturing industries to their U.S. counterparts, and then to test hypotheses about low British productivity by determining whether they can explain differences among British industries in their productivity shortfalls. His results tend to confirm traditional hypotheses about the shortcomings of British management and the obstinacy of British labor. The toll on productivity taken by poor labor relations is proportional not so much to union membership as to the disruptiveness of labor relations (number of strikes and working days lost); and the problem is worse in the nation's older industrial regions. Although productivity is low in the more management-intensive industries, there is some evidence that U.K. managers have honed their skills in dealing with labor-relations problems. The statistical evidence also confirms certain specific costs of bitter and uncertain labor-management relations, such as extra capital tied up in inventories and perhaps some tendency of entrepreneurs to avoid building large-scale plants (in which labor relations are usually at their worst). The analysis implies that manufacturing activity in the United Kingdom will tend in the long run to shift from industries most crippled by the basic sources of Britain's low productivity to those less disadvantaged—from large-scale assembly industries to small-scale or process industries (even though the experience of other countries does confirm economies of scale) and to industries using female labor forces.

The next two papers investigate two other alleged trouble spots in the British economy—the structure of income taxation and the institutions of the capital market. In his study Joseph A. Pechman concludes that the system of income taxation displays some notable paradoxes. Although Britain's tax system is famous for imposing high marginal rates on relatively modest levels of personal income, various mitigating features (such as a rather light rate of effective taxation on corporate income) make the system not particularly progressive overall. Another paradox is that the United Kingdom's rather high tax burden does not seem to have reduced individuals' outlay of effort. But it clearly exacts other real costs. It induces the expenditure of resources on finding ways to avoid taxes; it promotes the growth of the "hidden economy" and diverts personal saving into forms that enjoy preferential tax treatment. In the absence of sweeping innovations, such as a wealth tax or expenditure tax, Pechman advocates a considerable simplification of the personal income tax and a broadening of the tax base, along with further reductions in the tax rates, particularly for the low- and middle-income brackets.

In his study Marshall E. Blume investigates the United Kingdom's financial markets against a background of concern that their imperfections may have shrunk flows of saving or diverted them from their best uses. By and large, Blume finds no basis for real worry. It is true that investment in the United Kingdom suffers from rather low efficiency—a given amount of extra capital yields less extra gross domestic product than in other industrial countries. But that paucity seems due to the low productivity of British enterprise rather than to the efficiency with which the capital markets select the projects to be financed. Given the uncertainties prevailing in the 1970s about future returns and the heavy borrowing requirements of Britain's public sector, it is hard to fault British savers or corporations for not acquiring and issuing more corporate liabilities during that time. The high rate of personal saving observed in Britain in the 1970s apparently reflected an effort by individuals to restore a desired relation between net worth and personal income in the face of falling market values for most financial assets. The government's heavy borrowing requirement no doubt raised the cost of financing in the private sector, but there is no evidence that it caused particular difficulties by preempting the long-term bond market and thus pushing enterprise to rely more on equity financing. The one valid concern about the United Kingdom's financial markets has to do with the increasing role of financial institutions in holding assets on behalf of individuals (for example, pension funds). Individual savers traditionally serve as the chief source of finance for small companies, and it is not clear whether institutional investors are taking up this role. British public policy has recently lost its 1960s fascination with the advantages of bigness in production units, and the evidence developed in Caves's paper weakly suggests that British productivity is relatively higher in the smaller-scale industries. Therefore a trend in the financial markets that is hostile to the funding of small companies causes concern, especially since the institutionalization of saving is partly induced by the tax system.

In a difficult decade the one bright spot for the British economy has been the discovery of oil and gas in the North Sea. In the final paper Hendrik S. Houthakker investigates some of its implications for Britain's wealth and explores the problem of managing the resource to maximize its value for the nation. The oil and gas should increase Britain's gross domestic product by about 3 percent in 1982, and royalties and the petroleum revenue tax should account for 7 to 8 percent of the current receipts of the central government. Houthakker points out that to maximize the value of a natural resource, one must extract it at a rate based on forecasts of future prices. His own model of the world energy sector does not imply a continued large rise in the real price of oil; a huge rise, such as a doubling in twenty years, is not very likely. For British policy, this conclusion implies principally that government intervention to slow the rate of extraction has no economic justification. Indeed, in the face of many uncertainties, Houthakker prefers to decentralize decisions about output in order to reduce the chance of "centralized mistakes." Britain's earnings from oil exports may drive up the pound sterling's value on the foreign exchange market, although a rise need not take place if Britain's foreign debts are reduced or foreign assets are accumulated. The prospective of exchange rate appreciation has caused concern among those who fear its negative effect on the output of Britain's traded-goods sector; but since appreciation would help in the fight against inflation, the merits of insulating the exchange rate from appreciation are not clear. In any case, Houthakker suggests that the macroeconomic consequences of North Sea oil have generally been overestimated.

Conclusion

The studies in this volume indicate that Britain's economic malaise stems largely from its productivity problem, whose origins lie deep in the social system. This finding points to two policy approaches that could be played in tandem. One approach would strike directly at the productivity problem itself by improving industrial relations (if that were possible), by increasing individual incentives, by improving the allocation of capital (for instance, to small firms), and the like. A few suggestions on how to accomplish these tasks are found in the individual papers. The other approach is less positive but no less important: policymakers could do a better job of living within the constraint implied and convincing the people to do likewise. It is bad enough to endure relative impoverishment; it need not be made worse by inflation.

RUDIGER DORNBUSCH AND STANLEY FISCHER

Sterling and the External Balance

IN THIS PAPER we analyze the behavior of the current account and the exchange rate in the British economy in the 1970s and discuss the outlook, as influenced by the availability of oil revenues, for exchange rate developments during the 1980s.

Trade behavior and exchange rate behavior are affected by and in turn affect general macroeconomic developments and policy problems. In the short term the chief macroeconomic problems of the British economy are its high rates of inflation and unemployment. These can be traced to the combination of expansionary domestic monetary and fiscal policies in 1972–73 and the concurrent worldwide boom, which fueled the inflation of 1974–75. The subsequent reduction of the inflation rate has been accompanied by an increase in the unemployment rate and, especially in 1976–77, a decline in the real wage. It is quite likely that attempts to restore the real wage during the next few years will lead to a resurgence of high inflation.

Over the long term the underlying problem for the British economy remains its slow productivity growth when compared with the economies of the major countries (except the United States) in the Organisation for

We received many helpful comments on early drafts from conference participants and from members of the National Institute of Economic and Social Research and the Department of Applied Economics, Cambridge University. Valuable research assistance was provided by David Germany and David Modest.

Economic Co-operation and Development (OECD). The question of the causes of low productivity growth is beyond the scope of this paper, but, at least to nonspecialist observers, the state of labor relations appears to be both symptomatic of the problem and a major barrier to improving performance.

Against this macroeconomic background, sterling depreciated in both nominal and real terms in the 1970s, and the current account was in substantial deficit from 1973 to 1976. Movements in the current account can be attributed to relative income growth, changes in U.K. competitiveness, and the impact of North Sea oil. Exchange rate movements have been far from regular but can, over long periods, be attributed to differential inflation rates and productivity movements. North Sea oil exploitation may be thought of in this context as a productivity increase.

In the first section of the paper, we review the macroeconomic developments of the 1970s as essential background for understanding the behavior of the current account and the exchange rate. In the second section we discuss the current account, emphasizing the role of manufactures and semimanufactures in U.K. trade. We review the behavior of measures of competitiveness and the role of relative income growth, and conclude the section with an examination of the relation between the current account and public sector deficits.

The behavior of the exchange rate is taken up in the next section. We examine the role of capital flows and the determinants of government intervention, as well as the effect of the depreciation of the exchange rate on domestic inflation. In the final section we present concluding remarks, including a discussion of alternative exchange rate policies for exploiting the availability of North Sea oil and a discussion of the mechanics of exchange rate management in a flexible rate system.

Two major themes underlie our detailed examination of trade-related issues. First, the laws of economics continue to work in the United Kingdom: low domestic demand and improved U.K. competitiveness help the balance of payments, improved U.K. competitiveness causes the exchange rate to fall less rapidly, and so on. And second, the achievement of Britain's macroeconomic goals depends on the behavior of both nominal and real wages. The inflation rate will not remain low unless the rate of change of nominal wages does; full employment with stable prices and current account balance will not be achieved unless real wage growth is restrained or productivity growth increases.

An Overview of Macroeconomic Developments

A knowledge of macroeconomic developments is essential for understanding the behavior of the exchange rate and the external balance. But these developments are also of independent interest: during the 1970s the United Kingdom experienced its highest inflation and unemployment rates of the post–World War II period and has been IMFed. Although the economic performance of all the major OECD countries was worse in the seventies than in the sixties, the seventies were especially bad years for Britain.

Inflation, Unemployment, and the Output Gap

Figure 1 shows the combinations of inflation (of the retail price index) and unemployment that occurred from 1970 through 1978 in the United Kingdom and in the group of seven major OECD countries.[1] As can be seen, the United Kingdom and the group of OECD countries start from quite similar initial conditions in 1970 but soon exhibit very different macroeconomic performances.

By 1971 and 1972 the United Kingdom was already experiencing inflation and unemployment rates above those of the OECD group. Britain appeared to weather the commodity and oil price increases relatively well in 1973 and 1974, with its unemployment rate remaining low. But in 1975 the unemployment rate in the United Kingdom rose substantially as the inflation rate reached 24 percent, compared with under 10 percent in the group of OECD countries; by 1976 the United Kingdom had a higher unemployment rate and a substantially higher inflation rate than the OECD group.

Only in 1978 did the British inflation rate fall below 10 percent, but the unemployment rate was still close to its postwar high. The key features of British macroeconomic performance in the 1970s, then, are an inflation rate that on average is much higher than that of the group of OECD countries and a long period of high unemployment, which continued even into 1979.

Table 1 presents measures of the output gap (the shortfall of output from its full employment level), together with the unemployment and

1. See note a of figure 1 for the list of the seven countries.

Figure 1. *Inflation and Unemployment Rates in the United Kingdom and in the Group of Seven Major OECD Countries, 1970–78*

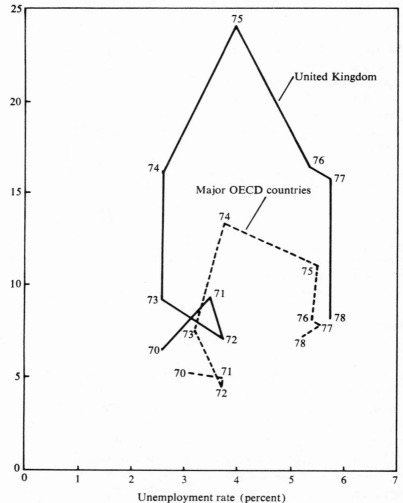

Inflation rate (percent)

Unemployment rate (percent)

Sources: Data for the United Kingdom are from Central Statistical Office, *Economic Trends*, no. 312 (London: Her Majesty's Stationery Office, October 1979), pp. 36, 42; inflation rates are calculated on a CPI basis, and unemployment rates exclude school leavers. The 1970–76 data for the major OECD countries are from Organisation of Economic Co-operation and Development, *Towards Full Employment and Price Stability* (Paris: OECD, 1977), p. 42; the 1977–78 inflation rates are authors' calculations based on data from International Monetary Fund, *International Financial Statistics Yearbook, 1979* (Washington, D.C.: IMF, 1979), using consumption in 1970 as weights; the 1977–78 unemployment rates are authors' calculations based on data from U.S. Department of Commerce, *International Economic Indicators*, vol. 5 (September 1979), using estimates of the labor force in 1977 as weights.

a. The seven countries are the United States, Canada, Japan, West Germany, Italy, France, and the United Kingdom.

Table 1. *Rates of Inflation and Unemployment, the Output Gap, and Growth Rates of Gross Domestic Product, United Kingdom, 1970–77*
Percent

Year	Inflation rate	Unemploy-ment rate	Output gap		Growth rate of gross domestic product
			Total (1)	Manufacturing (2)	
1970	6.4	2.6	2.8	3.5	1.8
1971	9.4	3.4	3.7	6.5	1.7
1972	7.1	3.7	1.1	6.4	2.3
1973	9.2	2.6	0.0	0.4	6.5
1974	16.1	2.6	3.4	1.8	−1.5
1975	24.2	3.9	7.7	11.2	−1.6
1976	16.5	5.3	8.8	12.9	2.3
1977	15.8	5.7	9.6	14.8	1.0

Sources: Inflation and unemployment rates are from Central Statistical Office, *Economic Trends*, no. 312 (October 1979), pp. 36, 42; inflation rates are calculated on a CPI basis, and unemployment rates exclude school leavers. Data for total output gap are authors' calculations using a 2.5 percent growth rate of potential output and a zero gap for 1973; data for output gap in manufacturing are from J. R. Artus and A. G. Turner, "Measures of Potential Output in Manufacturing for Ten Industrial Countries" (Washington, D.C.: International Monetary Fund, 1978). Growth rates are derived from the "average" estimate of GDP at 1970 factor cost, Central Statistical Office, *Economic Trends*, no. 299 (September 1978), p. 6.

inflation rates. Column 1 shows the output gap derived by assuming that 1973 represented a year of full employment and that the trend growth of potential output was 2.5 percent for the seventies. Column 2 shows estimates of the output gap in manufacturing only, derived from production function estimates that take into account measures of actual factor accumulation. Both columns indicate that the early 1970s was a period of economic slack, that 1972–74 was a period of high resource utilization, and that thereafter economic activity declined through 1977. In this context it is interesting to note that real income measured by gross national disposable income (which included an adjustment for terms of trade changes and net current transfers abroad) returned only in 1978 to its 1973 level.

The growth rate of the gross domestic product, shown in the last column of table 1, tells much the same story as the measures of economic slack. Against an estimated growth rate of potential output of about 2.5 percent, GDP growth rates for 1970–72 fell short of the trend rate. Growth in 1973 exceeded that of potential output, and the gap was accordingly eliminated. But growth was negative in 1974 and 1975 and even in 1976 and 1977 remained below potential, thus building up a sizable output gap.

Recovery got under way in 1978, but the unemployment rate and the output gap still remain very high. Output would have to grow at a rate of nearly 5 percent for four years to restore the economy to full employment.[2] The record of the last ten years suggests that such growth is most unlikely. An obviously important current policy issue concerns methods for dealing with present levels of unemployment.

The Current Account and the Exchange Rate

Table 2 presents the current account surplus of the United Kingdom as a percentage of GDP, and, for comparison, the U.S. current account surplus as a percentage of GNP. The dollar and effective exchange rates are multilateral trade-weighted average exchange rates against foreign currencies. The massive current account deficits of 1974 and 1975 and the rapid depreciation of sterling require explanation, which is deferred until later in the paper. The substantial improvement of the current account from 1977 to 1978 (not shown in the table) is likewise worthy of note.

Fiscal, Monetary, and Incomes Policies

Variables related to fiscal policy and monetary policy, for 1970 through 1977, are presented in table 3. The most striking feature of the table is the very large public sector borrowing requirement, or deficit (PSBR), particularly for the 1973–76 period. The change in the deficit from 1976 to 1977 was associated with the IMF loan of December 1976, the terms of which we discuss below. The public sector deficit or borrowing requirement includes borrowing to finance investment by public corporations and is thus not directly comparable to the deficit of the government sector in the U.S. national income accounts.

The share of current (noninvestment) government spending on goods and services hovered at about 21 percent of GDP up through 1973 and rose thereafter; total government expenditure was, of course, a much

---

2. Of course, if the natural unemployment rate now exceeds 2.5 percent, growth would have to be less for full employment to be restored. U.S. studies have shown an increase in the natural rate of unemployment in the seventies, but we are unaware of such studies for the United Kingdom. This is an issue of considerable importance that has apparently not generated much discussion in Britain.

Table 2. *The Current Account Surplus in the United Kingdom and the United States and Exchange Rate Indexes for Sterling, 1970–77*
Indexes, May 1970 = 100

Year	Current account surplus as percent of income		Sterling exchange rate indexes	
	United Kingdom	United States	Dollar rate[a]	Effective rate
1970	1.7	0.2	99.8	99.8
1971	2.2	−0.1	101.8	100.0
1972	0.2	−0.5	104.2	96.7
1973	−1.6	0.5	102.2	87.5
1974	−4.9	0.1	97.5	84.8
1975	−2.0	1.2	92.6	78.3
1976	−1.0	0.3	75.3	66.3
1977	0.2	−0.8	72.7	63.0

Sources: Based on data contained in Organisation for Economic Co-operation and Development, *Main Economic Indicators* (Paris: OECD, various issues); Central Statistical Office, *Economic Trends* (various issues); International Monetary Fund, *International Financial Statistics* (various issues).
a. Exchange rate of the pound against the dollar.

larger share of GDP, and one that increased over the period. Table 3 also shows two OECD-calculated measures of fiscal impact.[3] Positive numbers indicate an expansionary effect. In 1970 fiscal policy was tight, but it loosened up progressively from 1971 through 1974. Only in 1975 and 1976 did fiscal policy turn mildly contradictory. The fiscal impact measures thus confirm the impression given by the PSBR/GDP measure —that fiscal policy was expansionary through at least 1974, from 1971 on. Note also that the largest fiscal impulse came in 1972, a year of world-wide expansion.

On the monetary policy side, we consider the growth rate of M_3 as the basic policy measure.[4] As figure 2 shows, the behavior of domestic credit

3. The basic impact attempts to measure the first-round (that is, without multiplier) effects of changes in government and spending on GNP. The discretionary measure calculates the first-round impact of changes in government spending and changes in tax *rates*, interpreting inflation-induced changes in tax brackets as policy changes. Note that the fiscal impact variables attempt to measure the effects of changes in fiscal policy; they are thus akin to *changes* in the full employment budget deficit, rather than in the *level* of the deficit.

4. M_3 is perhaps best described for U.S. residents as being basically pre-1980 U.S. M_4 (M_2 plus large negotiable certificates of deposit), but also includes holdings by U.K. residents of nonsterling deposits. Sterling M_3 excludes the latter deposits. One serious problem in interpreting U.K. monetary policy is the divergent behavior of M_1 and M_3 in the important years 1972 and 1973.

Table 3. *U.K. Fiscal Policy and Monetary Policy Variables, 1970–77*

Year	Public sector borrowing requirement (PSBR) as percent of GDP	Fiscal impact as percent of GDP[a]		General government consumption as percent of GDP	Government investment as percent of GDP	General government expenditure as percent of GDP	Growth rate of M_3[b]	Short-term interest rate	Long-term interest rate
		Basic	Discretionary						
1970	0.0	-2.2	0.3	20.6	9.4	45.2	6.1	7.3	9.2
1971	2.8	1.2	1.3	20.7	9.0	44.1	12.6	4.6	8.8
1972	3.7	2.9	2.5	21.2	8.2	45.0	23.9	8.8	8.8
1973	6.6	1.3	1.7	20.8	9.0	45.2	26.9	16.1	10.7
1974	8.6	0.6	1.1	22.5	9.8	50.0	18.9	13.3	14.7
1975	11.4	-0.4	-0.04	24.8	9.7	51.5	9.6	11.3	14.6
1976	8.4	0.1	-1.0	24.3	9.2	51.0	10.4	14.9	14.4
1977	4.8	-0.7	n.a.	23.6	7.7	50.0	8.9	6.8	12.7

Sources: Based on data contained in Central Statistical Office, *Economic Trends*, no. 300 (October 1978), pp. 6, 14, 52; Central Statistical Office, *Economic Trends, Annual Supplement*, no. 2 (HMSO, 1977); Central Statistical Office, *Financial Statistics*, no. 195 (HMSO, July 1978), p. 13; Central Statistical Office, *Monthly Digest of Statistics*, no. 393 (HMSO, September 1978), p. 4; *Bank of England Quarterly Bulletin* (various issues); and "Budget Indicators," in *OECD Economic Outlook Occasional Studies* (Paris: OECD, July 1978).

n.a. Not available.

a. See note 3 of text for explanation.

b. See note 4 of text for definition of M_3.

was very similar to that of M_3, thus demonstrating that other sources, specifically the balance of payments, account for only a small portion of money creation. The monetary policy picture is similar to that for fiscal policy: through 1971 M_3 was growing at a rate of less than 10 percent a year; the growth rate then averaged about 20 percent for 1972 through 1974; and then from 1975 the growth rate of M_3 was kept below the Bank of England internal target level of 10 percent. Part of the increase in the growth rate of M_3 has been attributed to the adoption of "competition and credit control" monetary policy in 1971,[5] which removed quantitative restrictions on bank credit, permitting banks to compete vigorously for funds. Although interest rates rose, they by no means kept pace with accelerating inflation; ex post real interest rates were negative from 1974 through 1977. The ex post short-term real interest rate rose substantially from 1975 to 1976.

Figure 2 shows that the growth rate of money and the rate of inflation had no simple relationship to each other during the 1970s. The acceleration of money and credit growth started in 1972, and deceleration began in 1974. The period of very high inflation (and also the largest budget deficits) started only in 1974. The lag between money growth and inflation was thus substantial.

Some form of incomes policy has been in effect in Britain for most of the last twenty years. Table 4 gives details of the incomes policies pursued from 1970–78. The 1973–74 agreements in which pay was to be compensated for inflation after the inflation rate had passed a specified threshold have received blame for a substantial part (10 percent) of the 1974 wage explosion.[6] The 1976 and 1977 decelerations of wage inflation were accompanied by high levels of unemployment; it is thus difficult to disentangle the effects of unemployment and the social contract on wages. Nonetheless, there is prima facie evidence that the deceleration of wage increases in 1977 was related to the social contract.

Of special interest in the discussion of policy during the seventies is the package of measures adopted in December 1976 as part of the conditions

5. See "Competition and Credit Control," *Bank of England Quarterly Bulletin*, vol. 11 (June 1971), pp. 189–93 (text of a consultative document issued May 14, 1971).

6. See, for example, Michael V. Posner, "Problems of the British Economy," in Karl Brunner and Allan H. Meltzer, eds., *Public Policies in Open Economies*, Carnegie Rochester Conference Series on Public Policy, vol. 9 (North-Holland Publishing Company, 1978), pp. 5–32.

Figure 2. *U.K. Inflation Rates and Growth Rates of the Money Supply and Domestic Credit, by Quarter, 1970:1–1978:1*

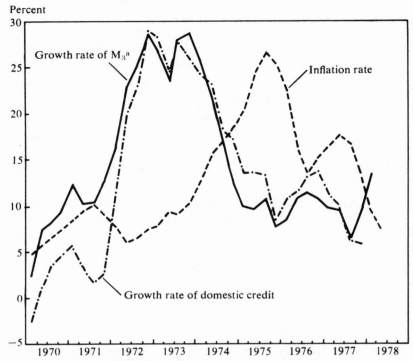

Percent

Growth rate of M_3[a]

Inflation rate

Growth rate of domestic credit

Source: Central Statistical Office, *Economic Trends* (various issues).
a. See note 4 of text for definition of M_3.

for obtaining the IMF loan to support sterling. An absorbing account of the maneuvering during the negotiations for both the June 1976 $5 billion standby credits (the bait) and the December $3.9 billion IMF loan is presented by Fay and Young.[7] The need for the loans arose from the behavior of the exchange rate, which we discuss later. But the proximate causes of the behavior of the exchange rate were the high rates of inflation and wage increase, together with the very large public sector deficit. Although monetary policy had already become relatively restrictive before the end of 1976, and fiscal policy had begun to turn restrictive, there seemed little prospect of a quick reduction in inflation without stronger

7. S. Fay and H. Young, "The Day the Pound Nearly Died," *Sunday Times* (London), June 1978.

fiscal measures. The conditions of the IMF loan included increases in taxes and cuts in spending designed to get the public sector borrowing requirement below 5¼ percent of GDP by 1978—a target that was met.[8] The end of 1976 marked the turning point for both the exchange rate and the inflation rate; however, (perhaps temporary) success on those fronts has been bought at the expense of continued unemployment.

Summary

In brief, the economic history of the 1969–78 period can be divided into four phases. The first, 1969–71, was the phase of slow growth, increasing inflation, and policy restraint, in which the budget actually showed a surplus (1971) and the unemployment rate was relatively low. Policy restraint reduced real growth below the rate of increase in potential output, and unemployment accordingly rose.

The next phase, 1972–73, was one of rapid monetary and fiscal expansion. Real growth rates rose substantially and during the world boom year of 1973 reached an extraordinary 6 percent. The budget deficit as a ratio of GDP increased to the 4 to 5 percent range. Inflation remained high under the impact of the expansion and accelerated in 1973. Unemployment declined to a level near full employment.

The third phase, 1974–76, saw the dislocation of the economy under the impact of the external supply shock, the decline in world demand, and the explosion of domestic inflation. Unemployment increased sharply, to more than twice the normal level. Inflation soared to nearly 25 percent in 1975. Real growth was negative, and the economic slack and measures of fiscal expansion widened the public sector deficit to more than 10 percent of the GDP. Thus 1974, 1975, and 1976 were extraordinary years by the standards of the postwar period.

In the final phase, the utter dislocation of the economy, including the serious external problems of a large deficit, low and falling reserves, and a sharply depreciating exchange rate, moved the authorities to accept the need for monetary and fiscal stabilization despite the high rate of unemployment. Starting in 1976 the budget deficit was reduced sharply and monetary growth was kept low. Along with growing unemployment the rate of inflation fell dramatically to below 10 percent in 1978. Externally,

8. OECD, *Economic Surveys: United Kingdom* (Paris: OECD, 1977), pp. 57–58, contains a summary of the IMF loan conditions.

Table 4. *Details of Incomes Policies and Effect on Average Earnings, United Kingdom, 1969–78*

Policy period	Pay restrictions	Implementation	Exceptions	Effect of policy	
				Rate of increase of average earnings (percent)	Year
1969–70	2½–4½ percent	Voluntary but with powers of delay	No ceiling on productivity bargaining; wage differentials and low-paid workers	12.8	1970
1971–72	(n − 1) policy	Voluntary, government-example public sector	None	11.1	1971
1972–73	Freeze	Compulsory	None	12.9	1972
1973	£1 plus 4 percent (12-month rule)	Compulsory	Settlements deferred by freeze	12.9	1973
1973–74	7 percent or £2.25 plus threshold payments	Compulsory	1 percent margin to deal with pay structures; "genuine" productivity schemes; premiums for "unsocial" hours	17.2	1974
Social contract, 1974–75	Compensation for price changes between main settlements	Voluntary	Low pay; elimination of discrimination, particularly against women	26.1	1975
1975–76	£6 maximum (12-month rule)	Voluntary	Equal pay	16.5	1976
1976–77	5 percent with £2.4 minimum, £4 maximum	Voluntary	None	10.2 15.5	1977 1978[a]

Sources: S. G. B. Henry and P. A. Ormerod, "Incomes Policy and Wage Inflation: Empirical Evidence for the U.K., 1961–1977," *National Institute Economic Review*, no. 85 (August 1978), p. 32; and Central Statistical Office, *Economic Trends* (various issues).
a. Third quarter of 1977 through third quarter of 1978.

the stabilization led not only to a current account surplus but also to an appreciating currency.

Our dry recital of the economic history of the 1969–78 decade should not be allowed to obscure the fact that policymakers in Britain had to cope with, and learn about, unprecedented problems, and that they adopted solutions that in 1968, when the previous Brookings book on the U.K. economy was published, would have been thought at best unlikely. The period started with the adoption of floating exchange rates; in the middle of the decade the Bank of England adopted a monetary growth rule; and a few years later the chancellor of the exchequer and the prime minister both argued that Keynesian methods were dead.

The Current Account

Our aim in this section is to explain fluctuations in the balance of payments on current account and to discern any trends and their implications. We first present an overview of the facts, examining the behavior of the components of the current account, the increasing importance of international trade, changing patterns of trade, and the importance of oil. We then discuss measures of British trade competitiveness and, after that, relative income growth. This is followed by an econometric analysis of the current account using competitiveness and relative incomes. Finally, we examine long-term trends and the relation between the current account and budget deficits.

Overview

Table 5 shows the current account in detail for the years 1970–77 and in outline for selected earlier years. The outstanding features, which have of course long characterized the British current account, are the persistent deficit in visible trade and the surplus in invisible trade, the only exception being the visible trade surplus of 1971. Particularly noticeable are the decreasing current account deficits from 1968 through 1971, the large deficit of 1974, and then the improvement of the current account from 1975 through 1977, a year in which a modest current account surplus occurred.

Table 5. *The U.K. Current Account, Selected Periods, 1913–77*

Millions of pounds

Period	Services				Interest, profits, and dividends		Transfers		Invisible balance	Current balance
	Visible balance	General government	Private sector and public corporations	Balance of goods and services	General government	Private sector and public corporations	General government	Private		
1913	−134	n.a.	n.a.	n.a.	n.a.	n.a.	n.a.	n.a.	340	206
1927–29	−373	n.a.	n.a.	n.a.	n.a.	n.a.	n.a.	n.a.	480	107
1937–39	−388	n.a.	n.a.	n.a.	n.a.	n.a.	n.a.	n.a.	355	−33
1952–60	−168	n.a.	n.a.	n.a.	n.a.	n.a.	n.a.	n.a.	273	105
1961–66	−220	n.a.	n.a.	n.a.	n.a.	n.a.	n.a.	n.a.	166	−54
1967	−567	n.a.	n.a.	n.a.	n.a.	n.a.	n.a.	n.a.	273	−294
1968	−682	n.a.	n.a.	n.a.	n.a.	n.a.	n.a.	n.a.	396	−286
1969	−172	n.a.	n.a.	n.a.	n.a.	n.a.	n.a.	n.a.	635	463
1970	−42	−309	720	369	−269	825	−177	−17	773	731
1971	261	−315	850	796	−204	709	−205	−6	829	1,090
1972	−722	−351	937	−136	−142	676	−210	−53	857	135
1973	−2,383	−409	1,031	−1,761	−199	1,419	−359	−99	1,384	−999
1974	−5,235	−538	1,341	−4,432	−352	1,634	−320	−121	1,381	−3,591
1975	−3,236	−620	1,771	−2,085	−514	1,277	−379	−154	1,644	−1,855
1976	−3,589	−757	2,739	−1,607	−648	1,963	−792	−53	2,452	−1,137
1977	−1,709	−788	3,589	1,092	−685	1,123	−1,127	−114	1,998	289

Sources: Data for 1913–66 are from Richard N. Cooper, "The Balance of Payments," in Richard E. Caves and Associates, *Britain's Economic Prospects* (Brookings Institution, 1968), pp. 149, 151. Data for periods longer than a year are averages at an annual rate. Data for 1967–77 are from Central Statistical Office, *Economic Trends*, no. 299 (September 1978).

n.a. Not available.

Table 6. *Current Account Patterns in the United Kingdom and Selected Countries, 1970–78*

Year	United Kingdom	United States	West Germany	Italy	France	Japan	U.K. visible exports as percent of GDP
		Current balance as percent of GDP					
1970	1.7	0.2	0.5	1.2	0.3	1.0	18.7
1971	2.2	−0.1	0.4	1.9	0.4	2.3	18.3
1972	0.2	−0.5	0.3	1.9	0.2	2.2	17.1
1973	−1.6	0.5	1.2	−1.8	−0.5	−0.0	18.9
1974	−4.9	0.1	2.6	−5.1	−4.2	−1.0	22.3
1975	−2.0	1.2	0.9	−1.6	−1.7	0.6	20.8
1976	−1.0	0.3	0.9	−1.7	−1.9	0.6	23.0
1977	0.3	−0.8	0.9	1.2	−1.0	1.6	25.7
1978	0.2	−0.7	1.6	n.a.	0.9	1.8	25.0

Sources: OECD, *Main Economic Indicators* (various issues); *OECD Economic Outlook* (various issues); Central Statistical Office, *Economic Trends* (various issues); International Monetary Fund, *International Financial Statistics* (various issues); International Monetary Fund, *Balance of Payments Yearbook* (Washington, D.C.: IMF, various issues); and *Bank of Japan Statistic Annual, 1978.*

In the 1970s there were systematic deficits by the government sector in the invisible account. There were government deficits in the service,[9] the interest, profit, and dividend, and the transfer accounts; however, the private sector and public corporations' surplus in these accounts, and particularly in the service account, grew sufficiently rapidly to produce a surplus in the invisible balance.[10]

Table 6 places the balance of goods and services in perspective by reporting it as a share of GDP; comparative data for the United States and several other countries are also reported. Table 6 also includes the ratio of U.K. exports to GDP, which has grown rapidly since 1970, particularly after 1973. The table confirms that the deficit or surplus experience has been quite uneven among major industrialized countries in this period, especially in 1974. The data in table 6 also show, at least superficially, no evidence of a trend deterioration in the U.K. external balance.

The 1970s saw significant changes in the pattern of British trade. U.K. exports to members of the European Community and of the Organization

9. Note that public corporations are not included in the government sector in table 5, although their borrowing is part of the PSBR in earlier tables.

10. For more detail on invisible exports, see Department of Industry, "Trends in Invisibles in 1977 and the First Half of 1978," *Trade and Industry*, vol. 33 (October 6, 1978), pp. 31–33.

Table 7. *The U.K. World Trade Pattern, 1970, 1974, 1977*

Percent of total

Trade flow and year	European Community	Rest of Western Europe	United States and Canada	Remaining developed countries	OPEC	Rest of world
U.K. exports						
1970	30.0	17.1	15.0	12.0	5.8	21.1
1974	33.7	16.7	13.7	10.4	7.4	9.3
1977	36.9	15.1	11.7	6.5	13.4	16.3
U.K. imports						
1970	28.2	14.9	20.9	10.1	7.2	18.5
1974	35.0	14.3	13.6	7.5	15.8	13.8
1977	40.2	13.6	13.3	7.3	10.1	15.4

Source: Department of Industry, *Trade and Industry*, vol. 32 (September 8, 1977). Figures are rounded.

of Petroleum Exporting Countries increased substantially between 1970 and 1977, as can be seen in table 7; the corresponding reductions were in exports to Canada and the United States, the remaining developed countries, and non-OPEC developing countries. There has been a very large decrease in the proportion of imports from Canada and the United States. Note that the European Community's share in U.K. imports has risen more than its share in U.K. exports.

The composition of U.K. external trade shows a heavy concentration in manufactures on the export side. Semimanufactures and finished manufactures constitute between 80 and 85 percent of exports. On the import side Britain is a substantial importer of food, fuels, and raw materials. Industrial materials (excluding fuels) and finished manufactures account for 65 percent of imports.[11]

British exports of manufactures have long constituted a declining proportion of total world trade in manufactures,[12] and the early part of the seventies showed no exception to that trend. Table 8 presents volume indexes for the manufacturing exports of industrialized countries and of the United Kingdom, as well as the United Kingdom's value share in manufactures' trade. The table shows that U.K. export growth fell short of the

11. For a more detailed account of the commodity composition of trade, see Department of Industry, *Trade and Industry,* vol. 33 (November 24, 1978), pp. 411–16.

12. See the analysis by Lawrence B. Krause, "British Trade Performance," in Richard E. Caves and Associates, *Britain's Economic Prospects* (Brookings Institution, 1968), pp. 198–228.

Table 8. *Volume Indexes of Exports of Manufactures for the United Kingdom and Industrial Countries, U.K. Unit Value Index, and U.K. Value Share, Selected Years, 1960–77*

1970 = 100

Year	Volume indexes		Relative U.K. unit value index[b]	U.K. value share (percent)
	Industrial countries[a]	United Kingdom		
1960	41	65	97.6	15.0
1965	60	76	103.3	12.6
1970	100	100	100.0	9.7
1974	148	128	94.4	7.9
1975	141	126	97.3	8.4
1976	157	133	96.2	7.9
1977	164	142	101.0	8.5

Source: United Nations, *Monthly Bulletin of Statistics*, vol. 32 (September 1978), pp. xx–xxi.
a. Includes the United Kingdom.
b. Ratio of U.K. export unit values to those of all industrial countries.

8.5 percent growth of exports by the industrialized countries as a group in the 1960–77 period: U.K. exports grew by less than 5 percent. However, the U.K. share did rise from 1974 to 1977. The relative price of U.K. exports, as measured by the ratio of U.K. export unit values to those of the industrialized countries (in a common currency), showed a decline from 1970 to 1976 but, because of appreciation and high inflation, increased in 1977.

Changes in the share of U.K. exports in industrialized countries exports reflect changes in both the volume of trade flows and relative prices. Thus the gain in 1977 may well be interpreted as the consequence of the slow adjustment to a decline in the relative price over the preceding years, leading to a relative increase in volume and at the same time an increase in the relative price. These minor fluctuations apart, there is little doubt that since the early 1960s—and of course even earlier—Britain has suffered a major decline in her world trade position. In the 1970s, though, the U.K. trade share has remained relatively constant. We discuss the causes of this decline later.

Table 9 casts an interesting light on the growth of trade. It shows the ratio of imports to home demand and the ratio of exports to manufacturers' sales, for a number of important sectors. Although there are some problems of interpretation, arising mainly from reexports, the data reveal

Table 9. *Home and Export Performance of U.K. Manufactures, Selected Years, 1968–77*[a]

Percent

			Engineering products				Chemicals and allied products	
	Vehicles		Mechanical		Electrical			
Year	(1)	(2)	(1)	(2)	(1)	(2)	(1)	(2)
1968	14	34	20	32	14	20	18	24
1970	12	33	20	34	17	21	18	25
1972	19	34	23	38	21	23	19	27
1974	25	41	29	40	29	29	27	34
1976	31	44	30	46	32	37	26	34
1977	36	45	30	45	35	40	27	37

Sources: Central Statistical Office, *Economic Trends*, no. 286 (August 1977), and Department of Industry, *Trade and Industry*, vol. 32 (August 18, 1978).

a. Column 1 under each heading represents the ratio of imports to home demand and column 2 the ratio of exports to manufacturers' sales.

a striking increase in both the ratios of imports to home demand and exports to sales.[13] This development is not of course peculiar to Britain; it reflects the growing importance of intraindustry trade, which becomes more pronounced as product differentiation increases and accounts for the increase in the ratio of trade in manufactures to income.

The behavior of manufacturing trade is further indicated in table 10, where we show volume indexes of disaggregated trade flows. The fact that has attracted attention is the very rapid increase in imports of finished manufactures. The 40 percent growth in imports from 1975 to 1978 is striking by comparison with the very modest growth of 10 percent in exports. This divergent trend is seen by some as a major long-term threat to British manufacturing.

Finally, in our review of the facts relating to the current account, we examine trade in oil and domestic oil production from 1972 through 1977. The immediate effects of the oil price increase of late 1973 are quite visible in table 11. Indeed, there is a coincidental similarity between the deficits on oil account in 1973 and 1974 and the current account deficits for those years, as seen in table 5. With the near quadrupling of oil prices from 1973 to 1974, the deficit on oil account almost quadruples; the recession of 1974 and 1975, combined with substantial inventory decumulation,

13. Table 9 helps explain the evolution of the ratio of exports to GDP in the last column of table 6.

Table 10. *U.K. Trade Volume Indexes, Selected Years, 1970–78*[a]
1975 = 100

Year	Semimanufactures		Finished manufactures	
	Exports	Imports	Exports	Imports
1970	82	75	75	56
1973	112	103	90	100
1976	117	110	104	109
1977	131	117	110	124
1978	135	133	110	140

Source: Department of Industry, *Trade and Industry*, vol. 34 (March 16, 1979), pp. 582–90.
a. Semimanufactures and finished manufactures refer to standard industrial commodity classifications 5, 6 and 7, 8, respectively.

reduced the value of oil imports in 1975, but only in 1977 was there substantial North Sea oil production, causing a large (nearly £ 1 billion) reduction in the current account deficit.[14] Note that investment activities associated with North Sea oil contributed to a current account deficit in the years before 1977; at the same time, however, they led to a capital inflow that more than balanced the contribution of North Sea oil to the current account deficit.[15]

The major facts outlined in this section are (1) the visible balance was in deficit in the years 1970–78 (as it has been historically), while there was a surplus on invisible account; (2) the government ran a deficit in the invisible account that was more than offset by a private sector surplus; (3) the current account was in surplus at the beginning of the decade, went into large deficit from 1973 through 1976, and was in surplus again in 1977; (4) the geographical composition of British trade moved toward the European Community countries and the oil-exporting countries of the Middle East and Africa and away from North America and the sterling area; (5) the commodity composition of British exports changed little at the aggregate level; fuel imports rose temporarily and manufactures remained the chief export; (6) the British share of manufactured exports in world trade were substantially lower than in the 1960s, even though exports in 1977 constituted a larger share of GDP than they did in 1970; (7) imports of finished manufactures rose very rapidly com-

14. The estimate is from "The Contribution of the UK Continental Shelf Oil and Gas Programme to the Balance of Payments," in Central Statistical Office, *United Kingdom Balance of Payments, 1967–77* (HMSO, 1978), pp. 64–66.
15. Ibid.

Table 11. *U.K. Trade in Oil and North Sea Oil Production, 1972–77*
Millions of pounds unless otherwise indicated

| | | | | | | North Sea oil and gas | |
Year	Exports	Imports	Balance on oil account	Balance as percent of imports	Average value per metric ton (pounds)	Value of sales	Contribution to current balance
1972	222	882	−660	6.5	6.4	…	…
1973	344	1,292	−948	6.5	8.3	134	−36
1974	711	4,136	−3,425	15.7	30.2	168	−194
1975	731	3,842	−3,111	13.7	35.3	248	−616
1976	1,172	5,145	−3,973	13.7	47.0	903	−323
1977	1,965	4,769	−2,804	8.3	53.7	2,543	958

Sources: Department of Industry, *Trade and Industry*, vol. 32 (September 8, 1978); OECD, *Economic Surveys: United Kingdom* (Paris: OECD, 1978); Central Statistical Office, *United Kingdom Balance of Payments, 1967–77* (HMSO, 1978), p. 66.

Table 12. *Indexes of Measures of U.K. International Competitiveness, 1963–77*[a]

1970 = 100 unless otherwise indicated

Period	Relative wholesale prices (1975 = 100)	Relative consumer prices	Relative average value of manufactured exports	Relative unit current costs	Effective sterling exchange rate (1969 = 100)
1963–67	n.a.	112.6	102.5	107.2	n.a.
1968	n.a.	98.1	98.1	94.6	n.a.
1969	n.a.	99.4	98.2	94.6	100.0
1970	105.2	100.0	100.0	100.0	99.0
1971	110.4	103.8	102.4	103.0	100.0
1972	107.7	101.6	102.1	100.0	95.2
1973	94.3	92.0	94.6	92.9	86.3
1974	95.0	91.5	93.3	95.5	83.6
1975	100.0	94.1	94.6	97.5	77.2
1976	93.1	86.2	92.1	94.3	65.4
1977	99.0	88.2	97.2	93.4	62.1

Sources: Relative wholesale prices are from International Monetary Fund, *International Financial Statistics* (various issues); effective exchange rates are from Central Statistical Office, *Economic Trends* (various issues); other data are from "The International Competitiveness of Selected Countries," in *OECD Economic Outlook Occasional Studies* (Paris: OECD, July 1978).

n.a. Not available.

a. Prices and costs are measured relative to equivalent foreign variables, weighted by their trade shares and expressed in the same currency.

pared with exports of these products; (8) and, finally, the oil price increase raised the value of British oil imports from 1973 to 1974 by about 4 percent of 1973 GDP; only in 1977 did North Sea oil production begin to contribute significantly to improving the current account.

In brief, the mixture contains much that is old as well as two new features—oil and membership in the European Community.

Competitiveness

The competitiveness of British exports and domestic production plays a role in explaining the behavior of the current account. Table 12 reports four measures of competitiveness for the United Kingdom.[16] All are exchange rate–adjusted indexes of *relative* (to the rest of the world) price

16. See C. A. Enoch, "Measures of Competitiveness in International Trade," *Bank of England Quarterly Bulletin*, vol. 18 (June 1978), pp. 181–90, for a discussion of the measures.

Figure 3. *Indexes of U.K. Import and Export Prices Relative to Domestic Prices, by Quarter, 1972–77*[a]

1975 = 100

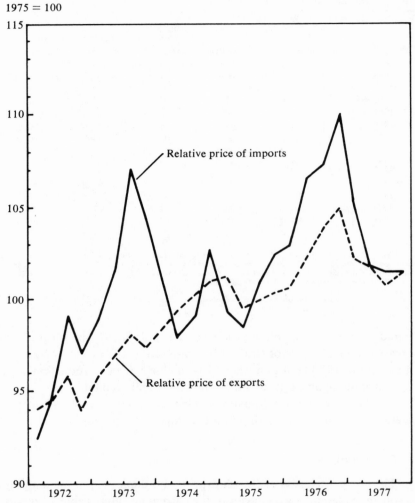

Sources: Central Statistical Office, *Economic Trends* (various issues); and Department of Industry, *Trade and Industry* (various issues).
a. Ratio of unit value of exports and imports to the domestic wholesale price of manufactures.

or cost. All show that the United Kingdom has become more competitive since 1970, though the extent of the improvement differs among the indexes.

Figure 4. *Index of U.K. Manufactures Terms of Trade, by Quarter, 1971–77*[a]

1975:2 = 100

Source: Department of Industry, *Trade and Industry* (various issues).
a. Ratio of unit values of U.K. manufactured exports to manufactured imports, which is the real exchange rate.

Figure 3 shows the price of traded goods relative to domestic goods. It presents the unit values of manufactures—exports and imports—relative to the domestic wholesale price of manufactured goods. There has clearly been a substantial increase in the prices of traded goods relative to domestic prices, although the shift since 1972 has by no means been smooth.

Figure 4 shows the ratio of the unit value of manufactured exports to the unit value of manufactured imports, which is a measure of the manufactures terms of trade.[17] We note, just as in figure 3, the large fluctuations in relative prices that are due in part to exchange rate movements and in part, given exchange rates, to the large difference between U.K. and foreign rates of inflation. Figure 4 is of particular interest because it shows

17. Figure 4 can be derived directly from figure 3.

that the movements in relative prices, while large, have been short-lived. The sustained gain in competitiveness is relatively small.

Figure 4 is consistent with the argument that, perhaps because of real wage resistance, the United Kingdom cannot achieve a *sustained* improvement in competitiveness or change in the terms of trade.[18] However, figure 3 does seem to show a sustained change in the price of traded relative to domestic goods—and such a change would move resources into the export industries. There is, nonetheless, a question of whether the sustained change in the relative price of traded goods shown in figure 3 is due to the currently depressed state of domestic demand. It is quite possible that the traded goods sectors have been able to pay higher real wages and make profits as a result of depreciation, while the demand squeeze has meant lower profitability and real wages in the goods sectors as a whole. If so, a return to full employment would imply a fall in the relative price of traded goods and a worsening in the current account, as a result of both reduced competitiveness and expanded demand.

We have so far shown that there have been short-run changes in the terms of trade and an apparently longer term shift in the relative price of traded goods—though we leave open the question of whether this latter shift would persist with full employment. There remains the issue of whether changes in relative prices affect trade flows. Here the evidence is quite unambiguous. Many studies, including the recent work by Enoch, Odling-Smee and Hartley, Deppler and Ripley, and Artus, find evidence for a relative price response of U.K. trade flows.[19] The precise estimates of elasticities differ depending on commodity groups and measures of relative price, but the overwhelming evidence is that there is a substantial long-run response to relative price changes and that in the short run there is a J-curve effect.

The critical issue, then, is whether the domestic wage-price mechanism is sufficiently flexible to allow for changes in relative prices. This question

18. Perhaps, however, policymakers elected to allow the real exchange rate to appreciate as North Sea oil came on line.

19. Enoch, "Measures of Competitiveness in International Trade"; J. Odling-Smee and N. Hartley, "Some Effects of Exchange Rate Changes," H. M. Treasury Working Paper 2 (May 1978); Michael C. Deppler and Duncan M. Ripley, "The World Trade Model: Merchandise Trade," *International Monetary Fund Staff Papers*, vol. 25 (March 1978), pp. 147–206; and Jacques R. Artus, "The 1967 Devaluation of the Pound Sterling," ibid., vol. 22 (November 1975), pp. 595–640.

Table 13. *Growth Rates of Real GDP in the United Kingdom and OECD Countries, and the U.K. Current Balance, 1970–78*

Country	1970	1971	1972	1973	1974	1975	1976	1977	1978
				Growth rate (percent)					
United Kingdom	1.8	1.7	2.3	6.5	−1.5	−1.6	2.3	1.0	n.a.
Major OECD countries[a]	2.5	3.9	5.6	6.2	−0.1	−0.7	5.6	4.0	3.8
Other OECD countries	5.8	4.4	5.2	5.7	3.6	0.0	3.5	1.8	2.3
				Current balance as percent of GDP					
United Kingdom	1.7	2.2	0.2	−1.6	−4.9	−2.0	−1.0	0.3	0.2

Sources: *OECD Economic Outlook* (various issues), and Central Statistical Office, *Economic Trends*, no. 299 (September 1978). The U.K. growth rates are derived from the "average" estimate of GDP at 1970 factor cost; OECD growth rates are calculated by using centered three-year moving averages of GDP as weights.

a. The United States, Japan, West Germany, France, Canada, Italy, and the United Kingdom.

is emphasized in the study by Odling-Smee and Hartley, who state that the answer depends critically on the unemployment rates accompanying any induced (for example, by devaluation) changes in competitiveness.[20] The experience of the last few years, as summarized in figure 8 below, leaves one with considerable skepticism about the extent of real-wage flexibility at full employment.

Relative Income Growth

Table 13 shows the current balance as a fraction of GDP and comparative growth rates of real income in the United Kingdom and OECD countries. On average in the 1970–78 period, the growth rates in other OECD countries have been higher and recessions have been more moderate than in the United Kingdom. This fact would lead us to expect, other things equal, that the U.K. current account should have been improving over the period as exports increased in quantity or value (or both) relative to imports because of the differential pattern of growth.

Recent evidence on the income elasticities of imports and exports may be dated to the work by Houthakker and Magee, who report income elasticities of import demand of 1.5 and income elasticities of export demand of about 1.[21] Artus allows for separate trend and cyclical income responses

20. Odling-Smee and Hartley, "Some Effects of Exchange Rate Changes."
21. Hendrik S. Houthakker and Stephen P. Magee, "Income and Price Elasticities in World Trade," *Review of Economics and Statistics*, vol. 51 (May 1969), pp. 111–15.

Table 14. *Income Elasticities of Import and Export Demand for Manufactures, Selected Countries, 1978*

Country	Imports		Exports	
	Elasticity of demand	Time trend	Elasticity of world demand	Time trend
United Kingdom	1.32	0.034	0.9	0
United States	1.27	0.035	1.32	−0.024
West Germany	1.89	0.016[a]	1.11	−0.003[a]
Japan	2.04	−0.004[a]	1.45	−0.038
France	1.38	0.026	0.70	0.013

Source: Michael C. Deppler and Duncan M. Ripley, "The World Trade Model: Merchandise Trade," *International Monetary Fund Staff Papers*, vol. 25 (March 1978), pp. 178–79.
a. Statistically insignificant.

and distinguishes between finished and semifinished manufactures.[22] His results support those of the Houthakker-Magee study.

Deppler and Ripley have elaborated on this disaggregated approach.[23] They too attempt to distinguish between time trends and income effects, with results shown in table 14. This table is of interest in showing that the problem of income elasticities of imports (of manufactures) above those of exports is common to West Germany, France, and Japan as well as to Britain. The substantial difference is in the time trends. The United Kingdom has a significant positive time trend for imports and a zero trend for exports. Comparison of the Deppler-Ripley results with those of previous studies will show that differences in export and import income elasticities found by others are here attributed chiefly to time trends. We discuss the British time trends in more detail below.

The material presented in the preceding pages points to the importance of changes in competitiveness and relative incomes in explaining the U.K. current account. And figure 4, showing an increase in the relative price of traded goods, and table 13, showing the declining British relative income, suggest an explanation for the fact that the adverse time trends and income elasticities shown in table 14 have not worsened the current account.

An Econometric Analysis of the Current Account

Our econometric analysis of the current account (see equation 1 in the appendix) broadly matches the evidence we have so far reviewed. The

22. Artus, "The 1967 Devaluation of the Pound Sterling."
23. Deppler and Ripley, "The World Trade Model."

dependent variable is the ratio of the balance on current account to GDP; explanatory variables are the U.K. unemployment rate, U.K. competitiveness in manufacturing, OECD income, the real price of raw materials, and a time trend.

The analysis starts with the role of cyclical factors. Higher unemployment implies reduced income and spending and therefore should lead to a current account improvement. Such an effect is strongly evident. A 1 percentage point rise in the unemployment rate reduces the current account surplus (as a percentage of GDP) by about 0.25 percentage point. Demand expansion abroad also works in the expected direction: a 1 percentage point increase in OECD industrial production improves the current account ratio by about 0.17 percent. The equation thus confirms the effects of strong domestic and foreign cyclical factors on the current account.

We consider next the role of relative prices. Here we use two measures: U.K. competitiveness in manufacturing and the price of industrial materials relative to the GDP deflator. Both variables are significant in explaining the current account ratio. An increase in U.K. competitiveness —a rise in foreign relative to U.K. prices of manufactured goods—will improve the current account ratio over two years. There is an initial adverse effect, thus confirming the J-curve, that is more than compensated for as time passes. But the dynamics of this adjustment cannot be specified with confidence. The combined effect is estimated with more precision: a 1 percent gain in competitiveness will eventually improve the current account ratio by about 0.25 percentage point.

The real price of raw materials affects the U.K. current account ratio adversely, since these are predominantly import items with inelastic demand. Our estimate is that a 1 percent increase in the real price of raw materials worsens the current account ratio by 0.1 percent. The effect is thus quite sizable and it is also quite precisely estimated.

Finally, we note the role of a time trend. There is evidence of a very strong adverse time trend, at the rate of 1.6 percent of GDP a year. But it should be appreciated that (the log of) the level of OECD production, which enters the equation, is growing at a trend rate. If the equation were to include deviations of OECD production from trend, rather than the level, the coefficient on the time trend itself would be reduced by about half. Nonetheless, the time trend remains powerful and significant for the period of the 1970s.

Current Account Trends

Our current account equation contains three variables that can change in trend fashion. The first is, of course, time itself—which is also present in the import equation for the United Kingdom estimated by Deppler and Ripley and summarized in table 14. The presence of an explicit time trend in an equation is a sign of the omission of other relevant variables, usually variables that are difficult to quantify. In this case the plausible omitted factors are nonprice competition and shifts in the pattern of competitive advantage.[24] Nonprice competition includes such factors as delivery lags and the availability of servicing for manufactured exports.[25] Shifts in the pattern of competitive advantage hurt the United Kingdom in its role as domestic producer and exporter of manufactured goods; such shifts may be taking place as technology and industrial capacity spread not only to Japan and Europe but also to nonindustrialized countries.[26] Quantitative measures of the importance of these two factors are not available, but we do not doubt their importance.

A particular change in the pattern of competitive advantage that could affect the adverse time trend for the United Kingdom is the exploitation of North Sea oil. This is certainly a relatively long-run phenomenon that may be expected to have a favorable impact on the current account at least through the next decade and probably beyond. (We discuss later the policy choices made possible by British oil production.)

Two other factors, the relatively slow growth of the U.K. economy and the increase in the price of traded goods relative to that of home goods, have favorably affected the behavior of the current account over a long period. The key issue in determining the future behavior of these trend terms in the current account equation is the rate of productivity growth. If productivity growth were higher, real output could grow more rapidly with fewer adverse effects on the current account, and British exports would tend to become more competitive. Table 15 shows measures of productivity growth for the United Kingdom, three other members of the European Community, and the Community as a whole, for 1960–77.

24. By competitive advantage we mean costs of production at a given real wage.
25. See David K. Stout and others, *International Price Competitiveness, Non-Price Factors and Export Performance* (London: National Economic Development Office, 1977).
26. Shifts in the pattern of comparative advantage might also be expected to have effects on U.K. competitiveness.

Table 15. *Productivity Growth Rates for the European Community as a Whole and Selected Member Countries, 1960–77*
Percent a year

Country	1960–65	1965–70	1970–75	1976	1977
West Germany	4.5	4.7	2.7	6.5	4.6
France	5.0	4.9	3.2	5.7	3.8
Italy	6.1	5.9	2.1	4.9	2.6
EC countries	4.3	4.5	2.6	5.1	3.0
United Kingdom	2.4	2.7	1.8	2.6	1.1

Source: *Enlargement of the Community: Economic and Sectoral Aspects,* Supplement to *Bulletin of the European Communities* (Belgium, Secretariat of the European Communities, March 1978).

Throughout those years the productivity growth of the U.K. economy was below that of the other economies shown in the table and was substantially lower during the sixties.

To point to the rate of productivity growth as an important issue for the future behavior of the current account—and indeed for the behavior of the economy as a whole—is hardly novel. And, unfortunately, we do not feel qualified to add to the many discussions of the reasons for the poor U.K. productivity performance.[27] But that poor performance to date is a fact, and its continuance would imply a continued adverse trend for the current account. Such a trend would in part be self-stabilizing because of the reduced growth that lower productivity growth implies for the economy as a whole. Part of the adverse trend, however, would have to be offset by a depreciating real exchange rate.

Current Account and Budget Deficits

One of the two major planks of the "New Cambridge" manifesto for the British economy is that there is a close, almost one-to-one, link between the budget deficit and the current account deficit. This could mean that the private sector as a whole keeps its financial surplus balanced at the margin, so that changes in the budget do not lead to changes in the private sector's acquisition of assets.

There are, of course, good macroeconomic reasons for expecting links between the budget and the current account deficits. First, to a significant extent, the actual budget reflects the operation of automatic stabilizers. If an external shock worsens the current account, thereby reducing the level

27. For a readable summary, see Posner, "Problems of the British Economy," pp. 12–15. See also the paper by Caves in this volume.

of income, the budget will also go into deficit. But this is only one possibility, since other disturbances, such as a reduction in domestic demand, will improve the current account as the budget deficit worsens. Second, expansionary fiscal policy that raises income will worsen the current account. Here again the link is not certain: the tightness of the link will depend on the particular policies being followed. For instance, a reduction in tariffs will have very different effects on the current account than an increase in road construction.

The third point concerns the effects of changes in the budget on competitiveness. An expansionary fiscal policy will raise aggregate demand and thereby worsen competitiveness. The deterioration will arise in part from the behavior of domestic wages, but could also arise from anticipatory exchange rate movements combined with the J-curve. This mechanism too is not certain to operate in the direction necessary to validate the New Cambridge view.

It is apparent, therefore, that whether a close relation exists between the budget and current account deficits is an empirical matter that depends on whether the private sector runs a marginally balanced budget, that is, whether the private sector has a marginal propensity to spend, on consumption and investment together, of unity. The New Cambridge view is based on an empirical finding by Cripps, Fetherston, and Godley, and by Fetherston that private expenditure does exhibit a unitary marginal propensity to spend.[28]

Rather than examine their evidence directly, we compare the budget and the current account deficits. Figure 5 shows the relation for the years 1964–78; the two series certainly appear remarkably closely linked. However, the scales on the two axes are different, and over the period the current account deficit does not increase on a one-to-one basis with the budget deficit. The simple regression of the annual current account deficit against the budget deficit for the longer period 1956–77 yields the following estimate: a one pound increase in the budget deficit worsens the current account by about one-quarter to one-third of a pound sterling (see equation 2 in the appendix).

28. Francis Cripps, Wynne Godley, and Martin Fetherston, "Public Expenditure and the Management of the Economy," in *Public Expenditure, Inflation and the Balance of Payments,* Ninth Report from the Expenditure Committee, House of Commons, Session 1974 (HMSO, 1974), pp. 1–12; and Martin Fetherston, "Estimation of Simultaneous Relationships: A UK Private Expenditure Function" (Cambridge University, 1975).

Figure 5. *U.K. Current Account and Public Sector Budget Deficits,* *1964–77*

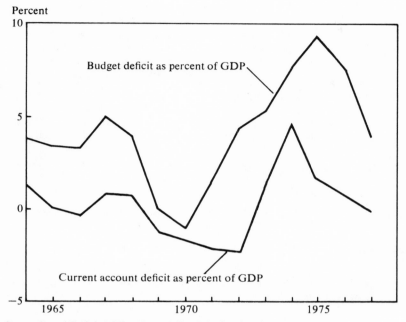

Source: Central Statistical Office, *Economic Trends* (various issues).

Although it is clear from both figure 5 and our regression that the two series are not identical, there is nonetheless a correlation between them. With regard to policy implications, there is good reason to think on other grounds than figure 5 that a tight fiscal policy will improve the current account. However, it should not be assumed that the link between the two series is automatic and independent of the causes of the budget deficit. We believe the observed correlation is consistent with the operation of the three macroeconomic forces we have outlined above rather than the reflection of a tight structural relation.

The Exchange Rate

In this section we first review the behavior of the exchange rate and analyze the factors responsible for that behavior. Second, we study capital

Table 16. *Indexes of Exchange Rates for Sterling, the U.S. Dollar, and the Deutsche Mark, 1971–78*

May 1970 = 100

Year	Sterling exchange rate indexes		U.S. dollar effective exchange rate index	Deutsche mark exchange rate indexes	
	Dollar rate	Effective rate		Dollar rate	Effective rate
1971	101.8	100.0	98.8	105.3	103.6
1972	104.2	96.7	89.8	114.8	107.1
1973	102.2	87.5	82.3	138.2	119.3
1974	97.5	84.8	84.2	141.5	125.5
1975	92.6	78.3	83.5	149.1	127.6
1976	75.3	66.3	87.7	145.5	132.3
1977	72.7	63.0	86.7	157.8	143.1
1978[a]	80.5	63.3	76.6	182.3	150.5

Source: International Monetary Fund, *International Financial Statistics* (various issues).
a. Figures for the third quarter of 1978.

flows and intervention. Third, we discuss the extent to which domestic inflation has been affected by exchange depreciation. The second and third topics are interdependent, since exchange rate movements are both caused by and cause changes in the inflation rate.

A Review of Exchange Rate Behavior

The depreciation of sterling in terms of currencies of major industrialized countries was far from even during the seventies, and the extent of changes in the exchange rate are hard to associate with only a few independent variables. Table 16 shows indexes of the dollar exchange rate and the IMF version of the effective exchange rate that takes into account multilateral trade patterns. Relative to the dollar, sterling depreciated by almost 20 percent between 1970 and the third quarter of 1978.

On an effective exchange rate basis the depreciation has, of course, been greater—more than 35 percent. The divergence reflects the appreciation of the deutsche mark and northern European currencies in terms of the dollar, since these currencies play an important role in U.K. trade relations. Table 16 shows for comparison the effective exchange rate of the dollar, with a depreciation of 25 percent, and the dollar and effective exchange rates of the deutsche mark, which show appreciations of 82 and 50 percent, respectively, over the period.

Figure 6. *Changes in the Effective Exchange Rate for Sterling, 1971–78*

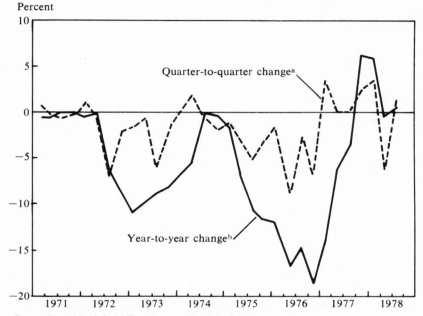

Percent

Quarter-to-quarter change[a]

Year-to-year change[b]

Source: Central Statistical Office, *Economic Trends* (various issues).
a. At a quarterly rate.
b. Change relative to same quarter of previous year, at an annual rate.

The timing of the depreciation of sterling is shown in figure 6, which exhibits both the depreciation or appreciation from quarter to quarter, at a quarterly rate, and the depreciation relative to the same quarter of the previous year, at an annual rate. The second series shows a relatively smooth trend of depreciation, while the first points to the timing of large exchange rate movements, which can be associated with major events or policy decisions. Among the latter we might note, for example, the brief presence of sterling in the tunnel arrangements for fixed exchange rates against European countries in May–June 1973, the oil shock of late 1973, the peaking of inflation in mid-1975, the policy of keeping sterling competitive in early 1976, the stabilizing impact of the IMF program at the turn of 1976–77, and renewed floating of the exchange rate in the fall of 1977.

There are three simple views of exchange rate behavior, each of which provides part of the explanation of the behavior of sterling exchange rates

Table 17. *U.K. External Balance, Official Financing, and Changes in Effective Exchange Rate, 1970–77*

Billions of pounds

Year	Current balance	Basic balance[a]	Official financing	Percentage change in effective sterling exchange rate
1970	0.7	0.6	1.3	n.a.
1971	1.1	1.1	3.1	0.2
1972	0.1	−0.6	−1.3	−3.3
1973	−1.0	−1.2	−0.8	−9.5
1974	−3.6	−2.4	−1.6	−3.1
1975	−1.9	−1.7	−1.5	−7.7
1976	−1.1	−1.2	−3.6	−15.3
1977	0.3	2.9	7.4	−4.8

Source: Central Statistical Office, *Economic Trends* (various issues).
a. Includes overseas investment by the U.K. public sector, private investment, and official long-term capital flows.

shown in figure 6 and table 16. The first view would explain depreciation by excess money creation. The second, for reasons based on purchasing power parity, would link depreciation directly to differential inflation.[29] The third would link depreciation to external imbalance as measured by the current balance or the basic balance. None of these three views is by itself adequate to explain exchange rate behavior. Money growth, for example, was running particularly high in 1972–74 and inflation peaked in 1975. Depreciation, however, peaked in 1976. Of course, allowance must be made for the rest of the world, where money growth was also high in 1972–73 and where inflation was high in 1973–74, but even with that allowance these simple theories do not go very far by themselves in explaining the magnitude *and* timing of depreciation.

Table 17 shows the relation between the external balance and the depreciation of sterling. Neither the current balance nor the basic balance is closely correlated with the behavior of the exchange rate. The largest deficits were recorded in 1974, when sterling moved very little, whereas considerably smaller deficits occurred in the year of peak depreciation, 1976. Part of the discrepancy between the behavior of the current balance and that of the exchange rate can be explained by examining capital move-

29. Presumably proponents of the first view would incorporate the second in any explanation of the effects of money on the exchange rate.

Table 18. *Net Sterling Liabilities, by Type of Holder, 1973–78*
Billions of pounds, end of period

| Year | Total | Central monetary institutions | |
		Total	OPEC
1973	5.7	3.4	1.0
1974	7.1	4.7	3.2
1975	6.9	3.7	2.8
1976	5.7	2.2	1.4
1977	7.1	2.1	1.4
1978[a]	7.0	1.7	1.0

Source: Central Statistical Office, *Economic Trends* (various issues).
a. End of third quarter.

ments, in particular foreign official holdings of sterling balances, of which the OPEC holdings were most important. Table 18 shows that OPEC holders accumulated sterling balances rapidly in 1974, when the exchange rate stayed up despite the current account deficit, and decumulated their holdings rapidly in 1976, when the exchange rate fell most rapidly.

This brief review thus suggests that a broader approach is required—one that takes into account not only the trend behavior of prices and the current account but also macroeconomic variables that affect the speculative outlook. These include interest rates, the adequacy of reserves, reserve use, and changes in official holdings of sterling.

Broader perspectives on exchange rate developments have been adopted in studies with quite different orientations, including in particular the work of Batchelor, Bilson, and Burns, Lobban, and Warburton.[30] The last study emphasizes medium-term exchange rate developments based on sectoral price level trends due to differential productivity growth and price arbitrage for traded goods. The Bilson studies take a relatively monetarist approach in studying the pound sterling–deutsche mark exchange rate. The explanatory variables include lagged exchange rates, relative money

30. R. A. Batchelor, "Sterling Exchange Rates 1975–76: A Cassellian Analysis," *National Institute Economic Review,* no. 81 (August 1977), pp. 45–66; John F. O. Bilson, "The Monetary Approach to the Exchange Rate: Some Empirical Evidence," *International Monetary Fund Staff Papers,* vol. 25 (March 1978), pp. 48–75; Bilson, "Rational Expectations and the Exchange Rate," in Jacob A. Frenkel and Harry G. Johnson, eds., *The Economics of Exchange Rates: Selected Studies* (Addison Wesley, 1978), pp. 75–96; and T. Burns, P. W. M. Lobban, and P. Warburton, "Briefing Paper: Forecasting the Real Exchange Rate," *OECD Economic Outlook* (October 1977).

supplies, the forward premium, and a time trend. Batchelor's work is desirably eclectic. It includes as explanatory variables short- and long-term interest rates, the trade balance, the lagged rate, and a time trend. The dependent variable is the deviation of the exchange rate from its level adjusted for changes in purchasing power, using either consumer or export prices.

The recent empirical work on exchange rates has not settled on any unique specification of the determination of exchange rates. In equation 3 of the appendix, we present our formulation of the determinants of the behavior of the sterling exchange rate over the period.

The equation explains the current effective exchange rate on a quarterly basis. The explanatory variables are the lagged effective rate, the lagged level of reserves, the covered interest differential of interbank Eurodollars against sterling, changes in OPEC sterling assets, and the dollar–deutsche mark exchange rate. Estimated over the period from the fourth quarter of 1971 through the third quarter of 1978, the regression performs quite well, although an important role is played by the lagged exchange rate. The equation shows that an increase in reserves, OPEC holdings of sterling, and the covered differential lead to an appreciation of sterling. A loss of competitiveness and an increase in the dollar–deutsche mark rate, on the other hand, lead to a depreciation.

The equation shows that a higher level of lagged reserves leads to an appreciation. The role of the reserve level in the equation can be interpreted both as a measure of cumulative balance of payments performance including borrowing and as a measure of the authorities' ability to intervene.

The covered differential appears as an indicator of speculative pressure. An increase in the differential in favor of the United States leads to a depreciation. The extent of the depreciation, however, is very imprecisely estimated. U.K. competitiveness affects the exchange rate in that a gain in competitiveness leads to an appreciation. A 1 point change in the competitiveness index leads to a 0.25 point change in the effective exchange rate index. Finally, the dollar–deutsche mark rate appears as an explanatory variable. An appreciation of the mark leads to a depreciation of the effective sterling rate.

The role of the dollar–deutsche mark rate in this context reflects the side effects on sterling of shifts in confidence in the dollar. The evidence suggests that the pound assumes an intermediate position, since the de-

Table 19. *U.K. Capital Transactions, Official Financing, and External Financing, 1970–77*

Billions of pounds

Year	Basic balance	Short-term capital flows[a]	Official financing	External financing	
				Change in official reserves[b]	Official borrowing
1970	0.6	0.7	1.3	−0.1	−1.3
1971	1.1	2.0	3.1	−1.5	−1.7
1972	−0.6	−0.7	−1.3	0.7	0.4
1973	−1.2	0.4	−0.8	−0.2	1.8
1974	−2.4	0.4	−1.6	−0.1	1.8
1975	−1.7	0.2	−1.5	0.7	0.8
1976	−1.2	−2.2	−3.6	0.9	2.8
1977	2.9	4.4	7.4	−9.6	2.2

Source: Central Statistical Office, *Economic Trends* (various issues). Figures are rounded.
a. A minus sign indicates outflow.
b. A minus sign indicates an increase.

preciation of the effective rate is substantially smaller than the change in the dollar–deutsche mark rate.

Capital Flows and Official Financing

Before table 19 is examined, some explanation is in order. Since sterling was effectively floating during most of the period 1970–77, the item "official financing" reflects exchange market intervention in each year and thus reflects a policy choice of the authorities. Under flexible rates neither the basic balance nor short-term capital flows are exogenous or predetermined, but are determined jointly with the exchange rate. In the absence of intervention, an autonomous demand disturbance might generate an increase in the basic balance deficit and bring about a depreciation (relative to anticipated exchange rates) of sufficient magnitude to call forth short-term financing at prevailing interest rates. The depreciation would, in turn, affect the basic balance through price and substitution effects.

In the table the basic balance, short-term capital flows, and official financing are shown, as well as the breakdown of external financing between changes in official reserves and official (short-term and medium-term) borrowing. The table indicates that official financing has been an

Table 20. *U.K. Outstanding Short- and Medium-Term Borrowing and Official Reserves, 1971–78*

Billions of dollars at end of year

Year	Borrowing			Total	Reserves
	International Monetary Fund	Other borrowing by Her Majesty's Government	Other public sector borrowing		
1971	1.1	...	0.4	1.4	6.6
1972	...	...	0.4	0.4	5.6
1973	...	...	3.0	3.0	6.5
1974	...	1.5	5.6	7.1	6.8
1975	...	2.5	6.4	8.9	5.4
1976	2.1	2.5	9.6	14.2	4.1
1977	4.0	4.0	10.0	18.0	20.6
1978	2.2	4.4	9.3	15.8	15.7

Source: *Bank of England Quarterly Bulletin* (various issues).

important part of external financing. One way of looking at the external accounts is to ask whether short-term capital flows have financed the basic balance or whether they have added to the imbalance, the latter, of course, being possible only if official intervention is sufficiently large. By this test, only in 1973, 1974, and 1975 did capital flows contribute toward financing the basic balance deficit. For the remaining years, particularly 1971, 1976, and 1977, capital flows and the basic balance had the same sign.

What determines the extent to which the authorities choose to finance the external imbalance rather than force self-financing through capital flows or adjustment? Essentially, the financing is an attempt to mitigate the rate of depreciation or appreciation of the exchange rate.

A natural question to ask is why the authorities should have invested so much in attempts to stabilize sterling. Table 20 shows the *net* official external position and confirms that external borrowing has been extensively used to finance the foreign exchange intervention of the last few years. There are essentially three arguments for exchange rate intervention.

The first, the concern for financial stability, much like the concern that leads to stabilizing interest rates, is at best an argument for smoothing the path of exchange rates. Of course, the ability to distinguish temporary disturbances from trends is not widespread.

The second argument for exchange rate intervention is to control inflation. Exchange rate movements brought about by financial disturbances affect import prices and thereby, as will be seen below, affect domestic inflation. Attempts to stabilize inflation would thus benefit from an accompanying policy of exchange rate stability.

The third argument concerns the competitiveness of industry. Excess depreciation, compared to differential underlying inflation trends, enhances competitiveness and thereby increases employment and improves the current account. British commentators have remarked optimistically on the role of undervalued German and Japanese exchange rates in promoting exports in the 1950s and 1960s.[31] Initially, such overdepreciation comes at the expense of price stability.

The relative importance of the three factors has varied. In early 1976, for example, sterling was depreciated deliberately to promote competitiveness.[32] In 1977, by contrast, exchange rate stability and slight appreciation helped stabilize inflation. By 1979 continuing high unemployment and a worsening of the competitive position in manufacturing made a real depreciation appear desirable, though perhaps hard to get in the face of sterling's oil-backed strength.

The scope for exchange rate intervention as an independent policy instrument should not be exaggerated. Intervention can successfully control the exchange rate only to the extent that there are compatible domestic monetary and fiscal policies. Exchange rate intervention is sometimes necessary to demonstrate the intent to follow particular domestic policies, but it cannot function long without their backing.

The Exchange Rate and Inflation

Two related questions are of particular concern here. Do exchange rate movements provide an exogenous source of domestic inflationary pressure? Are exchange rate changes an effective tool for payments adjustments? The second question is equivalent to asking whether exchange rate movements are offset by domestic inflation.

One view is that monetary and fiscal policies are largely exogenous

31. For example, Posner, "Problems of the British Economy."
32. See Fay and Young, "The Day the Pound Nearly Died."

(or that they can or should be?) and that they determine the rate of domestic inflation, with the exchange rate following on average a purchasing power parity path. The alternative view, which commands more widespread support, is that exchange rate movements frequently arise for reasons unrelated to current monetary or fiscal policies, that these exchange rate movements affect domestic inflation through import prices, and that this induced inflation invites at least partial accommodation by the authorities in an attempt to stave off the (short-run) deflationary effect of increased inflation for a given growth of money and a given tax structure. The accommodation validates the exchange rate movement.

The question, then, is whether there are exchange rate movements independent of domestic monetary and fiscal policy actions and whether there is accommodation. Little doubt exists on either of these scores. We may simply note the case in which a foreign tightening of policies causes an immediate change in exchange rates and increased domestic import prices. Further, monetary and fiscal policies will, to some extent, be conducted with real goals in view and therefore will automatically adjust to "exogenous" exchange rate movements.

We now look at the relation between exchange rate movements and changes in inflation and competitiveness during the seventies. Figure 7 shows the relation between movements in the nominal effective exchange rate and the real (wholesale price–adjusted) exchange rate, or competitiveness. The figure indicates that in the short run movements in nominal rates bring about changes in real rates in the same direction, although of a smaller magnitude. Over time, though, real rates do not show a trend, so that the changes in real rates are not large and persistent. The extent and persistence of measured real exchange rate movements depend on the particular price index used in defining the real rate. Movements of the real rate appear most significant for measures based on value-added, unit labor costs or consumer prices (as is implied by table 11 above).

Whether nominal exchange rate changes can move long-run real exchange rates is not a theoretical puzzle but largely a question of circumstances. If exchange rate movements, arising because, say, of a financial disturbance, are fully matched by monetary changes, so that unemployment remains constant, then one would expect a full adjustment of domestic prices more or less rapidly. But this example represents only the "pure" inflation part of the exchange rate movements, not the part that could serve to bring about real adjustments in relative prices and thereby

Figure 7. *Indexes of Nominal Effective and Real Exchange Rates for Sterling, by Quarter, 1970–78*

1975:1 = 100

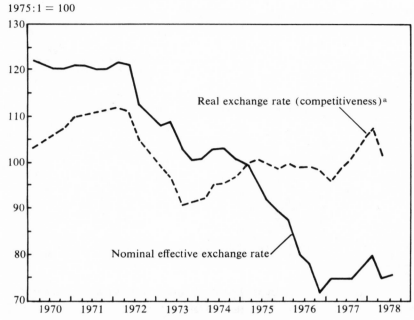

Source: Central Statistical Office, *Economic Trends* (various issues).
a. Wholesale price–adjusted rate.

in the current balance. For that part the essential question is whether there is flexibility in real wages to achieve a movement in relative prices. If the flexibility exists, there are further questions about how much unemployment over how long a period, and how large a nominal exchange rate movement, are needed to achieve a given relative price change.

The adjustment to the external imbalance of 1973–75 is brought out in table 21, which shows indexes of real wages and inflation rates. The full employment condition of 1973 combined with the sharp gain in real wages implied a lack of competitiveness and the need for a *real* depreciation to reverse the current balance. In the ensuing period, nominal depreciation and restrictive aggregate demand policies together reduced real wages.

The main question at the time of writing is whether exchange rates have merely run ahead of wages, which will soon catch up, or whether the real wage has been permanently reduced relative to trend. One indication of the answer is the pressure now (1979) occurring for wage settlements in

Table 21. *U.K. Inflation and Depreciation Rates and Indexes of Real Earnings, 1970–78*

Indexes, 1970 = 100

	Inflation rate (*percent*)			Effective rate of sterling depreciation (*percent*)	Indexes of real earnings[a]	
Year	Wholesale prices	Retail prices	Average earnings		(*1*)	(*2*)
1970	7.2	6.4	12.7	1.3	100.0	100.0
1971	9.1	9.4	11.2	0.9	101.8	102.0
1972	5.2	7.1	12.9	3.4	109.2	106.9
1973	7.4	9.2	12.9	10.7	114.8	110.6
1974	22.6	16.1	17.2	4.2	109.7	111.7
1975	22.2	24.2	26.1	7.7	113.2	113.4
1976	17.3	16.5	16.5	15.4	112.4	113.3
1977	19.7	15.8	10.3	5.5	103.5	107.9
1978	9.1	8.2	14.1	−1.4	116.1	114.2

Sources: Central Statistical Office, *Economic Trends* (various issues); and International Monetary Fund, *International Financial Statistics* (various issues).

a. Average earnings (manufacturing) deflated by the wholesale price index (column 1) and by the retail price index (column 2).

the range of 12 to 15 percent. The further question is whether, even if at present unemployment levels there were no pressure for gains in real wages (both catch-up and trend?), it would be possible to maintain the present real wage level if full employment were restored. One must be very skeptical on that score; accordingly, the hope of rising productivity or the use of fiscal policy to make available noninflationary real wage gains seem the only possibilities for maintaining real wages as unemployment falls.

How important have exchange rate movements and the induced changes in import prices been in the inflationary process? Table 22 provides an account of the sources of consumer price inflation for the 1972–77 period, with the accounting based on 1972 input-output tables. The interesting aspect of this table is the very uneven contribution of import price inflation. Only in 1974 do import price increases stand out as the single most important source of inflation. In 1975–77 wage inflation dominates with only a minor contribution from import prices. In these years taxes account for as much inflation as do import prices.

An alternative procedure to determine the importance of exchange rates and import prices for the domestic inflationary process is to assume that import prices can be taken as an exogenous independent variable in

Table 22. *Contributions to Consumer Price Changes in the United Kingdom, 1972–77*

Percent a year

Item	1972	1973	1974	1975	1976	1977[a]
Income from employment[b]	2.9	3.6	7.0	15.5	7.0	5.25
Other costs[b]	3.6	4.1	3.1	2.75	4.0	3.25
Taxes less subsidies[b]	0.2	0.1	−0.6	3.25	3.25	3.5
Price of imports	0.2	3.3	8.6	3.5	3.75	3.0
Residual	−0.2	−2.6	−2.0	−1.5	−2.75	−0.5
Consumer expenditure deflator	6.7	8.5	16.1	23.5	15.25	14.5

Source: OECD, *Economic Surveys: United Kingdom* (Paris: OECD, various issues).
a. Based on data to the third quarter of 1977.
b. Per unit of output.

a price equation. In equation 4 in the appendix, we relate the quarterly rate of inflation of retail prices to current and lagged inflation rates of wages (average earnings) and import prices. The equation is estimated for the period 1967–77 and explains nearly 70 percent of the variation in quarterly retail price inflation. The cumulative effect of a 1 percentage point increase in wage inflation is to raise retail price inflation by 0.79 percent. A 1 percent increase in import price inflation, cumulatively, raises retail price inflation by 0.18 percent. The combined effect of increased wage and import price inflation is thus to generate an equal increase in retail price inflation. The lag structure with which wages and import prices affect retail prices is not very sturdy, except that the mean lag for import prices appears shorter (1.6 quarters) than that for wages (2.7 quarters). This is quite sensible, since the effect of wages on retail prices arises to a large extent after an intermediate effect on wholesale prices.

We thus find a clear link between cost variables—import prices and wages—and the resulting domestic inflation. We would like to establish evidence for the proposition that inflationary expectations, the level of real wages, and the rate of unemployment affect the rate of increase in money wages. In figure 8 we show the level of real wages—average earnings deflated by the retail price index. Important to note are the great variability in the real wage since 1973, possible because of high and variable inflation, and the decline in real wages from 1975 to mid-1977.

It is generally agreed that at present there is no known *stable* wage

Figure 8. *Index of Real Average Earnings in the United Kingdom, by Quarter, 1967–78*[a]

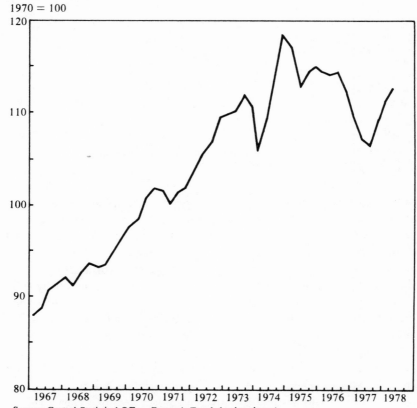

1970 = 100

Source: Central Statistical Office, *Economic Trends* (various issues).
a. Average earnings (all industries) deflated by the retail price index.

equation for the United Kingdom. A 1978 memorandum of the NIESR said:

> Even so, there is no wage equation which fits the experience of the last seven years at all adequately in this country; indeed, given the form which wage bargaining has taken in recent years and is likely to take, it is open to question whether there is a sensible wage equation at all.[33]

This statement diverges from an earlier view, presented by Henry, Sawyer, and Smith, that equations estimated through 1974, using as independent

33. National Institute of Economic and Social Research, "The Proposed New EEC Monetary System," Minutes of Evidence, November 3, 1978, Expenditure Committee, House of Commons.

variables a time trend, the level of net real earnings, and lagged inflation, performed well and were stable over subperiods.[34] In particular, the authors noted that a high level of net real earnings tended to reduce wage inflation and that no evidence existed of an effect of unemployment on wage inflation as the earlier Phillips curve model had maintained.

British wage behavior has been influenced by a number of factors whose relative importance has varied over time. First, there are inflationary expectations. Standard representations that rely on lagged inflation as a measure of expectations run of course into trouble because of the sharp acceleration of inflation in 1974–75 and the subsequent equally sharp deceleration. Second, unemployment rates have more than doubled since the late sixties and should thus exert a substantial dampening effect on wage inflation. To the extent that this is not the case, one must ask whether important changes in benefits have raised the natural rate of unemployment.[35] Third, relative wages have traditionally been taken as an important element in the wage formation process. This suggests that it is very difficult to change the wage structure as between manufacturing that is trade-oriented and services. To the extent that manufacturing wages rise with the prices of traded goods they may exert pressure on the general wage structure through a relative wage effect. Fourth, real net earnings have been taken as an important element in the wage bargain. Labor has a target real wage, and real wage resistance implies that a decline in real wages will in subsequent bargaining rounds lead to a catch-up. There is some question of the degree to which fiscal policies have to be taken into account in measuring the target real wage. Finally, incomes policy certainly exerts an important effect on the timing of wage and price changes and may even exert a durable effect on real wages.

In the appendix we report one of our estimates of a wage equation. Equation 5 explains quarterly changes in average earnings in terms of lagged inflation of retail prices, unemployment, and deviations of real wages from a time trend. The equation is satisfactory for this sample period but is not very stable when estimated over a substantially longer sample period. A good wage equation is essential, since we view the behavior of wages, relative to productivity, as crucial to the British stabili-

34. S. G. B. Henry, M. C. Sawyer and P. Smith, "Models of Inflation in the United Kingdom: An Evaluation," *National Institute Economic Review*, no. 77 (August 1976), pp. 60–71.

35. On this point see J. S. Flemming, *Inflation* (London: Oxford University Press, 1976).

zation problem. Wage inflation is central to domestic inflation and the external value of sterling, to the competitiveness of manufacturing, and thereby to the full-employment current account. The resurgence of high wage inflation in 1979 indicates that it is as yet impossible to depreciate the exchange rate in real terms to any significant extent or for any length of time, and that, accordingly, none of the basic problems of the seventies has found a permanent solution, even though oil revenues could finance a temporary solution.

The Outlook

What is the outlook for the U.K. economy, and in particular for the external sector? At the end of 1978 unemployment remained very high; inflation had declined substantially but was still around 8 percent. The budget deficit had declined under the auspices of the IMF to about £4 billion, and the current account showed a surplus, reflecting adjustment of relative prices, the effects of oil development, and the substantial slack in economic activity. In the wake of dollar weakness sterling had fully stabilized in terms of the effective exchange rate. Thus everything except unemployment seemed well under control.

However, none of the fundamental problems has been resolved.[36] At present, the major issue for policymakers is how to make the transition, aided by the temporary availability of oil revenues, toward self-financing noninflationary growth at full employment. Current account balance can be maintained in the 1980s if domestic demand is kept low and the unemployment rate high. The difficult decisions turn on the questions of how and when—and whether it is possible—to expand employment without increasing inflation and driving the current account into deficit.

Two possible scenarios mark the range of opportunities. The first has been strongly espoused by the Cambridge Group,[37] which advocates pro-

36. As this is written, in 1979, there are signs of trouble ahead in the form of increased wage inflation and an increased budget deficit.

37. See, for example, Nicholas Kaldor, "The Effect of Devaluations on Trade in Manufactures" (Cambridge University, 1977); Wynne Godley and Robert M. May, "The Macroeconomic Implications of Devaluation and Import Restriction," *Economic Policy Review,* vol. 3 (March 1977), pp. 32–42; and Francis Cripps, "Causes of Growth and Recession in World Trade," ibid., vol. 4 (March 1978), pp. 37–43.

tectionism or trade planning to solve the long-standing problem of manufacturing industry and employment.[38] The argument is that exchange rate
adjustment, because of the pass-through of inflation into wages and costs,
is not an effective means of changing competitiveness and employment.
This view has been strongly put by Cripps, who concludes:

Although international trade has certainly assisted the development and dissemination of productive technology, further increases in interdependence
will not necessarily be beneficial, because tendencies to structural imbalance
make it very difficult to maintain trade at a sufficiently high level. There must
therefore come a point at which the ability to regulate trade propensities is
at least as important as that they should be high. For many countries and from
a point of view of the trading system as a whole that point may now have been
reached.[39]

This view has rightly been challenged on efficiency grounds. Most important, it is not apparent why reducing real wages through protectionism
does not affect workers in the same way as reducing real wages through
depreciation.

At the other end of the policy spectrum is a trade-based policy that
views oil revenues as the source for an upgrading of industrial structure
and adopts a trade-oriented strategy. That approach would typically go
hand in hand with increased European Community participation and
membership in the European Monetary System. Such a policy has in the
short term to deal with the issue of whether exchange rate policy should
be managed to allow the oil revenue to float sterling up and inflation
down, or whether, in the interest of manufacturing, the real exchange rate
should be kept pegged, or better yet, undervalued.

The question of manufacturing and how to make or keep that sector
competitive is central to short- and medium-term policymaking. The
choice of a real exchange rate is important, as is the question of investment and growth in industrial productivity. The short-term factor of the
low level of domestic demand, including in particular the low level of
(nonoil-related) investment, operates against the policy goal of a strong
manufacturing sector. The other factor operating against an increasingly
vigorous manufacturing sector is the failure to achieve a depreciation in
the real exchange rate. The undervaluation that was a growth factor in
West Germany during the 1960s has been impossible because of the

38. Of course, minor forms of protectionism and pervasive exchange controls
have long been in force in the United Kingdom.
39. Cripps, "Causes of Growth and Recession in World Trade," p. 43.

Table 23. *Basic Balance Prospects for the United Kingdom, Selected Years 1978–85*

Billions of 1977 pounds

Year	Interest and capital repayment on official borrowing	Oil impact on current balance
1978	2.1	4.5
1980	5.0	7.5
1982	3.7	8.5
1985	1.5	9.5

Source: *Bank of England Quarterly Bulletin*, vol. 18 (September 1978), tables 23.2, 23.3; and OECD, *Economic Surveys: United Kingdom* (Paris: OECD, 1978), p. 56.

combination of persisting relatively high inflation and appreciation, the latter due to the slack in domestic demand and the prospects of a substantial current account improvement because of oil. These factors have caused sterling to keep from depreciating significantly in real terms and therefore have failed to give rise to an export boom and check on the growth of imports.

Table 23 shows the official liabilities, capital and interest, that fall due in 1978 and over the next few years. These liabilities peak in 1980 at about £5 billion. Estimates of the impact of oil exploitation on the current balance are reported in the second column. It is quite apparent that the order of magnitude of the oil impact substantially dominates the external debt service and repayments and that consequently leeway exists in the current account either for demand expansion—consumption or investment—or for appreciation. Given the pervasive concern with inflation, there is reason to believe that a course involving both (real) appreciation and increased investment will be chosen, but that substantial demand expansion is not really in sight.

The elimination of exchange rate control would clearly be another option in offsetting the effect of North Sea oil on sterling and manufacturing competitiveness.[40] If elimination of exchange rate control led to stability of the real exchange rate or even to some depreciation, without at the same time lowering asset prices relative to replacement cost in manufacturing, then one might see in this policy both a means to increased employment and a move toward more efficient resource allocation. It cannot really be presumed that this is *not* a good time to open up the economy.

40. This step was taken in late 1979 with the elimination of restrictions on domestic ownership of foreign securities and the elimination of the investment sterling market. The effects in the right direction appear to have been small.

North Sea oil by itself has contributed strength to the exchange rate and has kept the real exchange rate and the terms of trade at a high level. The question arises how to bring about a real depreciation and thus gain in competitiveness and increased manufacturing employment under these conditions. There seems very little doubt that fiscal ease will deteriorate the current balance and thus bring about a real depreciation. The details of the fiscal policy are, of course, important from an allocative point of view and from a perspective of medium-term competitiveness, but will not be discussed here.

Can increased investment together with some real depreciation solve the employment problem? Investment may well make labor more productive and thereby create external demand; at the same time, though, investment is likely to be laborsaving and to that extent results in an offsetting reduction in employment. Real depreciation induces the expansion of exports and checks import growth. On balance, therefore, it is not apparent that the employment problem will be fully answered by an investment-oriented strategy; but if demand is to be expanded (as it should be), policies that encourage investment—and thus tend to increase productivity—should be preferred.

Appendix

This appendix brings together the empirical work discussed in the text. Many of these equations parallel work reported in the many British sources referred to above. All the equations are estimated by generalized least squares, using single equation methods.

Current Account Equation

Our equation for the current account was estimated on quarterly data for the period 1968:1–1977:4. The numbers in parentheses in all equations are t-statistics.

(1) $\quad CA/GDP = 0.29 + 0.024U + 0.17Y^*$
$\qquad\qquad\quad (0.56) \quad (5.9) \qquad (2.5)$

$$- 0.004TIME - 0.10P_M - 0.24COMP$$
$$\quad (3.8) \qquad\qquad (3.2) \qquad (3.9)$$

$\bar{R}^2 = 0.75$; Durbin-Watson $= 2.1$; rho$_1 = 0.66$; rho$_2 = -0.33$, where

U = unemployment rate
Y^* = log of the OECD index of industrial production
$TIME$ = time trend (1968:1 = 1)
P_M = log of the price of materials relative to the GDP deflator
$COMP$ = log of the IMF index of U.K. competitiveness in manufacturing entered as a second-order polynomial with seven
lags.

The Budget and the Current Account

Using annual data for the period 1956–77, we estimated an equation
with the current account, CA, as the left-hand side variable and the
budget deficit, BD, as the explanatory variable.

(2) $$CA = 340.5 - 0.23BD$$
$$(2.13) \quad (5.14)$$

$\bar{R}^2 = 0.57$; Durbin-Watson = 2.35; $rho_1 = 0.34$; $rho_2 = -0.47$,

where rho_1 and rho_2 are the estimated coefficients in the correction for
second-order serial correlation.

The equation thus confirms strongly the effect of the budget deficit on
the current account, but the coefficient is less than one-third.

Exchange Rate Equation

Our exchange rate equation was estimated for the period 1971:4–
1978:3.

(3) $EER = 1.91 + 0.94EER_{-1} + (4.1E - 6)R_{-1}$
$\quad\quad (1.6) \quad (14.6) \quad\quad\quad (1.2)$

$\quad\quad + 0.01D - 0.25COMP_{-1} - 0.15(\$/DM) + (4.5E - 5)S$
$\quad\quad\; (1.5) \quad\quad (1.2) \quad\quad\quad (1.4) \quad\quad\quad\quad (2.0)$

$\bar{R}^2 = 0.98$; Durbin-Watson = 2.21; $EER = 0.03$,

where

EER = log of the effective exchange rate
R = level of exchange reserves
D = covered differential against sterling (interbank Eurodollar)

$/DM$ = dollar–deutsche mark exchange rate

S = OPEC holdings of sterling assets, after 1972.

The equation explains the effective exchange rate in terms of the lagged rate, lagged reserve holdings, the interest differential against sterling, U.K. competitiveness, the dollar–deutsche mark exchange rate, and OPEC holdings of sterling assets. We note that the coefficients on the lagged exchange rate and OPEC holdings are quite precisely estimated. Competitiveness has the expected sign—a loss of competitiveness leads to depreciation—but the coefficient is very imprecisely estimated. The same is true of the level of reserves and the covered differential. The dollar–deutsche mark rate is introduced, along with the covered differential, as a measure of speculative activity. The equation suggests that a dollar depreciation relative to the mark leads to an appreciation of the effective sterling rate.

The Price Equation

Our price equation was estimated for the period 1967:1–1977:4. The dependent variable is the quarterly inflation rate of the retail price index. The explanatory variables are distributed lags on wages and import prices.

$$(4) \qquad R\dot{P}I = 0.0 + 0.79\dot{W} + 0.18\ I\dot{P}$$
$$\phantom{(4) \qquad R\dot{P}I = } (0.03)\ (5.0) \qquad (2.8)$$

$$\bar{R}^2 = 0.66;\ \text{Durbin-Watson} = 1.89,$$

where

$R\dot{P}I$ = quarterly inflation rate of retail prices

$\dot{W}$ = wage inflation

$I\dot{P}$ = inflation of import prices.

Wage and import price inflation are entered as second-degree polynomial distributed lags with respectively five and four lags. The equation supports the notion that exchange rate management through the resulting influence on import price inflation exerts a strong, systematic, and rapid effect on domestic inflation. Reducing the rate of import price inflation by 5 percentage points reduces domestic price inflation *directly* by 1 percentage point. There will be further deceleration of inflation to the extent that money wage inflation declines.

Wage Equations

Equations for quarterly average earnings inflation were estimated for the period 1970:1–1978:1. We report here only one typical equation:

$$(5) \qquad \dot{W} = 0.38 + 0.36R\dot{P}I - 0.025U + 0.36\bar{W} - 0.09\Delta U$$
$$\quad (3.6) \quad (7.2) \qquad (3.0) \qquad (3.3) \qquad (3.7)$$

$$\bar{R}^2 = 0.76; \text{ Durbin-Watson} = 2.01; SER = 0.01,$$

where

$\dot{W}$ = wage inflation

U = log of the unemployment rate, second-degree polynomial with seven lags

ΔU = quarter-to-quarter change in U

$\bar{W}$ = real wage deviation

$R\dot{P}I$ = annual inflation rate of retail prices.

In the equation $\bar{W}$ represents the difference between real wage earnings, fitted along a quadratic time trend, and the lagged level of real earnings. With the fitted value being interpreted as a target real wage, the real wage gap is used as one of the explanatory variables.

The equation reflects both the impact of protracted unemployment and of current changes in unemployment as dampening factors in wage inflation. A higher level of the real wage gap, $\bar{W}$, exerts an accelerating effect while higher inflation raises the rate of wage increase. All coefficients are significant and have the expected sign. The equation is surprising, given the discussion in the literature, in that it shows a substantial effect of unemployment on wage inflation. The most serious problem, however, with an equation such as 5 is that it has very little stability when estimated over a longer sample period.

Comments by Alan Budd

IN THEIR introductory comments, Dornbusch and Fischer remark that "the laws of economics continue to work in the United Kingdom." Ironically, the field they survey is one in which there has been fierce debate about what the laws of economics actually are. The authors have made important contributions to that debate,[41] but with excessive modesty they do not cite their own work. Nor do they use the theories, which they have helped develop, to explain events in Britain. This too seems excessively modest. Although it is clear that naive versions of monetarist theories do not explain short-term behavior, the economic history of the last decade fits well into an approach (which I call "structural") that incorporates long-run properties similar to those of monetary models.

The shift to the structural approach (which has occurred in H. M. Treasury, among other places) has occurred both because of a revolution in economic theory and because of the series of economic disasters that Dornbusch and Fischer succinctly describe. (The revolution, like so many in economics, has involved rediscovery as much as discovery.) The shifts have been reflected in major changes in economic policy. It is instructive to look back to the earlier Brookings study on Britain to see how much ideas have changed in the past ten or so years.

The prospects in 1968 were gloomy enough, though there was far worse to come. Cooper listed a number of possible solutions to Britain's balance-of-payments problems, including a change in the exchange rate.[42] (The devaluation of 1967 occurred before the previous Brookings volume was published, but it was too early to know what its effects would be.) The analysis of the required devaluation was made in the conventional framework of the time, namely in terms of import and export price elasticities. Cooper calculated that a 6.4 percent devaluation would have been adequate to remove Britain's underlying balance-of-payments deficit. The 14.3 percent devaluation of 1967, on his estimates, would improve the balance of payments by over £800 million on a full-employment basis.[43] One could describe the analytical approach that led to this conclusion as the "income elasticities" approach. The approach was derived from the partial analysis embodied in the "Marshall-Lerner" conditions, but it had been extended, for example by Johnson and Meade, to incor-

41. See, for example, Rudiger Dornbusch, "Currency Depreciation, Hoarding, and Relative Prices," *Journal of Political Economy*, vol. 81 (July 1973), pp. 893–915; and Dornbusch, "Devaluation, Money, and Nontraded Goods," *American Economic Review*, vol. 63 (December 1973), pp. 871–80.

42. Richard N. Cooper, "The Balance of Payments," in Caves and others, *Britain's Economic Prospects,* pp. 147–97.

43. Ibid., p. 192. An account of British calculations in the same tradition is found in G. D. N. Worswick, "Trade and Payments," in Sir Alec Cairncross, ed., *Britain's Economic Prospects Reconsidered* (London: Allen and Unwin, 1971), p. 61.

porate the income effects of changes in the exchange rate. In Cooper's paper the potential effect on aggregate demand was estimated to require a reduction in domestic demand of £100 for every percentage point of devaluation.[44]

Although the income elasticities approach was an advance over the straightforward elasticities approach,[45] it still represented only a partial analysis of the problem. Most notably the analysis did not incorporate a full consideration of the effects of a devaluation on costs (including wages) and prices. Nor did it include a full consideration of the induced changes in financial markets, especially in the market for money. Cooper did in fact recognize that there might be an induced rise in wages and included an estimate by Lipsey as part of his calculations.[46] However, it is fair to say that the possible effect on wages was added as an afterthought rather than embodied in the analysis.

Although the income elasticities approach provides only a partial analysis of the balance-of-payments problem, at the time of the 1967 devaluation this approach was the only one incorporated in the macro-economic forecasting models in operation in the United Kingdom. Since those models were used in the process of producing complete forecasts of U.K. national income, the partial nature of the analysis was disguised by the weight of national-income and balance-of-payments forecasting that accompanied it. Further, the partial analysis was acceptable because it was generally assumed, at least for the United Kingdom, that wage inflation could be treated as autonomous and that a possible link between devaluation and wages was of secondary importance. In addition, the models and forecasting systems in use at the time paid little or no attention to the role of money in the economy and relied largely on an income-expenditure approach to macroeconomics. (Such was the state of opinion at the time on the "laws of economics.")

The opposition to the income elasticities approach was based originally on a model that was, admittedly, both artificial and incomplete. The model assumed the instantaneous adjustment of real markets, including those for labor, and incorporated a naive view of the demand for money. This simple monetarist approach led to very different conclusions from those of the income elasticities approach. First, it implied that a balance-of-payments

44. Cooper, "The Balance of Payments," p. 190.
45. The use of Marshall-Lerner conditions in analyzing devaluations is criticized in Dornbusch, "Currency Depreciation, Hoarding, and Relative Prices," p. 898.
46. Cooper, "The Balance of Payments," pp. 191–92.

deficit is a sign of monetary disequilibrium, of which one cause is excessive credit creation. A devaluation alters the balance of payments in the following way: the increase in prices in the devaluing country reduces its real money balances; with unchanged credit policy, the reduction in real balances causes a fall in expenditure that in turn causes an improvement in the balance of payments. Second, the monetarist approach implied that under fixed exchange rates inflation is an international rather than a domestic problem.[47] Either a small country has to accept the inflation that is thrust upon it or it must leave the currency system. The freedom to determine one's own rate of inflation requires a flexible exchange rate; under such a rate a country's rate of inflation will depend on the growth of its money supply. Finally, this approach implied that since balance-of-payments deficits are a monetary phenomenon, they cannot be resolved by such policies as import controls.

When the battle over these theories raged in the United Kingdom, particularly in the early 1970s, the two sides seemed to be unequally armed. The income elasticities approach (and the income-expenditure approach to national-income forecasting that accompanied it) had the big battalions in the form of large-scale econometric models. The opposition (one would describe the two sides as "Keynesian" and "monetarist" had those expressions not become so uninformative) had only its simple theories and hardly a regression to its name. Yet it is not a complete exaggeration to say that David has defeated Goliath and that the conventional wisdom has absorbed much, if not all, of the new ideas. (I am not of course suggesting that this acceptance establishes the truth of these ideas.)

As to the income-expenditure approach, the most notable official pronouncement on it has been that of Callaghan in September 1976:

We used to think that you could just spend your way out of a recession and increase employment by cutting taxes and boosting government spending. I tell you in all candour that that option no longer exists, and that insofar as it ever did exist, it worked by injecting inflation into the economy. And each time that happened the average level of unemployment has risen. Higher inflation, followed by higher unemployment. That is the history of the last twenty years.[48]

47. See, for example, Alexander K. Swoboda, "Monetary Policy under Fixed Exchange Rates: Effectiveness, the Speed of Adjustment, and Proper Use," in H. G. Johnson and A. R. Nobay, eds., *Issues in Monetary Economics* (London: Oxford University Press, 1974), p. 61.

48. Prime Minister James Callaghan, speech delivered at the Labour party's annual conference, Blackpool, Lancashire, September 28, 1976.

As for the income elasticities approach to exchange rate changes, one may quote Chancellor of the Exchequer Denis Healey's Mansion House speech of October 1978:

Some people used to see depreciation as an easy way of restoring price competitiveness. But hard experience confirms the findings of economic research— that the price increases generated by a fall in the exchange rate are tending to feed through a good deal faster into rising labour costs than they used to. Depreciation can no longer be treated as a soft option.[49]

The view of the exchange rate mechanism has shifted from one in which its main purpose was to affect relative prices and real flows of goods to one in which that purpose is to control inflation.

Why have these changes occurred? As Dornbusch has pointed out, the implications of the simplest Keynesian approach, which assumes complete specialization and unchanged domestic prices, and the implications of the simplest monetarist approach, which assumes instant adjustment of goods markets and a naive demand for money function, are both theoretically correct. It is equally clear that the underlying assumptions of each model are empirically false. The changed point of view undoubtedly owes much to the experiences of the disappointing response (in terms of general expectations before 1967) first to the devaluation and then to the floating of sterling. Events have corresponded more closely to the implications of the monetary model than to the implications of the income elasticities approach. As a result, economists, particularly those who construct and use econometric models, have reexamined the behavioral assumptions and long-run implications of their models. In so doing they have absorbed many of the monetarist ideas. (If the analogy is not too farfetched, one may say that David defeated Goliath by allowing Goliath to swallow him.) It has now been shown that the long-run implications of a "structural" model are the same as those of monetary models.[50] By structural model is meant a model that includes in its macroeconomic framework markets for goods, labor, and financial assets. It is assumed that at least some goods and financial assets are traded in international markets. By "market" is meant some system in which relative prices respond to excess demand. The laws of economics can then be limited to the laws of supply

49. Denis Healey, speech delivered at the Lord Mayor's Banquet for Bankers and Merchants, London, October 19, 1978.

50. See, for example, Michael Beenstock, *The Foreign Exchanges: Theory, Modelling and Policy* (London: St. Martin's Press, 1979).

and demand, over which there is considerable agreement. Disagreement can be limited to the precise dynamic specification of the behavioral equations.

The H. M. Treasury model is structural in this sense. Its development corresponds to the changes that have occurred since the first Brookings study. Then conventional wisdom said that fiscal expansion could reduce unemployment and that devaluation changed the real exchange rate. Now both beliefs have been officially abandoned. The paper by Dornbusch and Fischer provides many illustrations of why this has happened.

One may start with the point illustrated by figure 4 in their paper, which shows that the real exchange rate (measured in this case by the ratio of the prices of manufacturers exports to imports) responds only briefly to a change in the nominal exchange rate. The same result is apparent in other measures of the effect of exchange rate changes, although there are reasonable disagreements about how rapidly the competitive advantage is eroded. The authors attribute this result to "real wage resistance" and provide a simple model that incorporates it. Their model, however, raises a number of problems. The only useful meaning of real wage resistance would seem to be the failure of real wages to adjust to the excess demand or supply of labor. There may well be such resistance, but it is not obvious what connection it has with attempts to cut real wages simply by lowering the nominal exchange rate. And also if "full employment" is something that cannot be reached because of real wage resistance, it would seem important to reconsider what is meant by full employment in such a context.

Within a structural model one would expect considerable, and eventually complete, erosion of gains in competitiveness in the markets for traded goods following a devaluation. This is consistent with the evidence provided by Dornbusch and Fischer.

In assessing the role of money in exchange rate movements, the authors suggest that the "simple theories do not go very far by themselves in explaining the magnitude *and* timing of depreciation." That is undoubtedly true, but it would be very surprising if the simple theories did work in the short run. Within the structural approach one would expect to find other significant explanatory variables operating in the short run, including price movements. The authors present an eclectic equation that appears to support this view and that does not specifically incorporate monetary variables. At the technical level the equation has some worrying features.

With a highly significant coefficient of unity on the lagged value of the exchange rate, it seems clear that the equation relates to the change in the exchange rate and could be presented as such. The definition of the covered differential includes, presumably, the spot exchange rate and is therefore explaining the exchange rate partly by itself.

There is a general methodological point to be made about this equation and others presented in the paper. Equations like equation 3 in the appendix have variables on the right-hand side that are clearly endogenous to the economic system as a whole. Such equations do not by themselves tell one anything about the underlying causal mechanisms in the economy. One cannot, for example, learn from such equations whether wages cause inflation. (Still less can one answer such questions by comparing price and wage changes in a single year.) One needs to know what causes wages to change, and this can only be done by examining the full properties of the model. In the case of the exchange rate equation it would be necessary to know both what caused changes in competitiveness and what caused changes in the covered differential. Such single equations are by no means inconsistent with the view that, in the long run, exchange rate changes, inflation, and balance-of-payments movements are monetary phenomena.

Finally, Dornbusch and Fischer also observe that competitiveness has improved (on a number of measures) since 1970. (The results are shown in figure 3 and table 12.) In terms of competitiveness, if one compares 1977 with 1970 one observes the following ratios:

Export average values	0.97
Wholesale prices	0.94
Unit current costs	0.93
Consumer prices	0.88

This is what one might expect from the analysis of Balassa, for example.[51] It cannot be assumed, of course, that either 1970 or 1977 represents an equilibrium, but the figures suggest that export prices are largely set in world markets. Wholesale prices, by contrast, include an element of non-traded goods. Since the United Kingdom has a below-average growth of productivity, one would expect relative wholesale prices to fall more than relative export prices. The ratios of unit current costs and wholesale prices are almost the same. Consumer prices contain a yet greater share

51. See Bela Balassa, "The Purchasing-Power Parity Doctrine: A Reappraisal," *Journal of Political Economy*, vol. 72 (December 1964), pp. 584–96.

of nontraded goods and therefore show an even greater apparent gain in competitiveness. The tendency for relative consumer prices to fall more than relative export prices has been apparent since the 1950s, and indicates that under fixed exchange rates the United Kingdom would be expected to have a lower-than-average rate of inflation.

The rise of export prices relative to wholesale prices during this period does, however, appear to show a break with past trends. On the assumption that compositional changes were not significant, this is likely, as the authors say, to have been a favorable factor for exports.

If one contrasts the Dornbusch and Fischer paper with the earlier paper by Cooper, one is most struck by the far less confident way in which problems are diagnosed and cures proposed. That seems exactly right. If nothing else we all should have gained some Socratic wisdom in the last ten years. It would perhaps have seemed a dereliction of professional duty to have concluded that there is nothing to be done; but on the basis of the evidence and of the theoretical contributions by the authors and others, that would seem a more correct answer—as far as macroeconomic measures are concerned—than the solutions offered (albeit tentatively) in this paper. For example, the perceptive discussion of the problem of how to make manufacturing more profitable (which is assumed to be a policy objective) is introduced by the comment, "The choice of a real exchange rate is important, as is the question of investment and growth in industrial productivity." Surely the experience of the past ten years has shown that we cannot choose our real exchange rate or that at least conventional macroeconomic measures do not provide that choice except in the short run. Macroeconomic policy can perhaps determine the rate at which the economy returns to equilibrium after a shock (though there are cool reminders scattered through the paper of how unsuccessful short-term intervention policy has been). It can perhaps offer a choice of the rate at which inflation can be reduced. As the authors point out, that choice has been much eased by North Sea oil.

Experiences since 1967 have shown that the balance of payments was not a separate problem related to an overvalued currency but part of the problem of the sustainable pressure of demand in the British economy. One would like macroeconomic models to show at what level of unemployment the economy can achieve balance-of-payments equilibrium under fixed exchange rates or stable inflation under flexible exchange rates. Few would doubt that the level is higher now than it was in 1967. Few should doubt that it will not be lowered by macroeconomic solutions based on a partial analysis of the economy. Dornbusch and Fischer make that clear. If the resulting level of unemployment is politically unacceptable, the important problem is to discover the microeconomic reasons for this, and to derive, if need be, the microeconomic solutions.

DAVID C. SMITH

Trade Union Growth and Industrial Disputes

It is commonly said that trade unions cause inflation: however that may be, it is quite clear that inflation causes trade unions.

JOAN ROBINSON AND FRANK WILKINSON[1]

The failure to achieve reasonable growth in living standards in recent years has led to the militant and obstructive trade union activity from which Britain has suffered. Hence this has been a consequence of Britain's economic failures. It has not caused them.

ROBERT BACON AND WALTER ELTIS[2]

FROM 1968 through 1977 Britain experienced higher inflation, slower economic growth, more rapid growth of unions, and increased strike activity than it had in the previous decade (table 1). Issues of trade unionism also dominated British public policy debates to a greater extent, leading to an intensive search for new measures in labor-management relations. (Appendix A lists the major steps in this search.) Undoubtedly, the concern about trade unions has arisen largely because of the assumed relationship between their growth and behavior and the nation's economic problems.

Among those who have given assistance and advice in the preparation of this paper, I wish to thank in particular George S. Bain and his associates at the SSRC Industrial Research Unit at the University of Warwick, S. W. Creigh of the Department of Employment, and my colleague Michael G. Abbott.

1. "What Has Become of Employment Policy?" *Cambridge Journal of Economics,* vol. 1 (March 1977), p. 9.

2. *Britain's Economic Problem: Too Few Producers* (London: Macmillan, 1976), p. 8.

David C. Smith

Table 1. *Trade Union Expansion, Work Stoppages, Inflation, and Economic Growth, United Kingdom, 1958–77*

	Annual average (*thousands*)		Annual growth rate (*percent*)	
Item	*1958–67*	*1968–77*	*1958–67*	*1968–77*
Working days lost in work stoppages	3,274	10,136	...	...
Trade union membership	...	...	0.4	2.4
Retail price index	...	...	2.9	11.3
Real gross domestic product	...	...	3.1	1.9

Sources: Trade union membership and work stoppages are from Department of Employment and Productivity, *British Labour Statistics, Historical Abstract, 1886–1968* (London: Her Majesty's Stationery Office, 1971), pp. 395, 396; Department of Employment, *British Labour Statistics Year Book, 1975* (HMSO, 1977), pp. 304, 308; and *Department of Employment Gazette*, issues for 1976 and 1977; retail price indexes are from Central Statistical Office, *Monthly Digest of Statistics*, issues for period indicated; real gross domestic product is from Organisation for Economic Co-operation and Development, *Main Economic Indicators* (Paris: OECD, 1957 and subsequent years).

On the one hand, it is usually argued that growth in the strength and militancy of trade unions pushed up prices faster and inhibited adjustment processes required for longer-term improvements in productivity. However, the precise nature and strength of the links between trade unionism and the economy are not known. For example, an extension in the organization and economic power of unions would be expected to initially influence relative wages and prices in particular sectors; some increase in average wages and prices might then result, particularly in a period of widespread growth of union strength. But an expansion of monetary demand conditions would be necessary for a sustained, large rise in inflation.

On the other hand, it can be argued that the influence went the other way, namely, that higher inflation and slower economic growth caused the increase in the strength and militancy of trade unions. (The two epigraphs above suggest this line of reasoning.) Public policy responses to these economic conditions, including attempts to modify trade union impacts on them, might also have affected the growth of trade unions. From this standpoint, trade unionism is not an independent institutional phenomenon that influences, without being influenced by, its economic environment.

The contribution of this latter thesis to a better understanding of the 1968–77 period of crisis in British industrial relations is the primary subject of this paper. More specifically, two issues are examined. First, for many years after World War II trade unionism in Britain, as in Canada and the United States, was in a period of stagnation, and even slight decline, with regard to the proportion of the labor force unionized. But beginning in the late 1960s, British trade unionism entered a period of rapid growth. Was this spurt related to the more severe problems of economic instability of the economy and to government measures to deal with them or was it essentially independent of such influences? Second, Britain has an image of being highly strike prone, an image that has not been weakened by evidence of an upward shift in strike activity beginning in the late 1960s. Is it clear that Britain has a serious and deteriorating strike problem and one that has been aggravated by recent economic events?

Union Growth

In Britain trade union membership as a proportion of the civilian labor force rose by about 20 percent between 1968 and 1976; in the United States this measure of union density fell by about 5 percent over the same period. However, as figure 1 shows, from 1900 through the mid-1960s unionization in the two countries took approximately the same course. The period preceding, during, and immediately following World War I was one of substantial growth in both countries, with the United Kingdom starting at a higher level of unionization and experiencing a larger increase in unionization. From about 1920 to the mid-1930s unionization was in decline in both countries, but this period was followed by one of rapid expansion in unionization that extended into the early post–World War II years. From the late 1940s in the United Kingdom and from the early 1950s in the United States, union density figures remained roughly constant or declined slightly through to the mid-1960s. At that time, the extension of unionization into the public sector brought a moderate increase to the U.S. figure, but it soon began to decline.

The recent surge in British unionism occurred despite the continuation of longer-term postwar shifts in the industrial and occupational distribution of employment away from sectors in which trade unionism has traditionally been stronger. For example, as Price and Bain have pointed out,[3] employment shifted between 1948 and 1974 toward industries with tradi-

3. Robert Price and George S. Bain, "Union Growth Revisited: 1948–1974 in Perspective," *British Journal of Industrial Relations,* vol. 14 (November 1976), pp. 339–55.

Figure 1. *Trade Union Membership as a Percentage of the Civilian Labor Force, United Kingdom and United States, 1900–76*

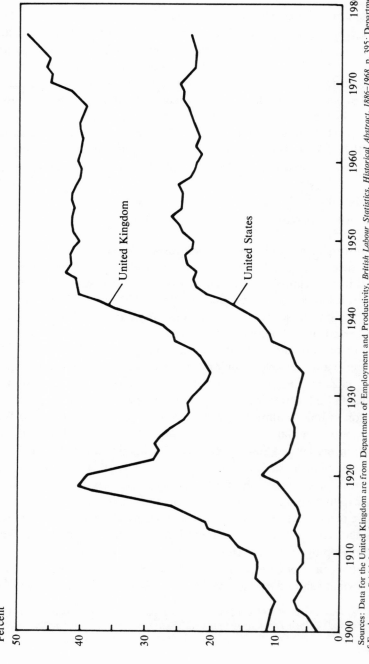

Sources: Data for the United Kingdom are from Department of Employment and Productivity, *British Labour Statistics, Historical Abstract, 1886–1968*, p. 395; Department of Employment, *British Labour Statistics Year Book, 1975*, p. 304; and *Department of Employment Gazette*, issues for 1976. Data for the United States are from U.S. Department of Labor, Bureau of Labor Statistics, *Handbook of Labor Statistics*, 1950 ed., bulletin 1016 (Government Printing Office, 1950), p. 139; ibid., 1978 ed., bulletin 2000 (GPO, 1979), p. 507.

tionally lower union density rates—such as professional and scientific services; insurance, banking, and finance; education; and distribution—and away from industries that had much higher union density rates—such as railways, coal mining, cotton textiles, and national government. (This shift was even more marked between 1971 and 1974.) They argue that "if the industrial distribution of employment had not changed between 1948 and 1974, union membership and density would have been greater by about 8 per cent."[4] Moreover, their data show a shift in the occupational distribution of the labor force toward a higher proportion of white-collar workers. This shift by itself would have decreased the aggregate union density figure because white-collar workers have been less strongly unionized than manual workers, but it was not associated with this effect because union density among both white-collar and manual workers rose substantially from the end of the 1960s. Thus factors that have been cited for the relative decline of unionization in the private sector in the United States—employment shifts toward traditionally less unionized industries and the relative rise in white-collar employment—have also been important in Britain, but did not have the same effect. Instead, British aggregate union density figures rose from the late 1960s because of a pervasive rise of union membership within major industrial and occupational classifications of employment.

Many questions that might be considered relevant to an explanation of this recent expansion of British trade unionism can be grouped—not always precisely—into two categories. One includes those questions that bear more strongly on the demand for union services. Was there a greater interest in joining unions to satisfy a taste for political or social expression? Did the "friendly society" benefits provided by unions become more attractive? Did the shift to higher inflation rates induce more workers to seek the protective security of unions or enhance the expected gains from collective bargaining? As the importance of the public sector increased, was there a greater incentive to join a union that would represent worker interests in the complex negotiations for benefits conferred by the state? The second category includes those questions that are directed more to changing influences on the supply of union services. Did the costs of union membership decline because of lower actual dues, less chance of losing a job through employer retaliation for joining a union, or lower organizational costs resulting from decreased employer resistance? Was there an

4. Ibid., p. 344.

expansion of protective measures for union organization that pressure or require workers to belong to a union? Did the government, perhaps in part to enlist more trade union support for other policy measures, introduce measures that made it easier for unions to expand?

Such questions show that unions can be considered a form of economic enterprise—though a very distinctive form—that depends for its survival and growth on the demand for services by workers and on the costs and organizational structure in the provision of services. Unions are notable for offering a great variety of services.[5] Some of the services, such as those based on mutual insurance, are private in that they accrue only to members. But as agents in the collective determination of wages and in the lobbying of governments, unions also produce collective services that can accrue to nonunion as well as union members. It is not surprising, therefore, that such arrangements as the closed shop,[6] which require membership of workers who might benefit from these services, are favored by union leaders and influence the existence and expansion of unions.[7]

Another problem for analysts of union growth has been that of agreeing on a reasonable assumption of maximizing behavior in the decision-making process of unions. Trade union leaders are constrained in their decisions by the need to retain the support of the rank and file, but the collective preferences of members are not always clear, since, for example, a goal of maximizing the wage per member would conflict with a goal of maximizing employment and number of members, and a goal of standardizing wages within the bargaining unit would not benefit all members.

5. For a useful discussion of the various types of private and collective services offered by unions, see John H. Pencavel, "The Demand for Union Services: An Exercise," *Industrial and Labor Relations Review,* vol. 24 (January 1971), pp. 180–90.

6. In Canada and the United States, the term *closed shop* usually means a plant in which only union members can be hired, and the term *union shop* means a plant in which nonunion members can be hired on condition that they then become union members. In Britain, the term *closed shop* normally covers both kinds of plants, although it is sometimes qualified by the terms *preentry* and *postentry* to distinguish between the two kinds.

7. Although in my view Olson overstated the need for coercive measures for the existence of unions, his imaginative analysis provides valuable insights into the role of such measures for the expansion of unionism. Mancur Olson, *The Logic of Collective Action: Public Goods and the Theory of Groups* (Harvard University Press, 1965). A subsequent analysis that questions Olson's emphasis on the need for coercive measures is in James Q. Wilson, *Political Organizations* (Basic Books, 1973).

I therefore attempt first to sift the evidence on recent factors that may have affected the attractiveness of trade union services and the costs and organizational opportunities in the provision of these services. I then consider the extent to which the hypotheses that emerge can be drawn together to throw some light on recent union growth.

Recent Demand for Union Services

On the demand side, the principal potential influences on union growth are (1) social and political appeal, (2) direct private benefits, (3) collective bargaining benefits, and (4) state benefits.

SOCIAL AND POLITICAL APPEAL. Trade unions attract some workers because they offer an outlet for social and political expression. This function, which in an economic sense is analogous to the services offered by a club, has clearly differed among countries and over time. Historians of the British labor movement have, at least until recently, placed considerable weight on it as a source of union growth. Undoubtedly early unions in many ways resembled social clubs for workers: meetings, for example, often took place in pubs, and much effort was devoted to developing a sense of worker solidarity. British unions also were instrumental in the development of the Labour party, which in the 1920s replaced the Liberal party as one of the two major political parties in the country. However, in recent reinterpretations of the historical development of British unions, the role of social and political attractions to union membership has tended to be downgraded. British unionism, it is argued, developed its greatest strength from efforts to improve pay and working conditions directly, not from efforts to advance political activity.[8]

Whatever may be the appropriate weight to attach to the social and political appeal of unions, is there evidence that it became more significant in the decade beginning in the late 1960s? Direct evidence on its role is obviously difficult to obtain, but some indirect pieces of evidence imply a negative answer, though each piece by itself is not conclusive. The rate of attendance at union meetings has not been particularly high or rising;[9]

8. For a useful review of important studies of British trade union development in the late nineteenth century and early twentieth century, see John Lovell, *British Trade Unions, 1875–1933* (London: Macmillan, 1977).

9. The Donovan commission estimated in 1968 that the average attendance at branch meetings was "well below ten per cent." Royal Commission on Trade Unions and Employers' Associations, *Report* (HMSO, 1968), p. 26.

Table 2. *Average Expenditure and Income per Member of Registered Trade Unions, United Kingdom, Selected Three-Year Periods, 1918–70*[a]

Pounds

Expenditure and income	1918–20	1928–30	1938–40	1948–50	1958–60	1968–70
Expenditure						
Friendly society benefits	2.247	5.445	3.821	2.211	1.637	1.805
Unemployment	0.544	1.971	0.883	0.087	0.066	0.078
Sickness and accident	0.473	1.131	0.754	0.574	0.380	0.645
Superannuation	1.008	1.697	1.346	0.905	0.649	0.451
Funeral	0.222	0.520	0.441	0.248	0.211	0.219
Other (such as education, legal expenses)	...	0.126	0.397	0.397	0.331	0.412
Dispute benefit (strike pay)	1.289	0.429	0.134	0.099	0.368	0.348
Political fund	0.096	0.200	0.123	0.236	0.168	0.164
Administrative expenses	2.192	4.411	4.268	4.599	3.838	5.065
Total	**5.824**	**10.485**	**8.346**	**7.145**	**6.011**	**7.382**
Income						
From members	5.941	10.857	9.765	8.182	5.867	6.501
Other	0.695	1.029	0.933	0.946	0.883	1.265
Total	**6.636**	**11.886**	**10.698**	**9.128**	**6.750**	**7.766**

Sources: Expenditure and income data are from John Gennard, *Financing Strikers* (London: Macmillan, 1977), apps. 2 and 3; data on registered trade union members are from George S. Bain; consumer price indexes are from Department of Employment and Productivity, *British Labour Statistics, Historical Abstract, 1886–1968*, pp. 172, 173, and Department of Employment, *British Labour Statistics Year Book, 1975*, pp. 114–15.

a. Values are adjusted to January 1974 prices; current values were multiplied by the ratio of the consumer price index of January 15, 1974, to the index of the current year.

the average political contributions per member, as table 2 indicates, have been both small and remarkably stable in recent decades; the growth of unionism flourished under both Labour and Conservative governments during the decade; strikes, as I argue later, appear to have been dominated recently even more by pay than by nonpay issues, although on occasion they have developed into serious political confrontations. Furthermore, if the general social and political attractions of membership are directly related to shifts in the public image of the value of trade unions to society, these attractions have not been rising. Since the early 1950s the British Gallup Poll has included the question: "Generally speaking, and thinking of Britain as a whole, do you think that trade unions are a good thing or a bad thing?" Figure 2 charts the percentage of people who thought unions were "a good thing" for the period 1954–77. Although there is considerable annual variation, the percentage declined between 1964 and 1977.

DIRECT PRIVATE BENEFITS. Another service, important historically in drawing workers into British trade unions, is the provision of various forms of mutual insurance benefits. Generally referred to as "friendly society" benefits, they include benefits related to sickness, accidents, un-

Figure 2. *Public Opinion on the Value of Trade Unions, United Kingdom, 1954–77*

Percent

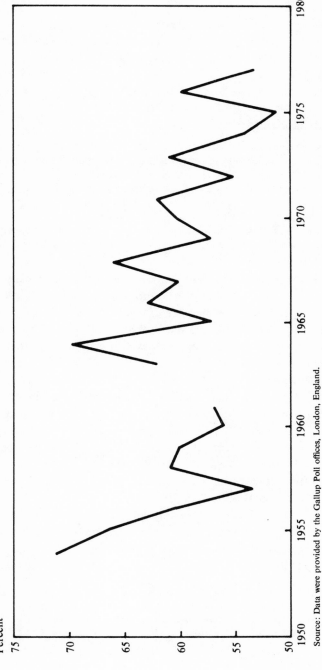

Source: Data were provided by the Gallup Poll offices, London, England.

employment, retirement, death, education, and legal expenses. Coverage requires union membership. But the importance of the service is limited by competition from other private organizations and, most important in recent decades, from the state. Employers have sometimes taken the initiative in attempts to forestall unionism, particularly among white-collar or supervisory staff. For example, in a study for the Donovan commission, Bain observed:

The best known device for discouraging staff unionism in private industry is the Foreman and Staff Mutual Benefit Society, a friendly society established in 1899 to provide pensions, life assurance, and sickness benefits to foremen and similar grades of staff in the engineering and shipbuilding industries. The Society has two kinds of members: contributory members or employers; and ordinary members, the eligible employees of contributory members. Contributory members pay at least half of the total contributions in respect of each ordinary member. . . . Under the Society's rules, an ordinary member may not belong to a trade union.[10]

Some evidence on the changing importance of friendly society benefits of unions is included in table 2. The principal categories of average income and expenditure per member of registered unions are shown for selected three-year periods since World War I, and the data have been adjusted for changes in the general price level. It can be noted that friendly society benefits per member were lower in the post–World War II periods than in the interwar periods. This decline undoubtedly reflects the growth in importance of government benefits in such areas as unemployment, health, and pensions. The 1968–70 average union benefit of £1.8 per member (in January 1974 prices) is not a large sum, although such averages conceal a great diversity among unions. As to other expenditures, no clear trend is observable in dispute benefits or in political contributions. Administrative expenses, on the other hand, have grown substantially in the post–World War II period.

Although it is doubtful that friendly society benefits were a stimulus to recent union growth, another type of direct private benefit to union members appears to have grown in importance. Membership in a union provides access to information that is costly for a worker to obtain on his own.

10. George S. Bain, *Trade Union Growth and Recognition*, Royal Commission on Trade Unions and Employers' Associations, Research Paper 6 (HMSO, 1967), p. 94. But with trade union support, a private bill was subsequently passed in the House of Commons that forced the Foreman and Staff Mutual Benefit Society to cease.

Through union officials a worker may get information relevant to his working conditions, such as the use of grievance procedures, legal claims, and alternative job opportunities, and information relevant to government benefits, such as unemployment compensation, injury benefits, and other social insurance claims. Unions are thus information brokers to their members. The growing complexity of rules, regulations, and benefits governing working conditions and the worker's relation to the state has expanded this function of unionism.

This other source of direct benefits is more difficult to measure, but, as seen in table 2, the growth of administrative expenses and of union per capita expenditures on "other" items under friendly society benefits (which include legal expenses) is not inconsistent with an increase in this type of benefit. The provision of information requires more and better-trained union officials and is often linked to legal advice and representation. The importance of the latter has been documented by Latta and Lewis. They estimate, for example, that in the early 1970s trade unions fought over 10,000 social insurance appeals a year on behalf of members, and they conclude that these and many other legal services to members have been expanding.[11]

Some direct private benefits from trade union membership have thus decreased and others have increased. The growth of government benefits in many areas traditionally covered by friendly society benefits has reduced that function of unionism, whereas the extension of governmental activities has increased the unions' information brokerage function.

COLLECTIVE BARGAINING BENEFITS. The primary function of a union in Britain, as in Canada and the United States, is to represent the collective economic interests of its members in negotiations with employers over terms of employment. However, institutional factors affect the way this function is carried out. Thus in Britain collective bargaining is frequently a two-level process in which a national agreement between a union and an employers' group or federation is supplemented by further negotiations at the local level. In Britain, too, the agreements are usually less formal and detailed than in Canada and the United States, and there is less emphasis on developing legally binding contracts for specified periods of time. The British approach to collective bargaining, despite recent steps to modify it, also reflects a stronger tradition of voluntarism. Neverthe-

11. Geoff Latta and Roy Lewis, "Trade Union Legal Services," *British Journal of Industrial Relations,* vol. 12 (March 1974), pp. 56, 70.

less, as Ulman pointed out, "the industrial relations systems in the United States and the United Kingdom have long shared certain family attributes which, notwithstanding very important dissimilarities, have served to place them, together with the Canadian system, in a distinctive international subset."[12]

Attempts to measure the effects of this function on union membership have usually concentrated on the pecuniary effects and, in particular, on the average wage differential between union and nonunion workers. Imprecise as such measures must be because of the difficulty of determining and holding constant other influences on wage differentials, the findings for Britain have not been very different from those for the United States. Pencavel, using data for 1964, found evidence of a union impact on hourly earnings ranging from 0 to 10 percent, and concluded:

Certainly, the range of values in this study is not out of line with estimates from American data: there is, for instance, Lewis's (1963) well-known estimate that, in the late 1950s, American unions had raised the average wage rate of union workers by some 10 to 15 per cent above that of non-union workers. Consequently, Phelps Brown's conjecture in his evidence to the [Donovan] Royal Commission (1966, pp. 1615–1616) that an estimate of the relative wage effects of British unions would not differ very much from Lewis's estimate from United States data is certainly not inconsistent with the results in this paper.[13]

It is not necessary, of course, to be a union member to benefit from this service, unless union membership is a condition of employment. In 1968 the Donovan commission estimated that the number of workers covered by collective bargaining was about 50 percent higher than the number of trade union members.[14] Data reported in another study indicate that the figure was approximately 44 percent in 1968 and 48 percent in 1973.[15]

12. Lloyd Ulman, "Collective Bargaining and Industrial Efficiency," in Richard E. Caves and Associates, *Britain's Economic Prospects* (Brookings Institution, 1968), p. 338.

13. John H. Pencavel, "Relative Wages and Trade Unions in the United Kingdom," *Economica*, vol. 41 (May 1974), p. 206.

14. Royal Commission on Trade Unions and Employers' Associations, *Report*, p. 10.

15. A. W. J. Thomson, C. Mulvey, and M. Farbman, "Bargaining Structure and Relative Earnings in Great Britain," *British Journal of Industrial Relations*, vol. 15 (July 1977), p. 177. The authors use New Earnings Survey data to estimate the proportion of workers covered by collective agreements to be 62.0 percent in 1968 and 71.8 percent in 1973, and cite data, used by Bain and Price in *Union Growth Revisited*, that showed the corresponding figures for the proportion of workers holding trade union membership to be 43.1 percent and 48.5 percent.

The second set of figures implies that the growth in union density during 1968–73 was not the result of bringing into the trade union fold nonunion workers previously covered by collective agreements, but, as will be discussed later, the more positive legislative encouragement to the closed shop since 1974 may have made this source of growth important subsequently.

If the number of workers covered by collective bargaining exceeds the number of union members—as it does in many sectors—it follows that estimates of positive union–nonunion wage differentials will be underestimates of the coverage differential, which is the wage differential between those workers covered by collective agreements and those not covered. (In other words, the ratio of union to nonunion wages is smaller because it includes among nonunion wages the wages of nonunion workers who, nevertheless, are covered by collective agreements.) Evidence of this larger coverage differential has been reported in recent studies.[16] More specifically, it appears that the coverage differential for most male manual workers has recently been about 25 to 30 percent, although for nonmanual workers it is not clear that the differential has been particularly large, or even positive.

Of particular interest for the subject of union growth is the evidence of an upward shift in the union–nonunion wage differential between the middle or late 1960s and the early 1970s. Layard, Metcalf, and Nickell find that the differential grew "sharply" between 1968 and 1972 and suggest there was further union pressure on it between 1973 and 1975.[17] Mulvey argues that "there is some reason to suppose that the differential may have increased between 1964 and 1973."[18]

Such findings may not be unrelated to the hypothesis, advanced and

16. See C. Mulvey and J. I. Foster, "Occupational Earnings in the U.K. and the Effects of Collective Agreements," *Manchester School of Economic and Social Studies,* vol. 44 (September 1976), pp. 258–75; Charles Mulvey, "Collective Agreements and Relative Earnings in UK Manufacturing in 1973," *Economica,* vol. 43 (November 1976), pp. 419–27; R. Layard, D. Metcalf, and S. Nickell, "The Effect of Collective Bargaining on Wages," Discussion Paper 11 (London School of Economics, Centre for Labour Economics, March 1977); David Metcalf, "Unions, Incomes Policy and Relative Wages in Britain," *British Journal of Industrial Relations,* vol. 15 (July 1977), pp. 157–75; Thomson, Mulvey, and Farbman, "Bargaining Structure and Relative Earnings," pp. 176–91.

17. "Effect of Collective Bargaining on Wages," pp. 10–14.

18. "Collective Agreements and Relative Earnings in UK Manufacturing in 1973," p. 426.

Table 3. *Unemployment Rate and Change in Retail Prices, United Kingdom, 1960–77*

Percent

Year	Unemploy- ment rate	Change in retail prices	Year	Unemploy- ment rate	Change in retail prices
1960	1.7	1.1	1969	2.5	5.4
1961	1.6	3.4	1970	2.6	6.4
1962	2.1	4.2	1971	3.5	9.4
1963	2.6	2.0	1972	3.8	7.1
1964	1.7	3.3	1973	2.7	9.2
1965	1.5	4.8	1974	2.6	16.0
1966	1.6	3.9	1975	4.2	24.2
1967	2.5	2.4	1976	5.8	16.6
1968	2.5	4.7	1977	6.2	15.8

Sources: Central Statistical Office, *Annual Abstract of Statistics, 1977*, no. 114 (HMSO, 1978), and *Monthly Digest of Statistics*, no. 234 (June 1965) and no. 390 (June 1978).

tested on U.S. data, of an inverse relationship between the union–nonunion wage differential and the level of economic activity.[19] As table 3 shows, the unemployment rate went up in the early 1970s and again in the mid-1970s, but the most striking change in the macroeconomic performance of the economy over the period was the shift to a higher and fluctuating rate of inflation. The annual rate of change of retail prices rose in the latter part of the 1960s and early 1970s, soared to a peak of 23.4 percent in 1975, and then declined to levels that were still high by historical standards.

This inflation is likely to have affected workers' perceptions of the expected returns from the collective bargaining services of unions, whatever may have been the actual effect of unions on wage differentials. A shift to higher and fluctuating rates of inflation raises uncertainty and the costs of information about appropriate specific wage increases, and it is likely to produce greater concern about unfairness in the determination of wage rates. Since some wages and prices do not adjust as flexibly as others, more unevenness in the movement of wages and prices occurs under these economic conditions, especially if the shifts in the inflation rate are largely unanticipated. Customary pay differentials tend to change, and evidence of higher pay settlements elsewhere spreads feelings of inequity.

19. See H. G. Lewis, *Unionism and Relative Wages in the United States: An Empirical Inquiry* (University of Chicago Press, 1963).

Moreover, with inflation as with real income increases, progressive income tax rates, applied to current values of income, take a larger fraction of pay. Even workers who receive above-average pay increases may thus be frustrated because after-tax real wage increases fail to match expectations.[20]

Under such conditions a collective organization can become more attractive as a vehicle for the expression of grievances, as a source of more specialized information, and as a safeguard for the interests of groups of workers. It has been argued that in the United States an inflationary situation may detract from the benefits of unionism because two- and three-year, legally binding, collective agreements cannot provide for an unanticipated increase in inflation. This point is less relevant for Britain since, as previously noted, collective agreements are less formal and more flexible and can be reopened as economic conditions change. And also, as the inflationary problem worsened in Britain in 1968–77, experiments with incomes policy became a prominent and persistent feature of national policy. (See appendix A for a condensed chronology of incomes policies since the mid-1960s.) Because incomes policies establish official rules for wage and price determination on the grounds that market forces are inadequate, they may in turn convince many people that wage determination is a highly administered system in which it is advantageous for groups to organize and develop their own administrative leaders. The system of wage determination in Britain, as, for example, Lipsey and Parkin argued,[21] has tended to become less responsive to demand forces during periods of incomes policy and, in this sense, to become more administered, regardless of whether the impact of the policy on average wage changes was positive, negative, or neutral.

STATE BENEFITS. The fourth potential source of benefits arises from the influence trade unions exert on governmental decisions affecting workers' interests. The close relation between the trade union movement and the Labour party does not necessarily give British unions a special advantage over unions in the United States. In Washington lobbying provides many ways for unions to influence political and administrative de-

20. It has been estimated that a married couple with two children, and with the father on an average wage, would have been assessed 3.3 percent in income tax in 1955 and 25 percent in 1975. Robert Taylor, *The Fifth Estate: Britain's Unions in the Seventies* (London: Routledge and Kegan Paul, 1978), p. 14.

21. R. G. Lipsey and J. M. Parkin, "Incomes Policy: A Re-appraisal," *Economica*, vol. 37 (May 1970), pp. 115–38.

cisions. But during the latter half of the 1960s and through much of the 1970s there was a greater interest in Britain—under both Labour and Conservative governments—in developing a closer partnership between government and labor (and business) than there was in the United States. In part this interest may have reflected the widespread conviction that some form of incomes policy was essential to curb inflation and that any enduring or politically popular form of such a policy needs broad support from trade unions. In addition, the strong tradition of voluntarism in industrial relations was important. Concern about strikes, inflation, and productivity growth stimulated proposals to increase the "responsibility" of unions by including them in public decisionmaking processes rather than to pass legislation affecting their activities. A notable exception to this trend was the Industrial Relations Act of 1971, which set out the first comprehensive legislative framework for trade unionism in Britain. But because it incurred the wrath of trade unions, it was replaced by legislation in 1974 and 1975 that was more acceptable to them.

The most dramatic example of the closer links between the government and trade unions was the so-called social contract of the mid-1970s. In essence, it was a deal between leaders of the trade union movement—one leader, Jack Jones of the Transport and General Workers' Union, played a particularly critical role—and the Labour government. Help in moderating wage demands was pledged in exchange for public policies more acceptable to unions. Begun inauspiciously in 1975, when average weekly wage rates rose by 29.5 percent, the social contract received credit for the sharp drop in their rise in 1976 and 1977, to 19.3 percent and 6.6 percent respectively. The idea was not entirely novel. A voluntary form of incomes policy also achieved some success in Britain in 1949–50, when several powerful union leaders agreed to help moderate wage demands in return for which the government agreed to postpone the lifting of price controls and subsidies on some key food items. Moreover, in the 1950s the Swedish economist Bent Hansen proposed a similar strategy for an incomes policy:

The method suggested here is that the State makes a declaration of its plans concerning future fiscal and monetary policy for the realization of full employment and a stable value of money with *alternative* future money wage rates. This declaration will include a promise that fiscal and monetary policy will be constructed in such a way that at one certain money wage rate, namely the one that the State considers suitable, wage earners will achieve the highest real disposable income, whereas at both higher and lower money wage rates their real disposable incomes will be lower. Normally it ought to be possible to make the "bribe" which is promised to the trade unions, if they direct their wage claims according to the wishes of the State, so high that the trade unions prefer this money wage rate to all others.[22]

But in contrast to Hansen's proposal, the recent British experiment appears to have been less an arm's length relationship of state to unions than an embrace over policy formulation.

Greater opportunities for union leaders to negotiate with the state do not, however, necessarily increase the incentives for workers to join unions. When such negotiations protect or advance the interests of large groups of workers, the benefits to an individual worker are independent of membership in a union; the well-known "free rider" situation applies, in a purer form than with collective bargaining services. Indeed, union leaders who spend much time on negotiations over general economic issues may soon find some erosion of their support among current rank-and-file members of their unions who, not irrationally, expect more specific returns from their financial contributions. This is a point that is frequently overlooked in proposals to involve trade union leadership in policy formulation on a more permanent basis in exchange for stronger union control over rank-and-file wage demands.

Although it probably affects the demand for union services very little, a closer relation between union leadership and government on policy matters can affect the structure of trade union organization and lead to policy measures more favorable to the recruitment of union members. Channels of communication and representation between the Trades Union Congress (TUC) and the government in the administration of incomes and other policies increase incentives to centralize the trade union movement. For example, the trade union of university teachers reversed its long-standing opposition to affiliation with the TUC largely because the union believed that its members would suffer relatively less in the application of incomes policy norms if it had TUC support. At the aggregate level, membership in unions affiliated with the TUC as a percent of total union membership increased from 87.1 percent to 91.8 percent between 1968 and 1976.[23] And union size becomes of greater importance when more issues relevant to unionism are being resolved within the TUC and

22. Bent Hansen, *The Economic Theory of Fiscal Policy,* trans. P. E. Burke (Harvard University Press, 1958), pp. 358–59.

23. Data on membership in unions affiliated with the TUC are given in the annual reports of the TUC.

through direct contact with the government. Size and political power are not unrelated. From 1900 to 1976 the number of trade unions declined from 1,323 to 493, while total membership rose from 2.0 million to 12.5 million. There have thus been longer-term trend factors causing an increase in the average membership of British trade unions. But the big increase came in later years: average membership rose by 54.3 percent between 1966 and 1976, whereas it rose by only 15.6 percent between 1956 and 1966 and by 22.3 percent between 1946 and 1956.[24] Finally, it is in the interest of trade union leaders to seek, in exchange for supporting government measures, more positive encouragement to unionism in the economic activities of governments and in legislation affecting union organization. But this encouragement would affect the supply aspects of union growth, to which I now turn.

Cost and Organizational Opportunities

On the supply side, the principal potential influences on union growth are (1) direct membership costs, (2) employer resistance, government action, and union security, and (3) union density and labor force characteristics.

DIRECT MEMBERSHIP COSTS. Direct costs of union membership have been lower on the average in Britain than in the United States, both as a proportion of earnings and in absolute terms. Troy has estimated that in 1970 the costs in the United States averaged about 1 percent of the annual income of union members.[25] In Britain the Donovan commission estimated that in 1966 weekly trade union contributions were about 0.39 percent of men's average weekly earnings, and Taylor, citing a TUC study, suggests the figure was about 0.28 percent in 1974.[26] Although not strictly comparable—the British figures, for example, do not include female workers, for whom the proportion of earnings spent on union membership appears to be higher—these estimates are consistent with other evidence

24. It is not suggested that a greater opportunity to negotiate on policy matters was the only new factor affecting an acceleration in the growth in size during 1966–76. For example, the Trade Union (Amalgamations, etc.) Act of 1964 made procedures for union mergers easier.

25. Leo Troy, "American Unions and Their Wealth," *Industrial Relations,* vol. 14 (May 1975), p. 141.

26. Royal Commission on Trade Unions and Employers' Associations, *Report,* p. 191; Taylor, *The Fifth Estate,* pp. 31–32.

that British unions usually spend much less than U.S. unions on administrative expenses and, in particular, on the hiring of union officials.

It is doubtful, however, whether the direct price of union services had much effect on recent shifts in British trade union membership. In table 2 data are included on the average income per member (adjusted for changes in the price level) that trade unions received. The three-year averages for the end of successive decades indicate a decline of nearly 50 percent from the late 1920s to the late 1950s and then an increase of about 10 percent to the end of the 1960s. More evidence is needed, but the rise in union contributions probably did not fully match the sharp acceleration of inflation in the early 1970s. Thus, although data on average costs do not reveal the relevant price that new members have recently paid, there does not seem to have been a dramatic decline (or rise) in direct membership costs in the decade following the mid-1960s. Moreover, to the extent that there was some change, a study by Pencavel supports the view that the demand for union services in Britain has not been highly sensitive to the price of union services.[27]

EMPLOYER RESISTANCE, GOVERNMENT ACTION, AND UNION SECURITY. Employer resistance indirectly raises the costs of unionism or lowers the benefits potential members might receive. Resistance can take the form either of opposing or delaying the recognition of unions in plants, thereby raising the organizational costs a union must bear, or of resisting cooperation with an established union on such matters as the automatic payroll checkoff of union dues, which a union might propose in order to reduce collection costs and increase pressure on maintaining membership payments. Employer attitudes also affect a potential union member's assessment of the risk of being moved to a less attractive job, or of losing it altogether if he or she joins or engages in organizing a union. Besides deterring unionism by raising individual and collective costs to its expansion, employers might directly encourage nonunion status by offering improved pay, fringe benefits, and job security, thereby providing the benefits that union organizers are promising to secure at a cost to members.[28]

The determinants of employer attitudes toward discouraging (or en-

27. Pencavel, "The Demand for Union Services."

28. The study by Bain for the Donovan commission, *Trade Union Growth and Recognition,* provides a fuller description of the various strategies employers have used. See esp. pp. 92–95.

couraging) unions are complex, but their significance is likely to be affected by the state of the labor demand. When employment opportunities are expanding, the potential cost to a worker of losing a job or of being shifted by the employer to a less attractive one is reduced. At the same time, because of the costs of securing and training replacements, business managers will have a greater incentive to try to satisfy and keep workers. Moreover, unemployed workers often tend to lose interest in maintaining the costs of union membership. Thus the strength of the British post–World War II commitment to full employment—a commitment that, despite recent periods of increase in unemployment, has usually been stronger than in Canada and the United States—has probably had a favorable effect on union organization.

Employer resistance is also affected by the government's position on union recognition. Clearly, as a major employer the government can influence unionization in the public sector. In Britain the rate of unionization in this sector is particularly high and has been for some time. It has been estimated that in 1974 approximately 83 percent of the labor force in the public sector was unionized, and the figure exceeded 90 percent in many industries: national government; air transport; port and inland water transport; railways; gas, electricity and water; and coal mining.[29] If the same classification of industries for the public sector is used to calculate the rate for 1948, the figure is about 70 percent. Unionization of the British public sector is therefore not a new phenomenon. In Canada and the United States it was not until the 1960s that a major expansion of unionization occurred in the public sector, even though in those countries the public sector is not as broad as in Britain, and unionization rates have traditionally been high in some of the industries that are not under public ownership there but are in Britain.

Of possibly greater importance for the spread of British unionism in recent years is the encouragement the government has given to unionization in the private sector. In times of crisis governments often seek more support from the labor movement. Bain has documented that the greatest previous advances in the unionization of white-collar workers (as well as of manual workers) occurred in the periods around World War I and World War II, when the British government, to gain the cooperation of trade union leadership, enhanced the status of unionism by involving the leadership in national administration and exerted pressure on private em-

29. Price and Bain, "Union Growth Revisited," pp. 342–43.

ployers to respond positively to unionization efforts.[30] During the recent period of economic instability, when both Labour and Conservative governments were seeking greater union support for policies to curb inflation, government encouragement of unionization in the private sector seems to have increased. In 1969 a Commission on Industrial Relations was established to review, among other things and on a continuing basis, problems of union recognition; its first general report made clear its support for the principle that employees should have an organization to express their collective interests.[31] The ill-fated Industrial Relations Act, which angered unions on other grounds, nevertheless established for the first time legal procedures for obtaining union recognition. In 1974 an Advisory, Conciliation and Arbitration Service (ACAS) was established to provide an independent conciliation service that would also assist in union recognition disputes. Through such measures, and through moral suasion, it appears that the government may have had some effect on lowering employer resistance to unionism.

The recent period has also been conducive to a strengthening of union security provisions that exert direct pressure on workers to maintain union membership and that have traditionally been less important in Britain than in the United States. These provisions range from agreements with employers for the automatic payroll deduction of union member dues to forms of the closed shop, whether of the postentry type, in which a new employee must join a union, or of the preentry type, in which an employee must be a union member in order to be eligible to be hired. The automatic checkoff was not widely practiced in Britain in the past, but its use increased after the mid-1960s. According to a TUC survey, the number of workers covered by a checkoff arrangement doubled between 1966 and 1972, rising from one-sixth to one-third of members.[32] Both forms of the closed shop were extended into new areas after the mid-1960s, although comparable measures of their significance over time are not available. McCarthy estimated in 1964 that about 16 percent of British workers—

30. George Sayers Bain, *The Growth of White-Collar Unionism* (Oxford: Clarendon, 1970), pp. 142–75.

31. Commission on Industrial Relations, *First General Report*, Report 9, cmnd. 4417 (HMSO, 1970), p. 9.

32. See Brian Weekes and others, *Industrial Relations and the Limits of the Law: Industrial Effects of the Industrial Relations Act, 1971* (Oxford: Basil Blackwell, 1975), p. 121. They suggest that these figures are underestimates because some affiliated unions did not respond fully to the TUC survey.

or about 39 percent of trade unionists—were covered by a closed shop agreement.[33] The Donovan commission reported in 1968 that, though the closed shop had been spreading among industries, employment had declined relatively in some industries where the closed shop had been most common. The commission therefore concluded that the overall extent of the closed shop was probably unchanged since 1964.[34] But on the basis of a survey, Brian Weekes and his associates found that between 1968 and 1971 the closed shop was expanding in coverage.[35] In 1971 the Industrial Relations Act outlawed the closed shop; instead it permitted an agency shop under which a worker did not have to belong to a union but had to pay a contribution for the services of the union or could designate that the contribution be paid to charity. The act was not effective in banning the closed shop but probably strengthened resistance to its expansion. The closed shop again became lawful under the Trade Union and Labour Relations Act of 1974 and the amendment to that act in 1976. Most commentators agree that this change has caused union membership to rise somewhat. Although time series data are not available to measure recent changes in the proportion of workers in closed shops, it is of interest that a survey in 1977–78 found that about 46 percent of all manual employees in manufacturing establishments were in closed shops.[36]

UNION DENSITY AND LABOR FORCE CHARACTERISTICS. Recent British trade union growth is the more remarkable from a North American perspective because Britain had already achieved a comparatively high level of union density and was also experiencing the types of shifts in labor force characteristics that have been regarded as inimical to the growth of private sector unionism in Canada and the United States. It appears that British unionism expanded despite these factors, or, in other words, that these factors exerted a negative impact on union growth that was more than offset by some of the positive influences that I have been discussing.

Higher union density is likely to inhibit further union organization,

33. W. E. J. McCarthy, *The Closed Shop in Britain* (University of California Press, 1964), p. 28.

34. Royal Commission on Trade Unions and Employers' Associations, *Report*, p. 39.

35. *Industrial Relations and the Limits of the Law*, p. 39.

36. Industrial Facts and Forecasting Ltd. and SSRC Industrial Relations Research Unit, "Work-Place Industrial Relations in Manufacturing Industry" (University of Warwick, 1978), p. 4.

which tends to take place first among those groups of workers who are the easiest to organize. Thus the proportion of unorganized workers who are more difficult to organize rises with levels of union density. A qualification to this point, however, makes the impact of union density on union growth less certain, particularly at low levels of density; namely, in the early development of unions, success in organizing one group of workers might have helped the organization of other groups because, for example, of economies of scale in organization and of reductions in uncertainty about the expected benefits relative to the costs of unionism.

Labor force characteristics, moreover, were not shifting recently in a direction usually regarded as favorable for labor organization. Female workers are less likely to belong to a union than male workers, and young workers are less likely to belong than older workers.[37] In the past it has been more difficult to organize white-collar workers than blue-collar ones. Yet in Britain, as in the United States, there has been a shift to a higher proportion of female workers, young workers, and white-collar workers. During the post–World War II period both countries also experienced a net shift away from industries that had a tradition of high unionization rates. These characteristics, therefore, were not the source for the rise in aggregate union density in Britain.

General Explanations of Recent Growth

The main conclusions of this part of the paper can be summarized briefly. The following factors in the demand for union services were probably not an important influence on the recent surge of British union growth: the attractions of a union as a means for expressing political and social ideas, as an agent for providing mutual insurance (friendly society) benefits, and as a route for influencing public policy. But it is suggested that the demand for collective bargaining services rose during this period of economic instability, particularly because of larger unanticipated changes in the rate of inflation. As far as the costs and organizational opportunities of unions are concerned, it is doubtful that changes in the direct costs of union membership were an important influence on union

37. Alan S. Blinder, "Who Joins Unions?" Working Paper 36 (Princeton University, Industrial Relations Section, February 1972). British evidence that young workers are less likely to be unionized than older workers is reported in George S. Bain and Farouk Elsheikh, "An Inter-Industry Analysis of Unionization in Britain" (February 1979).

growth. The indirect costs related to employer resistance, however, merit further investigation. On the one hand, a weakening in labor demand would be expected to raise employer resistance; on the other hand, there is evidence of considerable indirect and direct government support for the organization of unions that probably lowered employer resistance during the period and that permitted union organizers to bring stronger pressure on workers to join a union and maintain membership in it. Finally, it is suggested that the level of aggregate union density and the shifts in labor force characteristics were negative rather than positive forces on union growth.

Theories of union growth differ depending on the weight attached to these and other potential influences on demand and supply factors in the provision of union services. Currently, the leading model of trade union growth in the United Kingdom is the one advanced by Bain and Elsheikh to explain growth in the period 1893–1970; the general form of the model has also been applied to the United States and to Sweden and Australia.[38] In the model the annual rate of change of trade union membership ($\dot{T}$) depends on four variables: the rate of change of prices ($\dot{P}$), the rate of change of money wages ($\dot{W}$), the unemployment rate (U), and aggregate union density (D). The effect of prices is positive, with the qualification that, above some level of inflation, the price effect does not keep up with inflation. Therefore, an additional variable ($\dot{P}S$) is included that has the value of zero up to a 4 percent rate of inflation and above that point takes on (with a negative impact) the value of price increases. The effect of wages is positive; Bain and Elsheikh justify this largely on the grounds that workers (rightly or wrongly) regard increases in average money wages as evidence of the power of unions to improve or defend real wage rates. Recent unemployment rates have the expected negative effect, especially when they are expressed in terms of increases and decreases. The recent level of union density has a negative effect.[39] Reestimates of the model for the years 1894–1976 and 1950–76 are reported in appendix B.

38. George S. Bain and Farouk Elsheikh, *Union Growth and the Business Cycle: An Econometric Analysis* (Oxford: Basil Blackwell, 1976); Farouk Elsheikh and George S. Bain, "American Trade Union Growth: An Alternative Model," *Industrial Relations*, vol. 17 (February 1978), pp. 75–79.

39. Thus Bain and Elsheikh's model can be summarized as follows (positive and negative effects are shown in parentheses):

$$\dot{T} = f[\dot{P}, \dot{P}S, \dot{W}, U_{-1}, U_{-2}, D_{-1}].$$
$$(+)(-)(+)(-) \ (+) \ (-)$$

This model explains, with a remarkable degree of support from statistical tests, trade union growth over an eighty-year period as well as over the more recent twenty-five-year period. It places great weight on indicators of aggregate economic conditions and, in particular, on price changes, wage changes, and the unemployment rate. The findings are thus not inconsistent with the arguments in this paper that inflation and the state of labor demand are likely to have had a great impact on recent union growth. My arguments do imply, however, several modifications to Bain and Elsheikh's approach.

First, I argued that unanticipated increases in rates of inflation tend to increase the demand for union services both because of the effect on the dispersion of relative wage changes (and thus on rising concern about inequities in the system) and because of broader social tensions arising from the redistributional consequences of unanticipated inflation rates. Bain and Elsheikh's use of a threshold of 4 percent above which inflation has a declining effect is relevant to this point; some adjustment in expectations takes place at higher inflation levels. But my argument implies the replacement of the price change variable and the arbitrarily determined threshold variable by an expression for unanticipated price changes, difficult as it is to know how best to calculate it. And I drop the variable for average money wages. The rationale for including it as an indicator of the attractions of joining a union is not convincing except when it is considered in conjunction with average prices as a change in real wages. But then the variable would have a negative sign (rather than the positive sign that Bain and Elsheikh find) if the argument is that the free-rider problem is more easily resolved when potential union members feel their real wage position is deteriorating relative to what they have expected.

Second, Bain and Elsheikh found that it was not necessary to allow for the effect of government action on union growth.[40] I have suggested that the effect was important after the mid-1960s (and also, perhaps, around the World War I and World War II periods).

Third, Bain and Elsheikh's reliance on the unemployment rate as the indicator of employment conditions is worrisome. Questions can be raised both about the reliability of the data on unemployment rates for the early decades of this century and about changes over time in their economic significance as an indicator of labor market tightness. Moreover, since it is the rate of change of union membership that is being investigated, the

40. *Union Growth and the Business Cycle,* p. 105.

inclusion of the rate of change of employment as an additional variable merits further consideration. Greater disaggregation would be desirable to allow for changes in labor force characteristics that affect both the incentives to join unions and the organizational opportunities of unions. Bain and Elsheikh doubt that such disaggregation would make much difference: "Such variables as the industrial and occupational composition of the labour force exhibit little annual variation because they are dominated by their time trends, and hence they are irrelevant in a rate of change model such as ours."[41] Although they are engaged in further work that will permit greater disaggregation, data are not currently available over a sufficiently long period of time to modify the model in this direction.

I have attempted to reestimate Bain and Elsheikh's model with a few modifications that were introduced in light of the foregoing arguments. The statistical tests are reported in appendix B. The evidence is not inconsistent with the argument that unanticipated inflation has had an important impact on union growth both in the post–World War II period and over the longer period since the late nineteenth century. Unfortunately, agreement does not exist on how best to measure unanticipated inflation, and the tests were sensitive to the measure used. Inflation seems to matter, but the way it matters is not entirely clear.

The tests also do not conflict with the arguments that the rate of change of employment and, at times, government action have had positive effects on union growth. The measurement of government action raises special problems. In line with the method others have used to test for the effect of the Wagner Act on trade union growth in the United States after the mid-1930s,[42] I used a simple shift variable for the years 1969–76, even though, as I have argued, public policies toward unionism varied in Britain during that period.[43] But here, too, there can be much disagreement on how best to test for the influence of government action on organiza-

41. Farouk Elsheikh and George S. Bain, "Trade Union Growth: A Reply," *British Journal of Industrial Relations,* vol. 16 (March 1978), p. 99.

42. See, for example, Bain and Elsheikh, *Union Growth and the Business Cycle,* pp. 87–88, and M. G. Abbott, "A Model of Trade Union Growth in Canada, 1925–1972" (Queen's University, August 1977), pp. 16–18.

43. In the longer-term tests, I also introduced similar shift variables for the years 1911–20 and 1936–48 on the grounds that, amid the tensions preceding, during, and immediately following the two World Wars, the attractions of union organization rose: governments needed the support of union leaders to help unify the country and therefore more strongly favored union organization. The beginning and end dates were arbitrarily selected, however, and clearly more work on the institutional developments in these periods would be valuable.

tional opportunities of unions. The shift variable may be capturing negative and positive shifts in other determinants of union growth and may be masking the impact of governmental measures on the coefficients of variables included in the model.

In sum, the evidence seems to support the general argument that economic conditions and public policy have strongly influenced recent British trade union growth, even though, at the high level of aggregation used so far in statistical tests and with the limited and rudimentary proxies for some of the variables, it is obviously difficult to distinguish with great confidence among alternative hypotheses about the determinants of that growth. The tests have also not allowed for the possibility that union growth is simultaneously affecting the variables that are being used to explain it. There are a number of ways in which the relationships affecting trade union growth could be linked to a wider set of interrelationships. In the discussion that follows, I regard the recent pattern of British industrial disputes as being affected both by union growth and, more directly, by the economic conditions and public policies of the times.

Industrial Disputes

The development of British trade unionism and management's relations with the unions have produced, it is widely believed, a strike-prone country. Moreover, in the popular view the worsening of the strike record after the mid-1960s helps to explain the deterioration in the macroeconomic performance of the economy and is strong evidence of the need for basic reforms in the industrial relations system. But recent studies of the strike problem in Britain have frequently emphasized that its proneness to strikes is much exaggerated[44] and that fluctuations in strike activity are largely a result (not a cause) of changes in macroeconomic conditions.[45] What is the evidence of a serious and deteriorating strike problem

44. The following studies are particularly interesting: H. A. Turner, *Is Britain Really Strike Prone?* (Cambridge: Cambridge University Press, 1969); Michael Silver, "Recent British Strike Trends: A Factual Analysis," *British Journal of Industrial Relations,* vol. 11 (March 1973), pp. 66–104; C. T. B. Smith and others, *Strikes in Britain,* Department of Employment, Manpower Paper 15 (HMSO, 1978).

45. See, for example, John H. Pencavel, "An Investigation into Industrial Strike Activity in Britain," *Economica,* vol. 37 (August 1970), pp. 239–56; K. G. Knight, "Strikes and Wage Inflation in British Manufacturing Industry 1950–1968," *Bulletin*

David C. Smith

during the past decade? Have changes in strike activity reflected, as in the case of trade union growth, the economic conditions of the times or have there been other influences related directly to modifications in the institutional framework for collective bargaining, including the impacts of union growth and public policies? These are the two questions to which I now turn.

Recent Strike Activity

The most widely accepted measure of the seriousness of strike activity —the number of working days lost through industrial disputes per 1,000 people employed—does not place Britain at or near the top of international rankings in recent years. In table 4 data on this measure are shown for sixteen countries, with the United Kingdom ranking seventh in the period 1967–76. Canada, Italy, the United States, Australia, Finland, and the Irish Republic all had a worse record, but, with the exception of Italy, Britain had a less favorable record than any of its major European competitors. Although, as the table also shows, Britain was not alone in experiencing an upward shift in the seriousness of strikes after the mid-1960s, between 1964–66 and 1967–76 it did have the second highest percent increase in average working days lost (excluding the two countries for which there was a negligible level of strike activity in 1964–66).

Differences in statistical practices among countries in the recording of strike activity may affect these rankings somewhat, but they definitely reduce the usefulness of extending international comparisons to another general indicator of strike activity—the number of strikes. This indicator, which on the average also deteriorated in Britain in the 1967–76 period (despite a decline in the frequency of strikes in coal mining) and on which Britain has usually scored less well than the United States, is particularly sensitive to national differences in the criteria used to determine

of the Oxford Institute of Economics and Statistics, vol. 34 (1972), pp. 281–94; L. C. Hunter, "The Economic Determination of Strike Activity: A Reconsideration," Discussion Paper 1 (University of Glasgow, Department of Social and Economic Research, October 1973); R. Bean and D. A. Peel, "A Quantitative Analysis of Wage Strikes in Four U.K. Industries, 1962–1970," *Journal of Economic Studies,* new series, vol. 1 (November 1974), pp. 88–97; D. Sapsford, "A Time Series Analysis of U.K. Industrial Disputes," *Industrial Relations,* vol. 14 (May 1975), pp. 242–49; John Shorey, "Time Series Analysis of Strike Frequency," *British Journal of Industrial Relations,* vol. 15 (March 1977), pp. 63–75.

Table 4. *Comparison of Working Days Lost through Industrial Disputes in Mining, Manufacturing, Construction, and Transport, Selected Countries, 1964–76*

Country	Average annual days lost per 1,000 employed				Ranking in 1967–76	Ranking of percentage increase 1964–66 to 1967–76
	1964–66	1967–71	1972–76	1967–76		
United Kingdom	190	608	968	788	7	2
Australia[a]	400	796	1,502	1,131	4	6
Belgium	200	394	348[b]	373[b]	10	8
Canada	970	1,682	2,130	1,906	1	7
Denmark[c]	160	64	1,078	571	8	3
West Germany	[d]	80	32	56	15	. . .
Finland	80	886	1,028	957	5	1
France	200	313[e]	338	327[e]	11	9
Irish Republic	1,620	952	782	867	6	14
Italy	1,170	1,692	1,956	1,824	2	10
Japan	240	194	294	244	12	12
Netherlands	20	42	82	62	14	4
New Zealand	150	350	504	427	9	5
Norway	[d]	20	114	67	13	. . .
Sweden[f]	40	62	16	39	16	13
United States[g]	870	1,644	1,054	1,349	3	11

Sources: 1964–66 data are from Royal Commission on Trade Unions and Employers' Associations, *Report* (HMSO, 1968), p. 95; 1967–76 data are from "Industrial Disputes: International Comparisons," *Department of Employment Gazette*, vol. 85 (December 1977), p. 1342.

a. Includes electricity and gas.
b. 1976 figure not included in averages.
c. Manufacturing only.
d. Fewer than ten working days lost.
e. 1968 figure unavailable and not included in averages.
f. All industries included until 1971.
g. Includes electricity, gas, water, sanitary services.

which industrial disputes are too small to be classified as strikes. For example, in British data, work stoppages involving fewer than ten workers and those lasting less than one day are excluded from the statistics except when the aggregate number of working days lost exceeds one hundred.[46] In the U.S. data, on the other hand, work stoppages involving more than five workers are included in the statistics, but stoppages lasting less than

46. Other criteria used in the British definition of work stoppages can be briefly noted. Estimates of the number of working days lost and of the number of workers involved apply only to establishments in which the disputes occurred; working days lost through the indirect effects of disputes on other establishments are not included in the statistics. Strikes for political reasons, such as the demonstrations against the Industrial Relations Act, are excluded. Lockouts are not recorded separately from strikes; it has been estimated that lockouts, strikes by nonunionists, and unclassifiable disputes account for less than 4 percent of days lost from work stoppages. Silver, "Recent British Strike Trends," pp. 67–69; and "Stoppages of Work Due to Industrial Disputes in 1976," *Department of Employment Gazette,* vol. 85 (June 1977), pp. 579–80.

a day or full shift in length are excluded from them. Turner has estimated that the net result of applying the U.S. definition to British data in the mid-1960s would be a substantial decrease in the recorded number of British strikes and a reversal of the international rankings of Britain and the United States.[47] A problem thus emerges in defining the combination of length and size of a dispute that constitutes a strike. Moreover, records of short strikes are likely to be highly imperfect. They are compiled in Britain primarily from reports by local office managers of the Department of Employment, and there is evidence that in some industries many of the small, brief strikes go unreported.[48]

A low proportion of British strikes are recorded as "official," that is, as having been endorsed officially by the unions to which the strikers belong. The proportion was only 3.3 percent in 1964–66 and rose slightly to 4.8 percent in 1967–76, with an annual range in the later period of between 3.1 percent and 7.2 percent.[49] Silver has argued that such data have understated the relative importance of official strikes and suggests, on the basis of a 1966 survey of shop stewards, that perhaps about 15 to 25 percent of strikes should be classified as official.[50] Whatever may be the appropriate estimate, it should not be surprising that the decentralized, voluntary tradition of British industrial relations produces a high proportion of unofficial strikes and that the U.S. tradition of legally binding, detailed labor contracts produces a greater official role of union leaders in disputes, centered at the time of contract renegotiations, even though many unofficial, or wildcat, strikes may still occur. But it does not follow that the large proportion of unofficial strikes in Britain necessarily results in a much greater economic cost, because such strikes are highly unpredictable and widely scattered. Indeed, much publicity has been given recently to the Department of Employment's studies of the concentration of industrial stoppages. It found, for example, that in 1971–75, 98 percent of manufacturing establishments, employing about 80 percent of

47. *Is Britain Really Strike Prone?* p. 13. It can be noted that in Britain in 1976 about 20 percent of recorded strikes lasted not more than one day but accounted for only about 3 percent of working days lost "Stoppages of Work Due to Industrial Disputes in 1976," p. 584).

48. Silver, "Recent British Strike Trends," pp. 86–93.

49. See Royal Commission on Trade Unions and Employers' Associations, *Report,* pp. 97–98, and "Statistical Series: Industrial Disputes," *Department of Employment Gazette,* vol. 85 (October 1977), p. 1182.

50. Silver, "Recent British Strike Trends," pp. 86–93.

manufacturing employees, experienced no work stoppages in an average year.[51]

Such data raise doubts about the validity of the common belief that Britain suffers from an exceptionally serious strike problem. Undoubtedly, the notoriety of British strikes derives in part from the reporting by the media, at home and abroad, of seemingly trivial or silly issues that might precipitate only a short walkout but that make a good news story. "Industrial action" over how to slice the gherkins or the terms of a tea break, whether it titillates or infuriates the recipient of the news, attracts attention. There also seems to be much national introspection over the question why reasonable, responsible people should behave in what are viewed as unreasonable, irresponsible ways. Evidence of such human failings is newsworthy, especially when economic policy pronouncements in recent decades have often emphasized—and probably to a greater extent in Britain than in Canada and the United States—the need for a moralistic conversion in economic behavior rather than a change in the objective conditions under which economic markets operate.

Indicators of British aggregate strike activity, however, shed little light on issues in British labor relations that have caused much recent concern. For example, do British strikes have an especially adverse effect on productivity performance? Have strikes now become directed more toward influencing the policies of governments, with the result that key services to consumers are more likely to be interrupted by public sector strikes and that confrontations over public policies have become more common? Consequently, has the worsening of the British strike record after the mid-1960s reflected a new set of forces or simply a particular conjunction of unfavorable economic events that in the past have usually had an adverse effect on strikes?

As to the first issue, Richard E. Caves suggests in the next paper that British labor relations are an important factor in explaining relative weaknesses in British productivity. His statistical results demonstrate that the ratio of productivity in British industries to productivity in U.S. industries has a negative correlation to strikes in British industries. Caves also finds

51. "Concentration of Industrial Stoppages in Great Britain: 1971–1975," *Department of Employment Gazette,* vol. 86 (January 1978), pp. 9–10. These figures, however, are based on officially recorded strikes. If the many unreported short, small strikes could be counted, the percentage of manufacturing establishments unaffected by work stoppages in an average year would be lower.

Table 5. *Strike Activity in the Public Sector Relative to Total Strike Activity, United Kingdom, 1966–76*[a]

	Working days lost in public sector as percent of total working days lost		Work stoppages in public sector as percent of total work stoppages	
Year or decade	*Including coal mining*	*Excluding coal mining*	*Including coal mining*	*Excluding coal mining*
1966	12	7	37	8
1967	17	13	28	9
1968	15	14	19	10
1969	30	15	17	11
1970	32	22	18	14
1971	50	50	16	10
1972	48	3	17	8
1973	21	20	22	12
1974	48	10	21	15
1975	10	9	22	13
1976	18	16	29	15
1967–76	29	17	21	12

Source: C. T. B. Smith and others, *Strikes in Britain*, Department of Employment, Manpower Paper 15 (HMSO, 1978), tables 1, 13.

a. The public sector is defined as coal mining, iron and steel, gas, electricity, water, railways, road-passenger transport, air transport, postal services, telecommunications, education services, health services, public administration, and defense. Some "mixed" industries, such as road haulage and port and inland water transport, are not included because of the difficulty of separating the public sector and private sector components.

evidence that the ratio of British inventory-to-sales figures to those for U.S. industries are positively correlated with variables representing the state of labor relations in British industries. This second finding is consistent with the argument that the large number of short, unofficial strikes in Britain creates much uncertainty in the planning of output. Furthermore, Caves reports on the strong evidence that strike activity is related to the size of the plant.

As for the relation between strikes and government policy, it should first be noted that, contrary to some popular opinion, the public sector's share of strike activity in recent years has not been disproportionately high relative to employment. As table 5 indicates, the public sector accounted for 29 percent of total working days lost through industrial disputes and 21 percent of the total number of work stoppages over the ten years 1967–76. During this period employment in the public sector averaged about 27 percent of total employment. If strikes in coal mining are excluded from the public sector data, the relative share of strike activity drops considerably—to 17 percent for working days lost and to 12 percent for the number of work stoppages. Moreover, since the unionization rate is higher in the public than in the private sector, it follows that in 1967–76 union members in the public sector were not on strike more frequently or longer than in the private sector.

As the table also shows, however, the forces that led to a worsening of the British strike record at the end of the 1960s and the beginning of the 1970s had relatively more effect on the severity of strikes in the public than in the private sector. Whether as a result of the form of incomes policies or of other factors affecting the government's relations with its employees, the proportion of total working days lost increased for the public sector. The long-term decline in the number of coal mining strikes masks a similar shift to the public sector in the frequency of strikes, but the shift is apparent if coal mining is excluded.

A relationship between public policy and strikes in both the public and private sectors seems to have arisen because of occasional unrest over incomes policies, not because of demands for basic changes in the political and economic system. Political confrontations associated, for example, with the coal miners' strike of 1974 and the industrial unrest in the winter of 1978–79 were related to the government's pay policies. Strikes directly attributable to political factors, which are excluded in published strike data for Britain, were not numerous or severe and were prominent only at the time of demonstrations against the Industrial Relations Act. Moreover, data on reasons given for striking have been compiled, and though it is obviously sometimes difficult to pin down the precise reason for a strike, the data show the growing importance of strikes over wages relative to strikes for largely nonpay reasons. The latter include trade union matters and other working arrangements, rules, and discipline—reasons that might reflect dissatisfaction with economic and political organization. Thus, as table 6 indicates, disputes over wages accounted for 55.5 percent of the number of strikes and 75.0 percent of the working days lost in 1967–76, figures that are higher than in 1947–56 and 1957–66.

The effect of incomes policies on strikes is likely to vary with the form and stage of the policy. If pay norms are widely endorsed or enforced, the range of potential disagreement between employers and employees on expected wage increases tends to decline. But during the breakdown of such policies or when a new venture in incomes policy is expected, the

Table 6. *Strike Activity Due to Disputes over Pay Relative to Total Strike Activity, United Kingdom, by Decade, 1947–76*

Decade	Work stoppages over pay as percent of total work stoppages	Working days lost over pay as percent of total working days lost
1947–56	45.4	46.8
1957–66	47.1	68.5
1967–76	55.5	75.0

Source: C. T. B. Smith and others, *Strikes in Britain*, table 25.

range may actually widen because of uncertainties over what norms, if any, are appropriate to current negotiations. In addition, norms may increase union militancy, since they are viewed as a threat to the traditional functions of union leadership and may cause governments to take, directly and indirectly, a less flexible position in pay negotiations, to try to preserve these norms and avert political embarrassment. In this case the government may look to other measures to gain the support of union (and business) leaders or to give them a more direct stake in the success of national economic policies. But it is not surprising that the government's greater reliance on incomes policies since the mid-1960s and, in turn, its dependence on union support for these policies have increased the concern over the political implications of strikes.

Changes in the Level of Strikes

Two sets of institutional factors can thus be suggested as being especially relevant to strike activity during the years 1967–76. First, the more rapid growth of trade unions may have increased industrial conflict, because errors in negotiations are more likely in new or changing than in well-established bargaining relationships, because changes in the organization of participants in the labor market can be unsettling even to previously organized groups, or because a strike is sometimes necessary to test the union's ability to exercise economic power by controlling the supply of labor of newly organized workers. Institutional change in the organization of employers can, of course, also alter established bargaining relationships and increase the probability of disputes until both sides become more accustomed to the new channels for negotiation. Second, government policies have probably affected the pattern of strikes in recent years. In particular, the greater reliance on incomes policies since the mid-1960s and their on-again, off-again nature are likely to have influenced the short-term timing of strikes and also perhaps, though less clearly, the average level of strikes in the longer term.

Besides such institutional factors, economic conditions can have an impact on strikes, as much research has shown.[52] In a period of unexpectedly high inflation, for example, labor and management may diverge more than usual in their expectations of real wage increases, particularly if there is a tendency toward a larger dispersion of wage and price movements. Thus not only may there have been a direct link recently between union growth and strikes but also both may have been influenced by the same features of the economic environment.

Quantitative studies of British strike patterns have generally concentrated on explaining the frequency of strikes and have found much support for the argument that economic conditions are very important. Perhaps the best known is the study by Pencavel in which a model, developed and applied by Ashenfelter and Johnson to the U.S. experience, was used to explain reasonably well the number of strikes, on a quarterly basis, in British industries (excluding coal mining) over the period 1950–67.[53] The study emphasized the role of economic conditions—and, in particular, the role of the expected movement in real wages, the unemployment rate, and the ratio of profits to compensation—although it was recognized that institutional factors might have affected the upward trend in the number of strikes and that incomes policies and the political party in power also might have had some influence. In a later study John Shorey explored more fully a variety of hypotheses about the impact of economic conditions on strike frequency.[54] The conclusion he drew from tests on quarterly data for two periods, 1920–39 and 1950–67, was that economic conditions largely explain strike frequency.

Do such models adequately explain British strike behavior over the period 1967–76? Reestimates of these models, as reported in appendix C,

52. An early influential study on the subject is Albert Rees, "Industrial Conflict and Business Fluctuations," *Journal of Political Economy,* vol. 60 (October 1952), pp. 371–82.

53. Pencavel, "An Investigation into Industrial Strike Activity in Britain." For the U.S. study, see Orley Ashenfelter and George E. Johnson, "Bargaining Theory, Trade Unions, and Industrial Strike Activity," *American Economic Review,* vol. 59 (March 1969), pp. 35–49.

54. "Time Series Analysis of Strike Frequency."

yield much less satisfactory results for this period than for earlier ones. This does not, of course, mean that economic influences suddenly became less important; the ways in which economic conditions affect strikes may need to be respecified. But the results also seem to support the argument that greater consideration needs to be given to the recent impact of institutional variables on strike behavior.

The impact of union growth on strikes has been explicitly recognized in Hunter's modifications of Pencavel's model.[55] Using annual data for the period 1951–71, he found a positive relation between union growth and strike activity.

The impact of incomes policies and of the political party in power were further examined both by Hunter and by Robert Davies.[56] Hunter found evidence that some milder forms of incomes policy reduced strikes, although neither stronger forms nor the election of a Labour government appeared to have a dampening effect on strikes. Davies's study is of particular interest in regard to these issues. Using quarterly data for the period from the beginning of 1966 to the end of 1975, Davies found not only that economic conditions had a clear effect on strikes but also that incomes policies tended to moderate strike frequency over pay issues during the operational phases of the policies and to increase strike frequency over nonpay issues, that strikes tended to rise to above-average levels when an incomes policy broke down, and that "considered over their complete 'life cycle' incomes policies have been associated with a significant increase in the aggregate frequency of strikes."[57] These findings, Davies suggested, were not significantly affected by whether a Labour or Conservative government imposed the incomes policy.

Interesting and important as recent research on the subject has been, much is yet to be learned about the determinants of strike activity. Work on the underlying theoretical relationships is not greatly advanced, and so far British quantitative studies have concentrated more on explaining

55. Hunter, "Economic Determination of Strike Activity: A Reconsideration." Hunter suggests that union leaders intensify recruitment in anticipation of strike action in order to be in a stronger defensive position. In contrast, my argument is that union growth is influenced by several factors but that the probability of a breakdown in labor-management relations tends to be higher in a period of changes in the organization of participants in the labor market.

56. Ibid.; and Robert J. Davies, "An Economic Analysis of Quarterly Strike Activity in the United Kingdom, 1966–1975" (University of Warwick, Industrial Relations Research Unit, 1977).

57. "An Economic Analysis of Quarterly Strike Activity," p. 53.

the number of strikes than the number of working days lost. (The former, as Richard Caves's paper shows, has nevertheless had important independent economic significance.) More in the spirit of obtaining rough checks on the relevance of the arguments I have been examining than of trying to provide a new, well-tested set of clues for unraveling the mysteries of British strike patterns, I reformulated a simple model of strike frequency and fitted it to data for the period 1951–76. The unavailability of quarterly data on trade union membership required the use of an annual model. A description of the model and a report on the statistical tests are in appendix C.

The results are not inconsistent with a number of the hypotheses that have been discussed here. First, the results suggest that the level of strike activity is likely to be higher in a period of more rapid growth in the unionization of the labor force. As reported in appendix C, the variable for the percentage change in union membership has a positive and statistically significant coefficient. Disaggregation would be necessary to determine whether newly organized workers or previously organized workers, as a result of defensive attitudes and other tensions associated with trade union expansion, had a larger share in the more frequent breakdown of bargaining relations.

Second, the results suggest that official intervention in collective bargaining, such as through pay norms, can reduce strikes but that, in a period of increased uncertainty about the nature and effectiveness of this intervention, the overall level of strike activity may well rise. It is not clear how best to allow for this effect, particularly when annual observations are being used. Following the incomes and prices freeze and period of severe restraint in 1966–67, there was considerable uncertainty about the direction of incomes policy and much serious experimentation with various forms of it (see appendix A). I therefore included a shift variable for the period 1968–76. Its coefficient is positive and statistically significant. Obviously, however, that variable is not a very satisfactory means of capturing the average effect these policies had on strikes, and it may also reflect other influences that raised the level of strike activity in recent years.

Third, the results suggest that economic conditions influence strikes through several routes. The tests provide some support for the argument that higher rates of inflation tend to raise tension, which leads to more strikes, but show that this relation is not linear in that an allowance should be made for adjustments to higher inflation rates. I constructed a variable for real wage rates after tax by deflating average weekly wage rates by the retail price index and multiplying by the ratio of disposable income to personal income. Crudely constructed as this variable is, it nevertheless has the expected negative effect on the number of strikes when expressed as a rate of change lagged one year. But the variable lagged two periods is not statistically significant. Other studies have often included a variable for the state of the labor market. In the model reported in appendix C I used the change in the unemployment rate and found a significant, negative relation between a rise in unemployment and the frequency of strikes. Finally, Pencavel included a variable for the ratio of profits to wage and salary compensation in his model. As he noted, it is not obvious whether the expected sign on the coefficient should be positive or negative, that is, whether there is a positive relation between higher relative profits and strikes, because workers press harder for greater wage gains when profits are high, or whether there is a negative relation, because employers are more willing to concede to wage demands. In his tests the coefficient was positive, but in the results reported here it is negative.

Conclusion

Inflation has been the most pressing economic policy problem in Britain since the mid-1960s. Views continue to differ on the weight to attach to the growth and exercise of economic power of trade unions as a cause of this inflation.[58] Indeed, the meaning of *cause* in this context becomes less clear when one has recognized that, whatever may be the strength of unions in raising expectations of wage and price increases and in giving a push to wages, the persistence of inflation requires a mechanism through

58. A. G. Hines argued that trade union aggressiveness explained money wage rate increases and that trade union aggressiveness is closely related to the rate of change of unionization. ("Trade Unions and Wage Inflation in the United Kingdom, 1893–1961," *Review of Economic Studies,* vol. 31 [October 1964], pp. 221–52.) Although this argument has not been widely accepted among researchers in the field, it has produced a lively and continuing debate. See, for example, D. Dogas and A. G. Hines, "Trade Unions and Wage Inflation in the U.K.: A Critique of Purdy and Zis," *Applied Economics,* vol. 7 (September 1975), pp. 195–211; D. L. Purdy and G. Zis, "Trade Unions and Wage Inflation in the U.K.: A Reply to Dogas and Hines," *Applied Economics,* vol. 8 (December 1976), pp. 249–65; Charles Mulvey and Mary Gregory, "The Hines Wage Inflation Model," *Manchester School of Economic and Social Studies,* vol. 45 (March 1977), pp. 29–40.

which the necessary demand conditions and the monetary requirements for these conditions expand. Governmental responses through monetary, fiscal, and other policies, it is now more widely appreciated, are to a considerable extent induced and form part of the system of interdependent economic relationships.[59]

Trade unions, in discussions of these relationships, have usually been considered an exogenous factor, that is, one that influences but is not influenced by these relationships. Yet there is much evidence in recent British experience to support the argument that the growth and militancy of trade unions have been affected by economic conditions and public policy responses to these conditions. By recognizing this evidence and including institutions, such as trade unions and governments, in the system of interdependent economic relationships, one gains perhaps a useful perspective on the processes that have led to inflation and on the role of trade unions in its control. For example, suppose that an unexpected rise in inflation has strengthened union organization and increased industrial unrest. Governments are sensitive to this rise in inflation and strikes but for political reasons cannot neglect trade union pressure against allowing unemployment to rise substantially. To get the support of trade union leaders for curbs on inflation and strikes, governments may thus be willing to trade off some measures that permit greater future organizational opportunities for unions. To the degree that the upward pressure on average wage rates is higher in periods of greater union growth, these measures will produce even higher inflation rates than would otherwise occur. The stage is then set for a further round of private and public policy responses.

I do not wish to imply that the relationships suggested in this example provide an adequate explanation of the routes through which inflation has developed or that these relationships are rigid and deterministic. The emergence of the social contract in the mid-1970s, for instance, is not inconsistent with them, but it also depended on the position taken by leaders of the ruling Labour party and, in particular, by influential leaders of the trade union movement. Moreover, the characteristics of British trade unionism have changed significantly since the mid-1960s. Its tradition of voluntarism has been weakened, it is more secure under legislative protection, and it is more centralized within the Trades Union Congress.

59. See, for example, Assar Lindbeck, "Stabilization Policy in Open Economies with Endogenous Politicians," *American Economic Review*, vol. 66 (May 1976, *Papers and Proceedings, 1975*), pp. 1–19.

To the extent that current interest in extending industrial democracy favors the involvement of trade union as well as worker representatives in management decisions, new organizational opportunities may arise, but in many sectors of the British economy trade union organization of the work force is now virtually complete.

Appendix A: Public Policy toward Labor-Management Relations, 1964–77

1964 Trade Union (Amalgamations, etc.) Act (eased procedures for union mergers).

Joint Statement of Intent on Productivity, Prices and Incomes (signed by representatives of labor and employer organizations).

1965 Appointment of Royal Commission on Trade Unions and Employers' Associations (Donovan commission).

Trade Disputes Act (clarified legal protection to workers taking part in strikes).

Pay policy: National Board for Prices and Incomes established; a pay norm of 3–3½ percent, with four criteria for limited exceptions.

1966 Pay policy: a freeze for six months beginning in July, to be followed by six months of "severe restraint."

1967 Pay policy: after the period of severe restraint, ending on June 30, no pay norm established and all pay increases to be justified by the four criteria announced in 1965.

1968 Report of Royal Commission on Trade Unions and Employers' Associations (Donovan commission).

Pay policy: a 3½ percent average pay ceiling except for productivity agreements and pay restructuring.

1969 Commission on Industrial Relations established.

Department of Employment and Productivity, *In Place of Strife: A Policy for Industrial Relations,* white paper setting out the Labour government's proposals on the reform of industrial relations.

Pay policy: from the end of 1969 on, a pay norm to be 2½– 4½ percent.

1970 Pay policy: general pay policy disbanded with the election of a Conservative government, but the intention expressed to reduce the rate of advance of pay settlements in the public sector.

1971 Industrial Relations Act (comprehensive legislation on industrial relations; features unpopular with trade unions included the prohibition of closed shop agreements and registration requirements).

1972 Pay policy: a statutory pay freeze announced in November as part of stage 1 of a new incomes policy.

1973 Pay policy: Pay Board established; in March, stage 2 limited pay increases to £1 plus 4 percent a week, with an upper limit of £250 a year; in November, stage 3 set the maximum pay increase at 7 percent or £2.25 a week, with 1 percent for exceptions, an upper limit of £350 a year, and a provision for threshold agreements.

1974 Social contract: endorsed by Trades Union Congress.

Trade Union and Labour Relations Act (replaced the Industrial Relations Act and eliminated or modified many of its features that were unpopular with trade unions).

Advisory, Conciliation, and Arbitration Service (ACAS) established (to provide an independent conciliation service that would also assist in union recognition disputes).

Pay policy: Pay Board and controls disbanded with the election of a Labour government; under the social contract, pay increases to compensate only for price increases and settlements to be at not less than twelve-month intervals.

1975 Employment Protection Act (expanded on rights of employees and ACAS established on a statutory basis).

Pay policy: maximum pay increase to be £6 a week, with a freeze on incomes over £8,500.

1976 Trade Union and Labour Relations (Amendment) Act (clarified and made more flexible the provisions for closed shop agreements that had been made lawful again under the 1974 act).

Pay policy: a 5 percent norm, with a minimum of £2.50 and a maximum of £4 a week.

1977 Pay policy: pay norm to be a maximum of 10 percent except in the case of special productivity agreements.

Appendix B: Trade Union Growth Models

The model of trade union growth, developed by George S. Bain and Farouk Elsheikh and applied to British experience for the period 1893–1970, was reestimated for the periods 1897–1976 and 1950–76; the results are reported in columns 1 and 2 of table 7. The following symbols are used: a dot (˙) over a variable indicates the annual percent change; T is trade union membership; P is the retail price index; S takes the value of 1 when $\dot{P} \geq 4$ percent and 0 otherwise; W is the wage earnings index; U is the unemployment rate; D is union density. The Cochrane-Orcutt iterative method has been used for these and other estimates reported in the table.

These reestimates indicate a considerable stability to the Bain-Elsheikh model. Chow tests for a structural break in the model after 1949 (and after 1968) show no statistical grounds for arguing that the applicability of the model has shifted. A troublesome point, which Richardson called attention to in 1977, is that the coefficients on most of the variables are not significant by conventional tests when the model is estimated for the post–World War II period (see column 2).[60] But as Bain and Elsheikh responded, this statistical finding might be due to the small number of observations and less independent variation in the explanatory variables in the test since 1950.[61]

Estimates of a modified model are reported in columns 3 and 4 of table 7. The following additional symbols are used: $\dot{P}_e$, an estimate of the expected rate of inflation, is assumed to be determined by a distributed lag of the rate of change of prices over the previous three years; E is civilian employment; G is a shift variable that takes the value of 1 in the years of the subscript and 0 in all other years.

The results, as seen in the table, indicate some support for the modified model, but they must be treated with great caution. The estimates were sensitive to alternative specifications of the variable for expected inflation. The shift variables, and in particular that for 1969–76, were not always statistically significant. The employment data prior to 1948 are based on a linear interpolation between decennial census years. In short, much further work is needed, and it is not suggested that the model is clearly superior to the Bain-Elsheikh model on statistical grounds.

60. Ray Richardson, "Trade Union Growth: Review Article," *British Journal of Industrial Relations,* vol. 15 (July 1977), pp. 279–82.
61. Elsheikh and Bain, "Trade Union Growth: A Reply," p. 101.

Table 7. *Estimates of Determinants of Annual Rate of Change of Trade Union Membership in the United Kingdom, 1897–1976*[a]

Independent variable and summary statistic[b]	1897–1976 (1)	1950–76 (2)	1897–1976 (3)	1950–76 (4)
Variable				
Constant	7.91	26.47	8.47	21.15
	(4.18)	(2.18)	(2.84)	(2.77)
$\dot{P}_t$	0.60	−0.004	...	...
	(6.17)	(−0.013)		
$\dot{P}S_t$	−0.49	0.16	...	...
	(−3.60)	(0.717)		
$\dot{P}_t - \dot{P}_{et}$	...	...	0.18	0.29
			(2.06)	(2.62)
$\dot{W}_t$	0.43	0.29	...	...
	(4.18)	(1.67)		
U_{t-1}	−0.51	0.80	−0.61	(0.42)
	(−1.87)	(1.29)	(−2.84)	(0.74)
U_{t-2}	0.46	0.31	...	...
	(1.74)	(0.44)		
$\dot{E}_t$	...	...	0.78	0.42
			(2.67)	(2.12)
D_{t-1}	−0.23	−0.68	−0.20	−0.50
	(−5.07)	(−2.22)	(−2.73)	(−2.68)
$G_{1969-76}$	...	...	4.43	2.71
			(1.77)	(2.79)
$G_{1911-20}$	...	...	8.42	...
			(3.73)	
$G_{1936-48}$	...	...	4.01	...
			(2.13)	
Summary statistic				
$\bar{R}^2$	0.73	0.57	0.66	0.59
Durbin-Watson	1.98	1.93	1.83	1.86
Standard error of estimate	3.51	1.28	3.97	1.21
Rho	0.21	−0.04	0.39	−0.34
	(1.90)	(−0.19)	(3.81)	(−1.87)

Sources: Author's calculations. Data on trade union membership, retail prices, wage earnings, the unemployment rate, and union density are from George S. Bain and Farouk Elsheikh, *Union Growth and the Business Cycle: An Econometric Analysis* (Oxford: Basil Blackwell, 1976), and updates of the series were kindly provided by Bain. The unemployment rate for 1892–1948 was taken from C. H. Feinstein, *National Income, Expenditure and Output of the United Kingdom, 1855–1965* (Cambridge: Cambridge University Press, 1972), pp. T125–27. Employment is defined as the civilian labor force excluding the unemployed, employers, and the self-employed.

a. The numbers in parentheses are *t*-statistics; regressions were estimated by the Cochrane-Orcutt iterative method.

b. See appendix text for definition of variables.

Table 8. *Estimates of Determinants of Number of Strikes (Excluding Mining) in the United Kingdom, 1950–76*[a]

Independent variable and summary statistic[b]	Pencavel quarterly model 1950:1–1967:2 (1)	Pencavel quarterly model 1967:3–1976:4 (2)	Shorey quarterly model 1950:1–1967:2 (3)	Shorey quarterly model 1967:3–1976:4 (4)	Independent variable and summary statistic	Modified annual model 1951–76
Variable					*Variable*	
Constant	−98.23 (−1.16)	1,137.58 (2.23)	−244.03 (−4.03)	21.94 (0.11)	Constant	5,919.18 (6.93)
N_1	79.12 (6.14)	−22.26 (−0.51)	73.40 (4.97)	9.75 (0.15)	$\dot{T}$	116.79 (2.55)
N_2	31.93 (2.64)	81.58 (1.77)	6.92 (−0.51)	−136.67 (2.45)	$\dot{P}_t$	90.66 (1.80)
N_3	0.30 (0.02)	−21.36 (−0.42)	−7.50 (−0.51)	−35.65 (−0.52)	$\dot{P}_t^2$	−8.31 (−3.24)
U_t	−37.65 (−2.55)	−133.66 (−2.73)	...	...	$\dot{R}A_{t-1}$	−93.44 (−2.02)
V_t	6.51 (2.65)	−22.30 (−1.47)	...	...	$\dot{R}A_{t-2}$	26.01 (0.65)
$\sum_{i=1}^{6} \dot{R}_{t-i}$	−44.61 (−4.26)	−75.57 (−1.70)	...	...	$U_t − U_{t-1}$	−550.70 (−3.84)

T_R	5.43 (14.15)	5.29 (0.99)	...	...	...
P_R/P_t	...	...	0.26 (4.38)	0.15 (0.81)	...
$\dot{W}_{t-1}$	...	...	−14.38 (−1.67)	−0.14 (−0.01)	...
$\dot{P}_{t-1}$	...	...	10.59 (1.61)	−10.65 (−0.57)	...
P_t	...	...	1.28 (2.34)	−0.02 (−0.05)	...
SOM_{t-1}	...	...	0.54 (5.64)	0.81 (6.89)	...
V_t					−202.84 (−5.84)
G_{6876}					1,133.61 (5.22)
Summary statistic					
$\bar{R}^2$	0.89	0.70	0.88	0.63	0.93
Durbin-Watson	1.93	2.11	2.02[c]	1.90[c]	2.17
Standard error of estimate	36.42	110.01	37.50	121.87	293.41
Rho	0.22 (1.92)	0.52 (3.72)	−0.17 (−1.39)	−0.24 (−1.47)	−0.41 (−2.23)

Sources: John H. Pencavel, "An Investigation into Industrial Strike Activity in Britain," *Economica*, vol. 37 (August 1970), pp. 239–56; John Shorey, "Time Series Analysis of Strike Frequency," *British Journal of Industrial Relations*, vol. 15 (March 1977), pp. 63–75. Gross trading profits of companies and wages and salaries are for 1948–54 from L. R. Klein and others, *An Econometric Model of the United Kingdom* (Oxford: Basil Blackwell, 1961), p. 282, and for 1955–76 from *Monthly Digest of Statistics*, for dates indicated. Data on the number of work stoppages beginning in each period, the unemployment rate, weekly wage rates, and retail prices are from *Department of Employment Gazette* (which earlier carried the titles *Employment and Productivity Gazette* and *Monthly Labour Gazette*).

a. The numbers in parentheses are *t*-statistics; regressions were estimated by the Cochrane-Orcutt iterative method.

b. See appendix text for definition of variables.

c. Biased toward 2 because of the use of a lagged dependent variable.

Appendix C: Strike Frequency Models

Estimates of the strike frequency model used by John Pencavel is reported for two post–World War II periods in columns 1 and 2 of table 8. Similarly, estimates of John Shorey's model are reported in columns 3 and 4. In both cases the dependent variable is the number of strikes, other than those in mining, on a quarterly basis.

The following symbols are used: N_1, N_2, N_3 are seasonal dummy variables; U is the unemployment rate; V is the ratio of gross trading profits to wage and salary compensation; R is real wages; T_R is a trend variable; P_R/P is the ratio of profits to retail prices; W is the weekly wage rate; SOM is the number of strikes other than those in mining.

The statistical fit of both models is less satisfactory for the second period, and for both models the evidence is consistent with the determinants of strike frequency having shifted between the earlier post–World War II years and the 1967–76 period.

A modified model was tested on annual observations of the number of strikes other than those in mining. (Data on union membership are available only on an annual basis.) The following additional symbols were used: T is trade union membership; RA is the real wage after tax estimated as the ratio of weekly wages to retail prices multiplied by the ratio of disposable income to personal income; G_{6876} is a shift variable that takes the value of 1 for 1968–76 and 0 for other years.

The principal hypotheses that underlie the modified annual model are (1) a more rapid growth of trade union membership ($\dot{T}$) will increase strikes because of a greater chance of disputes in new or extended bargaining situations; (2) the rate of inflation ($\dot{P}$) affects strikes because of its impact on tensions over an appropriate wage structure, although adjustments to larger average price changes ($\dot{P}^2$) take place; (3) a higher rate of increase of real wage rates after tax ($\dot{R}A$) tends to decrease strikes because of greater satisfaction over the advance in standards of living; (4) a deterioration in the unemployment rate ($U_t - U_{t-1}$) decreases strikes; (5) it is not clear on a priori grounds whether a ratio of profits to wage and salary compensation (V) increases or decreases strikes; (6) the period 1968–76 has been one of considerable change in public policies affecting collective bargaining and an allowance for a shift in strike activity (G_{6876}) is made.

Comments by Derek Robinson

DAVID SMITH has used statistical and econometric techniques to shed light on two aspects of British industrial relations: trade union growth and industrial disputes. As with all such approaches, the analyses and explanations are limited by the availability and suitability of the data. Further difficulties arise from the nature of the processes of industrial relations. For example, does the growth in the size and power of trade unions merely reflect the greater weakness of employers, and, if so, ought the factors that explain any increase in trade union power also explain the decline in employers' power? Or might there be some factors that weaken employers but do not increase the power of trade unions?

There can be difficulties over the meaning of *trade union,* particularly in the two contexts considered here. The meaning is fairly straightforward when trade union growth is discussed; one need only define the organizations that are to be regarded as trade unions. It is less clear when industrial disputes are the subject. It does not follow that a group of workers, even if they are all trade union members, ought to be considered a trade union when taking some forms of action. For example, the recent strike action by some craftsmen was directed as much at their own trade union and the joint bodies of other trade unions to which their union belonged as it was at their employers. If the employers had prevented the strikes by conceding the demand for separate bargaining units for craftsmen, some of the unions would undoubtedly have taken official strike action. In what sense would such action be the result of trade union decisions? Similarly, the fact that most strikes in Britain are unofficial raises problems of terminology and analysis when one tries to relate trade union growth to trade union activity.

Trade Union Growth

Granted that the most useful measurement of trade union growth is density—the proportion of the work force that is unionized—it is unfortunate that so far it has not been possible to produce either trade union membership or density figures by standard industrial classification order. Since much of the recent increase in trade union membership has been in white-collar occupations, the use of aggregate density percentages leads to difficult problems if the percentages are related to changes in the earnings of manual workers only.

It is not uncommon to associate, if not equate, increases in the numerical strength of unions, measured either in simple numbers or as a density percentage, with increases in bargaining strength and militancy. But at present no measure of bargaining strength or militancy exists. It might be possible to assess union strength by comparing union wages with some baseline that represents a nonunion position. It is doubtful, however, whether there are data in the United Kingdom that permit such assessments to be made with any great degree of reliability. The attempts to use the New Earnings Survey data are interesting, but these data differentiate on the basis of trade union bargaining coverage rather than membership. No satisfactory examination has been made of the relative levels of earnings in unionized and nonunionized employments in Britain. If strong views on comparability or fairness in wage increases, as well as in pay levels, exist, then it may be that trade unions can increase pay and that the nonunionized firms will also increase pay either because of fears of labor shortages and the loss of some employees to unionized firms or because of equity considerations. This might be an even stronger possibility given schedule 11 of the Employment Protection Act and the Fair Wages Resolution. These provisions build in coercive comparisons so that firms without full bargaining recognition may obtain union levels of pay. They may also have the effect of encouraging nonunionized employers to keep in line.

The question of militancy raises yet further complications. Either militancy is the same as strength and therefore can be subsumed under union bargaining strength and its results presumably picked up in the measurement of changes in union density (or whatever measure is used), or it is something more than strength, perhaps the propensity to use strength, however that might be quantified. In the second case the measure of trade union strength does not in itself explain wage changes. It becomes necessary to introduce another variable to explain militancy, that is, the extent to which unions sometimes use their strength to the full and why at other times they do not do so. One can therefore distinguish between the *ability* to exert bargaining pressure and the *willingness* to do so.

To the extent that strength and militancy are functions of events external to a trade union (for example, rate of change of prices generally or of the general level of unemployment), one might expect *all* trade unions to be affected equally, at least so far as militancy is concerned. Profits or rate of return on capital might be expected to affect unions in the private sector more than in the public sector. On the other hand, if these external factors mainly influence union strength—that is, recruitment and retention of members—one might well expect them to be non-linear, not least because, as the density percentage rises, union strength cannot so readily be increased among those groups that are already highly organized.

Without having detailed figures on which to base a case, one might still argue that, though the extension of trade union organization is a function of external variables, internal factors are also important, as are noneconomic factors that cause certain discontinuities in union organization. This approach seeks to show that a considerable amount of trade union growth in Britain in recent years has been the result of extending trade unionism on a substantial scale to occupations and industries that have not previously been well organized. The simple broad example is the organization of middle-grade white-collar employees in the private sector.

Significant internal factors might relate to threats of takeovers or actual takeovers, organizational change (particularly greater formalization of managerial structures), the greater formality and rigidity in salary structures and reduction of flexibility to give incremental-scale salary rises on an individual or personal basis (the result of income policy provisions), and the squeezing of internal differentials. As large companies became more like the public sector in their employment relationship with middle-grade executives, these executives became more like their public sector counterparts and joined trade unions. In this respect the United Kingdom should perhaps be seen as following a Scandinavian pattern.

The climatic change whereby membership in a trade union—though frequently a special trade union that carefully distinguished itself from those catering to blue-collar workers—became acceptable to many middle-class private sector employees is not amenable to measurement, and indeed whether it is important or even relevant is ultimately a matter of judgment. However, I believe that this change in attitude did play a part in trade union growth and that three factors, among others, brought it about.

First, emulation had a strong effect. The apparent success of blue-collar trade unions in improving the conditions of their members and in reducing pay and other differentials, and the apparent success of some professional quasi trade union bodies, such as the British Medical Association, in supporting their members, suggested that unions had something to offer the middle grades, particularly when traditional paternalism was disappearing.

Second, and a point ill-suited to quantitative analysis, Clive Jenkins emerged as a well-known public leader of the professional classes. Jenkins both created and exploited supremely well the opportunities for the expansion of his union. The response to him, by employers, other unions, and potential recruits, led to the growth of trade unionism outside his own organization. Probably the expansion of white-collar unionism in general would have been considerably less, and slower in taking place, had it not been for Jenkins.

Third, new legislation and new organizations or machinery to encourage the extension of trade unions and collective bargaining helped to change the climate of opinion. These include not only bodies such as the Commission on Industrial Relations and the Central Arbitration Committee of the ACAS but also legislative provisions that limit employee participation to trade union representatives (where they exist), for example, on health and safety committees. If employee representatives on company boards are confined to trade union representatives, one should expect a further boost to trade unionism among the managerial and executive grades.

Bain and Elsheikh reported that they were unable to find statistical grounds for including these various developments in the explanation of trade union growth at the aggregate level, although it may well be that they had an impact at a disaggregated level in some industries for some occupations.[62] The Commission on Industrial Relations concluded that the provisions for union recognition had a favorable impact on union growth.[63] It would be ironic if subsequent work by Bain did not establish that government intervention had an effect at a disaggregated level. Bain's work influenced the Donovan commission and subsequent events more than anything else, and led to the view that if unionism and collective bargaining were to be extended, it was necessary for government to provide specific and positive assistance. Consequently, both the Conservative

62. *Union Growth and the Business Cycle.*
63. Commission on Industrial Relations, *Trade Union Recognition: CIR Experience,* CIR Study 5 (HMSO, 1974).

and Labour parties decided that the government should not be neutral on the question of the extension of collective bargaining but should declare that an extension was desirable.

The decision to join a trade union is influenced by internal and external factors. The density percentage depends on decisions to join made by those who have not previously been organized (or decisions by others to resign) plus employment shifts toward or away from occupations, industries, and firms that are highly organized. In the United Kingdom the second factor means that shifts toward public sector employment will increase the density percentage—and this is true irrespective of sex or age. The "measles" effect is strong; people who work in a highly organized office or plant have a much higher propensity to join a union than those who work in poorly organized or unorganized places.

My own view is that the relation between unions and government has little effect, if any, on the decision to join a trade union, although it might influence a union's decision whether to affiliate with the Trades Union Congress. (The classic example is the First Division Association.) Such a decision might, in fact, lead to a decrease rather than an increase in membership. Indeed, there might be danger to all trade unions in a closer identity with government, except perhaps in cases where union membership is compulsory. If government makes concessions in, say, taxation policy as a result of discussions with trade unions, it is very unlikely that politicians will allow trade union leaders to claim all the credit. Politicians will naturally seek to persuade the public that the tax reductions were the result of a government decision so that they can obtain the political advantage. Moreover, tax concessions are not confined to union members; it is difficult to persuade people to join a union on the grounds that they will then receive tax concessions obtained by the TUC. A built-in conflict exists when unions become involved in bipartite or tripartite discussions that lead to unions having to modify their behavior to obtain some advantages. The existing leadership of the union is exposed to internal criticism and challenge.

Affiliation with the Trades Union Congress might also be much influenced by the recruiting tactics of other affiliated unions. One advantage of membership in the TUC is the protection of the Bridlington Agreement covering interunion recognition and recruitment rights.

The modifications made by Smith to other models of trade union growth seem attractive in their appeal to intuitive views of explanatory factors as well as on statistical grounds. As he points out, the problems of disaggregation are severe, and it is at disaggregated levels that one might expect to find clearer evidence of the relevance and causal relationship of the various factors. I doubt whether it will prove possible to make much more progress in the use of proxies for various policy and attitudinal changes, but this doubt may well say more about my own approach to industrial relations than about the methodology and reliability of the statistics used in this sort of analysis.

Smith, in the first part of his paper, has therefore dealt in a constructive way with the question of why people join trade unions, and has added to our understanding. But the question of what determines the strength of trade unions once people have joined is answered somewhat obliquely and only in part. The question of what determines the way in which trade unions use their strength, or the militancy aspect of trade unionism, forms the second part of his paper.

Industrial Disputes

It is usual to regard statistics of industrial disputes as indicators of union strength or militancy or as signs of a breakdown in the industrial relations system. Without an analysis and assessment of the results of industrial disputes, one should be chary of drawing any conclusions about union, or employer, strength on the basis of dispute statistics. In particular, statistics of the number of disputes as recorded by the Department of Employment and year-to-year changes in them depend on so many factors that they ought not to be regarded as having much sensitivity to relatively small changes in other variables.

As to disaggregated data, it is clear that the dominant element related to the propensity to strike in British manufacturing industry is the size of the establishment. For example, as Smith points out, in a typical year (in the 1971–75 period) only 2 percent of establishments in manufacturing, employing 20 percent of the work force, were affected by stoppages, but the figures rise to something like one-third of establishments and half the work force for plants employing 1,000 or more. In part this difference is due to the higher probability of a plant with 1,000 employees being affected than one with 99, as well as to unofficial strikes and fragmented bargaining on multiunion issues. However, it is also clear that size is a real problem in that the larger the plant the more disputes and various forms of industrial action are likely to occur. Small plants are also much less likely to be organized.[64]

It appears from the preliminary results of a survey carried out by Industrial Facts and Forecasting for the SSRC Industrial Relations Research Unit that there is considerable underreporting of industrial action in the Department of Employment statistics.[65] Some of this is due to the exclusions in the department figures and some, no doubt, to failure to report to the department. And also a considerable amount of action other than strikes (for example, overtime bans) takes place.

Again, size seems important. Some form of industrial action was reported in one-third of plants with 50 to 99 employees and in 87 percent of those with more than 1,000. (It appears that these figures refer to 1977 and 1978 together and include all forms of industrial action.) But if the data are classified by size of plant and expressed as incidents per 100,000 manual employees, small plants have a higher ratio of industrial action than large plants. The survey also indicates that union membership density figures seem to have little effect on the incident ratio, but the presence of shop stewards, particularly full-time stewards, seems important, although causal relationships are not claimed in the preliminary findings.

It is clear that the Industrial Relations Research Unit's complete results and analysis, which are to appear later, may shed considerable light on various aspects of strike activity at plant level.

The relation between union expansion and strike activity is unclear but possibly important. If a firm causal relation exists, that might also shed some light on the distinction between official and unofficial strikes, for it is very unlikely that newly recruited members in a new bargaining unit would go on unofficial strike. It is here that the official strike decision ought to be expected. This is supported by the IFF-SSRC findings: "There is a tendency for industrial action to occur more often in establishments where unions have a secure base and where employers are organised but this is far from universal."[66] It is not clear, however, to what extent industrial action here means strikes and to what extent it refers to some other form of activity.

64. Price and Bain, in *Union Growth Revisited,* assume at one stage that there are no union members in plants with fewer than 100 employees and do not believe that this assumption seriously distorts their analysis.

65. "Work-Place Industrial Relations in Manufacturing Industry."

66. Ibid.

The pay system and bargaining unit can also be expected to affect the use of the official strike. Where there is a single industry-wide wage bargaining unit with centrally determined pay levels and grades, one would expect official strikes to dominate, at least in terms of number of days lost. In this regard, the introduction of productivity bonuses at the local level might lead to the reemergence of unofficial strikes in coal mining.

Further work needs to be done on the importance of size of plant in connection with the industrial relations issues, and, if possible, some efforts should be made to assess the importance, or relative irrelevancy, of industrial action, not just strikes, on economic performance. But researchers should probably not be working on the conflict between the economic-based or technologically possible economy of scales and the institutional and industrial relations–relevant social diseconomies of scale. Moreover, researchers ought perhaps to consider whether size of plant relates directly to strike incidence or whether size of plant is indicative of the type of work organization (for example, assembly lines), which is the underlying cause of industrial unrest. In that case, changing the organization of work might reduce the incidence of strike activity in large plants.

RICHARD E. CAVES

Productivity Differences among Industries

SINCE WORLD WAR II Britain has suffered a prolonged slide in its rank among industrial countries in level of income per capita. This decline is a suspected cause of many other ills, such as inflationary pressure for higher money incomes and the political anguish of settling for a peripheral role in international affairs. The slow growth in income per capita is closely allied to a slow expansion of productivity; indeed, one can so define "productivity" to make it equivalent to income per capita. Hypotheses abound in Britain about the basic cause of its difficulties, with the culprits ranging from microeconomic malfunctions through inappropriate public policies to fundamental traits of culture and society. "If Britain were different in respect of X, would productivity grow faster?" Orderly tests of these hypotheses have been few and largely confined to international comparisons on one feature at a time. Can the main trouble be strikes if the United States has more? Can Britain's leading companies be too small to compete internationally if Sweden's are smaller? And so on.

This paper uses a different approach to test the explanations of Britain's low or slow-growing industrial productivity. I measure how much the productivity levels of British manufacturing industries differ from those in another major industrial country—the United States—and seek to explain why the productivity shortfall of Britain's industries varies from

I am indebted to Mitchell Rodman for computational assistance.

135

industry to industry. This approach is of no help in evaluating forces that affect all British industries alike, such as the frequent changes in tax laws. But since many alleged causes of poor productivity performance potentially weigh more heavily on some industries than others, I seek to measure those factors and test their effects on productivity at the level of the individual manufacturing industry.

The Statistical Record

The familiar facts about Britain's productivity and its growth receive only a brief review here. As early as 1907, physical product per person employed in representative British manufacturing industries was on average no more than half of that for their U.S. counterparts.[1] Over the last century output per head in Britain has grown more slowly than in other industrial countries. Maddison's data suggest a fourfold growth in output per head for the United Kingdom over 1870–1976; fifteen other industrial countries averaged nearly an eightfold increase and only one grew more slowly. West Germany's gross domestic product per capita, 36 percent less than Britain's at the turn of the century, had become 29 percent higher by 1973. Over the same period Italy's GDP per capita climbed to equality with Britain's from a level 63 percent lower.[2] Productivity is only one source of growth in overall income, but one important enough to have a major influence on these national differences.

The story is similar when the period since World War II is examined closely. Jones compared the United Kingdom and the original members of the European Community in the growth of gross value added per man-hour in manufacturing as well as of gross value added per person employed overall. He found that in 1955 total labor productivity in the United Kingdom was 15 percent higher than in France and West Germany and 40 percent higher than in Italy, although it was 15 percent lower than in Belgium and the Netherlands. By 1961 the United Kingdom had

1. E. H. Phelps Brown with Margaret H. Browne, *A Century of Pay: The Course of Pay and Production in France, Germany, Sweden, the United Kingdom, and the United States of America, 1860–1960* (London: Macmillan, 1968), pp. 59–60.

2. A. Maddison, "Phases of Capitalist Development," *Banca Nazionale del Lavoro Quarterly Review*, no. 121 (June 1977), p. 107; D. T. Jones, "Output, Employment and Labour Productivity in Europe since 1955," *National Institute Economic Review*, no. 77 (August 1976), p. 84.

been overtaken by France and Germany and in 1973 was passed by Italy. In the manufacturing sector the picture is worse. France and Germany attained higher labor productivity in 1955, and Italy reached the United Kingdom's level in 1968.[3]

International comparisons of productivity in specific industrial settings add to the tale of woe. Many multinational companies have compared output (variously measured) per unit of labor input in their British plants to output of similar products per labor input in their plants in other industrial nations. These comparisons are valuable because the products compared should be identical, and the management of a multinational company should not be intrinsically more or less capable in one country than another. Pratten collected comparisons from a hundred companies and calculated the following unweighted averages for the percentage differentials between other industrial countries and Britain: United States and Canada, 50 percent; West Germany, 27 percent; Italy, 16 percent; France, 15 percent; Sweden and Denmark, 22 percent; Spain, −11 percent; Australia and New Zealand, −15 percent; Brazil, −15 percent.[4] Pratten also undertook a comparison between fifty United Kingdom companies and fifty Swedish companies, matched as far as possible for product mix. The Swedish companies, on average half as large but more export-oriented, attained labor productivity about 50 percent higher than their British counterparts.[5] A study of the automobile industry by the Central Policy Review Staff placed British labor productivity on comparable vehicle models about 30 percent below that in West Germany, France, and Italy. Vehicle assembly was found to take almost 100 percent more man-hours in Britain than on the Continent, and the production of power-train components 50 to 60 percent more.[6]

3. Ibid., pp. 72, 73.
4. C. F. Pratten, *Labour Productivity Differentials within International Companies,* University of Cambridge, Department of Applied Economics, Occasional Paper 50 (Cambridge: Cambridge University Press, 1976), pp. 5, 6. The differences from Britain are statistically significant for the United States and Canada, West Germany, and France, p. 8.
5. C. F. Pratten, *A Comparison of the Performance of Swedish and U.K. Companies,* University of Cambridge, Department of Applied Economics, Occasional Paper 47 (Cambridge: Cambridge University Press, 1976), p. 131.
6. Central Policy Review Staff, *The Future of the British Car Industry* (London: Her Majesty's Stationery Office, 1975), pp. 79, 81. Other comparisons of productivity, in particular manufacturing activities, are mentioned by Sir Alec Cairncross, J. A. Kay, and A. Silberston in "The Regeneration of Manufacturing Industry," *Midland Bank Review* (Autumn 1977), pp. 9–18.

Table 1. *Annual Rates of Growth of Productivity in Manufacturing Industry, United Kingdom and West Germany, 1954–76*
Percent

	Labor productivity		Total factor productivity	
Period	United Kingdom	West Germany	United Kingdom	West Germany
1954–59	2.2	3.6	0.8	2.1
1959–63	2.0	4.3	0.9	2.0
1963–68	4.2	5.8	2.7	3.4
1968–72	3.1	4.5	0.6	3.0
1972–76	3.8	4.9	1.2	2.5

Sources: Ian Elliot and Alan Hughes, "Capital and Labour: Their Growth, Distribution, and Productivity," in M. Panić, ed., *The UK and West German Manufacturing Industry 1954–72: A Comparison of Structure and Performance*, NEDO Monograph 5 (London: National Economic Development Office, May 1976), p. 38; Ian Elliot, "Total Factor Productivity," in ibid., p. 64; and data supplied by NEDO.

Productivity differences may in part reflect differences in knowledge and skills that have the potential of being easily erased; therefore, the laggards can cherish some hope of catching up with the leaders. Jones's comparison between Britain and the original members of the European Community offered a wisp of hope. Between 1955 and 1973 Britain's rate of growth of labor productivity in manufacturing accelerated from 2.2 percent annually in 1955–60 to 3.2 percent in 1960–64, 3.4 percent in 1964–69, and 4.5 percent in 1969–73. The growth rates for the six original Community members were higher throughout (4.6 percent, 4.8 percent, 5.9 percent, and 4.6 percent in these same four periods) but showed no trend.[7] The salt loses its savor, however, when the comparison is updated to 1976 and extended from labor productivity to total factor productivity. Data developed by the National Economic Development Office (see table 1) fail to identify a clear upward trend for Britain, especially in total factor productivity, and show the United Kingdom's productivity growth no less inferior to West Germany's in the 1970s than in the 1950s.

Lagging Productivity: The General Explanations

The British have offered numerous explanations for the country's productivity performance. If hypotheses about the causes of the United

7. Jones, "Output, Employment and Labour Productivity," p. 77.

Kingdom's lagging productivity were a marketable output, one wonders whether the "productivity problem" would vanish. Papers entitled "What Is the British Predicament?" and "How British Is the British Sickness?" deal, as one would suppose, with failings of economic performance broader than industrial productivity. Nonetheless, low and slow-growing productivity is central to diagnoses that sweep together low incomes per capita, slow economic growth, chronic troubles with balance in international trade, and an inability of either the private or the public sector to bring off ventures of great scope and boldness.

A theme in recent writings is that simple and sweeping economic explanations of poor productivity performance can be discounted. For one thing, the explanations clash. Britain's productivity is said to be low because an elaborate class structure with wide income disparities denies economic harmony—and because egalitarian measures to redistribute income have dampened the incentives of managers and savers. Government may be discouraging output by too much intervention—or by too little planning and guidance. Growth and productivity may be stalled by institutions that are too resistant to change—or by public policies that change all too often as the party in power embraces a new policy fad, or a party newly in power jettisons its opponents' pet devices to install its own.[8]

Second, too many of these explanations run afoul of simple international comparisons, as Phelps Brown has recently shown.[9] For example, the government's large share in economic activity is considered hostile to growing productivity in Britain, yet there are several faster-growing industrial nations where the government's share is larger. Or, again, the size of the tax burden is believed to discourage the efforts of British executives and professionals, yet their counterparts in other countries pay out higher fractions in taxes from their (admittedly) higher pretax foreign salaries. Anyhow, British productivity was growing slowly long before there were high taxes. Personal income is not distributed more unevenly in Britain than in the United States, France, Japan, or West Germany. The entrepreneurial class is not closed to those who did not attend a public school or a university—indeed, executives in nonfinancial enter-

8. Samuel Brittan, "How British Is the British Sickness?" *Journal of Law and Economics,* vol. 21 (October 1978), pp. 245–68.

9. Sir Henry Phelps Brown, "What Is the British Predicament?" *Three Banks Review,* no. 116 (December 1977), pp. 3–29.

prises have usually worked their way up through the ranks after only a local secondary-school education or technical training. And whatever may be said of British labor relations, the proportion of working time lost to strikes is less in Britain than in the United States and some other countries (see the preceding paper by David Smith). The Japanese government may protect the interests of promising national industries more vigorously than the U.K. government, but the West German government is arguably less solicitous. The structures of industries in Britain are quite similar to those in other industrial countries. Britain has applied neither the most nor the least generous competition policy toward collusive arrangements among producers. Likewise, in the last half-century the amount of tariff protection given to British firms has not varied greatly from the practice of other industrial countries.

Inconsistencies among themselves and national counterexamples are not enough to strip all these explanations of their claims to validity, of course. Nevertheless, the feeling mounts that they lack generality, unity, and historical depth. The pattern of slow growth in productivity and net output per head that has persisted over a long period of time demands an explanation comprehensively rooted in characteristics of the British economy and society. Just such a set of traits may, in the eyes of many observers, be found in the continuity of British institutions and the values that they embody. For example, Phelps Brown uses history to explain the apparent preference of British trade unions for restrictive arrangements. Union members never experienced a revolution, a defeat in war, or a foreign occupation to dislodge them from ancient values and attitudes. Because, unlike their U.S. counterparts, U.K. trade unions never knew a period when plenty of jobs were available, the need for "keeping a place" was instilled in their members at the start. In the twentieth century the closing down of some of the oldest industries—coal mines, textiles—"may well have had its effect on the outlook of more than those who lost their jobs. . . . It seems that the concentration of hardship, the frustrated lives and stricken communities, made a greater impact than the diffusion of new employment that was in fact going on."[10]

But trade unions are only part of the fabric of British institutions—a fabric with a matchless record of continuity and accommodation. Neither external conquest and destruction nor internal discord has seriously rent this fabric in modern times. As a result, groups have coalesced and

10. Ibid., pp. 20–22.

claimed legitimacy to express and defend a wide range of interests in the political arena. As Olson stressed, the goals that these groups pursue— policies advancing or preserving the group's common interests—are collective goods for its members.[11] Because of the free-rider problem, such groups are formed only with difficulty and emerge only in a stable and tolerant environment. Once in place they are at their most effective in blocking changes that will affect them adversely. "The general citizen has a dispersed interest in change and efficiency spread over thousands of different decisions. Particular industries and interest groups have a much more concentrated interest in stopping change or in securing inefficient decisions for their own narrow benefit."[12] Rather than holding out for lump-sum compensation as the price for being on the losing end of a socially desirable change, such groups find the interests of self-esteem and stability better served by blocking the change itself. Although this process is most easily seen in politics, it also affects the pursuit of economic efficiency. Efficiency is to an important degree the ability to make optimal adaptations to changes in one's circumstances. An incrusted institutional structure is therefore likely to delay change and thus reduce the growth rate of productivity, as well as to frustrate the search for the most efficient and productive arrangements in any given set of circumstances.

For these factors to explain the United Kingdom's productivity performance convincingly, institutions and their goals must be consistent with values widely held in the society. The mutual tolerance that makes the daily life in Britain so attractive to many foreigners indeed prompts an acquiescence in things as they are and a willingness to cope with imperfection rather than make a scene. This tolerance plays into the hands of those who resist change because they have something to lose from it. Another supportive value is the low social importance given to advancing one's own economic welfare. Brittan argues that the visible trappings of the United Kingdom's social structure cannot be blamed for the productivity problem. But what does persist is a social pecking order that "has less to do with merely making money than in almost any other Western society."[13] Pratten notes that some American managers posted

11. Mancur Olson, "The Political Economy of Comparative Growth Rates" (University of Maryland, 1977).

12. Brittan, "How British Is the British Sickness?" p. 257.

13. Ibid., p. 263.

in England remark on the acceptance of low incomes in the working-class culture and—because of these low incomes—a lack of working-class contact with the business problem of managing fixed assets and taking risks.[14]

If this evaluation proves correct, what task does it leave for the economist who would explain Britain's productivity problem? And what hope for the gradualistic policymaker? The economist's first job is to test whether the institutionalist explanation in fact holds up, and, if so, which institutions weigh most heavily on the level and growth of productivity. The research design employed here attempts that step by recognizing that the drag of traditional institutions on growth and change should logically not be the same from one industrial sector to the next, so that differences among U.K. industries in productivity levels and growth rates may signal the importance of these institutional burdens.

The policymaker may also benefit from such an approach. First, a knowledge of what explains differences among industries in Britain's productivity performance is useful for predicting the future structure of the economy: industries with poor productivity performance should lose their grip on the nation's factors of production, while those with better-than-average performance should gain. That is, the losers should be dislodged from export markets and give up a share of the home market to imports (or otherwise price themselves out), while the winners should advance on these same fronts. Second, this knowledge about differences among industries can show the policymaker what institutional constraints impose the highest costs in efficiency. Renegotiation of the social contract never entirely stops, and those charged with pursuing the general economic interests need an up-to-date priority list.

Lagging Productivity: Industry-specific Forces

The specific influences on productivity can be regarded either as many separate items or as a few groups of interrelated forces. The second approach is pursued here because of the strong evidence that the various influences indeed do interact: one retardant of productivity tends to in-

14. C. F. Pratten, "The Efficiency of British Industry," *Lloyds Bank Review*, no. 123 (January 1977), p. 25.

dulge or promote another, so that the whole is, as it were, less than the sum of its parts. The areas considered are hostile labor-management relations, poor performance of business management, and inappropriate sizes of production units (plants and companies). My concern is less with the behavioral causes of these difficulties than with their economic effects.

Labor Troubles

Britain's system of labor relations in the workplace, rooted ultimately in class and social attitudes, has been found to impair industrial productivity in a number of ways.[15] The system both reflects and reinforces the preference of workers for a secure job and restrictive work rules, at the expense of higher wages. The preference for restrictive practices in turn makes adequate quality control more costly and delays the introduction of technological change. The lack of a binding legal framework deprives managements of contractual assurance about the short-run continuity of their labor supply and therefore about the levels of output they can achieve. In the last decade or two, quantitative evidence has brought increased understanding to the debate over labor relations in Britain, enabling the paths by which these relations may affect productivity to be charted. Strikes, restrictive rules, policy overtime, and the costs to management of dealing with labor-relations problems have been quantified and subjected to some international comparisons.

STRIKES. The loss of production through strikes is one element of industrial relations that does not indict the British system, despite some recent deterioration. Data covering the period since World War II fail to put Britain very high among industrial countries in the number of working days lost due to strikes per 1,000 employees. And Britain's relative performance improves if the comparison is confined to countries with relatively similar systems of industrial relations, such as the United States and Canada. But the experience of recent years has thrown Britain's strike performance more into question. Figures presented in Smith's paper show that its rank among countries in the working days lost to strikes has deteriorated faster than the rank of any other major industrial country. Britain still excels the United States and Canada, but by a smaller

15. Lloyd Ulman, "Collective Bargaining and Industrial Efficiency," in Richard E. Caves and Associates, *Britain's Economic Prospects* (Brookings Institution, 1968), pp. 324–80.

margin. The same deteriorating trend is apparent in the number of strikes per 100,000 employees. International differences in reporting practices make comparisons hazardous, but they suggest that from 1964–66 to 1973–75 the proportional number of strikes in the United Kingdom grew at twice the rate of those in the United States.

The incidence of strikes is usually expected to increase with the size of plant. In large plants relations between workers and management are less personal than in small plants and thus more disputes occur. There are also more interactions among work groups in large plants and therefore more bases for stoppages over jurisdictional issues, work rules, and the like. Prais has worked out a model of large plants' greater potential for disputes by positing that each plant contains a number of work groups, the number increasing with the plant's size. He also assumes a fixed probability that any one group will get into a dispute (with management, or with another employee group) during a given period of time. This model, he finds, predicts quite well the actual increase in the number of disputes with the increase in size of British plants. The relation between plant size and disputes should not be peculiar to Britain, of course, but Prais shows that it operates more strongly in Britain than in either West Germany or the United States.[16] Is it possible, he asks, that large plants are not built in Britain because of the excessive risk of strikes? As Prais demonstrates, two-thirds of the difference in strike-proneness among the seventeen principal divisions of the U.K. manufacturing sector can be explained by differences in their distributions of plant sizes.[17]

RESTRICTIVE RULES. A second quantifiable effect of the United Kingdom's industrial relations system is low on-the-job productivity because of work rules, overmanning, resistance to innovation, and the like. A number of investigations, both official and private, have looked into the sources of poor productivity in certain major "problem" industries— shipbuilding, chemicals, printing, motor vehicles, mechanical engineering, and textiles. For all sectors but textiles the reports regularly mention constraints on productivity due to such restrictive labor practices as demarcation rules (between crafts) and union rules involving the use of

16. S. J. Prais, "The Strike-proneness of Large Plants in Britain," *Journal of the Royal Statistical Society,* series A (general), vol. 141 (1978), pt. 3, pp. 368–84; Prais, "Labour Relations and Plant-Size" (chap. 6 of a forthcoming book on plant size and productivity in Britain). See also C. T. B. Smith and others, *Strikes in Britain,* Department of Energy, Manpower Paper 15 (HMSO, 1978), chap. 8.

17. Prais, "The Strike-proneness of Large Plants," pp. 368, 384.

assistants. Union structure is also mentioned as a problem for these sectors, as are strikes for shipbuilding and motor vehicles.[18] It may be that for structural reasons these are problem industries in other countries as well. Hence studies that have made international comparisons of productivity differences provide a valuable check; and they frequently report outright overmanning. This could mean a failure of management, though that seems unlikely when the comparison involves multinational companies, which should be able to apply the best available management practices in Britain. The fact that overmanning often occurs in auxiliary functions (maintenance, canteen services, and so on), where craft unions are important, seems to signify restrictive labor practices. Furthermore, some managements claim that apparent overmanning in the United Kingdom is necessary to check on quality—a reflection on British labor's comparative performance.[19]

Pratten, reviewing productivity comparisons that multinational companies have made among their international plants, hazards a guess about the maximum proportion of the productivity differences between Britain and other countries that could be attributed to labor relations. This maximum is roughly one-fourth of the United Kingdom's shortfall relative to the United States and Canada, one-third of that relative to France, and one-half of that relative to West Germany.[20]

POLICY OVERTIME. A third quantifiable effect of labor relations on productivity is the persistence of policy overtime—long workweeks demanded by low-wage workers to fatten their thin pay packets. Overtime would have no adverse effect on productivity, properly measured, if it were undertaken sporadically to meet temporary or unexpected increases in demand. But it can become a drag on productivity if it becomes built into the labor bargain *and* results in lower productivity than would a normal workweek (with other necessary adjustments made). Since evidently overtime in Britain fluctuates in response to aggregate demand, it

18. Information summarized in C. F. Pratten and A. G. Atkinson, "The Use of Manpower in British Manufacturing Industry," *Department of Employment Gazette,* vol. 84 (June 1976), pp. 571–76.

19. Central Policy Review Staff, *Future of the British Car Industry,* p. 82; Pratten, *Labour Productivity Differentials,* p. 52. According to the Central Policy Review Staff, the British auto plants require up to twice as much time for rectifying faults as continental plants (p. 84). And breakdowns of equipment cost twice as many hours as on the Continent, although in Britain identical machinery is maintained by 50 to 70 percent more plant maintenance personnel.

20. Pratten, *Labour Productivity Differentials,* p. 61.

is not caused solely by a degenerate wage bargain. Nevertheless, the number of overtime hours worked shows a significant negative relation to average hourly earnings in the United Kingdom, but not in the United States—a strong indication that overtime serves to fill out the weekly pay.[21]

The National Board for Prices and Incomes found substantial shopfloor pressure to maintain overtime hours. The board's questionnaire study did not find that trade unions press for overtime, but it did show that managers use overtime more frequently to meet normal demand than to meet peaks and that a large minority of manual workers expect it regularly.[22]

Policy overtime does seem to have adverse consequences for productivity in British plants. The National Board's report observed that "where overtime for men is high, it is much easier to find examples of industries and undertakings in which there is much scope for improving efficiency." True, only about one-fifth of employers think that productivity in overtime hours is slightly lower than during regular hours (two-thirds rate them equal). But, more disturbing, 31 percent of employers (employing 42 percent of workers in the establishments surveyed) said that the productivity of most workers during *regular* hours is at least occasionally affected adversely by the presence of overtime opportunities.[23]

OTHER RESOURCE COSTS. Productivity shortfall also results from the excess costs incurred by British management in dealing with labor relations. These costs may take the form of either outright drains on resources or decreases in the effectiveness of the company caused by increased uncertainty about the rate of output. Numerous types of such losses have been identified.

1. Because of strikes and disruptions at supplier companies—on an average day in 1973, fifteen suppliers of Chrysler U.K. were on strike—British managements find it necessary to hold larger inventories of raw materials and goods in process than managements of comparable firms in

---

21. Derek Leslie, "Hours and Overtime in British and United States Manufacturing Industries: A Comparison," *British Journal of Industrial Relations,* vol. 14 (July 1976), pp. 194–201.

22. National Board for Prices and Incomes, *Hours of Work, Overtime and Shift Working,* Report 161, cmnd. 4554 (HMSO, 1970), pp. 51, 104, 105.

23. Ibid., pp. 52, 106, 107. Cross-tabulations contained in a supplement to the report suggest in a variety of ways that the problem of policy overtime is worse in engineering and allied trades than in other U.K. manufacturing industries.

other countries. Executives interviewed in connection with this study speculated that inventory holdings in the United Kingdom might be inflated 15 to 20 percent, and the Central Policy Review Staff noted that one Continental vehicle plant dependent on British supplies held a twenty-day inventory, whereas a comparable Japanese plant might hold a few hours' worth. Similar evidence has appeared for other industries.[24]

2. Uncertainties about output rates leave the company unsure how much output it will have to sell, thereby reducing the effectiveness of the resources it allocates to marketing activities. Once again, the automobile industry supplies striking evidence. In Continental plants making auto components, monthly production rates seldom vary from planned output by more than 5 percent, whereas variances of 20 percent or more are common in British plants. Distribution channels become periodically underutilized, or final buyers lower what they will pay for the product because of the uncertainty of delivery. Unexpected brief disruptions of production are particularly hard on the stability of a company's cash flow, because all costs are fixed in the relevant short run.[25]

3. Companies bringing new equipment on stream face demands that the resulting productivity gains be shared with the work force. The dilution of the cost savings and reduction in the rate of return on the investment, when these demands are successful, may be less costly than the uncertainty about how long newly installed equipment may be kept idle by disputes over manning. A metal container company reported that a new line producing two-piece cans was running at 40 to 50 percent of capacity, largely because of difficulties in labor relations.[26]

4. The marked tendency for labor relations to deteriorate as plant size increases, Prais noted, might encourage U.K. companies to build plants smaller than would otherwise be indicated by technical economies of scale.[27] Surprisingly, all the manufacturing executives interviewed for this study agreed on the limit to the size of efficient plants. A 500-worker plant, they felt, could be managed successfully, but to construct one employing more than 1,000 workers is to invite disaster.

24. Central Policy Review Staff, *Future of the British Car Industry*, pp. 26, 75; Price Commission, *Metal Box Ltd.—Open Top Food and Beverage and Aerosol Cans,* HC 135 (HMSO, 1978), pp. 5, 28.

25. Central Policy Review Staff, *Future of the British Car Industry*, pp. 24, 71, 75, 95–96.

26. Pratten, *Labour Productivity Differentials,* pp. 55–56; Price Commission, *Metal Box, Ltd.,* pp. 7, 24.

27. Prais, "The Strike-proneness of Large Plants," p. 368.

5. Management time is diverted to problems of labor relations and away from other tasks. Plant managers in the British auto industry claim to spend almost half their time dealing with labor disputes, whereas their counterparts in Belgium and West Germany mention figures of 5 to 10 percent.[28] The fact that British managers must be more in evidence on the plant floor, to deal with the problems that arise, is itself a source of friction.[29] Perhaps more insidious, the uncertainty of labor relations affects the criteria for evaluating the plant manager's performance, marking for success the resourceful improviser who can scramble to keep things moving on a day-to-day basis. If such people continue to rise to positions in top management, this trait bodes ill for the attention given by British companies to long-range planning—often thought of as top management's primary task.

Size of Companies and Plants

Another factor related to industrial efficiency that may vary from industry to industry is the size of companies and plants. In the 1960s the British public went through a period of romance with corporate bigness. Size, efficiency, and advanced technology were declared inseparable; policy was frequently based on the belief that merging the leading companies in British industries would somehow both increase their efficiency and improve their ability to stand up to their foreign rivals. It is known that important economies of scale exist in selected industries, but there was never clear evidence of a pervasive relation between size and efficiency in British industry. Nor was there evidence that increasing the size of competitively ineffectual firms would make them mend their ways. Nor was the assumed connection between size and effectiveness in international competition based on analysis more subtle than analogies to dogfights.[30] In any case the winds of public opinion have shifted in the 1970s, wafting the gentle melody that "small is beautiful."

28. Central Policy Review Staff, *Future of the British Car Industry,* p. 99.

29. Pratten, *Labour Productivity Differentials,* p. 56.

30. There is a positive relation between plant or company size and export performance, but the nature of the causal relation is anything but clear. Companies and industries enjoying a comparative advantage on the international market are likely to grow large. And there are scale economies in international transactions themselves because of the greater fixed costs of information, but it does not follow that enlarging the domestic sales of a company does anything to help spread the overheads associated with export markets.

Whatever the shifts of opinion, does one have grounds for thinking that British industries systematically sustain companies of inappropriate sizes? There is—to make a long story short—no general reason for thinking that the size of a company does not in the long run adapt to the dictates of profitability. Small companies are at some disadvantage in the capital markets, where transactions costs are important, and lenders cannot costlessly diversify their portfolios across large numbers of small firms. But there is no reason to think that this disadvantage is greater in the United Kingdom than in other industrial countries, and it may well be less serious.[31] A company may be large either because its size is conducive to economies of scale or because its size is associated with a market share big enough to allow it to annex some monopoly rents. Given the absence of strong legal restraint on horizontal mergers in Britain, one finds no institutional barrier to the rise of large companies to enjoy either the sweet fruits of efficient scale or the bitter (to society) ones of monopoly profit.[32]

What is the evidence on efficiency and the sizes of companies? The most elaborate recent investigation stemmed from the Bolton committee's inquiry into small firms. Douglas Todd analyzed the efficiency (measured by a ratio of factor input costs to the net value of output) of a sampling of large and small companies classified according to broadly drawn sectors of British manufacturing. Using a procedure suggested by M. J. Farrell, Todd derived an efficiency frontier for each sector from the capital and labor input combinations of firms that get the most net output from their inputs, and calculated the efficiencies of both large and small firms relative to this frontier. Two of his findings support the view that there is no systematic efficiency gap between small and large firms. First, none of his calculated efficiency frontiers is derived entirely from the input-output combinations of large firms; that is, some small firms are always found producing net output with combinations of labor and capital inputs such that no large firm is found capable of operating with proportionally less

31. See Peter Johnson, "Policies Toward Small Firms: Time for Caution?" *Lloyds Bank Review*, no. 129 (July 1978), pp. 1–11, and Marshall Blume's paper in this volume.

32. Both effects seem to have been present in a sample of manufacturing industries that experienced increasing seller concentration along with horizontal mergers. See P. E. Hart, M. A. Utton, and G. Walshe, *Mergers and Concentration in British Industry*, National Institute of Economic and Social Research, Occasional Paper 26 (London: Cambridge University Press, 1973), pp. 110–34.

of both. Second, although most firms appear to use labor-capital input combinations that put them outside the efficiency frontier, there is no significant difference in the apparent inefficiency levels of large and small firms.[33] Of course, there are some sectors in which small firms would be at a severe disadvantage, and others in which large firms could not function efficiently. When the allocative mechanism is working properly, however, those firms simply do not exist.

A good deal of information has accumulated on the comparative sizes of U.K. plants and companies and those in other countries in the European Community. Because of a pervasive relation between the sizes of plants and companies and the sizes of their national markets, U.K. firms are more aptly compared to those in similar-sized Continental countries than to those in the United States. George and Ward, who analyzed the four leading firms in 41 industries, found the U.K. firms to be larger on average than their West German counterparts in 29 of these industries, larger than French firms in 37 industries, and larger than Italian ones in 40. They attribute the difference to laws that have discouraged collusion but permitted mergers in the United Kingdom, whereas the Continental countries are more tolerant of collusion and effect a good deal of coordination among erstwhile competing firms through banking connections.[34] Seller concentration is correspondingly higher in Britain: the four largest companies account for a weighted average share of 30 percent of shipments in Britain, 22 percent in France, and 19 percent in West Germany and Italy.[35]

33. Douglas Todd, *The Relative Efficiency of Small and Large Firms,* Committee of Inquiry on Small Firms, Research Report 18 (HMSO, 1971).

34. Kenneth D. George and T. S. Ward, *The Structure of Industry in the EEC,* University of Cambridge, Department of Applied Economics, Occasional Paper 43 (Cambridge: Cambridge University Press, 1975), chap. 3, esp. p. 23. Their conclusion about the differential role of mergers and concentration is supported by an analysis showing merger activity in Britain during 1967–72 to have been more extensive than in West Germany, and to have made a significant contribution to the seller concentration of U.K. industries during that period. See Alan Hughes, "Company Concentration, Size of Plant, and Merger Activity," in M. Panić, ed., *The UK and West German Industry: 1954–72: A Comparison of Structure and Performance,* NEDO Monograph 5 (London: National Economic Development Office, 1976), pp. 105, 109.

35. George and Ward, *Structure of Industry,* p. 17. The statistical analysis (p. 16) suggests that Britain's "excess" seller concentration may be less in those industries that are more concentrated in the continental countries, but the fact that seller concentration cannot exceed 100 percent makes any judgment on this point suspect.

Moreover, the United Kingdom invariably outscores West Germany when the largest European firms, not only the leading ones in individual industries, are taken into consideration. For example, in 1972 and 1973 Britain had over 160 of the 500 largest manufacturing and mining companies in Europe, whereas West Germany had just over 100. Britain's share has been eroding somewhat because of the country's slower growth, but also because of mergers and nationalization. (Of the 200 largest enterprises in Britain in 1948, 179 had disappeared by 1972—two-thirds by merger or acquisition.) Though, as has been often noted, Britain's largest firms are concentrated in a distinctively different set of industries from those in West Germany—food and drink, tobacco, textiles, paper, and building materials in Britain, and electrical engineering, chemicals, metals and metal products in Germany—one can surely not conclude that British companies are in general too small to stand up to their European rivals.[36]

In turning to comparisons between British and Continental plant sizes, one must remember that unfortunately, as indicated above, labor relations in Britain decay rapidly as plant sizes increase—a relation present but not so strong in other industrial nations. Despite this problem, there could conceivably be overriding advantages from scale economies accruing to the producer with the largest plants. Therefore, whether British plants are growing larger or smaller relative to those in other countries has no clear net significance for British productivity.

The sizes of the largest plants in a country, like those of the largest firms, tend to be related to the size of the national market. Hence it is no surprise that the largest British and West German plants in given industries are quite similar in size and are larger than plants in the other European countries. In 1975 George and Ward examined the 20 largest plants in each of 47 manufacturing industries, finding the average size (weighted by industry employment) to be 3,730 employees in West Germany, 3,130 in the United Kingdom, 2,090 in France, and 990 in Italy. In terms of employment, the leading German plants are larger than the leading British ones in 24 of the 47 industries. Hughes notes that in West Germany manufacturing became increasingly concentrated in large plants over 1958–68, while British manufacturing remained relatively un-

36. George and Ward, *Structure of Industry*, chap. 5; Hughes, "Company Concentration," pp. 88–91. Also see Pratten, *Comparison of the Performance of Swedish and U.K. Companies.*

changed.[37] This pattern could result from differences in the overall rates of economic growth in the two countries, but it could also result from the more troubled labor relations found in large British plants. Even so, large plants are still relatively abundant in the United Kingdom, and the proportion of small manufacturing plants is lower there than in any other industrial country. The Bolton committee, using 200 employees as the cutoff for small establishments, found that in the 1960s 31 percent of U.K. manufacturing employment was in small establishments compared with 34 percent in Germany, 39 percent in the United States, 47 percent in Canada, and 53 percent in Sweden.[38]

Because, at this stage, it is uncertain whether size is good or bad, it is not clear whether the various results obtained from comparing plant and firm sizes in industrial countries should be a source of glee or gloom in Britain. For what it is worth, plant sizes have been found positively associated with industries' trade performance in those countries, whereas seller concentration and firm sizes are not.[39] Even here the causation is not clear: a cost advantage that enables an industry to sell abroad profitably may be what promotes the construction of large plants.

Quality of Management

The third major area in which industrial efficiency may vary by industry is in the quality of management, because effective management and

37. George and Ward, *Structure of Industry,* pp. 29–30, and Hughes, "Company Concentration," pp. 110–13. See also Frederic L. Pryor, "The Size of Production Establishments in Manufacturing," *Economic Journal* (London), vol. 82 (June 1972), pp. 547–66; and G. F. Ray, "The Size of Plant: A Comparison," *National Institute Economic Review,* no. 38 (November 1966), pp. 63–66. The British steel industry does seem to perform badly in terms of efficiency. See Anthony Cockerill with Aubrey Silberston, *The Steel Industry: International Comparisons of Industrial Structure and Performance,* University of Cambridge, Department of Applied Economics, Occasional Paper 42 (Cambridge: Cambridge University Press, 1974), pp. 93–100.

38. Department of Trade and Industry, *Report of the Committee of Inquiry on Small Firms,* cmnd. 4811 (HMSO, 1971), p. 68. Figures for other countries are given (Belgium and France, 51 percent; Japan, 54 percent; Netherlands, 58 percent; Australia, 60 percent; Switzerland, 61 percent; Italy, 66 percent), but their comparability to the British figure is less certain than for those quoted in the text.

39. Nicholas Owen, "Scale Economies in the EEC: An Approach Based on Intra-EEC Trade," *European Economic Review,* vol. 7 (February 1976), pp. 143–63; Fareeda Maroof with Amin Rajan, "UK and West German Trade in Manufactures," in Panić, ed., *The UK and West German Manufacturing Industry,* chap. 5.

sophisticated control techniques may make more difference for productivity in some industries than in others. The well-worn hypothesis that the United Kingdom suffers from inferior management has been documented from the relatively low level of human capital committed to business management, the low-priority claim it has traditionally held on the nation's most able citizens, the low intercorporate mobility of managerial personnel, and the like.[40] The hypothesis that poor management causes low productivity is essentially unsatisfying. It leaves the entrepreneur to carry the residual burden of opprobrium after everyone else has either been absolved or stuck with some share of the guilt. Productivity could be low either because management really is ineffective or because management cannot triumph over hostile forces that have gone undetected by the investigator. Some recent evidence can help to narrow the issues.

The principal controlled-experiment evidence on managerial effectiveness comes from Dunning's studies of the performance of British companies in comparison with that of competing foreign enterprises, both in Britain and in Canada and the United States. Dunning's analysis of data for the years around 1960 showed that 51 of 80 subsidiaries of U.S. companies attained higher productivity than their U.K. competitors and earned correspondingly higher average profits (21.1 percent versus 15.0 percent, for the years 1958–61).[41] This comparison could be biased, however, since multinationals in general perform better than run-of-the-mill domestic companies of any nationality. Yet there is also evidence that subsidiaries of U.K. companies operating in North America did less well on average than their local competitors. Even joint ventures with local companies were on average slightly more profitable than fully owned subsidiaries.[42] This result still does not clinch the case against British management, because the lower profits of British subsidiaries in North

40. See Richard E. Caves, "Market Organization, Performance, and Public Policy," in Caves and others, *Britain's Economic Prospects,* pp. 302–06; and, a more recent evaluation, Derek F. Channon, *The Strategy and Structure of British Enterprise* (Boston: Division of Research, Graduate School of Business Administration, Harvard University, 1973), pp. 214–16.

41. John H. Dunning, *Studies in International Investment* (London: Allen and Unwin, 1970), chap. 9, esp. pp. 380–81. There is also some evidence of better performance by foreign subsidiaries in specific categories of decisionmaking, such as selecting a plant location. See Keith P. D. Ingham, "Foreign Ownership and the Regional Problem: Company Performance in the Mechanical Engineering Industry," *Oxford Economic Papers,* vol. 28 (March 1976), pp. 133–48.

42. Dunning, *Studies in International Investment,* chap. 6.

America, as Dunning pointed out, might be due to their tenancy in slower-growing and less profitable industries. One may still wonder, of course, why they remain stuck in these industries.

Dunning's more recent investigations have broadly confirmed this pattern, but some qualifications have begun to appear. Companies affiliated with U.S. parents remain more profitable than the U.K. companies that are their direct competitors, and the U.S. affiliates continue to use younger and more highly qualified executives. U.S. affiliates, however, are not concentrated in the most profitable industries: their average profit rate on sales would actually increase by 7 percent if they were distributed among industries in the same way as all U.K. quoted companies. And their overall profit rate on total capital has been falling relative to that of leading U.K. companies; it averaged 92 percent higher in 1950–54 but was only 20 percent higher in 1970–73.[43] Furthermore, an analysis of productivity in U.S. affiliates and U.K. domestic companies suggested that the U.S. superiority in labor productivity might be explained by the tendency of the U.S. affiliates to concentrate in the more capital-intensive industries.[44] This doubt about the productivity advantage of non-British firms is reinforced by Solomon and Ingham's study of foreign subsidiaries and indigenous companies in Britain's mechanical engineering sector. An application of discriminant analysis indicated that the two groups of companies differ primarily in three traits: the subsidiaries export a larger proportion of their output, employ a larger number of workers, and experience *lower* sales per employee.[45] Because the subsidiaries are unlikely to be more integrated vertically than domestic companies, this last conclusion implies that their labor productivity may be lower. The authors suggest that multinational companies, sensitive to the increasing cheapness of British labor relative to that of the other leading industrial countries, may be picking Britain (the new Hong Kong?) as a site for labor-intensive processes serving the world market. But it may also be possible

43. John H. Dunning with R. D. Pearce, *U.S. Industry in Britain: An Economists Advisory Group Research Study* (Westview Press, 1977), pp. 69–70 and tables II.1–II.11.

44. Ibid., pp. 71–72.

45. Robert F. Solomon and Keith P. D. Ingham, "Discriminating between MNC Subsidiaries and Indigenous Companies: A Comparative Analysis of the British Mechanical Engineering Industry," *Oxford Bulletin of Economics and Statistics*, vol. 39 (May 1977), pp. 127–38.

that foreign entrepreneurs are actually at a disadvantage in extracting physical productivity on (what is to them) foreign soil, but accept the situation because of offsetting advantages in nonproduction activities.

This last possibility is underlined by recent evidence that multinational companies may not outperform domestic companies in their labor relations. The Steuer report found nothing to choose between foreign-owned and domestic firms, and Forsyth's investigation of labor relations in Scotland concluded that foreign subsidiaries did worse, even after making allowance for differences in company size and in base industry.[46]

Overall, the evidence from comparisons between foreign affiliates and domestic companies still seems to support the hypothesis of inferior U.K. management performance—but not conclusively.

Several other features of productivity performance in British industry support the hypothesis of managerial deficiencies, even if they can also be explained in other ways. One feature is the apparently low productivity of new investment in British industry, as indicated by incremental capital–output ratios. Brittan notes that investment in manufacturing has borne about the same relation to value added in manufacturing in the United Kingdom as on the Continent, but the increment in net output per unit of investment seems substantially smaller.[47] Likewise, the time required for plant construction has been found to be much longer in the United Kingdom than in other industrial countries (in the steel industry, at least).[48] Low capital productivity can be partly attributed to labor practices, but managerial ineffectiveness should probably take some blame.

Recent evidence continues to suggest that British products suffer from either poor quality or excessive and cost-increasing variety. Evidence of low average quality comes from Stout's comparison of the unit values of British exports with those of competing West German and French exports. If these unit values are proportional to selling prices, they should indicate how buyers on world markets perceive the qualities of British goods relative to competitors' offerings. West Germany came out higher

46. M. D. Steuer and others, *The Impact of Foreign Direct Investment on the United Kingdom* (HMSO, 1973), p. 77; David J. C. Forsyth, "Foreign-Owned Firms and Labour Relations: A Regional Perspective," *British Journal of Industrial Relations,* vol. 11 (March 1973), pp. 20–28, and references cited therein.

47. Brittan, "How British Is the British Sickness?" p. 249.

48. Cockerill and Silberston, *Steel Industry,* p. 34.

in 29 of 35 industrial categories, France in 23 of 34.[49] Similar evidence
appears in comparisons of the unit values of British exports and imports;
in many sectors, and in more sectors than for either France or West
Germany, the imports apparently offer higher quality than goods that the
country makes and exports. Some new evidence also supports the long-
familiar hypothesis that British industry offers a particularly large number
of product variants, with a possible inflation of unit cost.[50] Low product
quality could be the rational choice of a management confronted with
labor relations that make quality control very costly. High levels of
product variety could be due to the complexity of Britain's social structure
and the resulting diversity of tastes (although one wonders, when the
product is chicken feed). They may also be due to incomplete collusive
arrangements among British producers that suppress price competition
and divert rivalry into nonprice factors such as the proliferation of product varieties. But, on the other hand, these traits may stem from shortcomings in British management, as has often been alleged.

A Statistical Test

In order to test the hypotheses set forth about influences on British
productivity, and to weigh the strength of these influences, I conducted a
statistical analysis of the determinants of productivity levels of a group
of British industries. It is very difficult, using readily available data, to
measure an industry's efficiency or productivity in a way that permits
comparison with other industries. There is a solution to the problem,
though, that is inexpensive and practical even if rough and difficult to
provide with a tight formal justification; namely, to express productivity
in a given British industry as a ratio to productivity in its counterpart in

49. David K. Stout, *International Price Competitiveness, Non-Price Factors
and Export Performance* (London: National Economic Development Office, 1977),
appendix B.
50. See Price Commission, *Allied Breweries (UK) Limited—Brewing and Wholesaling of Beer and Sales in Managed Houses,* HC415 (HMSO, 1978), p. 23; Price
Commission, *Prices, Costs and Margins in the Production and Distribution of
Compound Feeding Stuff for Cattle, Pigs and Poultry,* HC 338 (HMSO, 1978), p. 26;
Price Commission, *Perkins Engines Company, Diesel, Gasoline, Reconditioned and
Short Engines,* HC345 (HMSO, 1979), p. 3; Central Policy Review Staff, *Future
of the British Car Industry,* pp. 89–92.

the United States. The formal hypothesis underlying this procedure is that productivity in the United States is highly correlated with the maximum level of productivity attainable using the technological knowledge and management practices now available to the industrial countries. For this procedure to work, one need not assume that U.S. industries are perfect and always attain the highest productivity levels. It is necessary only that any institutional factors dragging down the productivity of U.S. industries be uncorrelated with the ones retarding productivity in their British counterparts. Not even this assumption is required if one can measure the relative strength of such a retardant force in both Britain and America. Thus, in brief, my procedure will be to express the productivity of a British industry as a fraction of that of its U.S. counterpart and seek to determine why this measure of productivity shortfall varies as it does among British manufacturing industries.

Only limited use has been made before of this method of testing hypotheses about productivity. The approach was used in three widely cited studies undertaken in the 1940s and 1950s—those by Rostas, Frankel, and Paige and Bombach.[51] All three studies were concerned more with establishing the magnitude of overall differences in productivity between Britain and the United States than with explaining why the differences varied from industry to industry. Some correlates of interindustry differences in productivity were uncovered, however. All three studies sought and found some evidence that differences in labor productivity are associated with capital per worker and, in the relevant sectors, natural-resource rents. Scale economies at the plant level were suggested as a source of productivity differences; more productive sectors turned out to have more output per plant but not more employees per plant, leaving the influence of scale somewhat in limbo. Finally, the correlation between output per head and total output was observed, although only later did it become fashionable in Britain to impute causality to this correlation.

51. L. Rostas, *Comparative Productivity in British and American Industry,* National Institute of Economic and Social Research, Occasional Paper 13 (Cambridge: Cambridge University Press, 1948); Marvin Frankel, *British and American Manufacturing Productivity: A Comparison and Interpretation,* Bureau of Economic and Business Research, University of Illinois Bulletin 81 (University of Illinois Press, 1957); Deborah Paige and Gottfried Bombach, *A Comparison of National Output and Productivity of the United Kingdom and the United States* (Paris: Organisation for European Economic Co-operation, 1959), chap. 5. A recent inquiry is Matthew D. Shapiro, "Productivity in Manufacturing Industry in the United Kingdom and United States" (B.A. and M.A. thesis, Yale University, 1979).

The promising research method introduced by these investigations was then dropped. The approach has seen some recent revivals, but for countries other than the United Kingdom.

My procedure starts by matching rather finely disaggregated U.K. manufacturing industries (as defined in the *Report on the Census of Production*) to their counterparts in the United States, using the standard industrial classification manuals of the two countries to guide the matching.[52] This procedure yielded seventy-one industries that were deemed sufficiently comparable over the years 1963–72. These years were chosen because of the timing of the census of manufactures in the two countries— 1963, 1967, and 1972 for the United States; 1963, 1968, and annually since 1970 for Britain. I am thus able to take averages of observations made over a decade, to dampen the influence of random factors on certain of my variables. The seventy-one industries cover about half of the U.K. manufacturing sector and seem to give reasonably equal representation to the various major segments ("orders") of the British standard industrial classification.

The Dependent Variable

The concept of productivity refers to some ratio of the market value of output to the social opportunity cost of the inputs necessary to produce it. The principal problems that arise in measuring productivity are how to value output comparably from industry to industry and how to aggregate the various inputs.

When productivity is measured in physical terms—input cost per bushel of wheat or per ton of steel—the problem of placing a market value on the output does not occur. When comparisons are to be made among industries, however, the problem becomes unavoidable. It would be hazardous to make a value-based comparison of productivity in, say, two industries making and selling bricks in different isolated geographical areas. The less productive industry would simply charge a higher price, and the ratio of the value of its output to the value of its inputs need be no different from its more productive cousin. One can escape this dilemma, however, if one makes the comparison among production units all selling competitively to the same group of buyers, so that they all face the same market price for their output. Hence a key assumption made in

52. See appendix A for the list of industries, and appendix B for complete sources of the data.

my analysis is that a given British or U.S. manufacturing industry is merely a component of a larger world industry and neither the British nor the U.S. one has a great deal of influence in setting the world market price. If this assumption held strictly, the values and volumes of output of the two industries would be proportional to one another. But because many distorting factors, such as tariffs, transportation costs, and elements of monopoly, can cause this assumption to fail, I have to take account of these factors in my analysis. Nevertheless, the assumption is, I believe, basically sound and warrants not only the use of the U.S. counterpart industry as a control but indeed the whole procedure of making value-based comparisons of productivity among industries.

It is difficult to measure inputs because any production process requires a variety of them. They must be aggregated, and to do this some assumption must be made about the relation between the payments that the suppliers of inputs actually receive and the opportunity cost of their services. Since all revenue of the firm is allocated as payments to some claimant, each production process is defined as just covering its costs if it is assumed that the payment made to each factor is equal to its social opportunity cost. On the other hand, if this assumption about a given input is not made, some other way must be found to aggregate it with its partners to secure the needed overall ratio of inputs to output. I follow the usual procedure of assuming that all material inputs are bought in competitive markets, so that they can be netted out of the values of both output and input. My output measure becomes value added (net output), and only the primary inputs need be dealt with (that is, labor and capital; land is assumed to be unimportant in manufacturing industries).

My productivity ratio is now down to net output in relation to capital and labor inputs. Lacking adequate and comparable capital-stock data for U.K. and U.S. industries, I opted for the procedure of employing net output per unit of labor input as the key dependent variable, but using as a control a proxy for the relative capital stocks of the two industries. Thus the main dependent variable used in the following analysis is

VPW: value of net output per person employed in the U.K. industry (summed over 1963, 1968, and 1972) divided by value added per person employed in the U.S. counterpart industry (summed over 1963, 1967, and 1972).[53]

53. Further discussion of this variable and the problems it creates appears in appendix B. The choice of time period for this and other variables is also discussed in appendix B.

Independent Variables

The independent variables used in the analysis will be explained only briefly, because their justifications follow from the hypotheses and evidence discussed above. The first variable needed, as was just indicated, is a measure of capital intensity in the British industry relative to such a measure in its U.S. counterpart. Net output per British worker could be low simply because he has little capital to assist him. Capital-stock figures for the U.K. industries have not been published, but in any case would not have much value, since inflation and differences in rates of real economic growth make it difficult to compare capital stocks across industries and countries. As a rough substitute, I averaged gross investment and labor input in two years for each British industry and its U.S. counterpart, then calculated a relative investment–labor ratio. The resulting variable is

CAP: ratio of gross investment to labor input, U.K. industry, 1968 and 1972, divided by ratio of gross investment to labor input, U.S. counterpart industry, 1967 and 1972.

Against its obvious faults, this variable can claim the virtues of avoiding the problem of assets valued at historical cost and providing some control for differences among industries in the rates at which their capital stocks are being consumed (what matters for the analysis is the flow of services from the capital stock, not the size of the stock per se). If *CAP* simply controls for differences in efficiently used capital stocks of British and American industries, its coefficient should indicate a positive relation to *VPW*. However, the incidence of manning restrictions on equipment and of underutilization of plant due to uncertain labor relations may make the shortfall of British productivity increase as the importance of capital in the production process increases. That tendency would produce a negative relation to *VPW*. Therefore, the sign of *CAP* cannot be predicted a priori.

The other independent variables used in my analysis fall into the three classes discussed above—industrial relations, size of production unit, and effectiveness of management. I take them up in that order. Poor labor relations might be designated by several variables that are partly alternative, partly additive as indicators of conditions in the workplace that are hostile to productivity. Two available measures of the disruption due to work stoppages are

WDLB: ratio of working days lost by strikes during 1971–73 to actual working days of operatives, 1972;

STRIKB: number of strikes reported beginning in the years 1972–75 divided by number of establishments classified to the industry, 1972.[54]

The fact that strikes occur frequently (indicated by *STRIKB*) may impair productivity above and beyond the actual idling of facilities (*WDLB*) because of the additional uncertainty strikes create for managers. Those variables do not fully indicate the potential for collective-bargaining agreements to include clauses that impair productivity. These are perhaps best represented by

UNIONB: proportion of manual employees covered by collective bargaining agreements, 1973.

The institutional evidence on labor relations in Britain also suggests that the separate influences on productivity embodied in these three variables may be interactive rather than additive. Hence I make use of the three interactions

$$LAB1 = WDLB \cdot STRIKB$$
$$LAB2 = WDLB \cdot UNIONB$$
$$LAB3 = STRIKB \cdot UNIONB.$$

In general, I expect negative regression coefficients for all these variables. It should be noted, though, that unions outside Britain are not believed to be inevitably harmful to productivity;[55] furthermore, unionism is more common among workers with higher levels of skills, and those skills give rise to higher value added per worker.

Three more variables seem important for identifying the social roots of any negative influence that poor labor relations may have on productivity. Attitudes restricting productivity and a preference for restrictive practices, a legacy from the depressed years of the interwar period (if not from the early history of the Industrial Revolution), may be more

54. There is evidence that the interindustry pattern of this variable is quite stable from year to year. For evidence covering 1966–73, see Department of Employment, *Strikes in Britain,* pp. 22–25.

55. See Charles Brown and James Medoff, "Trade Unions in the Production Process," *Journal of Political Economy,* vol. 86 (June 1978), pp. 355–78.

common in Britain's old industrial regions.[56] If so, productivity may be higher in newer regions where labor-management relations can start with something approaching a clean slate. I developed the variable

REGB: percentage of industry employment located (during 1972) in West Midlands, Yorkshire and Humberside, North West, North, Wales, and Scotland.

REGB should be negatively related to relative productivity (*VPW*). It may also interact with the variables defined above in its negative effect on productivity. In particular, any adverse effect of collective bargaining agreements on productivity may be especially evident in the old industrial regions. This effect should be captured by

LAB4 = REGB • UNIONB.

Another factor associated with the social conditions of production, and one suggested frequently in my interviews with British managers, was that the incidence of hostile labor-management relations and restrictive manning arrangements (the syndrome known as "bloody-mindedness") is much greater in industries with largely male labor forces. This suggests the variable

PCFB: female percentage of industry's labor force, averaged for 1968 and 1972.

In this research design, however, one cannot simply regress relative productivity on the variable *PCFB*. Female workers often possess less strength, training, and experience than male workers and are paid less for this reason (and perhaps, as well, because of discrimination). This effect would surely dominate any direct statistical relation between relative productivity and *PCFB* and obscure any positive influence of *PCFB* on productivity that may result because better labor relations can be attained with a female labor force.[57] Hence I regressed the logarithm of each of the labor-relations variables on *PCFB*. Because the regression coefficient was negative and significant in every case, I accept the hypothesis that

56. Phelps Brown, "What Is the British Predicament?" pp. 20–22; Department of Employment, *Strikes in Britain,* table 14 and chap. 4.

57. There are strong negative correlations between *PCFB* and all of the labor-related variables defined so far.

these potential sources of lowered relative productivity are less evident in industries with female labor forces.[58] To complete the test, I redefine each of my labor-relations variables so that they consist only of that part not associated with the female proportion of an industry's labor force.[59] A variable thus transformed is indicated by the prefix *F* (for example, *FLAB1*). My hypothesis is that the other labor-relations variables show a stronger influence on relative productivity once the influence of the female proportion of the labor force is controlled in this way.

Logically, turnover and absenteeism in an industry's labor force are potential sources of impaired productivity, although in previous comparative studies they have not been considered distinctive sources of Britain's productivity problems.[60] In my study, nevertheless, I include a measure of labor turnover in British industries:

TURNB: gross turnover of employees, measured as the sum of new engagements and discharges per hundred employees, 1972.

It should be negatively related to relative productivity (*VPW*) if turnover is especially high in British industry. On the other hand, it is quite likely that a high turnover rate is characteristic of certain industries (for example, those that employ women and unskilled workers and offer seasonal employment). If a British industry exhibits high turnover, then its U.S. counterpart probably does too, and relative productivity would not be associated with the British turnover rate.

The influence of the sizes of plants and companies on the relative productivity of British industry is, as was seen earlier, problematic. Large production units may improve relative productivity by the fuller attainment of economies of scale, or may impair it by fostering more divisive labor-management relations. Thus, though I am not certain about the direction of their influence, I employ the following variables:

LGPB: proportion of employment accounted for by plants with 1,000 or more employees, 1968;

58. The *t*-statistics lie between −5.3 and −5.8.
59. That is, I replaced the raw variables with residuals from the regression of the logarithms of each labor variable on *PCFB*.
60. See Pratten, *Labour Productivity Differentials*, pp. 56–57; Central Policy Review Staff, *Future of the British Car Industry*, pp. 97–98.

LGEB: proportion of employment accounted for by enterprises with 1,000 or more employees, 1968;

SMALB: proportion of employment accounted for by plants with fewer than 25 employees, 1968.

Scale economies in production should pertain to the plant rather than the company. But it is not clear whether difficult labor relations are strictly a matter of plant size or whether the impersonal character of the large enterprise is the source of difficulty. Hence the inclusion of both *LGPB* and *LGEB*. The variable *SMALB* is simply a check on the results of the other two variables, using the small end of the distribution of plant sizes. Prais's findings about the incidence of strikes in large British plants, summarized above, suggest not merely a negative influence of large plant sizes on relative productivity but an influence that should interact with an indicator of the troubled state of an industry's labor relations.[61] I employ the simple multiplicative interaction

$$SIZE1 = LGPB \cdot UNIONB,$$

and also another form of interaction that simply lets the variable *LGPB* take a different slope in industries with higher-than-average coverage of their members by collective bargaining agreements:

SIZE2 = LGPB if *UNIONB* is greater than its mean value in the sample, zero otherwise.

The variables *SIZE1* and *SIZE2* should both be negatively related to *VPW*.

The next group of variables is intended to embody the hypothesis that managerial personnel and techniques in Britain are a source of poor relative productivity. Several variables suggest themselves for this purpose. The most compelling circumstantial evidence of managerial failure in Britain has come from comparisons between the performance of foreign-controlled companies and their domestic competitors. Although some doubts have recently been cast on the superior productivity of foreign firms,[62] it seems appropriate to test the hypothesis that the produc-

61. Prais, "The Strike-proneness of Large Plants."
62. Solomon and Ingham, "Discriminating between MNC Subsidiaries and Indigenous Companies."

tivity shortfall of U.S. industries is less when they contain a high proportion of foreign-owned companies. I employ

FOSB: sales by enterprises classed as foreign owned, expressed as a percentage of industry sales, 1968.

Another approach starts from the premise that industries differ in the amount and quality of managerial skill they require, in which case the United Kingdom might experience larger shortfalls of productivity in those industries needing more numerous or more sophisticated managers, or both. Because the problem may be the use of too few managerial personnel in Britain, U.S. data should be used to make this discrimination among industries. Relative productivity should be negatively related to

MGRS: managerial and kindred employees as a percentage of total employees, U.S. counterpart industry, 1970.

I also considered that any managerial disadvantage of British industry might be compounded by the need to deal with difficult labor-management relations.[63] The large amount of time devoted to this problem in Britain may distract managers from the function of long-range business planning, thereby making U.K. managerial resources even less adequate than they would otherwise be. Hence an industry's productivity shortfall because of a need for large managerial inputs should be even greater where labor relations are difficult. Diverse labor-relations variables could be used to investigate this interaction. I simply allowed the variable *MGRS* to take a different slope when a larger than average fraction of employees is covered by collective bargaining agreements:

MGRHU = *MGRS* for industries in which *UNIONB* is greater than its mean value, zero otherwise.

A negative sign is expected for the variable.

Indictments of British management have often included the charge that replacement investment has been inadequate, so that British workers' productivity is held back by the geriatric deficiencies of out-of-date equip-

63. In view of the emphasis given to labor-relations problems, it should be noted that effective management is not just a matter of keeping the work force happy. For an arresting comparative case study, see Duncan Gallie, *In Search of the New Working Class: Automation and Social Integration within the Capitalist Enterprise,* Cambridge Studies in Sociology, no. 9 (Cambridge: Cambridge University Press, 1978).

ment. The well-known study by Bacon and Eltis did not support this charge, for the authors found that the ages of metal-working tools in British and American industries are quite similar. Nonetheless, their data do indicate some differences among a limited number of industries in the relative ages of these capital goods.[64] From this information I took the variable

AGEM: average age of machine tools, U.K. industry, divided by average age of machine tools in its U.S. counterpart.

AGEM should be negatively related to relative productivity.

I complete this list of independent variables with two that are included as controls for possible spurious influences on relative productivity. As noted earlier, the dependent variable is an accurate measure of relative efficiency only under a number of assumptions, one of them being that the U.K. industry and its U.S. counterpart sell at prices determined on the world market and, indeed, are themselves merely small segments of a competitive world industry. This assumption could be wrong because international trade fails to link national prices tightly together and because domestic prices may be elevated by highly concentrated industries. I consider the latter influence first. If monopoly profits are captured by an industry, they count as part of value added. A monopolized industry in Britain would therefore appear to attain higher productivity than a competitive industry (unless, of course, the monopoly fails to minimize cost of production). Hence the independent variables should include

C5B: proportion of industry sales accounted for by the largest five companies, 1972.[65]

It should have a positive effect on *VPW* if concentrated industries both earn excess profits and eschew consuming the potential profits in the form of a quiet life.

Relative productivity may be affected in rather complicated ways by flows of international trade. One might argue that the less international

64. R. W. Bacon and W. A. Eltis, *The Age of US and UK Machinery,* NEDO Monograph 3 (London: National Economic Development Office, 1974), pp. 15, 50.

65. It is an open question whether this variable should be expressed simply as the level of concentration in Britain, or whether instead I should have employed the ratio of concentration in the British industry to that in the American counterpart industry. Concentration levels are no doubt highly correlated in the two countries.

trade, the freer the prices in national markets are to depart from the prices set in the world market. But this departure could be either up or down, depending on the national industry's efficiency, competitiveness, and so on. In this context the influence of import competition cannot be identified simply by adding another variable to the regression equation; a supplemental test (reported below) is required. Import competition may, however, have a direct effect on relative productivity if the state of a British industry's comparative advantage is changing over time. If the share of the U.K. market held by imports has been rising, the earnings of some U.K. factors of production employed in the industry are likely to be depressed below their opportunity-cost levels in their best alternative employments. Value added in the British industry then contains a negative windfall component. To check for this effect I used the variable

IMPB: ratio of import share of domestic shipments in 1974 to import share of domestic shipments in 1963, the variable weighted by the average value of the 1963 and 1974 shares.

The weight gives recognition to the fact that a rapidly changing import share should have little effect if the share is small both before and after. The variable *IMPB* should be negatively related to relative productivity.

Statistical Results

Because my hypotheses do not devolve from rigorous models of economic behavior, and because the possible interactions among the independent variables are numerous, I frankly was forced to do a good deal of experimentation in the testing of these hypotheses. Table 2 contains ordinary least-squares regression equations relating *VPW* to a group of the variables defined above. These specifications seem to me the most informative.

If the labor-relations variables are entered in their raw, additive forms, the measures of strikes and working days lost (*STRIKB* and *WDLB*) take negative coefficients that are statistically significant at the 10 percent level or better.[66] The coefficient of *UNIONB* is quite insignificant and variable in sign. The maximum explanatory power results when I use *FLAB1*, the product of *WDLB* and *STRIKB*, adjusted for the female proportion of

66. One-tailed tests of significance are used for all labor-relations variables except *UNIONB*.

Table 2. Regression Analysis of Determinants of Relative Productivity of British Manufacturing Industries (VPW)[a]

Equation	Constant	CAP	FOSB	FLAB1	LAB4	MGRS	MGRHU	Other	R^2	Degrees of freedom
1	0.191 (9.13)	0.012 (0.26)	−0.264 (−0.85)	−0.107 (−1.55)	−0.375 (−1.77)	−0.010 −(3.57)	0.003 (1.94)	⋯	0.304	40
2	0.188 (7.71)	0.014 (0.30)	−0.269 (−0.86)	−0.109 (−1.54)	−0.375 (−1.74)	−0.010 (−3.23)	0.003 (1.88)	+0.020 (IMPB) (0.19)	0.287	39
3	0.194 (9.33)	0.009 (0.20)	−0.320 (−1.04)	−0.078 (−1.10)	−0.335 (−1.58)	−0.009 (−3.09)	0.003 (2.08)	−0.206 (LGEB) (−1.39)	0.320	39
4	0.200 (6.23)	−0.003 (−0.06)	−0.151 (−0.43)	−0.125 (−1.50)	−0.221 (−0.91)	−0.008 (−2.77)		−0.377 (LGPB) + 0.326 (SIZE2) − 0.002 (TURNB) (−1.16) (1.05) (−0.70)	0.225	35
5	0.177 (6.81)	0.009 (0.20)	−0.200 (−0.63)	−0.106 (−1.50)	−0.342 (−1.59)	−0.009 (−3.05)	0.003 (2.13)	−0.054 (IMPB) + 0.755 (SMALB) (−0.35) (1.23)	0.296	38
6	0.192 (6.78)	−0.005 (−0.10)	−0.176 (−0.56)	−0.115 (−1.58)	−0.330 (−1.53)	−0.010 (−3.44)	0.003 (2.05)	+0.830 (LGPB) − 0.002 (C5B) (1.31) (−0.59)	0.300	38

Sources: See appendix B.

a. The numbers in parentheses are t-statistics.

b. See text pp. 160–67 for definitions. To scale them conveniently, the coefficients of C5B, FOSB, IMPB, LGEB, LGPB, SIZE2, and SMALB have been multiplied by 1,000 and coefficients of FLAB1 and LAB4 have been multiplied by 100,000.

the labor force. It is weakly significant, about 6 to 7 percent, except when *LGEB* is included. I conclude that disruptions in the workplace probably do exact a cost in productivity and that the disruptions systematically increase as the male proportion of the labor force increases.

Although in itself the coverage of employees by collective-bargaining agreements has no net influence on productivity, such an influence emerges when the product of this variable and the proportion of employment in the older industrial regions, *LAB4,* are used. *LAB4*'s negative coefficient is significant at 5 percent in some specifications, 10 percent in most others. Finally, labor-force turnover (*TURNB*) is not a significant influence on relative productivity, although its coefficient is negative as expected (equation 4).[67]

Next I consider the variables related to the scale of production. Each of these usually takes the sign one expects if the British industry's productivity disadvantage is greater the larger its production units are. The pattern of signs disputes the attractiveness of large units for the sake of scale economies and affirms their unattractiveness for achieving workable labor relations. As is shown by equations 3 through 6, however, these variables are never significant at the 10 percent confidence level in a two-tailed test. I therefore characterize the evidence on plant and company size as weak, though persistent. In equation 4 I include the variable *SIZE2* to test the hypothesis that the difficulty with large production units is inherent in the collective-bargaining process itself. *SIZE2* allows *LGPB* to take a different slope in highly unionized industries. It is not significant but has a positive sign, contrary to what one expects if large plants are dysfunctional because they engender restrictive bargaining agreements. The coefficient of *LGPB* itself turns positive if concentration (*C5B*) is included (equation 6); the two variables are collinear.[68]

The hypothesis of deficient management is embodied in the variables *MGRS* (the industry's management intensity), *AGEM* (relative age of

67. Turnover has moderate negative correlations with *UNIONB, WDLB, STRIKB,* and *FLAB1.* This fact suggests that "exit" and "voice" are alternative strategies of employees dissatisfied with their terms of employment.

68. Some recent evidence reveals a mechanism that could explain how conditions in large U.K. plants translate into lower productivity. Panić finds that the capacity utilization of U.K. manufacturing industries bears a significant negative relation to average plant size. Capacity utilization could reflect both idleness from strikes and a variety of other constraints on management's ability to utilize its plant. M. Panić, *Capacity Utilization in UK Manufacturing Industry,* Discussion Paper 5 (London: National Economic Development Office, 1978), pp. 42–44.

machinery), and *FOSB* (foreign subsidiaries' share of sales). The negative coefficient of *MGRS* is always significant at the 1 percent level, which implies that a British industry's relative productivity falls as the industry's need for managerial sophistication rises. The interactive term *MGRHU,* however, is positive and significant at or near the 5 percent level (two-tailed test), which suggests that U.K. management has made some headway in dealing with its labor-relations problems. The variable *AGEM* is not shown in table 2,[69] but its coefficient varies in sign and is always quite insignificant. The finding of Bacon and Eltis is thus confirmed—the difficulty with British productivity does not stem from the capital goods themselves.[70]

I expected that *FOSB* would take a positive coefficient, in light of Dunning's evidence that foreign-controlled enterprises display superior managerial performance. In fact, the coefficient is always negative, although not statistically significant. This result is not without its antecedents, as was noted above,[71] but it is curious enough to provoke a search for clarifying information. First, I wondered whether multinational companies might be trapped by the apparent inability of manufacturers in Britain to use their capital equipment effectively. *FOSB* is uncorrelated with the absolute capital intensity of industries in Britain, although it is positively correlated with their relative capital intensity (*CAP*). However, a test for statistical interactions between *FOSB* and *CAP* proved unrevealing. I then considered whether foreign subsidiaries might exert a negative influence on relative productivity because they tend to operate large plants, and large plants have a poor record of labor-management relations. That proves to be somewhat the case; with plant size controlled, industries tenanted by the multinational companies have fewer strikes than other industries, although they lose proportionally more working days because

69. Observations on *AGEM* are available for less than half of the seventy-one industries, so that its inclusion seriously reduces the degrees of freedom in the regression equations. As it is, missing observations restrict the degrees of freedom in table 2 to well below the maximum that the industries would permit.

70. Bacon and Eltis, *The Age of US and UK Machinery.*

71. The result has been reported for other countries, where it is more easily explained. Several scholars have investigated the tendency of multinational companies to establish small-scale facilities in Canada's small manufacturing sector. See Ronald S. Saunders, "The Determinants of the Productivity of Canadian Manufacturing Industries Relative to That of Counterpart Industries in the United States" (Ph.D. dissertation, Harvard University, 1978), chap. 8.

of strikes.[72] Finally, I wondered if *FOSB* should be considered an endogenous variable determined in substantial degree by other variables in the system. When I employ two-stage least squares, replacing *FOSB* by its estimated value, its coefficient indeed does turn consistently positive (although the *t*-statistic never exceeds one). I conclude that the foreignness of the entrepreneurial unit by itself has no significant influence on relative productivity, although the prevalence of multinational companies is probably related to some of the other variables determining relative productivity.

The variable indicating relative capital intensity (*CAP*) is never significant, and its sign varies from equation to equation. Because my analysis is not set up so that input combinations can be compared through a formal production-function relation, this negative result cannot be taken to imply that British industries gain nothing by adding capital. Rather, the result merely indicates that observed differences in capital intensity (with capital badly measured) contribute nothing to explaining differences in relative productivity.

The remaining regression results have to do with the variables for import competition and seller concentration. The seller concentration ratio of the British industry (*C5B*) takes a regression coefficient with no stable sign and is never significant (equation 6). As equations 2 and 5 show, the tendency of industries with growing import competition to suffer negative windfalls and apparently low productivity is not confirmed.

The main effect of high seller concentration and the absence of import competition may be to let the British industry's productivity vary more widely from the level attained in other countries, rather than push relative productivity systematically in any direction. To test this hypothesis (and several others), I examined the residuals from the equations in table 2. They were taken both with their signs attached (to see whether they might be associated with any variables left out of the model) and as absolute values (to check for influences that might let the productivity of British

---

72. These conclusions are reached by comparing zero-order correlations between these variables with first-order partial correlations that hold *LGPB* constant. Between *FOSB* and *WDLB* these coefficients are respectively 0.233 and 0.120; between *FOSB* and *STRIKB*, 0.043 and −0.150; between *FOSB* and *UNIONB*, 0.193 and 0.033. It should be mentioned that the zero-order correlation between *VPW* and *FOSB* is strongly negative (−0.341), so that the negative regression coefficient does not depend on indirect channels of causation; indeed, it is mitigated by them.

industries get further out of line).[73] This exercise showed that relative productivity levels are indeed more variable when imports have a lower share of the British market; this conclusion is statistically significant at the 10 percent level. The raw residuals are uncorrelated with seller concentration ($C5B$), but their absolute values show a positive correlation with concentration that is significant at the 5 percent level. This conclusion implies that high concentration may lead to monopoly and technical inefficiency in combinations that vary from sector to sector.

Some other interesting conclusions emerge from the analysis of residuals. The collective-bargaining variable can be disaggregated to indicate the proportions of employees under national contracts, national contracts with supplemental local agreements, and purely local (plant, company, or district) agreements. Mulvey determined that national agreements had no effect on wage levels, whereas the other two kinds did.[74] I found that coverage by local agreements is positively correlated with the residuals from my equations (significance level is 7 to 8 percent), which may imply that local agreements permit the use of high wages to buy off restrictive practices and overmanning, whereas national agreements perpetuate these restraints. The proportions of workers covered by national agreements (with or without supplemental local ones) are always negatively correlated with the residuals, but the correlations are not statistically significant. Finally, the analysis of residuals shows that the larger the proportion of nonproduction workers in the U.K. industry's work force, the lower its relative productivity (statistical significance is 10 percent). This result lends some support to the hypothesis, noted above, that overmanning tends to be concentrated in the auxiliary and nonproduction functions within the plant.[75]

73. Residuals from several equations in table 2 were calculated and processed; it turns out to make no appreciable difference which are used.

74. Charles Mulvey, "Collective Agreements and Relative Earnings in UK Manufacturing in 1973," *Economica*, vol. 43 (November 1976), pp. 419–27.

75. One expects that the more nonproduction workers an industry employs, the higher the value added per worker, because nonproduction workers on the average possess higher skills and receive higher compensation. The correlation between value added per worker in Britain and the nonproduction-worker proportion of the industry's labor force is 0.386, and the correlation between value added per worker in Britain and compensation per nonproduction worker is 0.763. Given these facts, one would expect a positive correlation between relative productivity (VPW, the dependent variable in table 2) and the relative proportion of nonproduction workers in Britain to those in the United States. That correlation should obtain if the matched

I also examined the residuals used in the preceding correlation analysis to see if industries with the largest positive or the largest negative deviations have any common characteristics that might suggest causal influences omitted from the model. Four of the five industries with large positive residuals (higher productivity than my model predicts) are process industries—man-made fibers, abrasives, printing ink, and bricks and refractory goods. During interviews various business executives suggested that in Britain process industries with machine-paced technologies can be carried on more effectively than other industries. That seems to be an accurate assessment: four of the five industries with the largest negative residuals (lower productivity than predicted) turn out simple household goods—polishes, linoleum, brushes and brooms, biscuits. These are partly assembly operations, but also subject to product differentiation. Again, the list seems responsive to the general hypotheses, as reviewed above, about the sources of the varying productivity performance of British industries.

Because I found strong statistical evidence to support the negative influence on industrial productivity of both poor labor-management relations and deficiencies in British management, I wanted to investigate some of the channels through which these interacting forces operate to depress productivity—underutilization of equipment, excessive inventories, inefficiently slow reallocations of productive capacity from low-return to high-return activities, and so forth. I performed a simple test of the hypothesis that the uncertainty of output rates, attributable to poor labor relations, causes excessive inventories to be held. I collected data on finished-good inventories relative to sales in both the U.K. industries in the sample and their U.S. counterparts, and expressed the U.K. inventory-to-sales figure as a ratio of the comparable U.S. figure. One would expect this variable to be positively correlated with variables indicating the extent to which production is disrupted by strikes. The variable in fact has positive correlations statistically significant at the 1 percent level with all of my variables indicating poor labor relations, for example, $WDLB$ (0.578), $STRIKB$ (0.505), $LAB1$ (0.663), and $FLAB1$ (0.678). There seems no doubt that, as much circumstantial evidence indicates, British

---

U.K. and U.S. industries differed only in unobserved factors that make them have different optimal combinations of nonproduction and production workers. However, the actual correlation is slightly negative (−0.056), consistent with the result drawn from the analysis of residuals mentioned in the text.

firms hold higher inventories to cope with uncertainties in their rates of output.

Growth Rates of Productivity

Ideally, one would proceed from an analysis of the relative productivity levels of British industries to an explanation of differences in their growth rates of productivity. Several contrasting models might be applied to the relation between an industry's productivity growth and the divergence of its productivity from the best level attainable. In the spirit of Gerschenkron's concept of relative backwardness, one can point to the cheap access to improved performance available to the producer that imitates his more advanced rival's best practices and avoids making the rival's mistakes. This hope glows brightest where productivity's shortfall is due to a lack of intangible assets—management practices, technological knowledge, and so forth—that can be taken up at low cost.

On the other hand, one can argue that some factors causing low productivity also tend to preserve or exacerbate a shortfall. Being productive in a world of change demands an ability to alter course quickly when circumstances dictate. If low productivity results from social conditions and restrictive arrangements that preclude efficient production, they are very likely to shrivel the gains from responding to some external signal that best practice has changed. The aptness of this proposition to Britain's productivity problem struck the authors of *Britain's Economic Prospects,* and Olson has recently elaborated the idea that institutional constraints on efficiency and growth are closely interrelated.[76]

Each of these views can be translated into behavioral propositions and tested by a cross-section analysis of manufacturing industries, similar to that performed above. Although my effort here will be only exploratory, it does shed some light on the relation between productivity shortfall and productivity growth. First, however, I consider some findings from previous research on productivity growth in Britain. Denison found that the growth of overall residual productivity in Britain during 1950–62 was no higher than that in the United States and no better than equal to that in other European countries, although the level of residual productivity in

76. Caves and others, *Britain's Economic Prospects,* pp. 487–95; Mancur Olson, "The Political Economy of Comparative Growth Rates."

Britain was lower. Thus at that time there was no evidence that Britain was catching up.[77] Other studies that have used methods very different from Denison's nonetheless concur on this point. Christensen, Cummings, and Jorgenson found that between 1955 and 1973 Britain experienced a somewhat faster rate of growth of total factor productivity than did the United States, but all other countries outside North America that they examined had still faster growth rates.[78]

Several analyses of interindustry differences in productivity growth rates also may be noted, even though they were concentrated on the relation between productivity growth and total output growth, not of interest for my purposes. Wragg and Robertson, working with a sample of industries similar to mine, found that the growth of total factor productivity over 1963–73 was significantly lower in industries experiencing more strikes per worker, and that it also exhibited a weak negative relation to the proportion of the industry's labor force covered by collective bargaining agreements. The authors seem to have found a positive relation of productivity growth to the proportion of employees in large establishments and a negative relation to seller concentration, but I am disinclined to trust their conclusions.[79] They got generally similar results for the determinants of growth in labor productivity, with indications that poor labor relations are a drag on productivity growth and large plant size is a stimulant. In producer-good industries Wragg and Robertson also found that productivity growth is faster in industries with greater exposure to international trade, but apparently this influence does not appear in the consumer-good industries or in manufacturing as a whole.[80]

77. Edward F. Denison, "Economic Growth," in Caves and others, *Britain's Economic Prospects,* pp. 261–63, 274.

78. Laurits R. Christensen, Dianne Cummings, and Dale W. Jorgenson, "Productivity Growth, 1947–73: An International Comparison," U.S. Department of Labor, Bureau of International Labor Affairs, *The Impact of International Trade and Investment on Employment* (GPO, 1978), table 11.

79. Richard Wragg and James Robertson, *Post-War Trends in Employment, Productivity, Output, Labour Costs and Prices by Industry in the United Kingdom,* Department of Employment, Research Paper 3 (HMSO, 1977), chap. 7, esp. table K. Their analysis suffers from substantial statistical difficulties. First, they included independent variables with overlapping justifications and thereby built a good deal of multicollinearity into their model. Second, they used no control for differences among industries in their technological opportunities for productivity growth; these opportunities are probably collinear with some of the authors' independent variables (such as plant size).

80. Ibid., p. 57.

International comparative evidence on growth rates of productivity can be found in studies undertaken at the National Economic Development Office on productivity and growth in British and West German manufacturing industries. If West Germany lacks the productivity-curbing features of Britain's older industries, one would expect faster relative productivity growth for Britain in the newer industries with greater potentials for productivity growth. Britain would trail further behind in the older industries with less potential for raising productivity. These conjectures imply that the variance of productivity growth rates among industries would be less in West Germany than in Britain, assuming that the ranks of industries in order of productivity growth rates are similar in the two countries. That necessary assumption indeed holds empirically.[81] The coefficient of variation of the growth rates of labor productivity over 1954–72 was 0.49 for Britain but only 0.29 for West Germany. For total factor productivity the corresponding values are 0.90 and 0.57.[82] This result implies that British productivity growth is low in those industries where productivity is low relative to that of their foreign counterparts— a proposition that can be tested with my data.

I used the data published by Wragg and Robertson on growth of productivity to supplement my statistical analysis of productivity levels. First, by examining the correlation between the growth of total factor productivity in British industries and their shortfall of productivity from their U.S. counterparts, one can determine whether or not the worst-performing U.K. industries have been seizing an opportunity to catch up. For the industries that overlap in my sample and theirs, this correlation is 0.397. The value is statistically significant at the 1 percent confidence level; the positive correlation implies that the British industries performing well

81. Ian Elliot and Alan Hughes, "Capital and Labour: Their Growth, Distribution, and Productivity," in Panić, ed., *UK and West German Manufacturing Industry,* pp. 39, 65. The rank correlation coefficient across sectors for growth in labor productivity over 1954–72 was 0.83, and for total factor productivity it was 0.56; both are significant at the 5 percent level.

82. Ibid., pp. 38, 63, 66. In an inquiry similar in spirit, Murrell finds that the proportional differences in rates of growth of output between "young" and "old" industries are significantly greater in Britain than in West Germany. That difference is consistent with (and implied by) the greater variability of productivity growth rates found in the NEDO studies. See Peter Murrell, "The Comparative Structure of the Growth of West German and British Manufacturing Industry" (University of Maryland, February 1979).

relative to their American counterparts have been growing faster while those performing poorly have been falling further behind. No catching up is apparent; on the contrary, the result suggests that the factors favoring industries' levels of productivity may be favoring their growth as well.[83]

An ideal procedure would be to calculate growth rates in total factor productivity for the U.S. counterparts of my sampled U.K. industries and seek to explain the differences between them. This step is needed because differences in productivity growth among industries in the main reflect differences in their opportunities for technological progress. Omission of any control for technological opportunity may severely bias one's estimate of other influences on productivity growth because of a common underlying relation to technological opportunity. For instance, technical progress seems more rapid in industries that are capital intensive and utilize large plants. If so, a spurious positive relation may appear between large plant size and productivity growth—a serious bias in view of the results reported above. Although my resources did not permit the calculation of total factor productivity growth for U.S. industries, one could make a rough approximation by using the growth of labor productivity in the U.S. counterpart industries (1963–72).[84] That variable is called *GVPWS*. Another variable that I used in this analysis but did not previously define is *NPW,* the ratio of nonproduction workers to total employees in the U.K. industry divided by the same ratio for its U.S. counterpart. Nonproduction employees perform diverse functions, but they include both administrative and research personnel who are important for promoting productivity growth.

I did not find many significant relations between the growth of total

83. My figure for the level of relative productivity is averaged over years at the beginning, middle, and end of the period covered by Wragg and Robertson's growth rate, so that no "regression fallacy" is involved. The correlation between my variable *VPW* and their data for the growth of labor productivity is similarly high, 0.259. This result is consistent with the evidence in George and Ward, *Structure of Industry,* pp. 66–67, that the British industries with the faster-growing productivity have more or less kept up with their West German counterparts, while sectors with slower-growing productivity in Britain have fallen far behind their German competitors.

84. Wragg and Robertson found a correlation of 0.78 between the growth of labor productivity and total factor productivity, and they drew a blank in their search for significant influences on the difference between the two (*Post-War Trends in Employment,* pp. 42, 49). My variable *GVPWS* is undeflated for price changes, which makes it a rough approximation indeed.

factor productivity ($GTFPB$) and the structural variables used above, but the following equation is revealing:

$$GTFPB = 2.44 + 2.16\,GVPWS + 0.80\,NPW - 0.18\,MGRS + 0.035\,FOSB$$
$$\quad\;\;(1.22)\;\;(1.75)\qquad\quad(1.30)\qquad(-0.94)\qquad\quad(1.81)$$

$$- \;0.11\,TURNB - 0.0013\,STRIKB - 0.022\,REGB.$$
$$(-0.59)\qquad\;\;(-0.46)\qquad\quad(-2.04)$$

The equation has 39 degrees of freedom, and the R^2 value (corrected for degrees of freedom) is 0.116. The growth of British productivity appears to be significantly slowed for industries concentrated in Britain's old industrial regions ($REGB$), even after I control for technological opportunity. And there is weak evidence that productivity grows more rapidly in industries where foreign subsidiaries are present,[85] a conclusion that may in part redeem their negligible influence on the productivity levels revealed above. With technological opportunity and the multinational presence controlled, the relative prevalence of nonproduction workers shows a weak positive influence on productivity growth. The signs of the regression coefficients suggest negative influences for management intensity and labor disturbances, but these variables are not significant. If a measure is added of the proportion of employees in plants with over 1,000 workers ($LGPB$), its coefficient is positive but quite insignificant. Thus I do not confirm either the significant positive influence of large plant size or the significant negative influence of collective-bargaining agreements reported by Wragg and Robertson.

Implications: Industrial Structure and Industrial Policy

The results of my study have several implications for the future of the British economy and British policymaking.

Prospects for Industrial Structure

My sectoral approach to productivity suggests a seldom recognized consequence of Britain's lagging productivity for the future structure of the U.K. economy. Some of the most commonly offered explanations for

---

85. The coefficient of *FOSB* is significant at 10 percent in a two-tailed test.

the shortfall are indeed confirmed by my cross-section analysis. That confirmation implies that the productivity performance in Britain, compared with those of other countries, varies significantly and persistently from industry to industry. Furthermore, no evidence was found that the laggard sectors are catching up—if anything, the forces that make productivity low also make it grow slowly, and the low-productivity sectors are straying further from the pack. This pattern implies changes in the structure of the economy. For sectors not sheltered from international competition (by transportation costs or import restrictions), it can be predicted that the ones whose traits mark them for sustained disadvantages in productivity will face increased foreign competition, losing both domestic and foreign markets to their international rivals. Conversely, reallocations of factors of production within the British economy will carry them toward those sectors with the least productivity disadvantage. In short, trends in relative productivity are the stuff of international comparative advantage. For sectors sheltered from trade, the prediction instead bears on the future structure of relative prices. The relative productivity that matters here, however, is performance against other sheltered industries in Britain and not against counterparts in other countries. Although the calculation differs from the one made for the trade-exposed industries, the same general principle holds: industries with a deteriorating productivity level among the trade-sheltered industries will exhibit rising relative prices, whereas prices should fall for those experiencing better-than-average productivity trends.

What are the traits that mark U.K. manufacturing industries for slow extinction? Quite obviously, those stuck with the heritage of divisive labor-management relations and located primarily in the old industrial regions. My statistical evidence suggests that the difficulty lies not in union organization and the presence of collective bargaining agreements per se but in long-standing attitudes of the work force that sustain hostility to change and cooperation. Better performance can be expected of industries with largely female labor forces. Quite consistent with these statistical conclusions is one voiced frequently by British industrialists: productivity performance in Britain is relatively good in process industries or those in which the speed of work is machine-paced; it deteriorates in assembly-type industries where the pace of machines is not controlling and where disruptions at one link in a chain of sequential production stages can throw the others out of joint.

Other industries with poor prospects are those needing large managerial cadres or managers requiring high levels of administrative skill. My statistical conclusions leave room for doubt whether such industries will simply recede or whether domestic companies will yield up part of the market to foreign subsidiaries. The prevalence of subsidiaries shows no relation to industries' productivity levels, although foreign enterprises do turn up on the winning side when it comes to industries' rates of productivity growth. Hence it is not clear that foreign companies enjoy across the board a prospective efficiency advantage over British companies. Indeed, the evidence suggests that the probability of displacement by multinationals differs from sector to sector. Britain is, after all, a prominent home base of multinationals, and these seem to be concentrated in those industries least afflicted by the productivity-depressing forces that I have identified—food and beverage, tobacco, paper and printing, petroleum.[86]

A final implication of this study is that industries with substantial scale economies will recede in prominence. My own statistical analysis did not designate the large plant as the culprit (as against the large firm). However, other evidence on the exacerbated state of labor relations convinces me that market forces will compel resort to smaller plant sizes in Britain. Where diseconomies of small scale are modest, such a trend could leave an industry's relative productivity on the whole improved (with the higher costs incurred at smaller output scales outweighed by a reduced gap between actual and best-practice productivity levels). Britain's mix of industries should thus tend toward those in which the cost curve does not rise sharply as plants' employment levels are decreased below 1,000 workers.

The interindustry differences that I have found may also bear on the controversy under way in Britain over "deindustrialization," the alleged overabsorption of labor in the nonmarket sector of the economy (where commercial revenues need not cover payments to factors of production).[87] The differences I found among manufacturing industries may also

86. George and Ward, *Structure of Industry,* pp. 55–57, note that West Germany's largest companies occur in industries where German relative productivity appears the strongest—electrical engineering, chemicals, metals and metal products. Clearly there are grounds for expecting that any country's large and multinational firms will be distributed toward the industries of its greatest comparative advantage.

87. F. T. Blackaby, ed., *De-industrialisation,* National Institute of Economic and Social Research, Economic Policy Papers 2 (London: Heinemann Educational Books, 1979); Robert Bacon and Walter Eltis, *Britain's Economic Problem: Too Few Producers,* 2d ed. (London: Macmillan, 1978).

pertain to the manufacturing sector's position relative to other broad sectors of the economy. If the productivity deterrents weigh more heavily in manufacturing than in services, exportable services would tend to displace manufactures as sources of export earnings, and the long-term shift of final expenditure toward the services sector would proceed faster than otherwise. But the evidence does not show that the growth of productivity in British manufacturing, relative to the growth in the British service sector, is slower than in the United States.[88]

If valid, these conclusions about the evolving structure of the British economy would of course have many implications for public policy. For instance, they indicate an inexorable movement away from the old industrial regions of the industries that were their traditional lifeblood and point to the sizable task that regional policy will face if it tries to maintain the overall level of employment in those regions. Do firms in the industries structurally favored by the trends that I have identified do relatively better in the old industrial regions than firms in the traditional industries? I have seen no systematic evidence on this question, which my analysis suggests is of considerable importance.

Policies toward Productivity

To consider public policy toward productivity is a daunting task. There are countless influences on industrial productivity, and my evidence shows the most important among them to be embedded in the fabric of British society. Furthermore, there is no well-developed model of optimal policy toward productivity such as exists in areas like macroeconomic management, taxation, and pollution abatement.[89] Hence no policy instruments are commonly recognized as the natural tools for improving productivity.

88. The following annual growth rates of net output per employee can be calculated for the United Kingdom and the United States (percent):

	United Kingdom 1948–73	United States 1947–65
Manufacturing	2.84	3.00
Distribution	1.62	2.69
Finance and insurance	1.34	1.75

The figures are taken from G. Briscoe, "Recent Productivity Trends in the UK Service Sector," *Oxford Bulletin of Economics and Statistics,* vol. 38 (November 1976), p. 274; and Victor R. Fuchs, *The Service Economy* (National Bureau of Economic Research, 1968), p. 211.

89. Cairncross, Kay, and Silberston, "The Regeneration of Manufacturing Industry," p. 14.

Many policies lay claim to improving it, and many others are charged with inadvertently impairing it. If productivity is conceived narrowly as efficient utilization of resources at hand on the shop floor, almost no policies deal with productivity directly. If productivity is recognized as depending on the optimal combination of resources—including optimal investment policies—throughout the economic system, almost no policy leaves productivity unaffected.

This confusion about policy toward productivity can be cleared up by a few simple propositions of economic theory. Although the propositions will sound familiar enough once stated, they are often ignored in exhortations about productivity policy. Productivity, however defined, is a relation between outputs and inputs. In popular discussion it is usually equated with labor productivity. Because combining a given labor input with more of other factors of production leads to more output (up to a point), the usual recommendation is to increase the other inputs. Yet this is obviously wrong as a universal imperative for policy. If the average product of labor is raised by adding more capital, in general the average product of capital is simultaneously lowered. The economy at any one time possesses only limited stocks of each productive input. The most familiar propositions of neoclassical economics declare that these stocks should be combined in a certain optimal way. The levels of labor productivity observed in various economic activities then assume optimal (not maximal) levels corresponding to the resource combinations. Since British real wages are lower than those in a number of other industrial countries, enterprises that are combining inputs in cost-minimizing ways should come up with labor productivity levels below those in foreign factories. In that sense, enterprises in Britain are not to be faulted for displaying low labor productivity. For the same reasons, there is no necessary normative significance to differences among British industries in levels of trends of labor productivity; the variable simply is not a direct indicator of whether resources are ideally allocated.

When productivity is thought of, more properly, as a relation between total inputs and total output, the goal of maximizing productivity becomes another way of looking at the goal of minimizing costs of producing a given output. Even here, the concept of productivity does not lead one immediately to the right perspective on policy. The marginal adjustments that optimize the mix of inputs used in a given process (including all the relevant investment decisions) do not necessarily leave productivity at its maximum attainable value, when productivity is defined as an average input-output relation and not a total one. In short, the problem of productivity is that of maximizing the output from the available inputs, and success must be judged on marginal criteria. Whether productivity should be raised by encouraging more investment, promoting more advanced technology, and the like, depends on the social rates of return at the margin on these commitments of resources. The concept of productivity is at best a catchall, and policies addressed to improving productivity must attend not to average productivity but to margins of resource use that are not socially optimized.

These remarks leave one unsurprised at the absence of clear evidence about the effects of British policies on productivity and also warn one away from casual judgments. Little can be concluded about these policies except by way of rough a priori evaluations; I therefore confine myself to an annotated list of the leading types of policies.[90]

1. The Industrial Reorganisation Corporation was a prototype policy device of the 1960s—an independent agency with substantial funds to promote rationalization schemes through high technology and the encouragement of exports. It showed a predilection for promoting mergers among leading companies (electronics, computers, and so on) and for strengthening U.K. companies that found themselves in close competition with foreign multinationals. The National Enterprise Board (1975) appears to follow the tradition of the Industrial Reorganisation Corporation; its main activity so far has been to hold the government's shares in British Leyland.

2. The machine tool industry in the 1960s received various forms of aid from the Ministry of Technology: increased research and development contracts, orders for preproduction models that were then placed on free loan to potential users, and the encouragement of mergers and associations with electronics and control engineering firms.

3. The charges of agencies responsible for controlling prices have at times included determining the efficiency of industries or firms that sought price increases and recommending corrective measures where appropri-

90. More detail can be found in P. Mottershead, "Industrial Policy," in F. T. Blackaby, ed., *British Economy Policy, 1960–1974* (Cambridge: Cambridge University Press, 1978), pp. 418–83; D. K. Stout, "De-Industrialisation and Industrial Policy," in F. T. Blackaby, ed., *De-industrialisation,* chap. 8; and Cairncross, Kay, and Silberston, "The Regeneration of Manufacturing Industry."

ate. The Price Commission and (before it) the National Board for Prices and Incomes disseminated a good deal of free management-consulting service to selected industries with strong incentives for the advice to be taken.[91]

4. Declining industries (textiles, coal, shipbuilding) have received various forms of public support and intervention. The assistance has aimed more at effecting public absorption of the costs of adjustment than at raising productivity, but some productivity gains have probably been achieved.[92]

5. Sector working parties bring together management, labor, and civil servants to consider bottlenecks to growth in individual industries (mainly engineering, but also chemicals and textiles) and propose strategies for removing them. Their current incarnation dates from 1976, but they have been around in one form or another for three decades. There seems to be no systematic evidence about their accomplishments. Some sector working parties are said to promote the dissemination of effective practices, often picked up from foreign competitors, and to supply a forum for promoting standardization.

6. Two decades ago, competition policy underwent a major change that made ordinary collusive price-fixing agreements illegal. Their abandonment often led to price declines that were large (though frequently temporary) and to the departure of firms from the industry—despite the fact that the falling price should have increased the quantity of output demanded. It may be that competition policy expelled inefficient capacity from these industries, but it is also possible that firms simply merged in order to curb the outbreak of competition, without rationalizing their facilities and increasing productivity.[93] That same key issue—whether horizontal mergers reduce the competitive pressure for efficiency or create

91. Allan Fels, *The British Prices and Incomes Board,* University of Cambridge, Department of Applied Economics, Occasional Paper 29 (Cambridge: Cambridge University Press, 1972), esp. chap. 11; J. D. Gribbin, "The United Kingdom 1977 Price Commission Act and Competition Policy," *Antitrust Bulletin,* vol. 23 (Summer 1978), pp. 405–39.

92. See Wragg and Robertson, *Post-War Trends in Employment,* p. 24, on the textile sector.

93. Dennis Swann and others, *Competition in British Industry: Restrictive Practices Legislation in Theory and Practice* (London: Allen and Unwin, 1974), chap. 4; D. C. Elliott and J. D. Gribbin, "The Abolition of Cartels and Structural Change in the United Kingdom," in A. P. Jacquemin and H. W. de Jong, eds., *Welfare Aspects of Industrial Markets,* Nijenrode Studies in Economics, vol. 2 (Leiden: Martinus Nijhoff Social Sciences Division, 1977), chap. 16.

the opportunity for its attainment—has been fought over in many specific policy settings. The antimerger supporters of competition policy have usually come out second best despite the negative evidence on the ex post success of mergers. Happily, the winds of official thought have recently been blowing in the right direction.[94]

This is not the place to attempt an evaluation of any of these policies. I shall say only that, overall, they are not impressively responsive to the origins of the productivity problem—as that problem is defined by my statistical analysis and in recent thinking of British observers. One must wonder whether the net has been cast wide enough in the search for remedial policies. Does the mixed bag of measures labeled "worker participation" contain anything that could help the labor force to recognize the consequences of their actions and attitudes on industrial productivity, without further overloading the capabilities of British management? Or is worker participation bound only to give increased weight to the old dysfunctional attitudes?[95] Despite the grim record of 1979, is there any hope that the transfer of more activity into the nationalized sector might improve the climate of industrial relations? Or are there enough marks against the performance of public enterprises to render such a course highly dubious?[96] Do tax and salary arrangements allow managers to recoup the cost of receiving training in business administration, and is there a case for subsidizing this activity?

Because the productivity problem originates deep within the social system, one needs an optimistic disposition to suppose that a democratic political system can eliminate that problem. Perhaps the most useful advice the economist can offer policymakers is for them to recognize the constraints on economic change and progress found in British society, to understand how these constraints will alter the structure of the British

94. See *A Review of Monopolies and Mergers Policy: A Consultative Document,* cmnd. 7198 (HMSO, 1978), pp. 34–38.

95. See B. C. Roberts, "Participation by Agreement," *Lloyds Bank Review,* no. 125 (July 1977), pp. 12–23.

96. A recent study finds that the centralized administration of nationalized industries has in important cases impaired innovative performance by reducing the chances for competing new technologies to be tried and shifting the responsibility for performance from the makers of equipment to the nationalized industries that use it. See Chris Harlow, *Innovation and Productivity under Nationalisation: The First Thirty Years* (London: Allen and Unwin for Political and Economic Planning, 1977). There have been too few attempts at objective appraisal of the nationalized industries' performance to support a well-informed judgment of them overall, but their performance in industrial relations does not seem impressive.

economy over time, and to try to hold Britain's aspirations for consumption in line with what its system is willing to produce.

Appendix A: Selection of Industry Sample

The matched manufacturing industries used in this study were selected on the basis of information contained in the standard industrial classification manuals of Britain and the United States, chiefly those employed for the U.K. *Report on the Census of Production, 1968,* and the U.S. *1967 Census of Manufactures.* Starting from the United Kingdom's minimum list headings, all manufacturing industries were included in the sample that could be matched closely and that did not represent a "miscellaneous" or "not elsewhere specified" product group. Minor apparent discrepancies were tolerated, especially when they allowed the inclusion of an industry representing a product group that would otherwise be missing. In both the United Kingdom and the United States the industrial classification system underwent some changes in the 1970s. But these did not cause much difficulty, because they usually involved disaggregating industries that had previously been combined.

Table 3 presents the seventy-one industries in the sample, along with their industrial classification numbers for the United Kingdom in 1968 and the United States in 1967. The names of industries are those used in the British data.

Appendix B: Sources of Data

Numerous sources of data were used to construct the data base employed in this study. The sources consulted are listed below, with each followed by the variables for which it was used and the numbers of tables from which data were taken. Special problems with the construction of certain variables are discussed at the end of this list.

U.K. Government Sources

Department of Trade and Industry, Business Statistics Office, *Report on the Census of Production, 1968,* vols. 8–141 passim (London: Her Majesty's Stationery Office, 1972): *LGPB* (table 2).

Table 3. *Names and Standard Industrial Classification Numbers of Industries Matched between U.K. and U.S. Standard Industrial Classification Systems, 1967–68*

Industry	SIC number, United Kingdom	SIC number, United States
1. Bread and flour confectionery	212	2051
2. Biscuits	213	2052
3. Cocoa, chocolate, sugar refining	217	207
4. Fruit and vegetable products	218	2032, 2033, 2034, 2035, 2037
5. Animal and poultry foods	219	2042
6. Vegetable and animal oils and fats	221	2091, 2092, 2093, 2094
7. Brewing and malting	231	2082, 2083
8. Soft drinks	232	2086, 2087
9. Tobacco	240	2111, 2121, 2131
10. Mineral oil refining	262	2911
11. Lubricating oils and greases	263	2992
12. Pharmaceutical chemicals and preparations	272	283
13. Toilet preparations	273	2844
14. Paint	274	2851
15. Soap and detergents	275	2841
16. Synthetic resins, plastic materials, synthetic rubber	276	2821, 2822
17. Fertilizers	278	2871, 2872
18. Polishes	279 (1)	2842
19. Formulated adhesives, gelatin, etc.	279 (2)	2891
20. Printing ink	279 (5)	2893
21. Aluminum, aluminum alloys	321	3334, 3352
22. Copper, brass, other copper alloys	322	3351, 3362
23. Agricultural machinery, wheeled tractors	331, 380	3522
24. Metal-working machine tools	332	3541, 3542, 3544, 3545, 3548
25. Pumps, valves, compressors	333	3561
26. Textile machinery and accessories	335	3552
27. Mechanical handling equipment	337	3534, 3535, 3536
28. Office machinery	338	3572, 3574, 3579
29. Mining machinery	339 (1)	3532
30. Refrigerating machinery	339 (3)	3585
31. Food and drink processing machinery	339 (4)	3551
32. Photographic and document-copying equipment	351	3861
33. Watches and clocks	352	3871, 3872
34. Surgical instruments, appliances	353	384
35. Telephone and telegraph apparatus and equipment	363	3661
36. Radio and electronic components	364	367

Table 3 (continued)

Industry	SIC number, United Kingdom	SIC number, United States
37. Broadcast-receiving and sound reproduction equipment	365	365
38. Electronic computers	366	3573
39. Radio, radar, and electronic capital goods	367	3662, 3693
40. Motor vehicle manufacturing	381	371
41. Motorcycle, tricycle, and pedal cycle manufacture	382	3751
42. Hand tools and implements	391	3423, 3425
43. Bolts, nuts, screws, rivets, etc.	393	345
44. Cans and metal boxes	395	3411
45. Metal furniture	399 (1)	2514, 2522
46. Man-made fibers	411	2823, 2824
47. Spinning and doubling on the cotton and flax systems	412	2281, 2282, 2284
48. Weaving of cotton, linen, man-made fibers	413	2211, 2221
49. Rope, twine, net	416	2298
50. Hosiery, other knitted goods	417	225
51. Lace	418	2292
52. Carpets	419	227
53. Narrow fabrics	421	2241
54. Canvas goods and sacks	422 (2)	2394
55. Leather tannery and dressing and fellmongery	431	3111, 3121
56. Leather goods	432	3161, 3171, 3172, 3199
57. Weatherproof outerwear	441	2385
58. Men's and boys' tailored outerwear	442	2311, 2327
59. Hats, coats, millinery	446	235
60. Gloves	449 (2)	2381, 3151
61. Bricks, fireclay, refractory goods	461	325
62. Pottery	462	326
63. Glass	463	3211, 322, 3231
64. Cement	464	3241
65. Abrasives	469 (1)	3291
66. Wooden containers and baskets	475	244
67. Cardboard boxes, cartons, etc.	482 (1)	265
68. Linoleum, plastics floor coverings, etc.	492	3996
69. Brushes and brooms	493	3991
70. Toys, games, children's carriages, sports equipment	494	394
71. Miscellaneous stationers' goods	495	395

Sources: U.K. Department of Trade and Industry, Business Statistics Office, *Report on the Census of Production, 1968* (HMSO, 1972), various volumes; U.S. Executive Office of the President, Office of Management and Budget, *Standard Industrial Classification Manual, 1972* (Government Printing Office, 1972).

Department of Trade and Industry, Business Statistics Office, *Report on the Census of Production, 1968,* vol. 156 (HMSO, 1972): *VPW, SMALB* (table 1); *CAP* (tables 1, 2); *NPW* (table 3).

Department of Trade and Industry, Business Statistics Office, *Report on the Census of Production, 1968,* vol. 158 (HMSO, 1974): *LGEB* (table 42A); *FOSB* (table 44).

Department of Industry, Business Statistics Office, *Report of the Census of Production, 1972, Summary Tables,* Business Monitor PA 1002 (HMSO, 1977): *STRIKB, VPW, WDLB* (table 1); *CAP, INVN* (tables 1, 2); *C5B* (table 9).

Department of Employment, *British Labour Statistics, Year Book, 1972* (HMSO, 1974): *PCFB* (table 5); *REGB* (table 60); *TURNB* (table 74); *WDLB* (table 152).

Department of Employment, *British Labour Statistics, Year Book, 1973* (HMSO, 1975): *WDLB, STRIKB* (table 147).

Department of Employment, *British Labour Statistics, Year Book, 1975* (HMSO, 1977): *STRIKB* (table 141).

Department of Employment, *New Earnings Survey, 1973* (HMSO, 1974): *UNIONB* (tables 110, 111).

U.S. Government Sources

Department of Commerce, Bureau of the Census, *1967 Census of Manufactures,* vol. 1, *Summary and Subject Statistics* (Government Printing Office, 1971), pp. 1–80: *NPW* (table 1); *GVPWS, VPW, CAP* (table 3).

Department of Commerce, Bureau of the Census, *1972 Census of Manufactures,* vol. 1: *Subject and Special Statistics* (GPO, 1976): *CAP, INVN, VPW* (general summary table 3; appendix C).

Bureau of the Census, *Census of Population: 1970, Subject Reports: Occupation by Industry,* PC(2)-7C (GPO, 1972): *MGRS* (table 1).

Other Sources

Bacon, R. W., and W. A. Eltis, *The Age of US and UK Machinery,* NEDO Monograph 3 (London: National Economic Development Office, 1974): *AGEM* (table J).

Hughes, James J., and A. P. Thirlwell, "Trends and Cycles in Import Penetration in the UK," *Oxford Bulletin of Economics and Statistics,* vol. 39 (November 1977): *IMPB* (table 2).

Wragg, Richard, and James Robertson, *Post-War Trends in Employment, Productivity, Output, Labour Costs and Prices by Industry in the United Kingdom,* Department of Employment, Research Paper 3 (HMSO, 1978): *GTFPB* (table 7).

Some variables are available only for industry categories more aggregated than those shown in table 3. Where necessary, I used the value of an aggregated classification for any of the industries included within it unless general knowledge suggested that this procedure would be inappropriate in the particular case.

My strategy toward the year of observation for these variables needs to be explained. Ideally, one would pick a reasonably long and "representative" run of years and secure average observations on each variable over these years (assuming no hypotheses are involved that specifically require time lags). That practice is normally impossible in studies of this type because some variables are collected only now and then, and others may be available only for a single year (or be measured incommensurably in different years). My strategy was governed by the years for which full census-of-production (or census-of-manufactures) data are available in both the United Kingdom and United States—technically only 1963 and 1972, but I cheated by assuming that 1967 (U.S.) and 1968 (U.K.) could be regarded as the same year. Variables from the censuses of production or manufactures were averaged for these three years whenever feasible. Other variables were averaged for periods as long as possible within 1963–72, with the following exceptions: a few variables, such as *PCFB,* seemed likely to vary so little between years that averaging was not worthwhile; a few other variables were averaged over years running beyond 1972, because they came available only for recent years and seemed likely to vary enough from year to year to make averaging important.

The variable *UNIONB* (proportion of employees covered by collective-bargaining agreements) is in fact the sum of three variables given in the source: employees covered by national collective agreements only, employees covered by company, district, or local collective agreements only, and employees covered by national agreements with a supplementary local agreement. Each component pertains to the month of April 1973. Each figure is a weighted average of male and female manual employees when the data are given for both, but only for one group if the source provides no entry for the other. Sometimes individual industries are not shown, but single industries or small aggregates can be derived by subtracting published components from the totals given for "orders" (that is, broad sectors) in the standard industrial classification.

For some industries values of the variable $REGB$ (proportion of employment located in "old" industrial regions) are understated because details are suppressed in the source to conform to rules on disclosure. For most industries these understatements should be small, but that may not be the case when the total number of establishments in the industry is small.

Data for $FOSB$ (foreign-owned enterprises' share of sales) are given not for industry sales but for the principal products classified to each industry. These may in the aggregate account for significantly less than all industry sales. When the figure for some of an industry's principal products is suppressed on account of disclosure rules, the calculation was usually based on the remaining products. In a few cases independent evidence was used as the basis for a rough estimate of the missing value.

Published data on seller concentration ($C5B$) for some industries give the share of the largest six enterprises rather than the largest five. For these industries a figure for five-firm concentration was approximated. The method used varied slightly, but in general it involved establishing a minimum value on the assumption that the leading six firms are the same size, establishing a maximum value on the assumption that the sixth firm is as small as it could be and still be included in its employment-size class, and averaging the two.

A similar problem was posed by the variable $LGPB$ (proportion of employment accounted for by establishments with 1,000 or more employees), because the boundaries of the employment-size classes reported vary from industry to industry. Sometimes a class straddles 1,000 employees; more often, in industries with relatively small plants, the open-ended top category has a lower boundary less than 1,000. In these cases I calculated minimum and maximum estimates of the variable and averaged them. For instance, when the open-ended category has a lower boundary of 500 employees, the maximum employment in plants employing 1,000 or over would occur if the category contained the largest possible number of plants employing exactly 1,000 (given that the remaining ones must employ at least 500 on average). The minimum would result if all plants but one employed 999 and the remaining plant the balance of the category's total. The minimum is of course zero if the average plant is smaller than 1,000, and the maximum is the whole category if the average plant is larger than 1,000.

Appendix C: The Structure of the Regression Model

Cross-industry studies of production relations suffer from the disadvantage that the industries in question cannot reasonably be assumed to operate on the same production function. When one also lacks (as I do) sufficient information to estimate production-function relations for the individual industries in the sample, one is able to impose only very general constraints on the form of the cross-industry relation. My model supposes nothing more than that capital and labor are substitutes for one another and that observed input combinations are such that all factor marginal products are positive. Differences among industries in marginal rates of factor substitution are a source of random disturbance.

Hart has recently considered the problems of estimating efficiency in cross section by fitting a locus that relates labor inputs per unit of net output to capital inputs.[97] Not only does the standard procedure estimate a best-fit relation rather than an envelope, but also the usual linear specification neglects the diminishing marginal rate of factor substitution that one normally expects to prevail and for this reason alone could rank the observed units incorrectly on their efficiency. The problem that Hart identifies does not arise directly with my research design. With the dependent variable stated as relative labor productivity and regressed on relative capital intensity, I am in essence estimating how far the common unit isoquant describing the input-output relations of U.K. industries lies outside the one common to their U.S. counterparts. There is no obvious way to deduce a proper functional form for such a relation. As a check on the form used in the text, I inverted both the dependent variable and the variable indicating relative capital intensity and reestimated the equations, leaving all other variables in their original forms. Aside from the expected reversals of signs, no substantial change occurred from the results reported in the text.

97. P. E. Hart, "Farrell-Efficiency, Profitability and Industrial Structure" (University of Reading, 1978). See also Douglas Todd, *The Relative Efficiency of Small and Large Firms,* Committee of Inquiry on Small Firms, Research Report 18 (HMSO, 1971).

Comments by S. J. Prais

WE ARE ALL much in debt to Richard Caves for his threefold contribution: first, for his comprehensive survey of previous studies; second, for his own statistical analysis of variations among British industries in their productivity levels relative to these levels in their U.S. counterparts; and third, for his careful reflections on policy matters.

Before finer points are discussed, it is perhaps well to recall the overall size of the disparity between British and American productivity in manufacturing and for how long it has persisted. For 1935–39 Rostas, using a selected sample of manufacturing industries and mainly physical output data from the census of production, calculated that output per worker in the United States was 2.2 times that in the United Kingdom;[98] for 1950 Paige and Bombach carried out a more comprehensive calculation (also based on censuses of production) and found a factor of 2.7 in favor of the United States;[99] for 1970 a calculation carried out by D. T. Jones and myself (based on value added in manufacturing deflated by purchasing-power-parity exchange rates for manufactured goods) yielded a ratio of 2.85; and an extrapolation to 1978, using indexes of output and employment, yielded a ratio of 3.0.[100] Roughly speaking, one may therefore say that the British worker in manufacturing today produces each week only a third of what an American worker does. It is a mark of the failure of long-term British economic performance over the past forty years that this gap has not been removed but, if anything (and there are of course qualifications to such comparisons), may have widened.

Two small crumbs of comfort can be found. First, the American advantage is not as great in nonmanufacturing as in manufacturing (haircuts seem to require as many barber minutes on both sides of the Atlantic, and

98. Based on thirty-one industries, choosing years with roughly the same capacity utilization; for simplicity I quote, both here and subsequently, only the results for an ideal index based on British and American weights. L. Rostas, *Comparative Productivity in British and American Industry*, National Institute of Economic and Social Research, Occasional Paper 13 (Cambridge: Cambridge University Press, 1948), p. 27.

99. Deborah Paige and Gottfried Bombach, *A Comparison of National Output and Productivity of the United Kingdom and the United States* (Paris: Organisation for Economic Co-operation and Development, 1959), p. 33.

100. Details will appear in a forthcoming National Institute of Economic and Social Research Occasional Paper.

Britain has some exemplary retailing institutions, such as Marks and Spencer, Tesco, and Great Universal Stores). Consequently, for gross domestic product as a whole, the British disadvantage is fortunately not quite so catastrophic as it is in manufacturing alone. Second, average hours worked per week have fallen more rapidly in Britain than in the United States, though they remain slightly higher in Britain.[101] The American advantage in output per man-hour has thus not increased as rapidly as its advantage in output per man-week (a rise in the ratio from 2.7 in 1935–39 to about 3.2 in 1978 for output per man-hour, instead of from 2.2 to 3.0 for output per man-week).

The size of the differential of course varies from industry to industry. The British are especially poor at assembling motor vehicles (the Americans are about five times as productive per employee), but they are not bad at making glass, carpets, or bricks (a ratio of less than 2.0). The differential is kept within certain limits by the familiar factors governing international trade. Caves notes the relevance of the principle of comparative advantage, which of course ultimately governs international specialization: those industries in which U.K. productivity is relatively poor can be expected to disappear in Britain. He suggests that the economic commentator or analyst can do little to improve the situation: the analyst's role, in this view, seems to be limited to that of a prophet of doom who points his finger at those industries next in line for extinction— industries from which the faithful would do well to remove their trust and resources in good time.

Nevertheless, by comparing other differences in the "structure" of industries with their productivity differences, Caves has elucidated a number of factors deserving particular attention.

• *Quality of skills.* His most statistically significant result is that British productivity is lower in industries requiring technical and managerial skills. This is consistent with what is known of the skill content of international trade: U.S. exports tend to be more skill-intensive than British exports and, correspondingly, U.K. imports tend to be more skill-intensive than U.S. imports (as shown in a number of studies by Donald B. Keesing). Britain thus stands at a disadvantage in skills. But fuller investiga-

---

101. Probably about 5 percent more hours are worked by the average British than the average American employee in manufacturing. Curious as it may seem, statistics on average hours worked, taking into account part-timers, are not readily available in Britain.

tions need to be made before one can say just how great the skill shortage is and can describe its nature.

• *Capital intensity.* Earlier studies by Rostas and Frankel were not able to show, contrary to the authors' expectations, that America's superior labor productivity was related to a greater amount of capital per employee.[102] Caves's present results are similar: the effects of differences in capital intensity in the two countries are not statistically significant. A possible explanation is that capital-intensive industries tend to have large plants. In Britain, however, the greater contribution of capital in these industries is partly or wholly offset by the greater labor-relations problems that arise in larger plants. (The British motor and steel industries seem to illustrate this point.) Unfortunately the cross-sectional multiple-regression analyses in Caves's paper do not provide more than suggestive support for this proposition; such analyses have so far not yielded clearer results, partly because of measurement difficulties (as Caves notes), but possibly also because of a more difficult "identification" problem. For it is conceivable that those industries in which Britain had a poor productivity record were the ones in which it was investing heavily in the years considered—with a view to raising its productivity. The measure of capital intensity used by Caves, it will be remembered, was the ratio of gross *investment* per man in Britain to that investment in America. His equation might thus combine two results: (a) a negative relation between productivity and capital investment because business was investing most heavily where productivity was low; and (b) a positive relation between productivity and capital intensity because productivity was raised most where investment was greatest. Such a two-way relationship would require a rather more complex analysis than Caves provides.

A fuller analysis of the effects of capital intensity ought also to consider both the absolute *level* of capital per head in each industry (either in Britain or in the United States, or an average of the two), and the *ratio* of those levels in the two countries. In that way it could be explicitly shown whether the shortfall in British productivity is greater in capital-intensive industries (which might support the view that Britain is poor in capital-intensive industries because of an underlying technological back-

102. Rostas, *Comparative Productivity in British and American Industry;* Marvin Frankel, *British and American Manufacturing Productivity: A Comparison,* Bureau of Economic and Business Research, University of Illinois Bulletin 81 (University of Illinois Press, 1957).

wardness), or whether the shortfall in productivity is greater where a greater shortfall in capital investment exists—irrespective of whether the industry has a high or a low capital intensity—and so support the view that more investment would provide a remedy.

• *Strike activity.* Caves presents some statistical support for a finding that strike activity, measured in various complex ways, lowers productivity. This finding has an obvious element: if the labor force is on strike for three months in a year, one might expect it to produce something like one-fourth less than it would if it worked the whole year. The purpose of a regression analysis is to show whether the reduction in production is much greater than this expectation (because of consequential disorder), or whether, as some commentators suggest, it is smaller, since after a strike workers make up for lost production to some degree. It would be helpful if Caves would interpret his regression coefficient so as to cast light on this issue. I believe—as I think Caves also implies—that the loss to productivity attributable to strike activity, for example in the British car industry, is much greater than the 1 to 2 percent of working days lost a year that are recorded in the official statistics.

• *Size of plant.* It is not widely realized that manufacturing plants in Britain and the United States do not differ very greatly in their number of employees; for example, in Britain the median plant had 440 employees in 1973, and in the United States it had 380 employees in 1972. The problem with British productivity seems to be that organizational diseconomics of scale, which are exemplified by strike activity but which in reality are more deeply rooted, have become so great that they now often outweigh potential technical gains that should arise from producing on a larger scale. The correlation across industries between strike activity and median plant size in Britain is now as high as 0.85, which makes it difficult for a statistical analysis to separate the effects on productivity of size of plant from the effects of strikes. Although the analysis by Caves suggests that plant size and enterprise size probably reduce productivity, his results are not statistically significant. The lack of significance is possibly due to multicollinearity with strike activity, as just mentioned, or possibly to Caves's particular measure of plant size (the proportion of the industry's employment in plants with over 1,000 employees). I have had the benefit of seeing a very similar analysis (by Matthew D. Shapiro of Yale University) that related relative productivity in Britain and the United States to relative average plant sizes and that included other explanatory factors but not strikes. That analysis yielded an elasticity of productivity with respect to plant size of -0.20, which was significant at the 5 percent level.

I now turn briefly to a few statistical points of a more technical nature. First, some of Caves's explanatory variables are ratios of British to American values, but others relate only to British absolute values or only to American absolute values. I would have thought that ratios would normally be chosen, since his dependent variable is also a ratio (but there are exceptions, as in the case of capital intensity mentioned above). Second, Caves uses certain combinations of variables that lead to difficulties in sampling theory. For example, in removing the linear component of female participation from his strike variables, he derives a modified strike variable that, as I understand it, cannot be regarded as a fixed variable in the subsequent regression analysis; consequently, his tests of significance are no longer valid. The problem can be avoided by bringing female-participation rates directly into the regression as an additional variable. I am puzzled why Caves did not do so. Third, when comparing relative *rates of growth* of different industries with their relative productivity *levels,* he refers in note 83 to the possible dangers of a "regression fallacy," which, he says, he has avoided. But I think further reflection may convince him that he has avoided that trap only partially. He defined his levels as an average of the beginning, middle, and end of the period over which he measured the change; two out of three of the observations making up that average (namely, the middle and end observations) are thus definitionally correlated with the change. A positive correlation between the average level (as he defined it) and the change is thus almost inevitable; the trap can be avoided by correlating the change with the level taken at the beginning of the period only.

I return finally to more substantial issues. Taken as a whole, Caves's comparisons across industries suggest that Britain is particularly backward in those industries that (a) require a greater degree of managerial sophistication, (b) are organized on a large scale, and (c) are subject to strikes. This draws attention to two aspects of our industrial structure on which policy should be (and to some extent already is) focusing: first, the modification of our framework of industrial relations, which at present is such that production in large plants is particularly difficult; and second, the British labor force's relatively low level of technical and vocational training. In the concluding paragraph of his main text, Caves questions whether a "democratic political system can eliminate" a problem that "originates deep within the social system." But I remain hopeful that if economic research could convincingly show that Britain's poor manufacturing productivity was, to a measurable and substantial extent, attributable to such matters as the frequency of strikes and the paucity of our vocational training, then ways would be found to overcome them. Caves's paper is to be welcomed as providing an important stepping-stone for reaching that objective.

JOSEPH A. PECHMAN

Taxation

TAXATION is one of the most controversial issues of public policy in the United Kingdom. The tax philosophies of the two major political parties differ markedly, and each party makes adjustments in the tax system when it is in power; as a result, the tax structure has changed frequently in the postwar period. It is widely held that the tax system distorts economic behavior, though the degree of distortion is hard to quantify. How Britain deals with its tax problem may have a significant effect on its future economic performance and on the stability of its social and political system.

Elements of the Tax System

The U.K. system has all the important components of the tax systems of most of the industrialized world: a graduated individual income tax, a

I wish to acknowledge with gratitude the advice and assistance I received from R. W. R. Price of the National Institute of Economic and Social Research; Arnold Lovell, Douglas Todd, and L. J. H. Beighton of H. M. Treasury; Sir Donald Mac-Dougall and his associates of the Confederation of British Industry; Jonathan Shields of the British Embassy in Washington; and my research assistants, James G. Mc-Clave, Jr., who programmed the tax incidence calculations, Andrew S. Winokur, who prepared the comparisons of taxes in selected countries, and Timothy A. Cohn, who checked the manuscript for accuracy. I am also indebted to Ronald Barbach, Richard E. Caves, Richard Goode, Nicholas Kaldor, John A. Kay, Mervyn A. King, Lawrence B. Krause, Kenneth Messere, Neil Munro, Alan T. Peacock, Robert R. Nield, Alan R. Prest, Stanley S. Surrey, Terry Ward, and G. D. N. Worswick for comments on an early draft of this paper. Research on tax burdens in the United Kingdom and the United States was supported by a grant from the National Science Foundation.

capital gains tax, a corporation tax and an imputation system that provides relief for dividends at the individual income tax level, payroll taxes, a value-added tax, excise duties on specific commodities, a unified estate and gift tax, and a property tax to finance local government.

In 1976 the United Kingdom raised 43 percent of its combined national and local tax revenues from the individual income tax and the corporation tax, 26 percent from taxes on commodities and services, 19 percent from payroll taxes, 11 percent from property taxes, and 1 percent from death and gift taxes (table 4).[1] This structure more nearly resembled those of the United States, Japan, and Canada than those of the United Kingdom's European neighbors, which rely more heavily on consumption and payroll taxes and less heavily on property taxes.

The chief distinguishing features of the U.K. system are first, very high rates of individual income tax throughout the income scale, and second, generous allowances for capital investment. Although the income tax is highly progressive, the tax system as a whole is not progressive.

The Individual Income Tax

The individual income tax was introduced as a temporary measure in 1799 and made permanent in 1842. Originally, the tax was levied at a flat rate; in 1909 a surtax that applied to only the top 2 percent of income recipients was added. In 1973 the basic rate and surtax were unified into one graduated structure, but the basic rate still extended over a wide band of the distribution. For tax year 1978–79 the rates ranged from 25 percent on the first £750 of taxable income and 33 percent on the next £7,250 to a maximum of 83 percent on taxable incomes in excess of £24,000 (table 5).[2] A surcharge of 15 percent was also imposed on investment income above £2,250. For 1979–80 the 33 percent rate was reduced to 30 percent, and the band to which it applied was widened to include taxable incomes up to £10,000, while the top rate was reduced to 60 percent on taxable incomes over £25,000. The threshold of the 15 percent surcharge was also raised to £5,000.[3]

1. Tables 4–16 appear in the appendix to this paper.
2. The British income tax year runs from April 6 of one calendar year through April 5 of the following year.
3. In 1978–79 the first £1,700 of investment income was exempt from the surcharge, and the next £550 was taxed at a 10 percent rate. (The thresholds for the surcharge were higher for persons over sixty-five.) For 1979–80 the 10 percent rate was abolished and the £5,000 threshold was applied to all taxpayers.

The personal exemptions under the income tax, which have been indexed to the cost of living since 1977, are low compared with exemptions in other countries.[4] Married couples usually file joint returns, but if husband and wife agree, they may file separate returns and be taxed on their earnings as two single persons, with the wife reporting her earnings and the husband reporting the rest of their income.[5] On joint returns, an allowance is provided for earnings of working spouses up to the amount of the single person's exemption. Persons over sixty-five also receive an additional allowance, which is withdrawn at higher income levels.

A flat tax of 30 percent on capital gains was enacted in 1956,[6] but exemptions have gradually been introduced. In 1979–80 the first £1,000 of capital gains were tax exempt, and reduced rates were provided for gains up to £9,500 (table 5). When the tax was enacted, capital gains were deemed to be realized when transferred by gift or at death; in 1971 deemed realization was repealed for bequests and most gifts, but retained for gifts of businesses, assets used in businesses, or shares in a family company. Capital gains on the sale or gift of a family business by persons sixty-five or over are exempt up to £50,000;[7] gains on the disposal of owner-occupied principal residences are completely exempt.

Numerous special provisions have been adopted under the income tax. Through 1978–79 a tax credit at one-half the basic rate was provided for life insurance premiums up to one-sixth of total income. For administrative convenience, beginning in 1979–80 the government paid 17.5 percent of policyholders' premiums, up to one-sixth of total income, direct to the insurance companies; the policyholders paid the remaining 82.5 percent. Employee as well as employer contributions to approved pension plans are not subject to tax, and lump-sum payments from pension plans

4. The government has discretionary power not to index the exemptions in any year. The exemption for married couples is maintained at roughly 1.5 times the single person's exemption. For 1979–80 the exemptions were £1,075 for single persons and £1,675 for married couples. The exemption for children was phased out at the end of 1978–79, but a cash benefit is still paid directly to mothers.

5. Whether a married couple elects joint or separate taxation, either husband or wife can ask for separate assessment, in which case their total liability is unchanged but is split between them according to prescribed rules.

6. In 1978–79 a special tax of 80 percent was levied on land development gains over £160,000 in lieu of the capital gains tax. The first £10,000 of such gains were exempt, and the next £150,000 were taxed at 66⅔ percent. In 1979–80 the land development tax rate was reduced to 60 percent and the exemption raised to £50,000.

7. There is a sliding scale of relief for persons between sixty and sixty-five.

or from termination of employment are not taxable up to one and one-half times the final salary. Modest amounts of interest on special forms of saving, such as national saving certificates, ordinary deposits in national savings banks, indexed-linked savings certificates for retired persons, and save-as-you-earn schemes, are not subject to tax. Lottery winnings on premium bonds (which pay no interest) are also not taxable. Bonds issued at a discount with low-interest coupons ("low coupon" gilts) are subject to tax on the interest but not on the capital gain when they are redeemed or sold, if held for more than a year. Interest on one home mortgage up to £25,000 is deductible.

Taxes on wages and salaries are withheld at the source under the pay-as-you-earn (PAYE) system. The system operates on a cumulative basis, so that for most wage and salary workers the right amount is withheld by the end of the year. Annuities and interest paid by nonfinancial corporations are also subject to withholding.[8] Dividends are in effect subject to withholding as a result of the imputation system (see below); the operation of the credit within the imputation system ensures that basic-rate taxpayers have no further income tax liability on the dividends they receive.

An annual tax return is required only if a taxpayer's circumstances change or his or her tax situation is complicated. Taxpayers filing a return do not calculate their own tax liability; the return is merely a report of nonwithheld income, allowances, and sales of securities and property in the year just ended and a claim for allowances in the year just beginning. The Board of Inland Revenue adds the amount of withheld income to the return, checks the other items reported, computes the tax, and sends a refund or assesses the taxpayer any balance of tax due. It also calculates the code number for the taxpayer's allowances that is used by the employer in determining the amount of tax to be withheld under PAYE in the following year.

Self-employed persons and those receiving income from sources other than employment (or a pension) are not subject to PAYE. Instead, they receive an assessment from the Board of Inland Revenue—usually in the fall—and are required to pay the tax due in two equal installments, by the following January 1 or July 1. This assessment is based on the income or profits of the previous tax year.

---

8. Interest on building society deposits is paid net of a tax that is somewhat lower than the basic rate. Such interest (including the gross-up for tax paid by the building society) is subject to the rates above the basic rate and the investment surcharge.

The Corporation Income Tax

The basic rate of corporation tax is 52 percent, but in 1978–79 and 1979–80 profits of less than £50,000 were taxed at a rate of 42 percent and the full rate applied to profits above £85,000.[9] Capital gains realized by corporations are subject in effect to a flat 30 percent rate.

A 100 percent deduction is allowed in the first year for investment in plant and equipment. An initial allowance of 50 percent is given on the acquisition of an industrial building, together with annual allowances of 4 percent for twelve years and 2 percent in the thirteenth year. A special "stock relief" formula is provided in lieu of an adjustment of the tax base for inventory profits caused by inflation.[10] Investment grants are provided for approved investments in development areas and Northern Ireland.

Between 1965 and 1973 the corporation tax was a separate tax, and no allowance was made for the corporate tax at the individual income tax level (the classical system). In 1973 an imputation system was introduced to provide a tax credit under the individual income tax for a part of the corporation tax paid on distributed profits. A company making a distribution must make an advance payment on the amounts distributed at the basic individual income tax rate, and this payment is then credited against the corporation tax. Persons receiving dividends include the advance payment in their taxable income and are then allowed credit for the same amount against their own tax. The rate of advance corporation tax, and hence the amount of the tax credit, is fixed by reference to the basic rate of income tax in such a way that the shareholder liable to income tax at the basic rate finds that his liability is met precisely by the tax credit. In effect, the system eliminates the so-called double taxation of dividends to the extent of the basic individual income tax rate.

Payroll Taxes

In the United Kingdom, as in other countries, the social security system is financed largely from payroll taxes.[11] At one time, contributions by both

9. A notch rate of 66.3 percent applied to the amount of profits between £50,000 and £85,000, so that the tax leveled off at 52 percent of total profits at £85,000.

10. Firms were allowed to deduct the increase in the book value of their inventories during the year less 15 percent of their profits from 1973–74 to 1978–79 and 10 percent beginning in 1979–80.

11. The Treasury adds 18 percent of all contributions paid by employees, employers, and the self-employed, as a supplement to the national insurance fund.

employees and employers were paid at a flat amount per employee per week. Since 1975 the social security tax has been levied as a percentage of the employee's earnings. In 1978–79 the tax rate for fully covered employees was 6.5 percent; for their employers the rate was 10 percent on the first £120 of earnings a week for employees earning £17.50 a week or more.[12]

Beginning in April 1977, a surcharge of 2 percentage points was added to the tax paid by employers, and an additional surcharge of 1.5 percentage points went into effect on October 1, 1978. Because the surcharge is for general revenue purposes, it does not go into the national insurance fund.

In an attempt to divert labor from the service industries to production industries, a selective employment tax was in effect from September 5, 1966, through April 1, 1973. The tax, which ranged from £1.25 per employee per week in 1966–67 to £2.40 in 1969–71, was rebated to firms in the production industries.[13] The selective employment tax was the subject of considerable controversy and was repealed because of strong business opposition.

Consumption Taxes

The consumption taxes consist of value-added tax and excise and customs duties.

The value-added tax was introduced on April 1, 1973, to replace the selective employment tax and purchase tax that had been the mainstay of the consumption tax structure since 1940. The purchase tax was levied on a wide range of manufactured goods (automobiles, home appliances, furniture, and so forth) with variable rates that sometimes went over 100 percent of wholesale prices. The value-added tax was substituted partly because it was a move toward tax harmonization with the European Community and partly because purchase tax did not apply to services and discriminated, some people felt, against the taxed commodities. The value-added tax also has the advantage that, through the system of refunds to business, the tax can be confined to consumer goods.

12. A married woman may elect to pay at a reduced rate of 2 percent. In this case, she does not receive social security benefits, except insofar as she may be entitled to them by virtue of her husband's contribution.

13. In the early years of the tax, firms in manufacturing industries received a subsidy in addition to the rebate.

In 1978–79 the standard rate of value-added tax was 8 percent, and a 12.5 percent rate was imposed on gasoline, home appliances, boats and aircraft, cameras, furs, and jewelry. In 1979–80 the rates were consolidated and increased to a flat 15 percent. On top of that, a tax of 10 percent of the wholesale price is levied on automobiles. Not all goods and services are subject to the value-added tax: some are exempt and others are subject to a zero rate of tax.[14] The difference between the two categories is that refunds can be claimed for tax paid on component goods and services in the case of zero-rated items, but not in the case of tax-exempt items. Between the annual finance acts the Treasury is permitted by law to raise or lower the value-added tax rates by up to 25 percent.

The United Kingdom levies selective excise taxes on alcoholic beverages, tobacco, gasoline, and betting, and stamp duties on commercial and legal documents. A wide variety of products are subject to protective import duties, which are gradually being aligned with those of the common tariff of the European Community.

Capital Transfer Tax

Before 1975 transfers of property at death were subject to an estate tax, but lifetime gifts made three years before death were tax free. A capital transfer tax was introduced on gifts made after March 26, 1974, and on transfers at death after March 12, 1975.

The capital transfer tax is applied to a person's lifetime transfers as they are made, on a cumulative basis. The last stage of the cumulation is the inclusion in the tax base of property transferred at death. In 1978–79 no tax was due on the first £25,000 of the cumulative total. Thereafter, the rate scale began at 10 percent and rose to a maximum of 75 percent on the amount of transfers above £2,010,000. Lifetime transfers up to £510,000 are taxed at reduced rates, but the tax on gifts is included in the final capital transfer tax base. The tax does not apply to transfers between husband and wife during life or at death. Outright gifts of £100 to one person in any year are exempt from tax; transfers by any one person up to £2,000 per year (plus the amount by which such transfers fell short of £2,000 in the previous year) are also exempt. For capital

14. The value-added tax applies to only about half of total consumption. The exempt category includes land sales, postal services, insurance, gambling, health services, and education. The zero-rated category includes all exported goods, most foods, books and newspapers, fuel and power, construction, drugs and medicines.

transfer tax purposes, the value of small business and agricultural property is reduced by 50 percent and the value of minority shareholdings in unquoted companies is reduced by 20 percent.

Local Revenues

The only source of local tax revenue is the property tax, called the "rates," which are paid by the owners of property. In principle, the rates are levied on the net rental value of real estate (land and buildings in the open market). In practice, there are gross distortions in tax payments because revaluations are made infrequently (only three times since the end of World War II: 1956, 1963, and 1973), and for long periods assessments do not reflect changes in relative rental values of different properties. Agricultural land and buildings, church property, and property of local governments are not subject to the rates. Rebates of the rates are provided for low-income households.[15] In 1975, 28 percent of local government revenues came from the rates and 17 percent from rents and other nontax sources; the remaining 55 percent came from national government grants.

Tax Burdens

The aggregate tax burden in the United Kingdom, when compared with that in other developed countries, does not seem excessive. In 1976 U.K. tax revenues (including social security contributions) amounted to 36.7 percent of gross domestic product (at market prices), which was 2 percentage points lower than the median level for twelve other advanced industrial countries in Europe, North America, and Asia (table 6). Germany, Italy, Canada, the United States, and Japan had lower tax ratios—in the case of Japan, substantially lower. The ratios for Austria and France were slightly higher than that of the United Kingdom, and the ratios for the Scandinavian and Benelux countries were much higher.[16]

15. The rebate amounts to 40 percent for households whose income equals their needs requirement. The rebate is increased by 8 percent of the difference between needs and income if needs exceed income and is reduced by 6 percent of the difference if income exceeds needs. There are also rent and electricity rebates for low-income households.

16. Little has happened since 1976 to alter significantly the rankings shown in table 6.

Among the various revenue sources, only the individual income tax seems to be relatively high in the United Kingdom. Its individual income tax accounted for 14 percent of gross domestic product in 1976, which was higher than in all other countries except Sweden, Denmark, and Norway. Its consumption and payroll tax ratios were below average. Taxes on corporations and on wealth are relatively small sources almost everywhere, and the United Kingdom is no exception. Following Anglo-Saxon tradition, the United Kingdom relies more heavily on the property tax (for local tax purposes) than other European countries do.

Individual Income Tax

The individual income tax starts at a lower income level and has higher initial starting rates in the United Kingdom than in most other countries (table 7). The 1978–79 top-bracket rate of 83 percent on earned income was close to the highest in the world; the top rate of 98 percent on investment income was surpassed only in Algeria (which had a top rate of 100 percent).

For the average U.K. production worker, the *average* rate of income tax paid on 1976 earnings was 20 percent; if employee payroll tax rates are included, the average tax rate was 26 percent. The *marginal* rates were 35 percent for the income tax alone and 41 percent for income and payroll taxes. These rates were very high when compared with the rates in such countries as France, Germany, Italy, and the United States, but low when compared with the rates in Sweden and Denmark (table 8). The 1979 reduction in the basic rate to 30 percent will still leave the marginal rates on earned income of the average production worker at a higher level in the United Kingdom than in most European countries, Canada, and the United States.

At higher income levels, the U.K. income tax in 1978–79 was clearly among the highest in the world. For income that is entirely earned, the U.K. tax was not as high as the taxes in Sweden and (in most brackets) Denmark, but higher than in other European countries, Japan, and the United States (figure 1). For investment income, international comparisons are difficult because some countries (such as Sweden, Denmark, and West Germany) have wealth taxes, while the United Kingdom has the investment income surcharge. Nevertheless, the taxes paid by the wealthy on investment income were at least as high in the United Kingdom as in

Figure 1. *Effective Tax Rates on Earned Income for a Married Couple with Two Children, by Earned Income Level, Selected Countries, 1978*

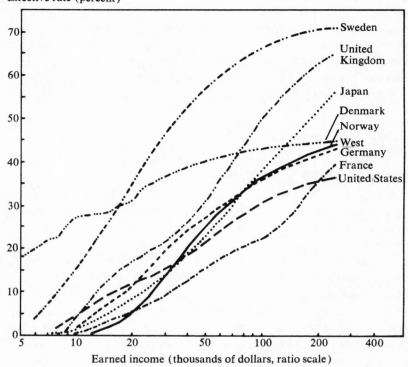

Effective rate (percent)

Earned income (thousands of dollars, ratio scale)

Source: Table 9.

a. Income has been converted to U.S. equivalents on the basis of the estimated ratios of relative earnings of production workers in 1978. Standard deductions and average employment deductions were allowed where applicable. Assumes there is only one earner in the family.

the Scandinavian countries and were certainly higher than in the other European countries.[17]

A major element in the public debate on taxation in the United Kingdom was the rise in real individual income tax burdens as inflation pushed people into higher tax brackets. The personal exemptions did not keep pace with inflation from 1973–74 to 1976–77, and tax rates were raised

17. Sweden has a maximum effective rate of 85 percent for the sum of income and wealth taxes. But because the wealth tax cannot be reduced by more than 50 percent, taxpayers with low incomes may pay a tax of more than 85 percent of their income. The United Kingdom has no maximum effective rate.

significantly in 1974–75 and 1975–76. From 1977 on, personal exemptions have been indexed; tax rates were reduced moderately in 1977–78 and 1978–79 and sharply in the top brackets in 1979–80. As a result, between 1973–74 and 1978–79 effective tax rates rose in real terms for practically all taxpayers. Thus a married person with two children paid a tax of 10.9 percent on an earned income of £2,000 in 1973–74.[18] In 1975–76, when the tax rates reached a peak, the tax on the same real income was 16.3 percent. Even though the rates were reduced, the tax in 1978–79 still amounted to 12.2 percent at the same real income level (figure 2).[19] For real earnings of £5,000 in 1973–74, there was a net increase in the tax burden of 3 percent of income over the five-year period; and for earnings of £8,000 and over, the increase amounted to 10 percent or more. The 1979–80 tax reductions reduced real tax burdens substantially below the 1973–74 levels for taxpayers with 1973–74 real earnings above £20,000, but those with real earnings between £5,000 and £20,000 still paid higher taxes in 1979–80 than in 1973–74, and those below £5,000 paid about the same taxes as in 1973–74.

To give some idea of the combined burden of all the elements of the U.K. individual income tax (income tax plus investment income surcharge plus capital gains tax), the effective income tax rates in the United Kingdom are compared with those in the United States in table 1. To make the comparison, the rates in both countries were applied to an estimate of the distribution of income in the United States in 1978.[20] Because a two-earner married couple in the United Kingdom may elect separate taxation of the wife's earnings, separate calculations were made for households with one earner and two or more earners. For purposes of these calculations, U.K. incomes were translated to an equivalent U.S.

18. The £2,000 level was slightly below the average 1973 earnings of manual workers in the United Kingdom. The tax calculations assume that the taxpayer had deductions (in addition to the personal exemptions) of 5 percent of his income and the children were under eleven years of age. The cash benefits for children introduced in April 1976 are treated as tax credits in these calculations, and the family's exemption is reduced by the "clawback" for the family allowance given to the second child.

19. The consumer price index rose 48 percent from 1973–74 to 1975–76 and 78 percent from 1975–76 to 1978–79 (calculated between the midpoints of the fiscal years). Thus an income of £5,000 was equivalent in real terms to £7,400 in 1975–76 and to £13,170 in 1978–79.

20. Because of the lack of data for the top brackets in the United Kingdom, it is impossible to calculate the effective tax rates when the U.S. and U.K. tax rates are applied to the U.K. distribution.

Figure 2. *Effective U.K. Tax Rates on Earned Income for a Married Couple with Two Children, by Real Income Level, 1973–74, 1975–76, 1978–79, 1979–80*

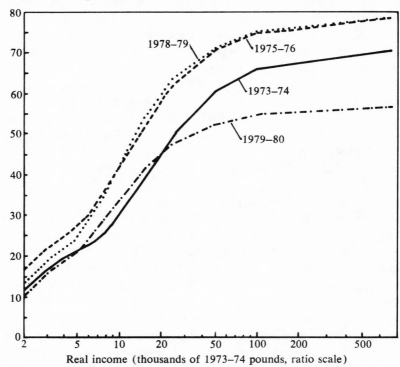

Effective rate (percent)

Real income (thousands of 1973–74 pounds, ratio scale)

Source: Table 10.

basis by using a 2.86:1 ratio, which in 1978 was approximately the ratio of average production worker earnings in the United States to those in the United Kingdom.[21]

Table 1 shows that in 1978, for the great majority of household units,

21. Average production worker earnings are assumed to represent relative incomes in the two countries. The classification in table 1 is by total money factor incomes plus realized capital gains. Income excludes the tax imputed to dividends, but the tax is net of the dividend credit. The income data were obtained by projecting the Brookings 1970 MERGE file to 1978. The file contains earnings figures for both spouses in a two-earner couple; the tax on such couples is on a separate and combined basis, whichever is lower. The U.S. figures include state and local income taxes.

Table 1. *Effective Rates of Personal Income Taxes for One-Earner and Two-or-More Earner Households, by Income Class, United Kingdom and United States, 1978*

		Effective rate (percent)			
		One-earner households		*Two-or-more earner households*	
Income class[a] (thousands of dollars)	*Cumulative percent of household units in United States*	*United Kingdom*	*United States*	*United Kingdom*	*United States*
0–3	20.8	0.6	−1.6[b]	3.8	−3.2[b]
3–4	23.6	4.9	−0.7[b]	6.4	−3.7[b]
4–5	25.9	10.7	1.6	4.5	−3.0[b]
5–7.5	33.0	12.1	5.4	5.4	−0.3[b]
7.5–10	41.0	17.1	9.1	9.1	3.2
10–12.5	49.3	20.3	11.5	12.0	5.8
12.5–15	57.6	21.8	13.2	14.8	7.6
15–17.5	65.7	23.6	14.9	16.7	9.2
17.5–20	72.6	24.0	16.7	16.7	10.6
20–25	82.6	25.1	18.0	16.7	12.0
25–30	89.3	26.0	20.0	17.2	14.0
30–40	95.2	29.0	22.3	15.6	15.5
40–50	97.4	31.6	27.0	16.4	17.9
50–60	98.3	35.3	26.9	17.6	19.3
60–75	99.0	41.2	35.3	22.2	21.7
75–100	99.5	49.5	29.3	30.9	25.5
100–500	100.0	52.2	36.4	48.9	35.0
500–1,000	100.0	45.3	45.9	59.9	47.3
1,000 and over	100.0	46.1	47.2	54.6	51.0
Total[c]	100.0	22.1	14.2	18.4	14.1

Source: Calculations based on Brookings 1970 MERGE file projected to 1978. U.K. incomes are translated to an equivalent U.S. basis by using a 2.86:1 ratio. Figures are rounded.

a. Money factor incomes plus realized capital gains. Income does not include tax imputed to dividends, but tax is net of the dividend credit.

b. Effective tax rates are negative, reflecting cash benefits for children in the United Kingdom and the earned income credit in the United States.

c. Includes household units with negative incomes not shown separately.

the U.K. income tax was clearly much heavier than the U.S. tax—particularly in so-called middle-income brackets. In the $10,000–$12,500 income class (which is close to the median household income in the United States), the average effective tax rate for a one-earner household was 20.3 percent at the U.K. tax rates and only 11.5 percent at the U.S. rates. For households at this income level with two or more earners, the U.K. effective rate was 12 percent and the U.S. rate 5.8 percent. Above the median, the U.K. rate for two-earner married couples flattened out because of the option to be taxed on their earnings separately;[22] as a result, the U.K. effective rate was lower than the U.S. rate for such couples with incomes between $30,000 and $60,000. Thereafter, the U.K. tax increased more rapidly and again exceeded the U.S. tax. In total, when applied to the U.S. income distribution in 1978, the U.K. income taxes were 56 percent higher than the U.S. income taxes for one-earner households (22.1 percent versus 14.2 percent) and 30 percent higher for households with two or more earners (18.4 percent versus 14.1 percent).

Taxes on Corporate Earnings

In contrast to the U.K. individual income tax, the U.K. corporation income tax is modest by international standards. The general tax rate of 52 percent is close to the rates usually adopted by the developed countries.[23] The capital consumption allowances and investment grants available in the United Kingdom are as generous as those in most other countries. In addition, full write-offs are allowed for plant and equipment; these write-offs and the stock relief provisions have virtually eliminated the corporate tax for industrial and commercial companies.[24]

Under the imputation system that was adopted in 1973, the portion of the corporate tax on distributed earnings that is equal to the basic individual income tax rate (33 percent in 1978–79 and 30 percent in 1979–

22. The flattening of the U.K. rate above the median is also the result of the wide basic rate band, which extends up to a taxable income of $27,000 for a married person.

23. The rates for 1978 were 56 percent in West Germany, 55 percent in Sweden, 50 percent in France, and 48 percent in Belgium, the Netherlands, and the United States. Only Japan had a substantially lower rate—40 percent. These are the rates for undistributed earnings. Some of these countries tax distributed earnings at lower rates or provide credits for dividends received at the individual income tax level, so that total effective tax rates on company earnings cannot be inferred from the corporate rates alone.

24. According to John Kay and Mervyn King, corporate tax liabilities of industrial and commercial companies declined from £1.5 billion in 1969 to £0.2 billion in 1976, while those of financial companies increased from £0.3 billion to £1.1 billion. The 1976 figures do not include £1.0 billion of advance corporation tax paid. See J. A. Kay and M. A. King, *The British Tax System* (Oxford University Press, 1978), p. 177; and Central Statistical Office, *Economic Trends, Annual Supplement,* 1979 edition (London: Her Majesty's Stationery Office, 1979), p. 150.

80) is regarded as an advance payment of tax by the corporation on behalf of the stockholder. The advance corporate tax is added to the dividend of the shareholder and included in his taxable income, but he is allowed to deduct it as a credit against his tax liability.[25] For example, a person who received a dividend of £48 in 1978–79 included £23.64 (33/67 × 48) of advance corporation tax in his taxable income and then received a credit of £23.64 against his final tax liability. Taxpayers with marginal tax rates of less than 33 percent (23.64 ÷ 71.64) received a credit or refund for the difference, while those with marginal rates of more than 33 percent paid additional tax to make up the difference. For 1979–80 the advance corporation tax and credit on a £48 dividend was £20.57 (30/70 × 48), and the break-even point at which no refund or additional tax was due was at a marginal income tax rate of 30 percent.

However, as a result of the 98 percent maximum rate in 1978–79, the top rate on *distributed* corporate earnings was higher in the United Kingdom than in any other country—higher even than in those countries where the classical system has been retained.[26] For example, in Sweden the corporate rate was 55 percent and the highest individual income tax rate (including local tax) was 83.8 percent. Together, the maximum combined tax on distributed earnings was 92.71 percent (55 + .838 × 45). In the United States, where the corporate rate was 48 percent and the top individual income tax rate was 70 percent, the maximum combined tax on distributed corporate earnings was 84.4 percent (48 + .7 × 52). The reduction of the top U.K. marginal rate to 75 percent in 1979–80 reduced the maximum rate on distributed earnings to 82.8 percent, which is slightly lower than the corresponding top Swedish and U.S. rates.

25. When originally introduced, the 52 percent corporate tax rate for the imputation system was chosen to give the same average yield as the 40 percent rate for the previous "classical" system.

26. The imputation system greatly reduces the taxes paid by shareholders on distributed corporate earnings in the lower income classes, but does very little for those subject to very high individual income tax rates (see table 11). For example, under the classical system, the combined effect of the corporate tax of 52 percent and the 1978–79 marginal individual income tax rates up to 98 percent ranged from 52 percent to 99.04 percent. The imputation system reduced the marginal rates on distributed corporate earnings from a range of 52–99 percent to 28.36–98.57 percent (table 11, column 6). The reason is that a shareholder who was not otherwise subject to tax benefited from the full reduction of 23.64 percentage points in the corporate tax; but at the top of the income scale, the 23.64 percentage point credit was taxed at 98 percent and thus, on balance, provided virtually no relief.

The actual combined tax paid on corporate profits depends on the degree to which profits are taxed at the corporate level and the percentage of after-tax corporate profits paid out in dividends. In the United Kingdom the effective rate of tax on corporate profits is very low because of the generous allowances for capital consumption and the adjustment that has been made in recent years to eliminate inventory profits from the tax base.[27] Dividend payout ratios seem to be 50 or 60 percent of the net profits of corporations as calculated for tax purposes, but only about 10 percent of profits before capital consumption and inventory allowances.[28] Thus, even though the theoretical maximum rate on distributed profits remains above 80 percent, the total tax burden on corporate earnings is in practice relatively low in the United Kingdom.

Table 2 compares the tax burdens on corporate earnings in the United Kingdom with those in the United States, by income class, for the year 1978. To make this comparison, retained profits and the taxes paid at the corporate level were allocated to shareholders, the marginal personal tax rates on the dividends (after the dividend credit, in the case of the United Kingdom) were calculated, and the sum of the taxes paid at the corporate and personal levels was then expressed as a percentage of the total corporate earnings in each income class.[29] Again, U.K. incomes were translated to an equivalent U.S. basis by using a 2.86:1 ratio.

As expected, at all income levels the total tax burden on corporate earnings is much higher in the United States than in the United Kingdom.

27. According to R. W. R. Price, the effective rate of tax on corporate profits net of interest payments but before capital consumption allowances varied between 14 and 23 percent in the period from 1960 to 1973. Since 1973 the effective rate has been less than 10 percent. See Price, "Budgetary Policy," in F. T. Blackaby, ed., *British Economic Policy, 1960–74* (Cambridge University Press, 1978), p. 164, for the figures from 1960 to 1973. Estimates for later years were kindly supplied to me by Mr. Price.

28. Mervyn King, *Public Policy and the Corporation* (London: Chapman and Hall, 1977), p. 168; and Central Statistical Office, *Economic Trends, Annual Supplement,* 1979 edition, pp. 150, 155.

29. The definition of corporate earnings follows the official definition of corporate profits in the U.S. national income accounts. The effective U.K. corporate tax rate was estimated by applying the U.K. depreciation allowances to U.S. capital stock figures and adding the net additional payment for advance corporation tax. It was assumed that the adjustments of inventories for inflation are, in the aggregate, roughly the same under the U.K. method of adjustment and the U.S. last-in-first-out (LIFO) method. The U.K. calculations assume that the dividend credit would not affect the U.S. dividend payout ratio. If payouts increased, the combined tax under the U.K. calculations would be lowered.

Table 2. *Effective Rates of Combined Personal and Corporate Income Taxes on Corporate Source Income, by Income Class, United Kingdom and United States, 1978*[a]

Income classes in thousands of dollars; rates in percent

Income class[b]	United Kingdom	United States
0–1	9.7	39.0
1–2	14.5	40.2
2–3	12.6	40.3
3–4	15.2	40.6
4–5	15.9	40.8
5–7.5	16.7	41.8
7.5–10	17.0	42.2
10–12.5	18.2	42.7
12.5–15	17.9	43.0
15–17.5	18.2	44.0
17.5–20	17.7	44.6
20–25	19.1	45.5
25–30	20.4	45.9
30–40	20.6	46.9
40–50	23.4	48.4
50–60	26.7	49.5
60–75	25.3	50.2
75–100	31.2	50.2
100–500	35.8	52.9
500–1,000	36.1	53.2
1,000 and over	35.8	52.6
Total[c]	26.5	48.6

Source: Calculation based on Brookings 1970 MERGE file projected to 1978. U.K. incomes are translated to an equivalent U.S. basis by using a 2.86:1 ratio. Figures are rounded.

a. Includes only household units with income from dividends.

b. Households are classified by their total money factor incomes plus realized capital gains plus retained corporate earnings and corporate tax allocated to shareholders.

c. Includes household units with negative incomes not shown separately.

In the lower-income classes the combined corporate and individual income tax (net of the dividend credit) in 1978 was about 40 percent of corporate earnings under the U.S. tax rates and 15 percent under the U.K. rates. The burden increased in both countries as incomes rose above this level; the rise in the United Kingdom was somewhat more rapid because of the faster rate of individual income tax progression. Nevertheless, the U.K. tax rate remained below the U.S. rate even at the highest levels. At the top of the income scale (incomes of $1,000,000 or more), the total tax burden on corporate earnings was 35.8 percent in the United

Figure 3. *Effective Rates of Total Taxes, United Kingdom and the United States, by Percentiles of Family Units Ranked by Adjusted Family Income, 1978*

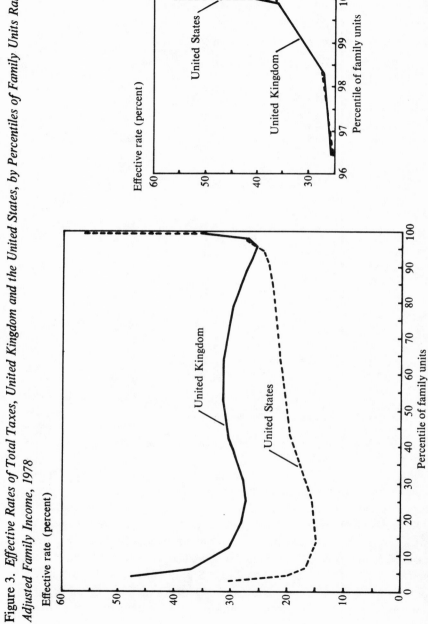

Sources: Tables 12 and 13.

Kingdom and 52.6 percent in the United States.[30] The combined personal and corporate taxes on all corporate earnings was 83 percent higher in the United States than in the United Kingdom (48.6 percent versus 26.5 percent).

Total Tax Burdens

The aggregate burdens of all taxes in the United Kingdom and the United States at 1978 tax rates are compared by income levels in figure 3.[31] Because payroll and consumption taxes were higher in the United Kingdom than in the United States, the total tax burden was much heavier in the United Kingdom at all levels except in the top 5 percent of the income distribution. For example, in the $10,000–$12,500 class, the total tax burden was 27.9 percent of income at the U.K. tax rates and only 15.8 percent at the U.S. rates. Beyond this point, the differences narrowed, with the rates converging between $60,000 and $75,000; above $75,000 the U.K. tax rates were lower than the U.S. rates. For the entire income distribution, taxes averaged 29.9 percent of income under the U.K. tax system and 23.8 percent under the U.S. system.

30. These figures do not allow for any capital gains tax that might be paid on the sale of corporate stock. In 1978 the maximum capital gains rate was higher in the United States than in the United Kingdom (40 percent versus 30 percent), so that the tax burden on corporate earnings including the capital gains tax was also higher at the top income levels in the United States. (In a few cases the maximum U.S. capital gains rate was as high as 49.25 percent.) In 1979 the U.S. capital gains rates were lowered to a maximum of 28 percent; this will narrow the differences in the taxes on corporate earnings between the two countries.

31. The income concept in these calculations is a comprehensive concept of economic income that includes money factor incomes, cash transfer payments, the value of fringe benefits, imputed income of owner-occupied homes, and corporate earnings allocated to shareholders, but excludes transfers in kind (such as medicare and medicaid). To avoid duplication, realized capital gains on corporate stock, which reflect undistributed corporate earnings, are omitted. Customs receipts and death and gift taxes are excluded. The assumptions used in allocating taxes are the progressive incidence assumptions generally associated with Arnold C. Harberger (that is, the personal income tax is borne by the taxpayer, and payroll taxes are borne by the workers; half the corporate tax is borne by the shareholders, and half by the owners of capital in general, including shareholders; the property tax on land is borne by the landowners, and the tax on improvements is borne by owners of capital in general; sales and excise taxes are borne by consumers). For the methodology used in this analysis, see Joseph A. Pechman and Benjamin A. Okner, *Who Bears the Tax Burden?* (Brookings Institution, 1974). The assumptions in figure 2 are the same as variant 1c in that book (see table 3-1, p. 38). U.K. incomes are translated to an equivalent U.S. basis by using a 2.86:1 ratio.

In 1978 the U.K. tax system was regressive for about the bottom quarter of the income distribution, became slightly progressive up to the median income, turned regressive again from the median to the 96th percentile, and was progressive in the top 4 percentiles. The U.S. tax system was regressive for the bottom quintile of the income distribution, mildly regressive up to the 98th percentile, and steeply progressive in the top 2 percentiles.[32] The large reduction in the high-bracket rates in 1979 undoubtedly increased the regressivity of the U.K. tax system in the top part of the income distribution.

Economic Effects of Tax Policy

It is extremely difficult to evaluate the effects of tax policy on the economic behavior of individuals and business in any country. As the other papers in this book indicate, many other policies besides tax policy have had a significant influence on Britain's economic performance. Moreover, the debate over tax policy reflects fundamental disagreements over equity and distributional objectives, although such views are often disguised as economic arguments. It is worthwhile, nevertheless, to review the principal areas of concern and to summarize the evidence to see whether a clear picture emerges.[33]

32. If the less-progressive incidence assumptions associated with Richard A. Musgrave are used (that is, half the corporate tax is borne by consumers and the property tax on improvements are taxes on shelter or passed on to consumers), both the U.K. tax systems are roughly proportional in most of the distribution except at the bottom. The U.S. average effective rates turn up at the very top of the distribution, but the U.K. rates remain flat as a result of the low corporate tax and the low capital gains rate.

The high degree of regressivity in the lowest income classes for both tax systems reflects the fact that consumption exceeds income at this end of the distribution. If income were measured over periods longer than a year, this regressivity would be greatly reduced or eliminated. See Pechman and Okner, *Who Bears the Tax Burden?* pp. 52–54.

33. The evidence is anecdotal as well as quantitative. My impressions about the effects of tax policy in Britain have been obtained from conversations with tax experts during frequent visits over the last fifteen years, from numerous interviews with political, business, and labor leaders and tax experts in the spring of 1978, and from the extensive literature on taxation (which is of very high quality).

The Labor Market

The effect of the tax structure on labor supply and productivity is a major issue in British tax policy. The high marginal tax rates on earnings are alleged to reduce work incentives, encourage the development of methods of nontaxable compensation (through the so-called perks), and promote widespread tax avoidance and evasion.

WORK INCENTIVES. With marginal tax rates exceeding 40 percent for the average production worker and 50 percent or higher for professional or managerial employees, the incentive to substitute leisure or nonmarket activity for paid employment in the United Kingdom is substantial.[34] Whether this incentive has been translated into reduced hours of work or lower work effort is difficult to establish. In the first place, the desire to maintain a given standard of living in the face of high tax rates (the income effect) offsets the negative influence of such rates on work and effort (the substitution effect), and it is impossible to predict which effect will predominate. Second, it is difficult to vary working hours and the quality of work in modern, industrial society. English economists have been trying to determine the substitution effects on the supply of labor by empirical means, but without any more success than economists in other countries have had.[35]

Oddly enough, the studies most frequently cited are by American economists. The earliest study, by George Break of the University of California, was based on intensive interviews of 306 English solicitors and accountants in 1956.[36] Some 40 percent of the respondents reported that taxation had, or would have, some influence on their work, but the posi-

34. Those who are beneficiaries of the welfare system or receive social security or unemployment benefits are subject to the highest marginal tax rates, creating a "poverty trap," which is the subject of great concern in the United Kingdom. However, reform of the welfare, social security, and unemployment systems is outside the scope of this paper.

35. Summaries of the results of the major studies undertaken in England and the United States over the past twenty-five years are provided in Organisation for Economic Co-operation and Development, *Theoretical and Empirical Aspects of the Effects on the Supply of Labour* (Paris: OECD, 1975); N. Stern, "Taxation and Labour Supply—A Partial Survey," in *Taxation and Incentives* (London: Institute for Fiscal Studies, 1970); and an unpublished paper by the Confederation of British Industry, "Managers' Pay—A Survey" (London, June 1978).

36. George F. Break, "Income Taxes and Incentives to Work: An Empirical Study," *American Economic Review,* vol. 47 (September 1957), pp. 529–49.

tive and negative effects almost canceled out one another. On the basis of this evidence, Break concluded that the net effect of taxation was small. In 1969 Donald Fields and W. T. Stanbury repeated the Break study, this time for a sample of 285 English solicitors and accountants.[37] The percentage of respondents reporting negative effects on their work rose, but the net effect after allowing for those reporting definite positive effects remained small.[38] Studies by other Americans, based on U.S. data, generally confirm these results.[39]

Another set of American estimates of the effect of tax policy on labor supply is based on the results of several negative income tax experiments conducted in the United States in the late 1960s and the 1970s. Under the negative income tax plans, the experimental group received a minimum income, but their earnings were taxed at 50 percent rates or higher. The conclusion reached in these studies is that a negative income tax would reduce the supply of labor, but the reduction would be substantial only for supplementary family earners (spouses and children) and relatively small for family heads. Unfortunately, these studies shed little light on the effect of the positive tax system on work incentives because the experimental samples were confined to the poor and near-poor and also because it was impossible to separate the substitution effect from the income effect in the empirical analysis.[40]

37. D. B. Fields and W. T. Stanbury, "Income Taxes and Incentives to Work: Some Additional Empirical Evidence," *American Economic Review,* vol. 61 (June 1971), pp. 435–43.

38. The percentage of respondents reporting some tax effect on their work in the two studies were as follows:

Study	Disincentives	Incentives
Break	13	10
Fields and Stanley	19	11

39. See, for example, T. H. Sanders, *Effects of Taxation on Executives* (Harvard University Graduate School of Business Administration, 1951); Robin Barlow, Harvey F. Brazer, and James N. Morgan, *Economic Behavior of the Affluent* (Brookings Institution, 1966); and Daniel M. Holland, "The Effect of Taxation on Effort: Some Results for Business Executives," in National Tax Association–Tax Institute of America, *Proceedings of the Sixty-second Annual Conference on Taxation, 1969* (Columbus, Ohio: NTA-TIA, 1970), pp. 428–517.

40. For a summary and evaluation of these studies, see Joseph A. Pechman and P. Michael Timpane, eds., *Work Incentives and Income Guarantees: The New Jersey Negative Income Tax Experiment* (Brookings Institution, 1975); and John L. Palmer and Joseph A. Pechman, *Welfare in Rural Areas: The North Carolina–Iowa Income Maintenance Experiment* (Brookings Institution, 1978).

The only large-scale study of the impact of taxation on work effort in England was conducted by C. V. Brown and E. Levin, who interviewed 2,068 weekly paid workers to find out whether taxation affected the number of hours of overtime work. The vast majority of workers reported that taxation had no effect on overtime hours. Among those who reported some effect, males who claimed they worked more overtime because of taxation slightly outnumbered those who claimed they worked fewer hours; females were much less affected by taxation, but more of them reported working fewer hours than those who reported working more hours.[41]

The Royal Commission on the Distribution of Income and Wealth (the Diamond commission) established that since 1969 there has been a large decline in the relative earnings of high-paid employees, both before and after tax.[42] The commission also concluded that U.K. managerial salaries before tax were above those in Sweden, about the same as in Australia and the Netherlands, and lower than in other countries of the European Community.[43] These trends have been exacerbated by the recent incomes policies, which have narrowed differentials between high-paid and low-paid workers. But there is no evidence that a decline in the work effort of business managers has occurred.[44] Nor do the data show any significant effect on migration of professional and managerial workers, despite the gap between top salaries in the United Kingdom and those in other countries.[45]

41. The percentage of respondents showing no effect and either a positive or a negative effect on overtime hours were as follows:

Sex	No effect	Positive effect	Negative effect
Male	74	15	11
Female	93	2	6

C. V. Brown and E. Levin, "The Effects of Income Taxation on Overtime: The Results of a National Survey," *Economic Journal,* vol. 84 (December 1974), pp. 833–48.

42. Royal Commission on the Distribution of Income and Wealth, *Higher Incomes from Employment,* Report 3, cmnd. 6383 (HMSO, 1976), pp. 5–43.

43. Ibid., pp. 44–85.

44. In a forthcoming study to be published by the Institute for Fiscal Studies, Brian Reddaway and associates were not able to detect any significant effect of the tax system on the mobility and performance of senior executives in ninety-four manufacturing firms. The interviews took place between February and October 1978.

45. Royal Commission on the Distribution of Income and Wealth, *Higher Incomes from Employment,* pp. 81–83, 185–207. Data from the Department of Employment indicate that net migration of managers and administrators increased from about 1,000 a year in the period 1965–73 to 4,500 in 1975 and 3,000 in 1976. *Depart-*

Several studies have attempted through the interview technique to find out how professional and managerial employees react to the high tax rates, but here again the results are inconclusive. As might be expected, the surveys do indicate that high-paid employees are unhappy about the decline in their real earnings and feel that the tax system treats them unfairly. But repeated studies have found that, despite the high tax rates and reduced differentials, the work performance of business executives has not been noticeably affected. According to their own responses, top managers have not changed their hours of work or work effort, their propensity to move on to other jobs, or their attitudes toward working overseas.[46]

NONTAXABLE FRINGE BENEFITS. It is not surprising that the high marginal tax rates have encouraged the development of methods of compensation that remove a large part of employee compensation from the tax base. Information submitted to the Diamond commission indicates that the nontaxable or lightly taxed portion of total remuneration of high-paid employees is two or three times as large in the United Kingdom as it is declared to be in France and West Germany.[47]

The largest and most widespread nontaxable fringe benefits are the pension arrangements. Contributions to approved pension plans by employees as well as employers are not taxable when they are made. An approved plan may provide a pension of as much as two-thirds of the employee's last year's salary, but an amount equal to one and one-half times that salary may be withdrawn in a lump sum free of tax.[48] This feature is especially valuable for high-paid employees and is apparently widely used.

---

ment of Employment Gazette, vol. 85 (September 1977), p. 904. Most of this increase is attributed to the employment opportunities in the Middle East, but the tax system may have had a marginal effect. In the Reddaway study for the Institute for Fiscal Studies, 5 percent of senior executives who left their firms in 1976 and 1977 accepted positions to work abroad. These executives accounted for only 0.3 percent of all senior staff at the time of interview.

46. See, for example, Opinion Research Centre, *The Motivation of Top British Management* (OPR, 1977).

47. Kay and King, *British Tax System,* p. 41, citing evidence submitted to the commission by Hay-M. S. L., Ltd., in 1976.

48. There is no limit on the amount of the lump-sum payment or on the annual pension benefits, and it is possible to inflate an employee's last year's salary without increasing his responsibilities.

In addition to pensions, business managers and directors have a number of highly visible, special perquisites, which receive considerable attention in Great Britain. Business firms pay the dues of their executives for private dining, health, and recreational clubs, serve expensive meals in executive dining rooms at little or no cost to the employee, reimburse the outlays of their top managers for admissions to theaters and sports events and for other entertainment expenses, and provide private medical insurance and low-interest mortgages for their higher-paid employees. Tax may be due on some of these benefits, but the amount taxed is much less than the cash value.[49]

The most obvious "perk" for the business manager is the company car, which is available to him for personal as well as business use. Until recently, the firm's expenditure on the car was taxable to the employee in the proportion of private to total mileage used. In practice, the proportion allocated to private mileage was small and, in any case, understated the value of the car to the employee. To reduce the tax advantage, new regulations adopted in 1976 require those who have company cars at their disposal to count as taxable income specific imputed amounts for the benefits they receive. But since the amount included may represent a small percentage of the use value of the car to the employee, the personal use of company cars is hardly being discouraged.[50]

The rank and file (in tax terms, those with salaries of less than £ 10,000 a year in 1979–80) also receive a variety of nontaxable fringe benefits, though such benefits are not as valuable to taxpayers in the lower tax brackets as they are to top-bracket taxpayers. Business firms often subsidize canteen meals for their employees and provide discounts

49. In the United States, outlays by business for the maintenance and operation of facilities such as yachts and hunting lodges were made nondeductible under the Revenue Act of 1978. Restrictions on the deductibility of other benefits of high-paid employees—such as country club dues, admissions to theaters and sports events, and first-class air travel—were proposed by the administration but were rejected by Congress.

50. For 1978–79 an employee who received a company car originally valued at more than £ 12,000 was required to include in his taxable income £ 880 if the car was under four years old. Such a car probably provided services of £ 3,600 a year (for insurance, operation and maintenance costs, and depreciation); even if only half the mileage of the car was for personal use, the understatement of £ 920 was equivalent to an annual gross salary of £ 5,412 at the top-bracket rate of 83 percent in 1978–79.

on purchases by employees of goods produced or distributed by the firm. Railroads and airlines allow their employees and their families to travel free of charge. Subsidized loans were provided tax free to employees before 1976, when the cash equivalent of the subsidy above a certain level was made subject to tax.[51] Until recently, many business firms paid the school fees of the children of their high-paid employees, but this practice may stop as a result of a ruling adopted in 1978 requiring that such awards be made available to the children of all employees on a nondiscriminatory basis.

TAX AVOIDANCE AND EVASION. The most serious development that has occurred in response to the high tax rates has been the growth of what has been called the "hidden economy," which may now represent as much as 7.5 percent of gross domestic product.[52] Many workers engage in moonlighting on jobs for which they insist on payment in cash. Plumbers, carpenters, painters, and other self-employed craftsmen routinely quote higher prices for their services if payment is to be made by check rather than in cash. (In such cases, the incentive to evade tax is the saving not only in income and payroll taxes but also in value-added tax.)

Besides outright evasion, tax avoidance is widespread in the United Kingdom. There are many tax consultants whose specialty is to devise wholly artificial transactions that exploit loopholes in the tax law in order to reduce or eliminate tax liability. As fast as the Board of Inland Revenue discovers a loophole and blocks it, others are found.

The amount of revenue lost through the various arrangements used to minimize taxes is not known, nor can the impact on economic efficiency be estimated.[53] It is clear, however, that such practices do have an effect on economic behavior and reduce taxpayer morale.

51. The interest subsidy on mortgage loans continues to be nontaxable, though the interest payment would, in any case, be allowed as a deduction (on mortgages up to £25,000).

52. Statement of Sir William Pile, chairman of the Bank of Inland Revenue, as reported in the *Financial Times,* March 27, 1979.

53. Estimates of the revenue effects of special provisions in the personal and corporation income taxes—called "tax expenditures"—have recently been prepared in the United Kingdom in a study sponsored by the Institute for Fiscal Studies: J. R. M. Willis and P. J. W. Hardwick, *Tax Expenditures in the United Kingdom* (London: Heinemann Educational Books, 1978). Most of the data used in these estimates are from the national income and product accounts and other official sources that do not provide any information on the type of nontaxable fringe benefits and tax avoidance and evasion schemes discussed in this section.

Saving and Investment

Many special provisions and preferences have been introduced into the tax law to promote particular types of saving and investment, including income tax deductions for specified personal saving items, preferential rates for capital gains and dividend relief, and generous investment and employment subsidies. These provisions have greatly moderated the effect of the nominally higher tax rates on unearned incomes and have also had the effect of channeling saving and investment into the preferred areas.

PERSONAL SAVING. Table 3 provides a list of the preferences under the U.K. income tax law for personal saving and an estimate of the revenue loss from each item in 1975–76. The largest item is the deduction for payment of interest on mortgage loans, which amounted to £865 million in that year.[54] This is followed by the deduction for life insurance premiums and the exemption for employee pension contributions, each of which amounts to one-quarter of the cost of the mortgage interest deduction. There are also deductions for a wide variety of savings, but the amounts are relatively small. In total, however, the value of all the saving preferences was not small: they reduced the income tax yield in 1975–76 by a minimum of 12 percent.[55]

Partly because of the preferential tax treatment, investment in owner-occupied housing, pension funds, and life insurance account for almost all net personal saving in the United Kingdom.[56] The result of this kind of saving structure is alleged to be a reduction in the savings that are available for risky investment and particularly for small business. Evidence exists that small business is much less important in the United Kingdom than in other industrialized countries and that it has lost a great deal of

54. This does not include the revenues from the exclusion of imputed net rent on owner-occupied homes (that is, rental income after the deduction of interest paid), which is at least as large as the revenue lost from the interest deduction alone.

55. The tax value of the preferences for which estimates are available in table 3 was £1,862 million, while total income tax, surtax, and capital gains tax collections amounted to £15,536 million in 1975–76. For the revenue estimates, see Board of Inland Revenue, *120th Report for the Year Ended 31st March 1977* (HMSO, 1978), p. 34.

56. According to calculations by Kay and King, these three forms of saving accounted for about 90 percent of total U.K. saving in the period 1972–76, as compared with 56 percent for the United States in 1974. See *British Tax System*, p. 60.

Table 3. *Income Tax Reliefs for Personal Saving in the United Kingdom,*
1975–76

Millions of pounds

Item	Tax treatment	Revenue loss
Home mortgages	Interest deductible on mortgages up to £25,000	865
Life insurance premiums	Relief provided for one-half the basic tax on premiums, up to one-sixth of total income	235
Pension contributions	Contributions by employees are fully deductible	289[a]
Pension fund accumulations	Income and capital gains not taxable	333[b]
Contribution by self-employed for retirement annuity	Contributions up to 15 percent of earnings are deductible, with maximum of £3,000	50
National savings certificates (maximum holding £1,500)	Interest untaxed	55
National and trustee savings banks	First £70 of interest untaxed	35
Save-as-you-earn (contractual saving of up to £20 a month)	Interest untaxed	c
Premium bonds[d]	Winnings untaxed	c
Building society accounts	Interest taxed at the estimated composite rate of depositors	c
Government securities	Capital gains exempt if held for a year	c

Source: J. R. M. Willis and P. J. W. Hardwick, *Tax Expenditures in the United Kingdom* (London: Heinemann Educational Books, 1978).

a. Does not include exclusion of employer's contribution from employee's income, which amounted to £1,000 million in 1975–76.

b. Extrapolated from Willis-Hardwick estimate for 1973–74.

c. Revenue loss is unknown, but amount is small.

d. No interest is paid on premium bonds; the interest equivalent on each issue is used to pay for winnings on the annual drawings.

ground in the last forty years.[57] But there is no way of knowing how much these trends have been affected either by the higher tax rates on earned income in the United Kingdom or by the special provisions for savings

57. A few years ago the proportion of manufacturing employment in establishments with less than 200 employees was the lowest in the United Kingdom among a group of thirteen countries. The number of small firms in the United Kingdom has been cut in half in forty years, while the number has doubled in the United States. Department of Trade and Industry, *Small Firms: Report of the Committee of Inquiry,* cmnd. 4811 (HMSO, 1971).

that are not available to small business. Furthermore, the United Kingdom, like other countries, provides tax relief to small business in many ways, but this policy has not had much success.[58]

Another trend that has been associated with the incentives in the tax system has been the institutionalization of stock ownership. According to Kay and King, stock ownership by individuals in the United Kingdom declined from 56.1 percent of the total in 1963 to 39.8 percent in 1975; the proportion owned by financial companies and institutions increased from 30.4 to 48.1 percent in the same period.[59] This trend, which is almost universal in the industrialized world, raises the cost of equity capital and probably reduces the supply of capital that would otherwise be available for risky investments. Again, there is no way of disentangling the effect of the tax factor from all the other factors that have contributed to this trend.

THE CORPORATE SECTOR. As already noted, the tax on corporation earnings is very low and must, therefore, have little effect on the economy as a whole (though not necessarily on such features of the corporation sector as debt–equity ratios and dividend payouts). The imputation system, which provides relief for almost one-half of the corporate tax at the individual level, greatly reduces the burden of the corporate tax for low- and middle-income shareholders (see tables 2 and 11). Even for those in the higher income levels, the combined effective tax rate on corporate earnings is moderate because the corporate tax on industrial and commercial earnings has been virtually wiped out by the first-year depreciation allowances of 100 percent for plant and equipment and 50 percent for industrial buildings (see table 14) and the adjustment for inventory profits, while only a small percentage of profits is paid out in dividends.[60] The low rates of tax on capital gains (a maximum of 30 percent, with reduced rates on gains of less than £9,500 in 1979–80) also make corporate investment attractive.

58. Special rates are provided under the corporation tax for firms with profits of less than £85,000; gains on the sale or gift of a family business are exempt up to £50,000 if the person is sixty-five or over; gains realized in the replacement of certain business assets are not taxed until disposal without replacement; and the value of small business firms can be reduced by 50 percent for capital transfer tax purposes. Many of the limits in these provisions were revised in the 1978 budget, at a cost of £204 million in a full year. H. M. Treasury, *Economic Progress Report,* no. 98 (HMSO, 1978), p. 3.

59. Kay and King, *British Tax System,* p. 67.

60. It should be noted that the immediate write-off for plant and equipment automatically eliminates the problem of underdepreciation in a period of inflation.

As King has pointed out, the 1965–72 tax structure encouraged U.K. corporations to rely heavily on retained earnings for their major source of finance, discouraged the issue of new shares, and increased the attractiveness of borrowing.[61] The adoption of the imputation system in 1973 encouraged dividend distributions and increased the attractiveness of equity financing. There does seem to have been an increase in corporate equity issues in recent years (see table 15), but the dividend payout ratio has not changed significantly. Thus retained earnings have remained the main source of equity finance in the corporate sector.

Despite the low rate of tax on corporate earnings, during the past few years the rate of return on U.K. corporate investment has been at the lowest level since the end of World War II. On a replacement-cost basis, the pretax return of industrial and commercial companies declined from over 10 percent in 1966–69 to less than 5 percent in 1974–78.[62] The after-tax return declined from 6 percent to less than 4 percent in the same period (figure 4). The share of profits of industrial and commercial companies in gross corporate product also declined in this period.[63] But even though profitability declined, private capital formation seems to have held up fairly well. Gross investment of industrial and commercial companies, which averaged 13.5 percent of gross domestic product in 1966–68, averaged 16.3 percent in 1976–77 (table 16). The sustained rate of investment in the face of declining profitability may well be due to the generous tax treatment accorded to private investment.

SUBSIDIES. The United Kingdom has experimented with a large variety of direct and indirect subsidies to promote investment or regional development or both. In contrast to the United States, which uses a modest investment credit (currently at its peak rate of 10 percent for equipment purchases only) and the asset depreciation range (ADR) system, the United Kingdom has used, at one time or another, accelerated depreciation, high initial depreciation allowances, investment allowances (up to 40 percent of the amount of the investment), and investment grants (which, in the case of investment in development areas, have been as high

61. King, *Public Policy and the Corporation*, pp. 204–27, and table 15 in this paper.

62. "Profitability and Company Finance, A Supplementary Note," *Bank of England Quarterly Bulletin*, vol. 19 (June 1979), p. 183. These calculations take into account the gains resulting from the reduced value of debt during the recent inflation.

63. "Measures of Real Profitability," *Bank of England Quarterly Bulletin*, vol. 18 (December 1978), p. 514.

Figure 4. *Real Rates of Return before and after Tax and Ratio of Gross Private Domestic Investment to Gross Domestic Product, Industrial and Commercial Companies in the United Kingdom, 1966–77*

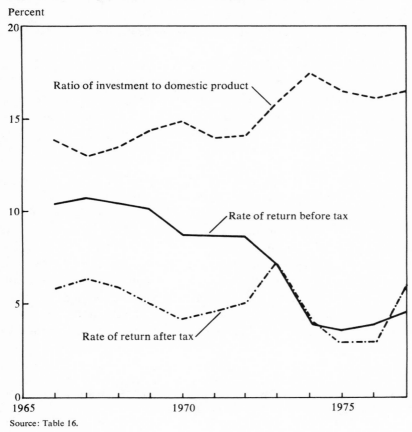

Percent

Ratio of investment to domestic product

Rate of return before tax

Rate of return after tax

Source: Table 16.

as 45 percent of the amount of the investment) and, in most instances, has applied these allowances and grants to plant as well as equipment expenditures in manufacturing and construction (table 12).[64] Employment subsidies have also been paid to industrial firms generally (under the Selective Employment Act of 1966, which expired in 1977) and to those located in designated development areas (under the regional em-

64. Initial allowances and accelerated depreciation cannot raise total depreciation taken over the life of an asset above its cost; investment grants are given on top of the depreciation allowances.

ployment premium from 1967 to 1971). Prest estimates that the cost of all subsidies amounted to at least £3,000 million in 1972 (almost 25 percent of total U.K. tax revenues in that year) and was rising sharply.[65] Mellis and Richardson estimated that a firm investing in plant and machinery can, in present value terms, recover between 41 and 63 percent of the cost of the investment.[66]

The effectiveness of these subsidies has been the subject of a great deal of research using interview as well as econometric techniques.[67] The numerous studies of investment incentives come up with a wide range of answers; P. J. Lund's summary concludes with the view that the most that can be said for these studies is that they "do not support any allegation that the incentives have been wholly ineffective."[68] On the contrary, most experts believe that the tax incentives have increased investment, and some even believe that capital subsidies have been carried to a point where reasonable returns on investment are difficult to obtain.[69]

Brian Reddaway's committee concluded that the selective employment tax (SET) reduced employment in wholesaling and retailing (which was subject to tax) and also resulted in a higher rate of growth of productivity in these industries than would otherwise have been the case. Whitley and Worswick have challenged this view, arguing that there was an acceleration of growth in manufacturing after SET was enacted and that some factor other than SET was at work to raise productivity in distribution as well as in manufacturing.[70] The regional employment premium has also

65. A. R. Prest, "The Economic Rationale of Subsidies to Industry," in Department of Industry, *The Economics of Industrial Subsidies* (HMSO, 1976), p. 66.

66. C. L. Mellis and D. W. Richardson, "Value of Investment Incentives for Manufacturing Industry 1946 to 1974," in ibid., p. 34.

67. For an excellent summary of this research, see Department of Industry, *Economics of Industrial Subsidies*.

68. Ibid., p. 261.

69. Geoffrey Maynard is a notable proponent of the view that taxation has helped to increase labor costs relative to capital costs, with the result that capital has been substituted for labor and the rate of profit on capital has declined in line with the fall in the real cost of capital. Unpublished memorandum, "A Non-Keynesian Model of Inflation, Unemployment and Balance of Payments Deficits as Applied to the U.K."

70. The dispute has not been resolved. See W. B. Reddaway and others, *Effects of the Selective Employment Tax, Final Report* (Cambridge University Press, 1973); J. D. Whitley and G. D. N. Worswick, "The Productivity Effects of Selective Employment Tax," *National Institute Economic Review,* no. 56 (May 1971), pp. 36–40; W. B. Reddaway, "Reply," ibid., no. 57 (August 1971), pp. 67–68; Whitley and Worswick, "Rejoinder," ibid., no. 58 (November 1971), pp. 72–75.

been judged to have been effective, although the actual increase in employment in development areas is disputed.[71]

Inflation

Though a great deal has been said and written in the United Kingdom about the impact of inflation on individual and business tax burdens, very little is said about the effect of taxation on inflation.[72] There is some evidence that labor bargains on an after-tax basis, so that some of the tax increases in recent years may have been shifted in the form of higher prices.[73] Inflation would be exacerbated if the high rates reduced productivity, but as already indicated the evidence on this is unclear. The corporation tax has been increasingly deemphasized in recent years, when inflation has skyrocketed, which indicates nothing about the effect of the corporate tax on prices except that other factors have been much more important.

The substitution of the value-added tax for purchase tax in 1973 was not intended, on balance, to raise revenues. In fact, the ratio of taxes on goods and services in the United Kingdom to gross domestic product actually declined slightly from 1973 to 1976,[74] which suggests that the authorities were aware that a rise in consumption taxes would be unwise

71. See B. C. Moore and J. Rhodes, "A Quantitative Analysis of the Effects of the Regional Employment Premium and Other Regional Policy Instruments," and R. R. MacKay, "The Impact of the Regional Employment Premium," and their comments on each other's papers in Department of Industry, *Economics of Industrial Subsidies*, pp. 191–244.

72. See, for example, Sandilands Commission, *Report of the Inflation Accounting Committee*, cmnd. 225 (HMSO, 1975); Institute for Fiscal Studies, *The Structure and Reform of Direct Taxation*, Report of a Committee chaired by Professor J. E. Meade (London: Allen and Unwin, 1978); and Kay and King, *British Tax System*.

73. See J. Johnson and M. Tinbrell, "Empirical Tests of a Bargaining Theory of Wage Determination," *Manchester School of Economic and Social Studies*, vol. 41 (June 1973), pp. 141–69; Organisation for Economic Co-operation and Development, *Public Expenditure Trends* (Paris: OECD, 1978), pp. 51–58, 81–87; and S. G. B. Henry and P. A. Ormerod, "Income Policy and Wage Inflation: Empirical Evidence for the U.K., 1961–1977," *National Institute Economic Review*, no. 85 (August 1978), pp. 31–39.

74. The ratio was 10.1 percent in 1972 and 9.7 percent in 1976. Organisation for Economic Co-operation and Development, *Revenue Statistics of OECD Member Countries, 1965–76* (Paris: OECD, 1978), pp. 93, 172.

in a period of inflation.[75] But in June 1979 the new conservative government accepted the inflationary consequences of a higher value-added tax in order to provide replacement revenues for cuts in the individual income tax. This was expected to raise the retail price index by 3.5 percentage points.

Increases in employment taxes have also contributed to inflation. The tax paid by employers was raised in two successive budgets—by 2 percentage points in April 1977 and 1.5 percentage points in October 1978 —to offset the revenue loss from tax cuts made elsewhere. These actions raised employment costs by about 3 percent, and it may be presumed that the increases were fully reflected in higher prices. The increase in October 1978 was forced on the government because the opposition parties insisted on a reduction in the basic income tax rate (from 34 to 33 percent) even at the expense of raising a tax that directly increased business costs.[76]

Distribution of Income and Wealth

Much effort has been devoted in Great Britain to the measurement of the inequality in the distribution of income and wealth and to the identification of the determinants of these distributions. The Diamond commission, which was appointed in 1974 to undertake an analysis of current and past trends, stimulated a great deal of research and has issued several reports and background memoranda on various aspects of its work.

The latest estimates of the Diamond commission reveal that the shares of total personal income received by the top 1 percent and top 5 percent dropped between 1959 and 1974–75 both before and after income tax. Before tax, the share of the top 1 percent declined from 8.4 to 6.2 percent, and the share of the next 4 percent declined from 11.5 to 10.6 percent. After tax, the decline was from 5.3 to 4.0 percent for the top 1 percent and from 10.5 percent to 9.7 percent for the next 4 percent. The average income tax burden increased 75 percent in the period (from 10.5 to 18.3

75. Specific duties on such items as tobacco and alcoholic beverages have not been raised for the same reason, even though their value has been eroded in real terms because of inflation.

76. This neglect of the inflationary consequences of payroll taxes is by no means confined to the United Kingdom. For example, the United States enacted a multistage payroll tax increase that will increase payroll tax receipts by $26 billion, or 20 percent, by fiscal 1983.

percent). But the increase in the top 5 percent was small (because they were already paying high taxes), while the increased burdens on the lower- and middle-income groups were very large.[77] The movement of the income distribution toward equality cannot therefore be attributed directly to changes in the income tax, and there is simply no way of determining how much, if any, of the declining share of income at the top is attributable to reduced work and saving incentives.

Wealth is much more concentrated than income in the United Kingdom (as it is elsewhere), but the inequality in the distribution of wealth has also been declining in the last two decades.[78] Between 1960 and 1975 the share of personal wealth owned by the top 1 percent of persons with recorded wealth (about half the adult population) declined from 28.4 percent to 17.2 percent and the share of the next 4 percent declined from 22.5 to 17.8. Inclusion of the value of occupational and state pension rights reduces the overall level of inequality, as might be expected.

According to the Diamond commission, the main influences at work on the distribution of wealth have been, first, the large and sustained rise in real incomes, which allowed many people to buy their own homes and to accumulate other assets, and, second, the impact of the estate duty, which reduced wealth inequality directly and also encouraged wealthy people to distribute their wealth before death.[79] According to Harbury and McMahon, however, the role of inheritance in the creation of the largest wealth holdings remains large, even if these holdings are account- ing for a smaller proportion of total wealth.[80]

It is still too early to evaluate the effect of the capital transfer tax,

77. From 1959 to 1974–75 the average income tax burden of the top 1 percent increased 9 percent, while the burden of the middle quintile of the distribution tripled. Royal Commission on the Distribution of Income and Wealth, *Third Report on the Standing Reference,* Report 5, cmnd. 6999 (HMSO, 1977), pp. 13–66, 199–204.

78. In fact, the movement toward equality in the wealth distribution goes back as far as 1911. See Royal Commission on the Distribution of Income and Wealth, *Initial Report of the Standing Reference,* Report 1, cmnd. 6171 (HMSO, 1975), p. 97.

79. Royal Commission on the Distribution of Income and Wealth, *Third Report on the Standing Reference,* p. 76, and *Initial Report on the Standing Reference,* p. 12.

80. C. D. Harbury and P. C. McMahon, "Inheritance and the Characteristics of Top Wealth Leavers in Britain," *Economic Journal,* vol. 83 (September 1973), pp. 810–33.

which replaced estate duty in March 1975. Technically, the capital transfer tax is much superior to the estate tax because it taxes all gifts (not just those made before death) as well as bequests, and the tax base for any one person is cumulative for all taxable transfers made during his or her entire life.[81] But the original legislation provided lower tax rates for lifetime gifts up to £300,000, and in 1976, 30 percent of small business property and 50 percent of agricultural property were excluded from the tax base. In 1977 the 30 percent exclusion for business property was raised to 50 percent and a new exclusion of 20 percent for minority shareholdings in unquoted companies was introduced. Further, while the top-bracket rate of 75 percent was carried over from the estate tax, the rate of graduation is less steep under the capital transfer tax—presumably in the expectation that gifts would make up the revenue loss. Thus far the effect of the exemption of interspousal transfers and of the lower tax rates has predominated: the estate tax produced £459 million in 1972–73, £412 million in 1973–74, and £339 million in 1974–75; in 1977–78 the capital transfer tax yielded £311 million and £87 million was collected from the estate tax for previous years.[82]

In 1974 the Labour government proposed the enactment of an annual net wealth tax to obtain some tax from wealthy people who are able to avoid present taxes and also to further reduce the concentration of wealth. The government's Green Paper, which outlined how a wealth tax would work, envisaged a threshold of £100,000, so that the tax would apply only to the top one-quarter percent of the adult population, and a progressive rate structure with a maximum rate of 2½ percent or 5 percent.[83] The paper did not say whether the revenues from the wealth tax would be substituted for revenues from other taxes or be a net addition to the tax structure. The proposal was considered by a Select Committee of the House of Commons and drew loud protests on grounds of tax policy as well as administration. The committee was not able to agree on a report, and the government postponed action on the proposal.

81. Moreover, the gift tax is included in the cumulative tax base gross of tax rather than net of tax.

82. Board of Inland Revenue, *121st Report for the Year Ended 31st March 1978* (HMSO, 1977), pp. 38–39.

83. Under the proposal, a taxpayer would be liable to pay the higher of the investment income surcharge and the wealth tax. See H. M. Treasury, *Wealth Tax,* cmnd. 5704 (HMSO, 1974).

Options for Change

The picture that emerges from the foregoing discussion of the burdens of the U.K. tax system and of its effects on economic behavior is one of sharp contrasts. On the one hand, the nominal tax rates on both earned and unearned incomes were pushed to inordinately high levels. On the other hand, the tax system contains all sorts of preferences and subsidies that are clearly designed to take the curse off the high rates and to promote particular kinds of activity. For an outsider, it is difficult to understand how a country that imposed a maximum nominal tax rate of 98 percent on investment income also adopted capital consumption allowances that virtually wiped out the corporate tax on industrial and commercial companies, provided relief for almost half the remaining corporate tax on any dividends that are paid, taxed realized capital gains at a maximum rate of 30 percent while providing reduced rates for the first £9,500 of gains, and exempted capital gains transferred at death. And it is not easy to understand why the marginal tax rates on earned incomes of the middle-income class were allowed to creep up above 50 percent, when at the same time a wealth tax was being considered, to cut down the wealth of the super rich.

How much economic damage the country did to itself by adopting such a policy cannot be quantified. Clearly, however, the tax system generated distortions in labor and capital markets and produced highly inequitable results for people and businesses in essentially the same economic circumstances. In addition, the system produced the inevitable tug-of-war between taxpayers who seek methods of getting out from under the high tax rates (through better fringes, improved perks, conversion of income into capital gains, and other devices) and the tax administrators who try valiantly to stem the tide—but with indifferent results. The growth of the hidden economy, in which taxpayers of modest means are now participating, is particularly disturbing.

Whether the economic limits of taxation had been reached or not, it is clear that the political limits were reached long before the sharp reduction in income tax rates made by the new conservative government in June 1979. Every budget in recent years contained tax proposals that mitigated the effects of the high tax rates on particular groups. Many of these provisions were second-best solutions to problems that should have been dealt with by rate reductions or by nontax methods.[84] The newspapers kept up a steady barrage of stories illustrating new loopholes, providing further evidence of cash dealings to avoid taxes, or reporting an Inland Revenue ruling that upset still another tax avoidance scheme. Social conversation frequently turned to discussions of the tax system, and the major political parties put tax reform at or near the top of their legislative agenda.

Now that the top-bracket rates have been cut, the next step in tax reform should be to reduce substantially the marginal tax rates for the large mass of wage and salary workers. And the investment income surcharge, which remains at 15 percent but with a threshold that was raised to £5,000, should be repealed outright.[85]

To maintain fiscal responsibility, large rate reductions for the lower- and middle-income classes would require substantial cuts in public expenditure or offsetting increases in taxes or both. Analysis of the U.K. budget is outside the scope of this paper, but most of the offsetting revenue will probably have to come from the tax side of the budget.[86] It should be emphasized that the question of offsetting tax increases is neutral with regard to the overall progressivity of the tax system: it should be possible to maintain progressivity where it is or to raise or lower it. The various tax options range from repairing the base of the present income tax to introducing new taxes to make up the revenue loss.

84. In the 1978 budget, full-year costs of over £200 million were for "tax proposals helpful to small business" and £65 million for relief for capital gains recipients. H. M. Treasury, *Economic Progress Report,* no. 98, p. 3; and *Financial Statement and Budget Report, 1978–79* (HMSO, 1978), p. 36.

85. In my view, the classical arguments in favor of taxing property income more heavily than earned income do not justify a large differential. The appropriate method of differentiation would be to provide a deduction or tax credit for the additional costs of earning income, but such an allowance would be modest compared with the 15 percent U.K. investment income surcharge. See Richard Goode, *The Individual Income Tax,* rev. ed. (Brookings Institution, 1976), pp. 238–42.

86. Reductions have already been made in public expenditure in recent years, and the new conservative government made additional reductions of about 3 percent in the June 1979 budget. Public expenditure was 46.5 percent of gross domestic product at market prices in 1975–76 and 42 percent in 1978–79. H. M. Treasury, *The Government's Expenditure Plans, 1979–80 to 1982–83,* cmnd. 7439 (HMSO, 1979), p. 5; and *Financial Statement and Budget Report, 1979–80* (HMSO, 1979), p. 13.

Broad-based Income Taxes

It is probably too much to expect the United Kingdom (or any other country, for that matter) to adopt fully comprehensive personal and corporate income taxes,[87] but there is plenty of room for movement between the present tax system in the United Kingdom and the theoretical comprehensive tax.[88] The exclusions for savings could be curtailed, the highly favorable treatment of pension contributions and benefits could be modified, the preferences for homeowners could be reduced or eliminated, economic depreciation could be substituted for the generous depreciation allowances now allowed, dividend relief could be repealed, and capital gains could be treated as ordinary income. Along the same lines, the capital transfer tax might be strengthened by reducing or eliminating the generous exclusions for small business and farm property from the tax base.[89]

Such changes, combined with the rate cuts, would increase tax equity and improve tax morale. But every one of the provisions has staunch defenders and change in any one of them will be strongly resisted. Furthermore, while it would be difficult to broaden the tax base at any time, it may be particularly difficult when inflation is still above 10 percent. The alternatives are to index the tax base so that only real rather than nominal incomes are subject to tax or to wait until the inflation has subsided. Fiscal officials are cautious about indexation because it might be seen as an official acknowledgment that inflation would be tolerated by the government; and tax administrators worry that indexation would

87. In the United States, President Carter campaigned for the adoption of a comprehensive income tax, but he gradually watered down his own proposals within a year after being elected and even these proposals were, for the most part, rejected by Congress. In the end, he signed a bill for a tax that was even further removed from a comprehensive income tax than the tax he had campaigned against. The debate over the bill indicated that there is little support for comprehensive income taxation in the United States.

88. For a detailed discussion of the major elements of a comprehensive income tax, see U.S. Department of the Treasury, *Blueprints for Basic Tax Reform* (Government Printing Office, 1977); Joseph A. Pechman, ed., *Comprehensive Income Taxation* (Brookings Institution, 1977); and Institute for Fiscal Studies, *Structure and Reform of Direct Taxation,* esp. pp. 127–49.

89. Even if the exclusions under the capital transfer tax were removed, small business would be better off if the savings preferences that channel personal savings into institutions were eliminated.

introduce significant complications for tax compliance and administration.[90]

Wealth Tax

If, as might be expected, the effort to broaden the income tax base is only partially successful, consideration might be given to the adoption of a low-rate, annual, personal net wealth tax. Because such a tax would reach wealth that has been lightly taxed or not taxed at all under the individual income tax, horizontal equity would be improved. Furthermore, a net wealth tax could encourage people to shift from safe, low-yield investments to riskier, high-yield investments. The receipts from a wealth tax, which would be confined only to the top wealth owners, could be used to finance a further reduction in the top marginal income tax rates. An annual net wealth tax with a top rate of 2 percent combined with an income tax with a top rate of 50 percent would be a substantial improvement over the income tax with a top rate of 98 percent or even the present 75 percent rate.

It would be virtually impossible to administer a wealth tax that applied to the mass of taxpayers, but the problems would not be insuperable if the tax were confined to the top 5 percent of wealth owners. Low-rate wealth taxes are already a standard element of many tax systems, though the revenues collected are generally small.[91]

Value-added Tax

The 1979 reductions in income tax rates were financed in large part by an increase in the value-added tax from the dual-rate structure of 8

90. For methods of adjusting the tax system for inflation, see Thelma Liesner and Mervyn A. King, eds., *Indexing for Inflation* (London: Heinemann Educational Books, 1975); Henry J. Aaron, ed., *Inflation and the Income Tax* (Brookings Institution, 1976); and Institute for Fiscal Studies, *Structure and Reform of Direct Taxation,* pp. 99–126.

91. The tax is now used in all the Scandinavian countries (Sweden, Norway, Finland, Denmark, and Iceland), Austria, West Germany, the Netherlands, the Swiss counties, the Indian subcontinent (India, Pakistan, and Sri Lanka), and in a few countries in Central and South America. Ireland recently introduced an annual net wealth tax but then repealed it. For a discussion of annual wealth taxation, see Alan A. Tait, *The Taxation of Personal Wealth* (University of Illinois Press, 1967); C. T. Sandford, J. R. M. Willis, and D. J. Ironside, *An Annual Wealth Tax* (London: Heinemann Educational Books, 1975); and Institute for Fiscal Studies, *Structure and Reform of Direct Taxation,* pp. 350–66.

and 12 percent to a flat rate of 15 percent. Additional revenue could be obtained from further increases in the new 15 percent rate. Such a large shift from income taxation to value-added taxation would increase the regressivity of the tax system. This could be avoided if the income tax base were broadened to include incomes in the higher income classes which are not now taxed. Aside from adding to the regressivity of the tax system and making it hard to prevent underreporting of sales by small service and retail establishments, heavier reliance on value-added taxation has the disadvantage of raising the price level and thus contributing to inflation. The 1979 value-added tax increase is a gamble that will pay off only if it does not exacerbate the wage-price spiral.

Expenditure Tax

Taxation of personal consumption expenditures instead of personal incomes is an old idea that has recently been revived by Nicholas Kaldor, the U.S. Treasury, the Meade committee, a Swedish legislative committee, and many tax experts in Britain and the United States.[92] Expenditure taxation is strongly supported by those who believe that the income tax excessively discourages saving. It is also supported as a method of taxing incomes not reached by the income tax. The tax would be levied at graduated rates, and could be used as a replacement for, or as a supplement to, the income tax.

92. The idea was repeatedly advocated by John Stuart Mill, who credits John Revans for originating it. Mill was skeptical, however, of the administrative feasibility of the exemption of net saving from an income tax. Irving Fisher was a vigorous supporter of the expenditure tax, but made few converts. Recent interest in the expenditure tax is credited to Nicholas Kaldor, who raised the issue in the early 1950s as a member of the Royal Commission on Profits and Income and later published a book on the subject, which is still a classic. William D. Andrews revived the idea in the United States in 1974. See John Stuart Mill, *Principles of Political Economy*, 5th ed. (Appleton and Company, 1874), vol. 2, pp. 425–29; Irving Fisher, *Constructive Income Taxation* (Harper, 1942); Nicholas Kaldor, *An Expenditure Tax* (London: Allen and Unwin, 1955; Westport, Conn.: Greenwood Press, 1977); William D. Andrews, "A Consumption-Type or Cash Flow Personal Income Tax," *Harvard Law Review*, vol. 87 (April 1974), pp. 1112–88; U.S. Department of the Treasury, *Blueprints for Basic Tax Reform;* Institute for Fiscal Studies, *Structure and Reform of Direct Taxation;* Kay and King, *British Tax System;* Sven-Olof Lodin, *Progressive Expenditure Tax—an Alternative?* A Report of the 1972 Government Commission on Taxation (Stockholm: LiberFörlag, 1978); and Joseph A. Pechman, ed., *What Should Be Taxed: Income or Expenditure?* (Brookings Institution, 1979).

There is sharp disagreement among tax experts over the equity of expenditure taxation and its practical feasibility. Proponents of expenditure taxation regard expenditures as the preferred base for taxation because it does not reduce the reward for saving and therefore makes future consumption relatively as attractive as present consumption. Proponents of income taxation believe that personal taxation should be based on the ability to pay of an individual, as measured by his total income, that is, by the amount he accumulates as well as the amount he consumes. Administration and compliance would be more difficult under the expenditure tax than under the income tax in some respects and easier in others. Taxation of large personal outlays, such as those on homes and consumer durables, would raise particularly difficult problems under the expenditure tax. On the other hand, the fact that receipts and expenditures would be counted on a cash flow basis under the expenditure tax would greatly simplify tax accounting for business and property incomes. Moreover, correction of the tax base for inflation would not be needed under an expenditure tax.[93]

Expenditure taxation would be a radical departure in taxation for the United Kingdom (or for any other country). It is hard to believe that it would be easier to tax expenditures on a comprehensive basis than it is to tax incomes on such a basis or that the political forces that make income tax reform so difficult would accept a shift to an expenditure tax.

Conclusion

The highest priority for tax revision in the United Kingdom should be to reform and simplify the income tax. The tax base should be broadened by removing the special provisions that erode the tax base and the revenue should be used to reduce the tax rates, particularly for wage and salary workers who are still subject to very high marginal rates. If the replacement revenues cannot be obtained through income tax reforms, other sources must be found. All the noninflationary alternatives seem impractical, but they are clearly better than the present state of affairs.

93. For a discussion of the pros and cons, both from the theoretical and practical viewpoints, see Pechman, ed., *What Should Be Taxed?*

Appendix: Statistical Tables

Table 4. *Distribution of Tax Revenues by Source, Selected Countries, 1976*[a]
Percent

Country	Income tax			Payroll	Goods and ser- vices[b]	Prop- erty	Wealth[c]
	Total	Indi- vidual	Cor- porate				
Denmark	57.7	54.1	3.5	1.1	37.0	3.5	0.1
Sweden	46.6	43.0	3.6	28.0	24.7	*	0.6
Canada	46.7[d]	34.8[d]	11.9	11.0	32.9	8.5	0.9
United Kingdom	42.8	38.1	4.7	19.4	26.3	10.6	0.9
United States	43.3	33.0	10.3	24.6	18.2	12.4	1.4
Japan	41.2	24.5	16.6	25.5	26.4	6.0	0.9
Norway	40.8	36.6	4.2	18.1	39.2	0.4	1.5
Belgium	38.3[d]	31.5[d]	6.8	31.6	29.4	*	0.7
Netherlands	34.0	27.0	7.0	37.8	26.1	1.3	0.9
West Germany	34.8	30.2	4.6	35.4	27.1	1.2	1.5
Austria	24.9	21.5	3.3	36.9	35.9	0.8	1.6
Italy	22.7	16.5	6.2	45.8	31.1	0.1	0.2
France	18.4[d]	12.6[d]	5.8	42.1	37.0	2.1	0.5

Source: Organisation for Economic Co-operation and Development, *Revenue Statistics of OECD Member Countries, 1965–76* (Paris: OECD, 1978). Data are for the calendar year except for the United States (fiscal year begins July 1, 1975) and Japan (fiscal year begins April 1). Figures are rounded.

* Less than 0.05 percent.

a. Includes national and local taxes. Receipts of public enterprises (other than fiscal monopolies) are excluded.

b. Includes sales, value-added, and excise taxes, taxes on imports, exports, and transfers of property and other securities, and transactions taxes paid by enterprises.

c. Includes annual net wealth taxes and death and gift taxes.

d. Adjusted to include unallocable income taxes in proportion to individual and corporation income tax revenues.

Table 5. *Personal Income Tax Rates in the United Kingdom, 1978–79 and 1979–80*

Income classes in thousands of pounds; rates in percent

Ordinary income[a]		Investment income surcharge[b]		Capital gains[c]	
Taxable income class[d]	*Rate*	*Investment income class*	*Rate*	*Capital gains class*	*Rate*
		1978–79			
0–0.75	25	*Under 65*		0–1	0
0.75–8	33	0–1.7	0	1–5	15
8–9	40	1.7–2.25	10	5–9.5	50[e]
9–10	45	Over 2.25	15	Over 9.5	30[e]
10–11	50				
11–12.5	55	*65 or over*			
12.5–14	60	0–2.5	0		
14–16	65	2.5–3	10		
16–18.5	70	Over 3	15		
18.5–24	75				
Over 24	83				
		1979–80			
0–0.75	25	0–5	0[f]	0–1	0
0.75–10	30	Over 5	15[f]	1–5	15
10–12	40			5–9.5	50[e]
12–15	45			Over 9.5	30[e]
15–20	50				
20–25	55				
Over 25	60				

Sources: H. M. Treasury, *Financial Statement and Budget Report, 1978–79* (London: Her Majesty's Stationery Office, 1978), pp. 33–34, and *1979–80* (HMSO, 1979), pp. 29–30; *Inland Revenue Statistics, 1978* (HMSO, 1978), p. 166.

a. Includes wages and salaries, self-employment income, and investment income.

b. Includes interest, dividends, and net rents.

c. In lieu of the regular capital gains tax, capital gains on the development of land was subject to a special tax of 80 percent in 1978–79 and 60 percent in 1979–80.

d. Income after personal allowances and deductions.

e. The high rate for the £5,000–£9,500 bracket is designed so that the tax at £9,500 is exactly equal to 30 percent. Thus, above £9,500, the 30 percent rate applies to all gains.

f. Rates and threshold apply to all taxpayers.

Table 6. *Tax Revenues as a Percent of Gross Domestic Product, by Source, Selected Countries, 1976*[a]

Country	Income tax			Goods and services[b]	Property	Wealth[c]	Total
	Individual	Corporate	Payroll				
Sweden	21.9	1.8	14.3	12.6	*	0.3	50.9
Netherlands	12.5	3.2	17.5	12.0	0.6	0.4	46.2
Norway	16.9	1.9	8.3	18.1	0.2	0.7	46.2
Denmark	24.2	1.6	0.5	16.6	1.6	0.4	44.7
Belgium	13.2[d]	2.8[d]	13.2	12.3	*	0.3	41.9
France	5.0[d]	2.3[d]	16.6	14.6	0.8	0.2	39.4
Austria	8.4	1.3	14.3	14.0	0.3	0.6	38.9
United Kingdom	14.0	1.7	7.1	9.7	3.9	0.3	36.7
West Germany	11.1	1.7	13.0	9.9	0.4	0.6	36.7
Italy	5.9	2.2	16.4	11.2	*	0.1	35.8
Canada	11.4[d]	3.9[d]	3.6	10.8	2.8	0.3	32.9
United States	9.7	3.0	7.2	5.3	3.6	0.4	29.3
Japan	5.1	3.5	5.3	5.5	1.3	0.2	20.9

Source: Organisation for Economic Co-operation and Development, *Revenue Statistics of OECD Member Countries, 1965–76* (Paris: OECD, 1978). Data are for calendar years except for the United States (fiscal year begins July 1) and Japan (fiscal year begins April 1). Figures are rounded.

* Less than 0.05 percent.

a. Includes national and local taxes. Receipts of public enterprises (other than fiscal monopolies) are excluded.

b. Includes sales, value-added, and excise taxes, taxes on imports, exports, and transfers of property and other securities, and transactions taxes paid by enterprises.

c. Includes annual net wealth taxes and death and gift taxes.

d. Adjusted to include unallocable income taxes in proportion to individual and corporation income tax revenues.

Table 7. *Starting and Maximum Rates of Individual Income Tax,*
Selected Countries, 1978
Income levels in dollars[a]

| | Starting rates | | Maximum rates | | | |
| | | | Earned income | | Investment income | |
Country	Percent	Income level[b]	Percent	Income level[b]	Percent	Income level[b]
Netherlands	20.0	6,510	72.0	83,560	72.0	83,230
Sweden[c]	27.0	1,020	83.0	35,720	83.0	35,720
Norway	6.0	11,480	48.0	65,680	48.0	65,260
Denmark[c]	40.8	720	68.8	16,750	68.8	16,490
Belgium[c]	29.7	18,670	76.3	130,560	76.3	129,120
Austria	23.0	2,220	62.0	135,570	62.0	135,130
France	3.6	8,560	54.0	125,470	60.0	110,690
United Kingdom	25.0	5,513	83.0	81,780	98.0	81,780
West Germany	20.0	7,480	55.0	134,180	55.0	134,180
Canada[c]	8.6	4,660	61.9	78,130	61.9	77,910
Italy	10.0	2,540	72.0	1,204,800	87.0[c]	1,204,800[c]
United States	14.0	8,000	50.0	58,750	70.0	253,750
Japan[c]	21.0	11,400	83.7	414,100	93.0	377,610

Source: Author's calculations. Tax rates are reduced by standard deductions where they are explicitly related to income.
a. Incomes are translated to U.S. equivalents on the basis of relative average production worker earnings in 1978.
b. Gross income before deductions for a married taxpayer with two children under eleven years old.
c. Includes local income taxes.

Table 8. *Average and Marginal Income and Payroll Tax Rates on Earnings of Average Production Workers, Selected Countries, 1976*[a]

Percent

Country	Average rates		Marginal rates	
	Excluding payroll taxes	*Including employee payroll taxes*	*Excluding payroll taxes*	*Including employee payroll taxes*
Netherlands	11	31	26	42
Sweden	35	35	63	63
Norway	20	27	34	42
Denmark	29	33	51	55
Belgium	11	22	27	37
Austria	1	14	19	28
France	...	10	6	16
United Kingdom	20	26	35	41
West Germany	11	27	18	34
Canada	14	16	30	30
Italy	6	14	15	23
United States	11	17	26	32
Japan	4	8	17	21

Source: Organisation for Economic Co-operation and Development, *The Tax/Benefit Position of Selected Income Groups in OECD Member Countries* (Paris: OECD, 1978), pp. 94, 96.

a. For a married couple with two children, assuming one parent earns all the income.

Joseph A. Pechman

Table 9. *Effective Tax Rates on Earned Income for a Married Couple with Two Children, by Earned Income Level, Selected Countries, 1978*[a]
Income in thousands of dollars; rates in percent

Income	United Kingdom	United States	Sweden	Denmark	Germany	Norway	France	Japan
5	b	b	b	18.1	b	...	...	...
6	b	b	3.6	19.9	b	...	...	...
7	b	b	7.0	22.0	b	...	...	0.1
8	b	1.5	9.9	22.8	b	...	...	0.4
9	1.0	3.1	12.6	25.4	b	...	...	0.7
10	3.9	4.5	15.1	27.4	1.3	...	0.3	1.4
12.5	9.1	7.0	20.9	28.3	4.6	0.5	1.9	3.3
15	12.5	9.2	26.1	28.6	7.1	1.7	3.4	5.0
17.5	15.0	10.6	30.7	30.3	9.0	3.1	4.5	6.7
20	16.8	11.7	34.9	31.3	11.0	4.7	5.5	8.3
22.5	18.2	12.6	38.4	33.6	13.3	6.7	6.5	9.7
25	19.4	13.4	41.4	34.9	15.5	9.0	7.4	11.0
30	21.1	15.1	46.2	36.7	19.3	13.4	9.1	13.7
35	23.2	16.7	49.6	38.0	21.9	17.0	10.9	16.3
40	25.6	18.3	52.8	39.0	23.9	20.2	12.5	18.6
45	28.3	19.8	55.2	39.7	25.6	22.6	14.0	20.7
50	30.8	21.2	57.2	40.3	27.1	25.0	15.5	22.8
60	35.7	24.0	60.1	41.3	29.6	28.5	17.7	26.6
70	40.0	26.3	62.2	41.9	31.5	31.1	19.3	30.0
75	41.8	27.2	63.0	42.1	32.3	32.2	19.9	31.5
80	43.3	28.0	63.7	42.4	33.1	33.2	20.5	33.0
90	46.7	29.3	64.9	42.8	34.4	34.9	21.4	35.5
100	49.5	30.4	65.9	43.1	35.5	36.2	22.2	37.8
125	54.6	32.3	67.7	43.6	37.9	38.5	24.9	42.5
150	57.9	33.6	68.9	44.0	39.4	40.1	28.9	46.0
175	60.3	34.5	69.7	44.3	40.5	41.2	32.5	48.9
200	62.1	35.2	70.3	44.5	41.3	42.1	35.2	51.5
250	64.6	36.2	71.2	44.7	42.4	43.3	39.0	55.7

Source: Author's calculations.

a. Income has been converted to U.S. equivalents on the basis of the estimated ratio of relative earnings of production workers in 1978. Standard deductions and average employment deductions were allowed for where applicable.

b. Tax rates are negative, reflecting children's cash allowances or tax credits.

Table 10. *Effective U.K. Tax Rates on Earned Income for a Married Couple with Two Children, by Real Income Level, 1973–74 to 1979–80*[a]

Real income in thousands of dollars; rates in percent

Real income 1973–74	1973–74	1974–75	1975–76	1976–77	1977–78	1978–79	1979–80
2	10.9	12.7	16.3	15.7	13.2	12.2	9.6
3	16.8	20.5	21.9	21.6	19.6	18.6	15.9
4	19.7	24.4	24.8	24.5	22.8	21.8	19.0
5	21.5	26.7	27.6	27.5	25.8	24.8	21.5
6	22.6	28.5	30.7	30.9	29.4	28.7	24.6
7	24.1	30.5	34.0	34.4	33.1	32.5	27.4
8	26.1	32.7	36.9	37.7	36.4	36.2	29.9
9	28.2	35.0	39.6	40.6	39.5	39.6	32.0
10	30.3	37.0	42.0	43.2	42.7	42.7	34.0
14	37.4	44.1	49.8	51.3	51.8	52.2	40.3
20	45.4	51.9	58.0	59.6	59.9	60.2	45.3
25	50.1	57.3	62.2	63.4	63.7	64.0	47.7
50	60.7	68.1	70.5	71.1	71.3	71.4	52.3
100	66.0	73.5	74.7	75.0	75.1	75.1	54.7
1,000	70.7	78.3	78.4	78.5	78.5	78.5	56.8

Source: Author's calculations.

a. Assuming the taxpayer has deductions of 5 percent of his income and children are under 11 years of age. The cash benefits for children are treated as tax credits in these calculations and the family's exemption is reduced by the "clawback" for the family allowance given to the second child.

Table 11. *Illustration of the Classical and U.K. Imputation Systems of Taxing Corporate Earnings, 1978–79 and 1979–80*

Marginal individual income tax rate (percent) (1)	Corporate income before tax (2)	Corporation tax at 52 percent (3)	Dividends received by stockholder (4)	Stockholder's individual income tax (5)	Total tax burden (6)	Additional burden of the corporation tax (7)
Classical system						
0	100	52	48	0	52.00	52.00
20	100	52	48	9.60	61.60	41.60
33	100	52	48	15.84	67.84	34.84
40	100	52	48	19.20	71.20	31.20
50	100	52	48	24.00	76.00	26.00
60	100	52	48	28.80	80.80	20.80
75	100	52	48	36.00	88.00	13.00
98	100	52	48	47.04	99.04	1.04
Imputation system, 1978–79 (standard rate: 33 percent)						
0	100	52	71.64	−23.64	28.36	28.36
20	100	52	71.64	−9.31	42.69	22.69
33	100	52	71.64	0	52.00	19.00
40	100	52	71.64	5.02	57.02	17.02
50	100	52	71.64	12.18	64.64	14.64
60	100	52	71.64	19.34	71.34	11.34
75	100	52	71.64	30.09	82.09	7.09
98	100	52	71.64	46.57	98.57	0.57
Imputation system, 1979–80 (standard rate: 30 percent)						
0	100	52	68.57	−20.57	31.43	31.43
20	100	52	68.57	−6.86	45.14	25.14
30	100	52	68.57	0	52.00	22.00
40	100	52	68.57	6.86	58.86	18.86
50	100	52	68.57	13.71	65.71	15.71
60	100	52	68.57	20.57	72.57	12.57
75	100	52	68.57	30.86	82.86	7.86

Source: Author's calculations.
Column 3 = 0.52 × column 2.
Column 4 = column 2 − column 3. Includes 23.64 (33/67 × 48) with standard rate of 33 percent and 20.57 (30/70 × 48) with standard rate of 30 percent.
Column 5 = column 1 × column 4. After deduction of credits of 23.64 or 20.57 under the imputation system.
Column 6 = column 3 + column 5.
Column 7 = column 6 − (column 1 × column 2).

Table 12. *Effective Rates of U.K. Taxes, by Income Class, 1978*

Income class[a] (thousands of dollars)	Cumulative percent of household units in the United States	Effective tax rate (percent)			
		Personal income tax	Corporate tax	Other taxes	Total taxes
0–1	1.1	0.7	3.5	[b]	[b]
1–2	1.9	1.6	1.8	[b]	[b]
2–3	3.0	1.0	1.1	[b]	[b]
3–4	4.4	2.1	1.2	[b]	[b]
4–5	6.4	0.6	0.7	36.3	37.5
5–7.5	12.7	1.4	0.7	28.1	30.1
7.5–10	18.9	3.6	0.6	24.0	28.2
10–12.5	25.0	4.1	0.6	22.6	27.4
12.5–15	31.0	5.2	0.6	22.1	27.9
15–17.5	36.9	6.8	0.6	21.8	29.1
17.5–20	42.6	7.8	0.6	22.2	30.5
20–25	54.3	9.1	0.5	21.7	31.4
25–30	64.1	9.8	0.6	20.9	31.3
30–40	79.8	9.7	0.7	19.2	29.6
40–50	89.1	9.5	0.8	17.3	27.5
50–60	93.4	9.1	1.0	16.1	26.2
60–75	96.4	9.2	1.2	15.0	25.5
75–100	98.3	11.2	1.7	14.3	27.1
100–500	99.9	19.7	3.8	12.4	35.9
500–1,000	100.0	20.9	7.5	12.2	40.6
1,000 and over	100.0	16.0	10.4	13.6	40.0
Total[c]	100.0	10.1	1.3	18.6	29.9

Source: Calculations based on Brookings 1970 MERGE file projected to 1978. U.K. incomes are translated to an equivalent U.S. basis by using a 2.86:1 ratio. Figures are rounded.

a. This is a comprehensive concept of economic income. See note 31 in the text.

b. Effective rates are unusually high in these classes, reflecting the low incomes of household units that may be in the class temporarily.

c. Includes household units not shown separately.

Table 13. *Effective Rates of U.S. Taxes, by Income Class, 1978*

Income class[a] (thousands of dollars)	Cumulative percent of household units in the United States	Effective tax rate (percent)			
		Personal income tax	Corporate tax	Other taxes	Total taxes
0–1	1.1	[b]	5.9	[b]	[b]
1–2	1.9	[b]	3.6	[b]	[b]
2–3	3.1	[b]	2.9	18.6	30.5
3–4	4.6	4.8	1.7	14.2	20.6
4–5	6.7	3.7	1.4	11.7	16.8
5–7.5	13.1	2.8	1.4	11.1	15.2
7.5–10	19.3	2.5	1.2	11.7	15.5
10–12.5	25.4	2.3	1.3	12.3	15.8
12.5–15	31.3	2.9	1.2	13.0	17.1
15–17.5	37.1	3.7	1.2	13.4	18.3
17.5–20	42.9	4.6	1.2	13.7	19.5
20–25	54.6	5.6	1.1	13.7	20.4
25–30	64.6	6.6	1.2	13.6	21.4
30–40	80.5	8.0	1.3	12.9	22.2
40–50	89.7	9.6	1.5	12.1	23.2
50–60	93.8	10.6	1.8	11.5	23.9
60–75	96.7	12.1	2.5	11.0	25.6
75–100	98.4	14.1	3.5	10.4	28.0
100–500	100.0	18.6	7.5	10.2	36.3
500–1,000	100.0	22.1	14.6	12.4	49.1
1,000 and over	100.0	20.1	21.2	14.7	56.1
Total[c]	100.0	9.1	2.3	12.4	23.8

Source: Calculations based on Brookings 1970 MERGE file projected to 1978. Figures are rounded.
a. This is a comprehensive concept of economic income. See note in text.
b. Effective rates are unusually high in these classes, reflecting the low incomes of household units who may be in the classes temporarily.
c. Includes household units not shown separately.

Table 14. Rates of Investment, Initial, and First-Year Allowances for New Assets in the United Kingdom

Percent

Period	Industrial buildings	Agricultural and forestry buildings and works	Ships	Mining works	Scientific research assets[a]	Fuel saving plant	Other plant and machinery	Dredging	Second-hand plant and ships	Private cars
Investment allowances										
4/8/59–11/5/62	10	10	40	20	20	20	20	10	...	...
11/6/62–1/16/66	15	15	40	30	30	30	30	15	...	...
Initial allowances										
4/8/59–4/2/63	5	...	...	20	...	10	10	5	30	30[b]
4/3/63–4/5/65	5	...	...	20[c]	...	10	10[e]	5	30	30[b]
4/6/65–1/16/66	5	...	d	20[c]	...	10	10[e]	5	30	...
1/17/66–4/5/70	15	...	d	40	...	30	30[e]	15	30	...
4/6/70–10/26/70	30[f]	...	d	40	...	30	30[e]	15	30	...
10/27/70–3/21/72	30[f]	...	...	40[c]	...	...	...	15	...	...
3/22/72–11/11/74	40	...	...	40[c]	...	...	...	15	...	...
11/12/74 and after	50	...	...	40[c]	...	...	...	15	...	...
First-year allowances										
10/27/70–7/19/71	...	...	d	...	...	60[g]	60[g]	...	60	...
7/20/71–3/21/72	...	...	d	...	...	80[h]	80[h]	...	80	...
3/22/72 and after	...	...	d	...	...	100	100	...	100	...

Source: Board of Inland Revenue, *Inland Revenue Statistics, 1978* (HMSO, 1978), p. 167.

a. From November 6, 1962, expenditure allowed wholly in the first year.

b. For cars costing more than £2,000 acquired after April 16, 1961, the initial allowance was restricted.

c. Free depreciation allowed in development districts (areas) and Northern Ireland.

d. Free depreciation.

e. Under the Industrial Development Act 1966, new plant and machinery in manufacturing industry qualified for a grant of 20 percent (40 percent in development areas). Writing-down allowances are given only on the net expenditure after deduction of grant. The (rate of) grant was increased to 25 percent (45 percent for 1967 and 1968).

f. 40 percent in development and intermediate areas and Northern Ireland.

g. Capital expenditure on new immobile plant and machinery for industrial purposes in development areas and Northern Ireland qualified for a 100 percent first-year allowance. Expenditure on other plant and machinery qualified for a first-year allowance of 60 percent and an annual writing-down allowance of 25 percent thereafter.

h. Capital expenditure on all new immobile plant and machinery in development areas and Northern Ireland qualified for a 100 percent first-year allowance.

Table 15. *Sources of Finance of Quoted Corporations in the United Kingdom, 1960–76*[a]

Percent

Year	Total	Retentions	Long-term debt	Bank borrowing	New stock issues
1960	100.0	74.8	2.4	8.8	14.2
1961	100.0	65.3	6.3	11.0	17.6
1962	100.0	66.8	20.7	5.4	7.1
1963	100.0	77.5	8.9	7.1	6.3
1964	100.0	76.8	9.0	8.6	5.5
1965	100.0	69.3	14.0	14.5	2.2
1966	100.0	68.8	18.7	9.5	3.0
1967	100.0	74.5	19.8	2.8	2.9
1968	100.0	75.7	7.2	8.5	8.6
1969	100.0	69.9	6.1	17.8	6.2
1970	100.0	70.2	8.4	19.3	2.2
1971	100.0	85.6	14.6	−4.0	3.9
1972	100.0	82.9	6.1	7.1	3.9
1973	100.0	70.0	8.4	21.1	0.6
1974	100.0	68.4	1.5	28.8	1.3
1975	100.0	83.4	5.6	−1.6	12.7
1976	100.0	64.5	16.5	10.9	8.1

Sources: 1950–72: Mervyn King, *Public Policy and the Corporation* (London: Chapman and Hall, 1977), p. 209; 1973–76: data supplied by Mr. King.

a. The data cover quoted companies in manufacturing, distribution, and other services.

Table 16. *Real Rates of Return before and after Tax and Ratio of Real Gross Private Domestic Investment to Real Gross Domestic Product, Industrial and Commercial Companies in the United Kingdom, 1966–77*

Percent

Year	Real rates of return, industrial and commercial companies		Ratio of gross private domestic investment to gross domestic product[c]
	Before tax[a]	After tax[b]	
1966	10.3	5.7	13.8
1967	10.6	6.3	13.0
1968	10.4	5.9	13.5
1969	10.1	5.0	14.4
1970	8.7	4.1	14.8
1971	8.7	4.5	14.0
1972	8.6	5.0	14.1
1973	7.2	7.2	15.8
1974	3.9	4.0	17.5
1975	3.5	3.0	16.5
1976	3.8	3.0	16.1
1977	4.5	3.6	16.5

Sources: "Profitability and Company Finance, A Supplementary Note," *Bank of England Quarterly Bulletin*, vol. 19 (June 1979), p. 183; and Central Statistical Office, *National Income and Expenditure, 1966–76* and *1967–77* (HMSO, 1977; 1978).

a. Non–North Sea gross trading profits less stock appreciation and capital consumption at replacement costs, expressed as a percentage of net capital stock at current replacement cost. Excludes foreign income and investment.

b. Same as note a, except that U.K. taxes are deducted from profits, with tax allowances computed by reference to the present value of current investment incentives.

c. Gross domestic product is expressed in market prices.

Comments by Mervyn A. King

FEW AREAS of the British economy have received more attention in recent years than the tax system. Discussion about both the structure and rates of taxation has featured prominently in public debate and academic research and played a leading role in the 1979 election campaign. Despite the many changes that the tax system has undergone in the past two decades, still more changes can be expected in the next two or three years.

The paper by Joseph Pechman, who is one of the leading overseas experts on taxation, is therefore especially timely in providing an "outsider's" view of taxation in the United Kingdom. Pechman divides his paper into three parts. First, he gives a description of the main features of the present British tax system, along with an assessment of the economic effects of the taxes. Then, in what to me is the most original part of the paper, he analyzes the distribution of the total tax burden among income groups. Finally, Pechman discusses some "options for change" and suggests the direction in which he thinks Britain should be moving.

A brief description of a tax system as complicated as that of the United Kingdom will inevitably produce some misleading impressions. Although Pechman's paper provides an excellent short guide to the main elements of the U.K. tax system, it does not bring out clearly what, I believe, is the most significant aspect of the British "income" tax system; namely, that it is a combined income tax and expenditure tax system. The concessions both to savings in such forms as pensions, life insurance, and owner-occupied housing and to physical investment in plant and machinery mean that the U.K. system is remote from any theoretical ideal of an income tax. This in itself would not matter were it not that many problems of the present system have arisen because Britain has neither an income tax nor an expenditure tax.

An example of such a problem is the "temporary" (with us since 1974) scheme for adjusting taxable corporate profits to allow for the effects of inflation on stock (inventory) values. Pechman implies that the "stock relief" scheme adjusts the tax base for the effects of stock appreciation. This is true only if one compares the total stock relief granted with the total value of stock appreciation in the economy, and even then there is no exact correspondence between the two; for individual firms, the effects may be very different. It is particularly important to point out that at the margin the present scheme allows both free depreciation on investment in

stocks and deductibility of interest payments on loans taken out to purchase those stocks. That has two consequences: the distribution of tax
burdens among companies may be very different from that which would
result from a proper inflation-adjusted system and at the margin there is a
strong incentive to invest in stocks.

What broad conclusions might one draw from Pechman's survey of the
tax system? His own conclusions are summarized in figure 1, which plots
effective tax rates on earned income (for a married couple with two children), by income level, in selected countries. Tax rates on earned income
in Britain are seen to be higher than those in most countries and are
particularly high at the top levels of earned income. But there are two
problems with drawing conclusions from this diagram. First, it ignores
taxes collected on consumption goods and national insurance contributions and so does not give an accurate picture of the relative values of
the tax "wedge" between earnings and consumption. Second, to evaluate
the significance of the diagram one needs to know the distribution of
earnings in different countries. It would seem that the incomes of the vast
majority of people in the United Kingdom would be well to the left in the
diagram; in this case the differences between countries are much less
marked. For example, the average earnings of male manual workers in
manufacturing in 1978 were about $12,000 (using Pechman's rate of
exchange), and at this level of income tax rates in Britain are by no means
exceptional. The design of the diagram tempts one to follow the lines upward and onward to ever higher levels of income and tax rates, although
there are few people in those ranges. Because the diagram is concerned
with effective average tax rates, and hence income distribution, one must
be careful to focus one's attention on those parts of it that are particularly
relevant.

The effects of the tax system on income distribution depend not only
on the taxation of earned income but also on the effective tax rates on
income from capital. One of the conclusions reached both by the Meade
committee and by John Kay and me in our own studies was that, because
of the great variation in tax rates on different types of capital income and
the interaction between inflation and tax burdens, the effective tax rate on
income from capital varies almost randomly from person to person and
year to year.[94] Although it is possible to say that the effective tax rate on
capital income is very different from the nominal tax rate, in fact very

94. Institute of Fiscal Studies, *Structure and Reform of Direct Taxation;* Kay and
King, *British Tax System.*

little is known about average effective tax rates on capital income in Britain or in other countries. That is one subject on which more research needs to be done.

In the second part of his paper, Pechman presents some very interesting calculations in order to assess the burden of the U.K. tax system on different income groups. He applies the income tax rate structure in Britain to a data file of the pretax distribution of income in the United States in 1978. It is of course strange to apply the tax system of one country to the pretax income distribution of another country, but unfortunately there is no file of individual data in the United Kingdom remotely comparable with the Brookings MERGE file. The Family Expenditure Survey, although extremely valuable in itself, contains an inadequate representation of households with large incomes; a study of the income, expenditure, and savings patterns of higher-income groups is badly needed.

The broad conclusion of Pechman's calculations is that, although effective tax burdens are greater in the United Kingdom than in the United States, the U.S. tax system seems to be more progressive. This conclusion may well be correct, but several factors need to be considered when assessing its validity. First, the effective tax rate for those on very low incomes depends upon a whole range of state benefits, which are not all taken into account in table 1. But even if they were, it would be difficult to assess the effects of the tax system on the distribution of lifetime income, since the need for many of the benefits depends upon the particular stage of the life cycle at which the household finds itself and upon "temporary" misfortunes. Furthermore, the income distribution is plotted for earned income plus the money value of capital income. In times of rapid inflation money-factor incomes are a poor indicator of real incomes; consequently, figures near the top of the distribution may be distorted. Finally, it is not known how much the pretax distribution of income reflects a particular tax system; it could therefore be misleading to compare the effects of two different tax systems on the pretax distribution of income under one of the systems. One needs to be particularly careful when examining the income distribution at the top end, because the effective tax rate on capital income in Britain depends critically on concessions to particular types of saving and investment. The division of capital income among different legal types of income may be very sensitive to the tax treatment of these different types, and consequently the distribution of *measured* income is very likely to be affected by the tax system. The numbers in table 1 are certainly very interesting but one should use caution when interpreting them. As Pechman indicates, there is need for further research in this area.

Turning to individual taxes, Pechman looks at the effect on tax burdens of the existence of a separate corporation tax. He shows that the imputation system has a much larger *absolute* effect on the tax burden of shareholders facing low personal tax rates than on the tax burden of shareholders facing the higher personal tax rates. Although that is true, it gives a misleading impression because the effect of the system on the *proportionate* change in liability is very different. One way of seeing this is to examine what I have elsewhere defined as the ACID (attempted corporate integration of dividends) test statistic:[95] the ratio of the maximum net dividend that the shareholder of a company could receive out of one unit of pretax profits to the maximum net dividend that would be received if the business were unincorporated. (This measure is shown in Pechman's table 11, column 4.) The ACID test statistic measures the extent to which the corporate tax system is a net addition to the taxation of dividends at the personal level, and it measures how successful the attempted integration of taxes has been. A value of unity means that the corporate tax system imposes no extra tax on dividends over and above the level of personal taxation, a value that is achieved only in Norway and West Germany. In the United States the value of ACID is about one-half; in the United Kingdom the present value is 0.69. This value is independent of the personal tax rates of the shareholders. As an aside, it may be worth adding that it would seem sensible to base the harmonization of corporate tax systems on some agreed range or band for the value of the ACID test statistic rather than on the rate of imputation. The harmonization of that rate, as proposed in 1975 by the Commission of the European Communities, would give the basic rate of income tax little flexibility. Even the recent change in the U.K. basic income tax rate from 33 percent to 30 percent (which appears marginal) is inconsistent with the Commission's proposals. In an area of active EC concern, it would seem highly desirable to give more thought to the principles on which harmonization is to be based.[96]

Table 2 has some interesting figures showing the effective tax rate on income from corporations for different income groups in the United King-

95. King, *Public Policy and the Corporation,* p. 57.
96. This issue is discussed further in ibid., p. 58.

dom and the United States. As is pointed out in note 29, the assumption behind the calculations is that the payout rate is independent of the opportunity cost of dividends in terms of retentions forgone. I would like to see the calculations reworked using those estimates of the elasticity of the payout rate with respect to the tax cost of dividends that have been obtained from econometric studies in the United Kingdom. These recalculations would show by just how much the tax liabilities in the U.K. column would be reduced. Another factor that needs to be considered is the importance of the U.K. tax-exempt institutions, which own a significantly higher proportion of equity than their U.S. counterparts.

Although the data in figure 3 on the distribution of total tax burden among income groups are subject to the criticisms noted above, they do lend impressive weight to the belief that the U.K. tax system is broadly proportional for most people. The fact that the tax burden is greater on employment income than on income from capital is shown by the concave shape of the curve for the top 75 percent of the U.K. population (but not the top 1 percent). Obviously these results depend upon the assumptions made about the incidence of various taxes. Pechman's comments suggest that alternative assumptions make little difference to the general picture. The next step in this sort of analysis, however, is to incorporate behavioral responses with the assumptions made about incidence—one of the aims of the Social Science Research Council program on taxation, incentives, and income distribution directed by A. B. Atkinson, M. A. King, and N. Stern. This program aims also to improve our knowledge of the incentive effects, the present evidence on which is well summarized by Pechman in the central part of his paper.

Before I turn to Pechman's conclusions, two further points merit a brief mention. First, the discussion of "tax expenditures" for personal saving does not really direct attention to the crucial question of the benchmark that is used to define a tax expenditure. This is, I believe, a major weakness in the Willis and Hardwick analysis cited in table 3. For example, employers' contributions to pension funds should be in the table and not in a footnote if, as table 3 implies, the benchmark is a comprehensive income tax. Second, it is worth emphasizing Pechman's point that the switch to the capital transfer tax in 1974 appears to have failed in its objective of increasing revenue from the taxation of transfers. The revenue from the transfer tax in recent years has actually been less than that from the old estate duty, and it is likely that the new concessions introduced in 1978 will reinforce this trend.

Pechman's survey of the British tax system and his analysis of its economic effects demonstrate that there is room for improvement in many areas, and Pechman argues forcibly for reform. He is sympathetic to the aims of a comprehensive income tax, but feels that such a tax has little political appeal. As Pechman says, in discussing the 1978 U.S. tax legislation, "the debate over the bill indicated that there is little support for comprehensive income taxation in the United States." In Britain, too, there seems to be little desire to introduce any of the measures necessary to move the present system nearer to a comprehensive income tax. And a common element in the legislation of the past twenty years is a shift to those features that are characteristic of an expenditure tax. I believe that this is not accidental and that it represents a genuine preference for expenditure-based rather than income-based taxes. The choice, therefore, is between moving gradually to a coherent personal expenditure tax or continuing with the present muddle.

My own preference is for a consolidation of the present system into a progressive personal expenditure tax. But the important conclusion to be drawn from Pechman's paper is that marginal changes in tax *rates* are less important than the reform of the tax *base*. It is toward this issue that debate in the United Kingdom should be directed.

MARSHALL E. BLUME

The Financial Markets

THE VIGOR of an economy has frequently been linked to the level of new investment. The United Kingdom, when compared with most other developed countries, has had a low level of new investment and in many areas the performance of the economy has been poor. One possible reason for such a low investment level is that the financial markets are not working properly, thereby curtailing the amount of capital available.

The purpose of this paper is to examine the financial markets in the United Kingdom. The paper begins with a comparison of the investment levels among various developed countries and then moves on to an overall description of the roles played by different U.K. participants in the financial markets in the provision and use of investment funds. Following this more general material is a detailed analysis of these participants, with comparisons to their U.S. counterparts where appropriate. Particular attention is paid to the venture capital markets and to the growing institutionalization of the equity markets.

I am grateful to the following persons for many useful comments on earlier versions of this paper: Colin L. Callegari, Richard E. Caves, Jean Crockett, M. J. Erritt, Irwin Friend, Wynne A. H. Godley, Richard J. Herring, Lawrence B. Krause, Paul Marsh, Bruce K. MacLaury, Morris Mendelson, Richard C. E. Morgan, J. L. Norton, Joseph A. Pechman, David A. Walker, Randolph Westerfield, and C. J. Wiles. Midland Bank Limited and J. Henry Schroder Wagg & Co. Limited supplied various unpublished data series from their internal files; William L. Bednarski, John Geewax, Dushyant Pandit, Richard Papetti, and Bruce Terker were responsible for most of the statistical analysis. I would also like to thank Rosemarie Moore for typing the several versions of this manuscript. Finally, the financial aid given by the Rodney L. White Center for Financial Research of the Wharton School is gratefully acknowledged.

The Amount and Quality of New Investment

In this section the level of new investment in the United Kingdom is compared, by various standards, with investment levels in the United States, Japan, and five of the six original members of the European Community (EC)—France, Belgium, West Germany, the Netherlands, and Italy.[1]

Percentage of GDP Devoted to Capital Formation

In 1960 the United Kingdom devoted 16 percent of its gross domestic product (GDP) to gross fixed capital formation, a somewhat smaller percent than did the United States, France, and Belgium and a much smaller percent than did Japan, West Germany, the Netherlands, and Italy (table 1). By 1970 the United Kingdom had increased this fraction to 19 percent, exceeding the United States by 2 percentage points. In comparison, these five original EC countries and Japan invested a greater percentage of their GDP in capital formation, ranging from 21 percent for Italy to 35 percent for Japan.

In 1977 the United Kingdom was still spending 18 percent of its GDP this way, the same level as the United States. The five EC members and Japan had either just maintained or decreased this percentage from the 1970 levels. At the extreme, the share of GDP put into capital formation by West Germany, the Netherlands, and Japan had dropped 5 percentage points in each country. Thus, by this measure, the United Kingdom is still not investing as much of its GDP as its EC colleagues and Japan. Nonetheless, the gap between the United Kingdom and these other countries narrowed during the seventies, largely because of a drop in the percentage of GDP that these other countries devoted to capital formation rather than because of an increase in the proportion for the United Kingdom.

Per Capita Capital Formation

In 1960 the per capita GDP of the United Kingdom exceeded that of any of these five original members of the European Community; never-

1. Britain became a member only in 1973.

Table 1. *Demand Categories Measured as Percentages of Gross Domestic Product, Eight Countries, 1960, 1970, and 1977*

Year and item	United King- dom	Bel- gium	France	West Ger- many	Neth- er- lands	Italy	United States	Japan
1960								
Private consumption	66	69	61	57	57	65	65	57
Government consumption	17	13	13	13	13	12	17	9
Gross fixed capital formation	16	19	20	24	24	22	18	30
Change in stocks	2	0	4	3	3	2	1	4
Net exports	−2	−1	2	3	2	−1	0	0
Gross domestic product	100	100	100	100	100	100	100	100
1970								
Private consumption	62	60	60	54	57	65	63	51
Government consumption	18	14	14	16	16	13	19	8
Gross fixed capital formation	19	22	23	26	26	21	17	35
Change in stocks	1	2	3	2	3	2	0	4
Net exports	1	2	0	2	−2	−1	0	1
Gross domestic product	100	100	100	100	100	100	100	100
1977								
Private consumption	59	62	61	56	58	65	65	59
Government consumption	21	17	16	20	18	14	19	10
Gross fixed capital formation	18	20	23	21	21	20	18	30
Change in stocks	1	1	1	1	2	1	1	1
Net exports	−1	−1	−1	2	1	−1	−2	1
Gross domestic product	100	100	100	100	100	100	100	100

Sources: 1960 and 1970 data are from International Monetary Fund, *International Financial Statistics*, vol. 31 (IMF, May 1978); 1977 data are from ibid., vol. 32 (May 1979). Figures are rounded.

theless, the United Kingdom ranked next to last in terms of per capita gross fixed capital formation (table 2). The United Kingdom surpassed only Italy among these EC countries, was substantially ahead of Japan, but trailed the United States by a large margin. Sometime in the late sixties Japan overtook the United Kingdom. Throughout the seventies Belgium and France increased their lead over the United Kingdom, while the United Kingdom maintained a roughly one-to-two relationship to West Germany, since Germany greatly decreased the proportion of its GDP devoted to capital formation.

Table 2. *Per Capita Gross Fixed Capital Formation for Eight Countries in Terms of Pounds Sterling, Selected Years, 1960–77*

United Kingdom = 100

Year	United King- dom	Belgium	France	West Germany	Nether- lands	Italy	United States	Japan
			Using foreign exchange rates					
1960	100	105.3	121.2	141.5	103.5	69.7	219.3	61.4
1965	100	117.4	147.3	152.8	114.4	63.6	197.8	81.4
1970	100	147.0	159.6	192.0	153.0	89.7	203.3	162.3
1971	100	141.4	157.8	202.5	156.9	82.9	197.3	160.2
1972	100	147.6	171.0	209.6	156.0	82.6	197.7	185.2
1973	100	159.0	184.2	219.8	166.3	86.5	184.7	222.6
1974	100	174.0	174.5	190.0	160.7	89.4	167.6	198.9
1975	100	173.2	180.7	171.9	155.2	79.4	141.8	165.2
1976	100	194.2	199.8	198.7	169.4	81.4	169.3	192.7
1977	100	207.5	203.6	219.9	204.0	86.4	190.3	229.9
			Using purchasing power parity rates					
1970	100	135.3	153.2	197.9	138.6	90.7	137.0	155.8
1973	100	160.2	195.4	230.9	179.8	91.5	177.6	200.2

Sources: Foreign exchange rates are from IMF, *International Financial Statistics*, vol. 31 (May 1978); 1960–76 figures for gross fixed capital formation and population are from ibid., and 1977 figures are from ibid., vol. 32 (May 1979); purchasing power parity rates are from Irving B. Kravis, Alan Heston, and Robert Summers, "International Comparisons of Real Product and Purchasing Power," *United Nations International Comparison Project: Phase II* (Johns Hopkins University Press for the World Bank and the United Nations, 1978), pp. 10, 18, 19.

Quality of Investment

Some concern has been expressed in the United Kingdom that not only are the levels of its new investment low in comparison to those of other countries but also that the quality and productivity of this investment are low.[2] A crude measure of quality that has been used before is the ratio of the percentage growth in some measure of output to the percentage of GDP devoted to capital formation. If all countries devoted the same percentage of GDP to capital formation, were obtaining the same relative output from their existing capital stock, and faced the same marginal efficiency of capital curves in terms of the percentage of GDP devoted to

2. See J. M. Samuels, Dr. R. E. V. Groves, and C. S. Goddard, *Company Finance in Europe* (London: The Institute of Chartered Accountants in England and Wales, 1975).

capital formation (as distinct from the absolute amount of capital), this ratio would be the same for all countries. If, however, these countries devoted different percentages of GDP to capital formation, this ratio would differ from one country to another, decreasing as the percentage of GDP devoted to capital formation increased. In that case, values of this ratio could not be compared among countries unless one knew the exact shape of the marginal efficiency of capital curves.

Yet in one case it is possible to interpret differences in this growth–investment ratio between two countries. Assuming that the first country devotes the same percentage or less of its GDP to capital formation as does a second country and at the same time has a lower value for the ratio, one could conclude one or both of the following: that the marginal efficiency of capital curve in the first country was lower than that of the second country or that the existing capital stock of the first country was not being used as effectively as in the second.

Over the 1970–77 period the real value of the United Kingdom's per capita GDP increased 10.0 percent and the average percentage of its GDP devoted to gross fixed capital formation was 19.4 percent, implying a value for the growth–investment ratio of 0.52 (table 3). The values of the ratio for Belgium, France, Germany, Italy, and the Netherlands were all equal to or greater than that for the United Kingdom; and at the same time, those countries devoted a greater percentage of their GDP to capital formation. Thus, based upon this crude measure, it would appear that the marginal efficiency of capital curve in the United Kingdom is below that of each of the five other countries or possibly that the United Kingdom is not using its existing capital stock as effectively.

In this type of comparison the United Kingdom does not come off well. It must be remembered, however, that besides the usual measurement errors that might invalidate the comparison, a basic problem exists in that the GDP, as conventionally measured, may not fully capture all the benefits to society of new investment. For example, if a greater proportion of investment in the United Kingdom were devoted to, say, environmental protection or improvements in workers' health and welfare, the percentage change in measured GDP would understate its true change from a social point of view. Finally, if the countries were starting with different capital bases, one might expect differences in the marginal efficiency of capital curves. Thus one should be very cautious in using this type of comparison to evaluate the functioning of the U.K. economy.

Table 3. *The Relation of Growth in Output to Investment in Eight Countries, 1970–77*

Country	Percentage change in per capita GDP from 1970 to 1977[a] (1)	Average percentage of GDP devoted to capital formation 1970–77[b] (2)	Ratio of column 1 to column 2
United Kingdom	10.0	19.4	0.52
United States	15.6	17.6	0.89
Japan	17.3	33.5	0.52
Belgium	24.6	21.6	1.14
France	25.0	23.5	1.06
West Germany	18.8	23.4	0.80
Italy	21.3	20.6	1.03
Netherlands	22.4	22.7	0.99

Sources: Column 1: gross domestic product and consumer price index figures for 1970 and population figures up through 1976 are from IMF, *International Financial Statistics*, vol. 31 (May 1978); GDP, CPI, and population figures for 1977 are from ibid., vol. 32 (May 1979). Column 2: estimates of gross fixed capital formation and gross domestic product for 1970 and 1971 were calculated using ibid., vol. 31 (May 1978), and for 1972–77 were calculated using ibid., vol. 32 (May 1979).

a. The numbers in this column are the ratios of 1977 GDP, deflated by the 1977 CPI and the population level, to 1970 GDP, deflated by 1970 CPI and the population level, and expressed as percentages.

b. The numbers in this column are averages of the yearly ratios of gross capital formation to GDP, expressed as percentages.

An Overview of the Capital Markets

One of the most publicized changes in the capital markets of both the United Kingdom and the United States in the recent past has been the growing institutionalization of the savings and investment process. In both countries individuals have on balance been selling their direct holdings of common stock, while institutions have on balance been buying. Nonetheless, individuals in both countries are still important stockholders in their own right and, in certain segments of the market, are undoubtedly the dominant investors.

This growing institutional presence, particularly in the equity markets, has led many commentators in both countries to express concern that the efficiency of the capital markets may have been impaired. Some of these commentators point to the potential economic power of institutions to affect the allocation of real resources. In the United Kingdom, for instance, some have asserted that institutions have used their economic power to thwart government financing plans to the detriment of society in general.[3] And in the United States some worry about the possibility that institutions might use their large holdings to control corporate management and therefore have called for laws to restrict institutional activities.[4] Another group of commentators, on the other hand, has argued that institutions with their large holdings may affect the very liquidity and operational efficiency of the capital markets and thereby cause an increase in the cost of funds to corporations as their liabilities become less desirable.

Although the Wilson committee has not formally come to any conclusions as of the end of 1979, the extensive work it did on the British financial markets found no persuasive evidence that institutional growth has hindered the ability of corporations to raise external funds.[5] The only exception may be small venture capital firms, but even here it is not clear that institutional growth is the principal reason that some of these firms may find it difficult to raise capital.

In the United States, the issue of the institutionalization of the financial markets and its potential problems has sometimes loomed so large as to dwarf other important issues connected with the markets. As an example, it is frequently forgotten that institutions were a dominant force in the elimination of fixed commission rates on the New York Stock Exchange, an action that would be expected to increase the operational efficiency of the equity market. Moreover, a recent study of investors in the United States concluded that, at the current level of institutional activity in the United States, further restrictions on institutional activities to curb their economic power would be unwarranted.[6] That study also found no evi-

---

3. Others would argue that if the government cannot issue debt on the terms it desires, the terms are just not competitive and the markets are working efficiently. For a statement of this position, see the lead editorial of *The Economist,* November 4, 1978.

4. In the United States there has been no important legislation passed in recent years to restrict the activity of institutions for the purpose of controlling their economic power. Perhaps the last major law designed to do so was the Taft-Hartley Act of 1947, which restricted union-dominated pension plans. The Teamsters scandal of several years ago, however, suggests that this law may not be as effective as intended. The Employee Retirement Income Security Act of 1974 (ERISA) was primarily designed to protect the rights of the beneficiaries of nonpublic pension plans—though in doing this, it may have placed some modest restrictions on institutional activities.

5. Committee to Review the Functioning of Financial Institutions, *Evidence on the Financing of Industry and Trade,* vols. 1–7 (London: Her Majesty's Stationery Office, 1977).

6. Marshall E. Blume and Irwin Friend, *The Changing Role of the Individual Investor* (John Wiley, 1978).

dence that institutional growth had impaired the liquidity of the market-place.

The primary purpose of this section is to put into perspective the changes in the capital markets that occurred in the United Kingdom during the years 1966–76. Where informative and equivalent U.S. data are available, the characteristics of the U.K. and U.S. markets are compared. The section begins with a short review of the historical pattern of returns on different types of assets in both the United Kingdom and the United States and then moves on to a look at the flows of funds among different sectors of the economy and, where possible, the balance sheets of these sectors.

Realized Returns

Over the six years ending in 1976, the realized before-tax total returns on the major types of U.K. financial assets did not keep up with inflation (table 4). With both dividends and capital gains and losses included, equity stocks realized the greatest return—10.3 percent per year—but were closely matched by the 9.1 percent per year realized on short terms. However, both these returns fell short of the 13.8 percent annual increase in the consumer price index.

In periods of unanticipated inflation, yields tend to rise and, correspondingly, the prices of long-term fixed-coupon instruments tend to drop, driving down the total realized return on bonds. This appears to be exactly what happened from 1970 to 1976 in the United Kingdom, giving long-term bonds the worst return. The gap between realized returns on financial assets and inflation was greater for the second half of the six-year period than for the first half. Finally, it might be noted that over this whole period capital gains accounted for only a fraction of the total return. Some types of financial institutions, like mutual funds or unit trusts, normally distribute dividend income, while other types, like pension funds, retain such dividends. The division of total return as between dividend and capital gain components may thus have implications for the relative growth of different types of institutions.

In the United States, by comparison, long-term corporate bonds over these years returned more than the inflation rate, because of their performance in the first half of the period.[7] Equity stocks turned in lower

---

7. During the sixties there was substantial unanticipated inflation in the United States, and bonds had negative returns for a number of years.

Table 4. *Annual Compound Rates of Return on Selected Financial Instruments and Annual Rates of Change in the Consumer Price Index in the United Kingdom and the United States, 1970–76*
Percent

Country and item	December 1970– December 1976	December 1970– December 1973	December 1973– December 1976
United Kingdom			
Consumer price index	13.8	8.6	19.3
Treasury bills[a]	9.1	6.8	11.5
Long-term corporate bonds[b]	4.9	5.1	4.6
Equity stocks			
Total return	10.3	6.3	14.6
Capital gain	2.4	1.9	2.9
United States			
Consumer price index	6.6	5.2	8.0
Treasury bills[a]	5.7	5.2	6.3
Long-term corporate bonds[b]	8.2	9.0	7.4
Equity stocks			
Total return	5.8	4.5	7.2
Capital gain	2.6	1.9	3.3

Sources: Long-term corporate bond returns for the United Kingdom are derived from the Financial Times actuaries index (twenty-year debenture and loan stocks); for the United States, from Moody's composite index. Equity stock returns for the United Kingdom are derived from the Financial Times actuaries index of industrial ordinary shares; for the United States, from Standard & Poor's composite index.
a. Realized return from reinvesting every three months in Treasuries.
b. Realized return from investing at the beginning of each year in a new twenty-year bond issued at par and then selling it at the end of the year.

total returns than bonds and did not beat the inflation rate. The price of any long-term instrument is positively related to the expected level of the cash payouts, such as coupons or dividends, and negatively related to the rate at which these payouts are discounted. Thus these differences in returns between bonds and stocks in the two countries might be taken as evidence that over the first part of the seventies investors judged the earnings prospects for U.K. equities more favorably than the earnings prospects for U.S. equities.[8]

8. Another explanation could be that the risk premiums on equities were substantially greater in the United Kingdom than in the United States. Because of the international flow of investment funds from one country to another, this explanation would require that the risk associated with equity investments be substantially greater in the United Kingdom than in the United States.

Table 5. *Net Changes in Financial Assets and Liabilities by Sector,*
United Kingdom and United States, 1970–77

Date	Central government and local authorities	Public corporations	Industrial and commercial companies	Personal sector	Rest of world	Balance and residual
			United Kingdom (millions of 1976 pounds)			
1970	3,526	−1,818	−2,431	2,283	−1,480	−80
1971	1,351	−2,314	63	2,281	−2,067	686
1972	−1,771	−1,379	2,083	2,468	−282	−1,118
1973	−3,034	−1,309	−1,344	4,597	1,527	−437
1974	−4,814	−2,293	−6,528	7,652	5,310	674
1975	−5,779	−3,425	−799	8,417	2,149	−564
1976	−6,109	−2,248	−1,279	8,034	1,137	483
1977	−3,920	−1,081	−2,079	7,544	−257	−206
			United States (millions of 1976 dollars)[a]			
1970	−28,200	...	−54,700	77,200	900	4,800
1971	−51,500	...	−50,600	72,300	19,600	10,200
1972	−24,000	...	−68,400	71,800	16,200	4,400
1973	−7,700	...	−91,600	82,500	4,000	12,800
1974	−28,300	...	−151,200	141,600	10,400	27,500
1975	−91,000	...	−4,100	107,400	−18,000	5,700
1976	−59,100	...	−32,600	80,700	−7,700	18,700
1977	−59,400	...	−57,500	64,400	20,600	31,900

Sources: For the United Kingdom, figures for 1974–77 are from Central Statistical Office, *Financial Statistics*, no. 191 (London: Her Majesty's Stationery Office, March 1979), table 1.1; figures for 1973 are from ibid., no. 188 (December 1977), table 1.1; figures for 1972 are from ibid., no. 176 (December 1976), table 1.1; figures for 1971 are from ibid., no. 140 (December 1973), table 2; and figures for 1970 are from ibid., no. 134 (June 1973), table 2. U.S. figures for central government and local authorities, industrial and commercial companies, personal sector, and rest of world are from Board of Governors of the Federal Reserve System, *Flow of Funds Accounts, 1st Quarter 1979* (The Board, 1979), pp. 12 and 14, 8, 6, and 12, respectively.
a. U.S. figures available only to tenths of billions.

The Flow of Funds

The seventies saw some dramatic changes in the flows of financial assets among the different sectors in the United Kingdom. Perhaps the most obvious change occurred in the government sector, which includes local authorities. In 1970 the government retired 3.5 billion more (1976) pounds of financial liabilities than it issued,[9] but from 1972 on, it became a net issuer of financial claims (table 5). By 1976 the government issued 6.1 billion more pounds of financial liabilities than it retired. To put this figure in perspective, £6.1 billion represented 4.9 percent of the gross national product of the United Kingdom in 1976 or 76.0 percent of the personal sector's net accumulation of financial assets. In 1977 the net

9. To facilitate comparisons across time, most pound figures in this section are expressed in 1976 pounds, and most dollar figures in 1976 dollars. Consumer price indexes from International Monetary Fund, *International Financial Statistics*, vol. 31 (IMF, May 1978), were used to make these adjustments.

amount of financial liabilities issued by the government fell to £3.9 billion.

In the United States, by comparison, the government sector, including state and local units, was a net issuer of financial liabilities throughout the seventies. U.S. governmental bodies in the peak year of 1975 issued a net amount of $91 billion of financial claims.[10] This figure represented 5.6 percent of the gross national product of the United States in that year and 84.7 percent of the personal sector's net acquisition of financial assets.

During peak years both the United Kingdom and the United States made roughly the same use of the financial markets, measured as a percentage of GNP. But the average annual net issuance of financial liabilities by governmental bodies in the United States, as a percentage of GNP, was less than that of the United Kingdom. Thus since 1973 government in Britain has made greater use of the financial markets, as a percentage of GNP, than government in the United States. If everything else were equal, this greater governmental use in Britain would be expected to make the cost of funds to the private sector greater than in the United States. But everything else is probably not equal, and there could well be adjustments in other parts of the economy that might mitigate this effect.

Despite the heavy borrowing requirements of the U.K. government sector, in 1974 the private industrial and commercial sector was able to raise a net amount of £6.5 billion in the financial markets. This sum is almost five times the amount raised in the previous year and represents 5.4 percent of the GNP of 1974. As is well known in the United Kingdom, a great portion of this amount was used to finance short-term assets, such as work in process, whose values had increased substantially because of inflation, and much of it represented bank borrowings rather than money raised from longer-term sources. Nonetheless, regardless of the reasons for the large amount of new financing or of the particular form it took, the fact that the capital markets could accommodate this large, nonrecurring demand testifies to the adaptability of the U.K. financial system. Put simply, the financial markets were able to transfer a substantial amount of funds, as judged in an historical perspective, without raising the costs of funds to a prohibitive level.

Except in 1977 the net accumulation of financial liabilities by U.K. public corporations was fairly steady over the 1970–77 period and generally exceeded that of the private industrial and commercial sector.

10. See note 9.

Since many of the so-called public corporations in the United Kingdom belong to what are generally regarded as the more cyclical industries, this fairly steady net accumulation of financial liabilities might suggest that the operating plans of such corporations are less sensitive to market pressures than those of private corporations. The sometimes-exercised practice of converting a sick private firm to a public corporation in order to preserve employment would be consistent with this possibility. If so, this steady demand for funds on the part of public firms would, for a given level of savings, alter the costs of funds to the private sector from what they would have been in a competitive world as the borrowing requirements of public firms forced up the costs of funds in slack periods and decreased the costs in boom periods. Although this type of behavior might initially lead to some destabilizing effects on the costs of funds to the private sector, the overall effect of the actions of public firms on the economy would hinge also on their impact on aggregate demand and output.

During the 1970–77 period the personal sector was a steady net accumulator of financial assets in both the United Kingdom and the United States. However, in terms of 1976 currencies, the trends in the two countries differed markedly. In the United Kingdom the personal sector accumulated £7.5 billion of financial assets in 1977, down only slightly from the peak of £8.4 billion in 1975. In the United States, by contrast, the personal sector accumulated $64.4 billion of financial assets in 1977, slightly less than half the peak amount of $141.6 billion in 1974.

The Ownership of Company Securities

In Britain, as in the United States, corporations not owned by the public sector finance their activities from a broad range of sources. The most important are internal funds, short-term debt, long-term debt,[11] and equity. Here I examine the distribution of ownership of long-term debt and equity among different sectors of the economy.

In comparing figures for long-term debt in the United States and the

11. Differences between U.K. and U.S. terminology can be confusing. Long-term fixed-income debt is sometimes referred to as "loan stock" in the United Kingdom, whereas in the United States such debt is normally called a bond. In the United Kingdom the term "bond" is usually reserved for a short-dated instrument of roughly five years or less. Even government debt is sometimes referred to as "stock": for example, the 13 percent Treasury stock of 1990.

United Kingdom, one should keep in mind two major institutional differences between the two countries. The first difference is that almost all such debt in the United Kingdom is callable only in the final years before the redemption date, normally a five-year interval, whereas in the United States, most long-term debt, with the exception of that of the federal government, is usually callable on prespecified terms after a prespecified number of years, such as five or ten years. In the United States, therefore, a corporation can redeem or call its debt at a predetermined price many years before maturity and, if interest rates were to fall, refinance its debt at a lower interest rate. Consequently, in the United States long-term debt is a more flexible financing instrument for corporations than in the United Kingdom.

The second difference is that government debt in the United Kingdom is subject to different tax provisions from that of private debt. Government issues, if held for over one year, are not subject to capital gains tax, while private issues are subject to such tax. Likewise, capital losses on government issues held over one year cannot be used to offset capital gains from other sources, while capital losses on private issues can be so used. The tax treatment of interest income is the same for both government and private debt. Thus government debt selling at a discount enjoys a tax advantage over otherwise similar private debt. Indeed, the government has on occasion utilized this tax advantage by issuing long-term debt at a discount, with an appropriate below-market coupon.

BALANCE SHEETS. According to data prepared by the U.K. Department of Industry from a survey of stockholder registers,[12] individuals at the end of 1975 directly held 37.5 percent of the market value of all listed U.K. registered ordinary shares (table 6). The four major institutional investors—insurance companies, pension funds, investment trusts, and unit trusts—held 42.9 percent of this type of stock. If other financial institutions, such as property companies or unlisted investment trust companies, were included, this figure would jump to 45.8 percent.

These aggregate figures hide the fact that individuals are the major investors in smaller companies. Thus, as of December 31, 1975, individuals owned 56.8 percent of the market value of smaller listed companies, defined as those with equity market values of less than £4 million. The

12. The Department of Industry conducted a survey of nominal holders and then allocated the resulting shareholdings back to the beneficial holders. These beneficial holdings are what are reported in the text.

Table 6. *Percentage Distribution of Market Value of Shareholdings by Type of Beneficial Holder and Size of Issue, 1975*
Percent of total

| | Size of issues[a] | | | | | |
Beneficial holder	Over £130 million	Over £40 million to £130 million	Over £4 million to £40 million	£4 million and under	Miscellaneous issues[b]	Total issues
Persons	36.8	34.9	36.0	56.8	47.4	37.5
Charities and other non-profit-making bodies serving persons	2.7	2.2	1.7	1.8	1.3	2.3
Stockbrokers and jobbers	0.3	0.3	0.4	1.9	0.4	0.4
Banks	0.6	1.4	0.3	0.5	0.1	0.7
Insurance companies	15.2	17.0	19.3	5.5	12.1	15.9
Pension funds	17.9	20.1	14.2	6.4	12.8	16.8
Investment trust companies	5.8	6.2	7.5	2.4	4.1	6.1
Unit trusts	3.4	4.0	5.6	5.0	3.9	4.1
Other financial companies	1.9	2.5	4.1	6.7	5.7	2.9
Industrial and commercial companies	2.3	4.5	6.8	8.0	1.9	4.1
Public sector	7.2	0.2	0.1	0.2	0.1	3.6
Overseas sector	5.7	6.8	4.0	4.8	10.2	5.6
Total (millions of pounds)	21,555	10,023	9,856	2,595	532	44,560

Source: Data provided by U.K. Department of Industry, December 31, 1975. Figures are rounded.
a. The strata relate to the market values of the equity on July 1, 1975, the date of the sampling frame used for the survey.
b. The unclassified share issues comprise ordinary share issues, of various market values, with voting and other rights that differ from those of the main ordinary share issues of their companies.

four major institutional investors together owned only 19.3 percent of these types of companies.

This pattern of ownership among listed companies, with institutions more heavily concentrated in the larger companies and individuals more heavily concentrated in the smaller companies, is very similar to the U.S. pattern. Moreover, in the United States, it is known that individuals are the dominant holders of unlisted issues, which usually are much smaller companies than those that are listed. If intercorporate holdings are excluded, it is estimated that individuals in the United States hold roughly 94 percent of the market value of all unlisted shares.[13] This pattern of ownership is consistent with the potential difficulties that an institutional investor might face in investing a large sum in a large number of small issues.

In the United Kingdom, unlike the United States, there is very limited information about the value and ownership of unlisted issues. But since individuals in the United Kingdom, as in the United States, are more heavily concentrated in smaller listed issues than in the larger listed issues and since U.K. institutions would face the same problems of investing in small issues as U.S. institutions, it might reasonably be hypothesized that individuals in Britain are even more heavily concentrated in unlisted issues than in the smaller listed issues. If one is willing to make some very rough assumptions, it is possible to estimate the proportion of all stocks, whether listed or not, owned by individuals in the United Kingdom. Estimates of personal wealth prepared by the U.K. Central Statistical Office indicate that individuals on December 31, 1975, held £17 billion of listed U.K. ordinary shares and £7 billion of unlisted U.K. ordinary shares.[14] Assuming a similar ownership pattern of unlisted shares in Britain as in the United States, these £7 billion would represent roughly 94 percent of all unlisted shares or, to be more conservative, 90 percent. On the basis of this smaller figure, the total market value of all shares would have to be £52.3 billion, of which individuals would own about 45 percent.

Although this figure of 45 percent is based upon a tenuous extrapolation, the pattern of holdings of listed stocks strongly suggests that the inclusion of unlisted shares would increase the proportion of stock owned by individuals in the United Kingdom.[15] This analysis also paints a much more complex picture of the institutionalization process than the aggregate figures reveal. The obvious implications for the provision of venture capital are explored below.

As in the United States, the proportion of stock owned by individuals in the United Kingdom dropped continuously during the sixties and

13. Blume and Friend, *Changing Role of the Individual Investor*, p. 173.

14. "Personal Sector Balance Sheets," *Economic Trends,* no. 291 (January 1978), p. 99.

15. Including over-the-counter stocks, the percentage of stock owned by individuals in the United States was somewhere between 53.4 percent and 66.9 percent in 1975. Blume and Friend, *Changing Role of the Individual Investor.*

Table 7. *Percentage Distribution of Market Value of Shareholdings by Type of Beneficial Holder, 1963, 1969, 1975*
Percent of total

Beneficial holder	1963	1969	1975
Persons	54.0	47.4	37.5
Charities and other non-profit-making bodies serving persons	2.1	2.1	2.3
Stockbrokers and jobbers	1.4	1.4	0.4
Banks	1.3	1.7	0.7
Insurance companies	10.0	12.2	15.9
Pension funds	6.4	9.0	16.8
Unit trusts	1.3	2.9	4.1
Investment trusts and other financial companies[a]	10.0	8.7	10.0
Industrial and commercial companies[b]	5.1	5.4	3.0
Public sector	1.5	2.6	3.6
Overseas sector	7.0	6.6	5.6

Source: M. J. Erritt and J. C. D. Alexander, "Ownership of Company Shares: A New Survey," *Economic Trends*, no. 287 (HMSO, September 1977), p. 100. Figures are rounded.
a. Includes property companies and unlisted investment trust companies.
b. Excludes property companies and unlisted investment trust companies.

seventies. Individuals owned 54.0 percent of all ordinary listed stock in 1963 (table 7). This percentage decreased to 47.4 percent in 1969 and, as already reported, to 37.5 percent in 1975. Institutions, including the four major ones, held 27.7 percent of all listed stock in 1963. This percentage increased to 32.8 percent in 1969 and, as already reported, to 46.8 percent in 1975. Because of the exclusion of unlisted stock, these percentages undoubtedly understate the individual share and overstate the institutional share, but even after allowing for these deficiencies, institutions have almost certainly increased their share. Finally, it might be noted that the share of stock owned by the overseas sector decreased from 7.0 percent in 1963 to 5.6 percent in 1975.

NET TRANSACTIONS. Since individuals and institutions tend to weight their portfolios toward different sectors of the market, part of this shift in ownership could theoretically be due to differences in performance of the different sectors of the U.K. equity market. But the special fifteen-year summary of the U.K. flow of funds shows that individuals were net sellers of ordinary equity every year from 1963 through 1976.[16] More specifically, over the period 1967–73 individuals' net sales in terms of 1976 pounds ranged from a low of £ 1.4 billion in 1969 and 1970 to a high of £ 2.5 billion in 1971 (table 8). In 1974 their net sales dropped to £ 1.1 billion from £ 2.4 billion the previous year. A substantial portion of this drop is probably attributable to the fall of stock market values in 1974.

In both 1975 and 1976 individuals sold less than £ 1 billion of equity. In view of the increase in security values for both of these years, these levels of net sales represent a substantial reduction from the levels of previous years. However, preliminary figures for 1977 indicate that individuals have increased their level of net sales from these lows.

Institutional Investors in General

The nominal value of the total assets administered by the four primary types of institutional investors increased dramatically from £ 18.4 billion in 1965 to £ 54.7 billion in 1976 (table 9). But when their assets are measured in 1976 pounds, using the CPI deflator, the story is quite different. From 1965 through 1970 the real value of their assets increased from £ 49.5 billion to £ 61.1 billion, but then decreased to £ 57.3 billion in 1975 and finally to £ 54.7 billion in 1976. Thus, during the 1970–76 period, the total real value of these institutional assets did not keep up with inflation—despite the substantial new money flowing into these institutions. Put another way, in that period the real return on their investments was negative.

These institutional investors place a large amount of their assets in equities. This type of investment represented about 34 percent of their holdings in 1976, a slight increase from the 33 percent in 1965. Likewise, they held roughly 18 percent of their portfolios in gilts or government securities in 1976, the same percentage as in 1965. Institutions increased their commitment to property investments from 6 percent in 1965 to 15 percent in 1976—perhaps the best performing assets of the period. Their commitment to other types of company securities, such as preferred stock or long-term debt, decreased from 15 percent in 1965 to 6 percent in

16. *United Kingdom Flow of Funds Accounts: 1963–1976* (Bank of England, May 1978), pp. 5–104.

Table 8. *Net Transactions of U.K. Company Securities in Secondary Market, by Sector and Type of Security, 1967–76*
Millions of 1976 pounds

Date and type of security	Public sector	Overseas sector	Personal sector	Nonfinancial companies	Financial companies
1967					
Ordinary share	13	18	−2,022	674	1,547
Fixed interest	...	88	93	212	732
1968					
Ordinary share	137	320	−1,778	742	1,513
Fixed interest	...	135	−217	198	655
1969					
Ordinary share	27	544	−1,420	421	949
Fixed interest	...	39	158	146	658
1970					
Ordinary share	13	359	−1,465	271	1,020
Fixed interest	...	97	−99	127	424
1971					
Ordinary share	155	484	−2,497	250	2,149
Fixed interest	...	254	−43	157	460
1972					
Ordinary share	26	268	−2,303	928	2,345
Fixed interest	...	323	−145	350	458
1973					
Ordinary share	25	706	−2,433	877	1,099
Fixed interest	...	307	−575	397	287
1974					
Ordinary share	46	837	−1,127	112	316
Fixed interest	...	113	−177	123	19
1975					
Ordinary share	665	217	−921	−59	1,789
Fixed interest	...	91	−38	98	76
1976					
Ordinary share	260	329	−801	232	1,153
Fixed interest	...	97	−102	112	13

Source: Derived from *United Kingdom Flow of Funds Accounts: 1963–1976*, table 5.9. Conversion rates are based on IMF, *International Financial Statistics*, vol. 31 (May 1978).

1976. This decrease parallels the declining importance of long-term debt —particularly, listed long-term loan stocks, to use the U.K. terminology— in the mix of new capital raised by corporations.

FOREIGN INVESTMENTS. In 1976 roughly 20 percent of institutional equity holdings consisted of non-U.K. securities, the bulk of which would

Table 9. *Total Assets and Percentage Distribution of Market Value of Assets of Major U.K. Institutional Investors, by Type of Asset, Selected Years, 1965–76*[a]

Percent of total unless otherwise indicated

Institution and date	Total assets Millions of current pounds	Total assets Millions of 1976 pounds	Net short term	Gilts	Property	Ordinary shares United Kingdom	Ordinary shares Over- seas	Other company securities	Other
Unit trusts[b]									
1965	500	1,346	2	1	...	84	9	4	0
1970	1,315	2,829	5	2	...	79	10	4	0
1975	2,555	2,979	10	1	...	71	15	3	0
1976	2,622	2,622	13	1	...	65	18	3	0
Investment trusts									
1965	3,119	8,399	2	1	...	57	35	4	1
1970	4,469	9,614	4	1	...	57	32	5	1
1975	5,705	6,652	6	3	...	49	36	4	2
1976	5,958	5,958	5	3	...	44	41	4	3
Insurance companies									
1965[c]	9,521	25,639	1	24	10	18	3	21	23
1970[c]	14,810	31,861	3	22	12	22	3	18	20
1975[c]	26,689	31,119	7	24	18	20	3	11	17
1976	28,508	28,508	7	21	20	24	5	7	16
Pension funds									
1965	5,253	14,145	2	18	2	41	1	15	21
1970	7,836	16,858	3	12	10	48	2	14	11
1975	14,166	16,518	7	15	16	47	4	6	5
1976	17,488	17,488	6	20	16	43	5	5	5
Total									
1965	18,393	49,529	2	18	6	33	8	15	18
1970	28,430	61,161	3	15	9	37	8	14	14
1975	49,115	57,268	7	18	14	34	8	8	11
1976	54,682	54,682	7	18	15	34	9	6	11

Source: Prepared by J. Henry Schroder Wagg & Co. Limited from various issues of *Financial Statistics* and *Business Monitor-M5* as well as from statistics provided by the Central Statistical Office on ordinary shares of overseas companies held by pension plans.

a. The four major institutional investors are described in detail on pages 284–90 of the text.

b. Excludes property unit trusts whose assets on December 31, 1976, had estimated book values of £452 million.

c. This is the distribution of assets by book value, as the market value of the assets of the insurance companies was not available before 1976. Total assets exclude the value of "agent balances."

be foreign currency securities treated for U.K. exchange control purposes as portfolio investments (as opposed to direct investments).[17] Up until October 23, 1979, Britain's balance of payments and official reserves were insulated from the effects of portfolio investment abroad by controls on transactions in such securities by U.K. residents; such investments could

17. Direct investments may be defined as those in which the investor establishes, expands, or consolidates an economic enterprise with the intention of participating in its management and operation; separate rules apply to the acquisition and disposal of such interests by U.K. residents.

not be acquired with foreign currency purchased in the official foreign exchange market, but would normally be purchased with "investment currency," or with borrowed foreign currency.

Investment currency was foreign currency originating mainly from the sale of U.K. resident–owned foreign currency securities; because supply was limited, it usually changed hands at a premium. From the beginning of 1978 until the elimination of controls, resident sellers of foreign currency securities obtained the full benefit of the premium; from 1965 until the beginning of 1978, 25 percent of any sale proceeds had to be sold at the official market rate of exchange, to the potential benefit of the official reserves. The level of the premium has fluctuated considerably: in 1978 it averaged some 42 percent, but by mid-1979 it had fallen to 13.5 percent, reflecting the easing of controls in the new budget. As of October 23, 1979, all controls were eliminated.[18]

As an alternative to the use of investment currency, professional managers of securities could with the Bank of England's permission borrow foreign currency for investment in foreign currency securities.[19] This largely removed exposure to the premium because securities in the borrowed portfolio were purchased with the borrowed foreign currency and once so purchased could be switched without resort to the use of investment currency. Exposure to the premium would have arisen only if the income from the securities were insufficient to meet the cost of the borrowing or, upon liquidation of the borrowed portfolio, the sale proceeds of the securities were insufficient to repay the borrowing.

CONCERN ABOUT INSTITUTIONAL GROWTH. As stated earlier, a frequent concern about the growth of institutional investors is the concomitant growth of their power and the potential that they may abuse that power. In evaluating this concern, it is useful to consider two separate issues. The first is related to the institutional investors' potential ability to affect in some adverse way the overall allocation of real resources. The second is related to potential conflicts of interest between the institutional investor and the beneficiary.

18. There was some modest easing of restrictions by the new Conservative government on July 18, 1979.

19. Such borrowings were sometimes made as one side of a back-to-back arrangement, under which, for example, a U.K. resident portfolio investor would borrow foreign currency from a nonresident and at the same time would lend an equivalent amount of sterling to the nonresident's U.K. subsidiary, to be used for its operations in the United Kingdom.

The propensity of institutions to hold specific assets, and perhaps the institutions' trading activity itself, might affect the relative prices of these assets as well as their general price level. The important question is whether institutions lead to a better allocation of resources or to a poorer one. In a competitive world in which each investor is fairly small, so that he acts as if he has no effect on the prices of individual assets, a competitive equilibrium would prevail, and most economists would agree that such an equilibrium is the best obtainable within a capitalistic system. The size distribution of institutional investors would seem, at least on the surface, to approximate this atomistic condition for a competitive equilibrium.

S. J. Prais of the National Institute of Economic and Social Research points out that the three largest insurance companies each had assets in excess of £1.5 billion at book value in 1973 and accounted for one-fourth of all insurance companies' assets.[20] Assuming that these three companies still accounted for about one-fourth of all insurance companies' assets in 1975 and that the composition of their portfolios were similar to the typical life insurance portfolio, the fact that insurance companies held roughly 16 percent of all listed equity in 1975 would imply that these three companies held about 4 percent of all listed equity in 1975. Similar calculations can be performed for other groups of institutional investors and show that no single institution accounts for a very large percentage of the total holdings in the market.

Nevertheless, some critics have argued that the competitive model does not hold because of a follow-the-leader mentality on the part of institutional investors. According to these critics, there are a limited number of leaders in the financial community who communicate their views to other institutional investors through market letters and the like, and these other investors blindly follow their advice. Support for this view is usually provided by an anecdote in which an institution recommends against purchasing some prominent new issue and the issue fails.

If the institutional recommendation were based upon a correct judgment that the terms of the new issue were noncompetitive, market efficiency would be enhanced. If the institution were frequently wrong in its judgment, its recommendations would have less and less influence. Thus

20. S. J. Prais, *The Evolution of Giant Firms in Britain: A Study of the Growth of Concentration in Manufacturing Industry in Britain, 1909–1970* (Cambridge: Cambridge University Press, 1976), p. 269, n. 53.

by a process of elimination those advisers that emerged as the leaders would tend to be those with the most frequently correct advice (assuming that there is in fact such a follow-the-leader behavior). Parenthetically, it should be noted that the generally greater research capability of institutions may allow them to make more informed judgments than individuals about market conditions and individual issues.[21] Hence it could be argued that increased participation of institutional investors might even enhance the efficiency of the market.

Those who express concern about the growth of institutions are not worried about the role played by institutions in driving prices to their correct level (except possibly for equity reasons), but rather about the possibility that institutions might be able to exercise oligopsonistic power against the issuers of financial claims, like the Bank of England. Overt collusion among the many institutional investors is farfetched, but a follow-the-leader mentality could conceivably mimic such collusion. It is hard to evaluate this argument empirically, since its proponents present only anecdotal evidence that is usually just as consistent with an efficiently operating competitive capital market as not.

The economic incentives facing such a large group of competitors would, however, make such a tacit arrangement very unstable. To profit as oligopsonists, a group of firms must be able to force a deviation of market rates from their competitive equilibrium through some common action, such as restricting the amount that they would finance of some new issue. In such a situation the competitive pressure to produce superior returns would give great incentive to a small institutional investor to break the cartel, and the rewards through increased management fees would be very great to such an investor. Therefore, until proponents of this cartel-type argument provide convincing empirical evidence of its validity, fears that institutions would be able to act as oligopsonists appear to be unwarranted. If the atomistic structure of institutional investors were to change dramatically, then there might be some justification for this fear, but not at the present time.

21. There is an equity question about who should profit from a disequilibrium situation. In the United States the regulatory bodies have generally taken the position that all relevant new information should be made available to all investors simultaneously. If taken literally, this position would probably result in a substantial reduction of private research effort, with a possible reduction in the efficiency of the market. A delicate balance must therefore be struck between equity and efficiency considerations.

Perhaps the most telling evidence about the effect of institutions on the market is their investment performance. If institutions do affect prices, either through superior insight or market power, one would expect institutions to outperform the market. A careful review of the literature by Elroy Dimson finds no persuasive evidence that unit trusts, institutions for which the public data are available, have outperformed the market.[22] The more extensive studies in the United States, with only a few exceptions, have reached a similar conclusion. If institutions in the United Kingdom have been attempting to manipulate asset prices, either overtly or through a follow-the-leader mentality, such actions do not appear to have had much effect.

It is also sometimes feared that institutional investors may be more interested in making money than in serving the public welfare. In a competitive society this amounts to a fear that private benefits differ markedly from social benefits and, if justified, ultimately becomes an indictment of the competitive system. It is hard to see what this indictment has to do with institutional growth.

The second major area of concern about institutions is the potential conflict of interest between beneficiaries and those responsible for the investment decisions. Here the competitive model may no longer hold. For example, an employee may not know, or may not devote the energies necessary to learn, what investment decisions his trustees are making. A beneficiary of a standard life insurance policy seldom knows exactly what investments are backing up the potential claims; he only cares that the claims be paid. The usual way to guard against these potential conflicts has been through some sort of regulation.

Although it is beyond the scope of this paper to analyze the adequacy of current regulations in the United Kingdom to cope with these conflicts, it might be noted that, while these potential conflicts of interest, such as self-dealings between a pension plan and the sponsoring corporation, may have serious equity effects,[23] their overall effect upon the entire allocation process is likely to be small. But laws and regulations designed to

22. Elroy Dimson, "A Review of UK Stock Market Research" (London Graduate School of Business, December 1977).

23. *The Economist,* November 4, 1978, pp. 109–15, contains examples of several pension plans whose investment strategies would be difficult to reconcile with the goals of the beneficiaries. *The Economist* called for greater disclosure as a way to reduce the incidence of such conflicts in the future.

thwart such conflicts, if not carefully conceived, may well affect the allocation of real resources.[24]

A Detailed Look at the Capital Markets

The last section examined the general trends in the capital markets. The purpose of this section is to take a more detailed look at specific participants in the U.K. capital markets to determine whether there are any institutional features of these markets that hinder market efficiency or lead to social inequities. The section begins with a close look at institutional investors, then turns to individual investors and private corporations, and ends with a brief examination of the primary and secondary markets for long-term securities.

Institutional Investors

From 1970 through 1976 the real value of the combined assets managed by the four principal institutional investors dropped in value; but contrary to this trend, the real value of pension fund assets increased slightly, from £16.9 billion in 1970 to £17.5 billion in 1976, all stated in 1976 pounds (table 9). The remaining three institutional types experienced a drop in the value of their assets, with investment trusts showing the greatest drop.

UNIT TRUSTS. Unit trusts are very similar to U.S. mutual funds in that they continually issue and redeem their shares at net asset value. But they are taxed in a totally different way from U.S. mutual funds, because they must pay corporate tax. In the United States, as long as virtually all the net income received by a mutual fund is passed through to the beneficiaries within a short period of time, the mutual fund is exempt from tax liability,

24. As an example in the United States, the comprehensive law ERISA was passed with the laudatory purpose of protecting the right of the beneficiaries of private pension plans. Though it is too early to evaluate the bill completely, even its proponents would recognize that it has had some undesirable effects. For political reasons the responsibility for administering the bill was divided between two government departments, which fact has created some very burdensome reporting and compliance requirements. Because of these reporting and compliance costs and certain other provisions of the bill, some smaller corporations have decided to cancel their pension plans.

either on its own behalf or on the behalf of its stockholders. Under the imputation system in the United Kingdom, income paid out by a corporation to a stockholder is divided into "franked" and "unfranked" investment income. Franked investment income is income that has been paid out after corporate tax, such as corporate dividends, while unfranked investment income is income paid out before corporate tax, such as interest. Any franked income that one corporation receives from another is not taxed further, but unfranked income is taxed. Thus a unit trust that takes the form of a corporation can pass dividends through with no additional tax liability but must pay tax on interest income.

This tax has effectively precluded the establishment of general type bond funds; it is usually more advantageous for an individual to hold a bond directly. Most of the assets of unit trusts are therefore in company securities yielding franked income (table 9). If, as in the United States, most holders of unit trusts are investors of low-to-moderate means, this tax structure may well preclude many smaller investors from investing in long-term debt instruments and in that way achieving further diversification. There seems to be no obvious reason to continue a taxation system that precludes a particular type of investment if the system can be changed with no loss of taxes, as would appear to be the case in the United Kingdom. It might be noted that, when the Carter administration was considering the elimination of the double taxation of dividends in the United States, a specific part of the program prepared by the Treasury Department would have treated mutual funds as agents for individual investors and subject to no taxes.[25]

Unlike the U.S. mutual fund industry, the unit trust industry has had continual net inflows of new money every year, partly owing to the prevalence of regular subscription schemes by which investors contribute a fixed amount at regular intervals. As a result of these inflows, unit trusts have been net purchasers of company securities over most of the 1968–77 decade (table 10).

INVESTMENT TRUSTS. Investment trusts are much like closed-end investment companies in the United States. They have a fixed capital structure, often with some leverage, and because of legal restrictions and tradition, do not as a matter of course redeem shares at net asset value.

25. See Marshall E. Blume, Jean Crockett, and Irwin Friend, *Financial Effects of Capital Tax Reform,* New York University Monograph Series in Finance and Economics, 1978-4 (New York, 1978).

Table 10. *Net Purchases and Sales of Major U.K. Institutional Investors in U.K. and Overseas Company Securities, 1968–77*[a]

Millions of 1976 pounds

Date	Unit trusts		Investment trusts		Insurance companies, United Kingdom and overseas[b]	Superannuation funds, United Kingdom and overseas
	United Kingdom	*Overseas*	*United Kingdom*	*Overseas*		
1968	477	18	245	30	1,012	848
1969	301	63	−36	−148	609	883
1970	95	37	−69	37	761	1,030
1971	161	24	225	52	937	979
1972	140	125	221	596	1,556	1,241
1973	88	50	−402	−206	722	788
1974	4	−68	−171	−458	56	333
1975	288	109	154	78	482	1,397
1976	56	−14	44	−86	238	1,108
1977	113	17	43	−72	484	1,213

Sources: Derived from the December 1973, December 1975, December 1978, and March 1979 issues of Central Statistical Office, *Financial Statistics*, tables 8.11, 8.12, 8.13, 8.14.

a. The four major institutional investors are described in detail on pages 284–90 of the text.

b. Values before 1974 do not include the slight expansion in the statistical base caused by the inclusion of nonmembers of the British Insurance Association at the beginning of 1974.

An investor wishing to sell his shares will usually sell them in the open market at whatever price he can obtain. There is no guarantee that the sale price will be the same as the net asset value of the trust—it could be greater or less but is usually less. Investment trusts are taxed in the same way as unit trusts and therefore confine most of their investment to company securities with franked income (table 9).

Because of the relatively fixed nature of their capital structure, investment trusts have not benefited, as unit trusts have, from a steady inflow of new funds. In fact, since 1975 investment trusts have redeemed more of their shares than they issued and currently represent a much smaller proportion of institutional assets than they did in the past. Though their nominal returns have probably been positive, their real returns over the last decade have clearly been negative.

INSURANCE COMPANIES. Although the real value of their assets decreased after 1970, in 1976 insurance companies were the most important institutional investor, with assets of £28.5 billion as against £17.5 billion for pension funds and £54.7 billion for the four main types of institutional investors combined (table 9). Insurance companies in the United Kingdom offer the standard package of insurance services ranging from casualty insurance to ordinary life policies. In addition, the U.K. tax structure makes life insurance companies a very favorable place in which to save. A fairly detailed knowledge of this tax structure is useful for understanding the personal saving process.

To begin with, premiums paid to life insurance companies generate a tax credit equal to one-half the "basic rate" times the premiums, subject to certain but generous limitations. If the basic rate were 33 percent, as it was in 1978, a premium of one pound would cost an individual only 83.5 pence in after-tax income.[26] To be eligible for this type of tax credit, the policy must be a so-called qualifying policy, which means, among other things, that the maturity of the policy is ten or more years.

Probably more important than the tax credit to an individual investor is the fact that by saving through life insurance policies, he can substantially reduce the effective tax rate on his investment income. Two provisions of the law make this possible. First, the proceeds of a life insurance plan are usually not subject to any individual income tax. Second, a life insurance company pays only 37.5 percent on unfranked investment income, rather than the normal corporate rate of 52 percent, and like any corporation pays no tax on franked income, such as dividends. Under the imputation system a life insurance company receives a net dividend but cannot itself use the tax credit attached to the dividend, so that the effective tax rate on dividends works out to be the basic rate.[27]

Life insurance companies have taken advantage of these tax laws to offer what are essentially contractual savings plans, which, to be in technical compliance with the law, have only a nominal link to what is normally considered a life insurance policy. For example, Prudential Assurance Company, the largest insurance company in the United Kingdom, offers through a subsidiary a unit-linked life insurance policy, the Vanbrugh Maximum Investment Plan. Under this plan a person aged thirty-five might purchase a policy with ten years to maturity. Only 0.5 percent of each premium would be used to purchase insurance, with the remainder being used to purchase units in what are essentially, though perhaps not technically, unit trusts or mutual funds. The policyholder would have a

26. As of April 1979 the mechanics of obtaining this rebate changed. Now the policyholder pays the contractual premium net of the tax credit, and the company reclaims the tax credit directly from the government.

27. The life insurance company must also pay tax on realized capital gains at an effective rate of 30 percent as of 1978. This rate is the same as the maximum rate of capital gains tax applicable to individuals in the United Kingdom. In 1979 individuals realizing gains of less than £9,500 were taxed at a lower rate. Formerly, the tax was the minimum of 30 percent or one-half the marginal tax rate.

wide choice of funds to choose from, ranging from equity funds to fixed interest and cash funds.[28] Moreover, he could reallocate his investment among the funds over time as he saw fit.[29] For this particular plan, the amount payable on death is the accumulated value of the units, with a floor of 75 percent of the total premiums payable during the life of the policy. In an inflationary period in which nominal interest rates are high, this floor would be expected to come into play only in the early years of the policy.

These contractual savings plans are not cheap. In the case of the Vanbrugh plan, there was a 5 percent spread between the bid and offer prices —equivalent to a 5.3 percent charge on the amount purchased.[30] There are substantial charges for early discontinuance of the plan, ranging up to the forfeiture of one year's premium.[31] Similar types of contractual savings plans, but ones involving mutual funds, were widely sold in the United States during the fifties and early sixties with what amounted to big cancellation penalties. Owing to substantial publicity about the disadvantages of these plans to investors and the recommendations of the U.S. Security and Exchange Commission that these plans be curtailed, they became less popular in the mid-1960s and nowadays are insignificant.[32] Without a detailed study, it is not possible to know how widespread the losses from these prepayment penalties might be in the United Kingdom. If one judges

28. Because the proceeds of a policy are not generally taxed, a life insurance company is not penalized from investing in corporate or government bonds as would be a unit trust.

29. Perhaps the most persuasive evidence that the individual investors regard these policies as contractual savings plans is that the unit prices of these funds are published daily in such places as the *Financial Times* and *Daily Telegraph*. Moreover, captive life companies have been set up in order to sell units in "managed funds," which are structurally the same as unit trusts, but with the favorable tax treatment accorded life insurance companies; examples are Hambros Life and Schroder Life.

30. The administrative and investment charges for this particular plan are 0.5 percent of the value of the funds under management, which is similar to what these charges would be in the United States.

31. In addition, some of the favorable tax treatment of these types of investments may be withdrawn. In the early seventies insurance companies sometimes guaranteed such generous surrender values that there was a risk that the commitments could not be met. Indeed, some companies failed in those years; subsequent legislation, however, has mitigated that particular problem.

32. In the United States there are now limitations on the maximum amount that a mutual fund can retain upon cancellation; and perhaps because of these limitations these savings plans are no longer being marketed aggressively.

from the U.S. experience, the losses may be great—and more prevalent among lower-income families.

In the United Kingdom, the picture is slightly more complicated in that these contractual savings plans have substantial tax implications that they did not have in the United States. One way to ameliorate this problem is to allow insurance companies to issue qualified policies with premiums that can be varied over time as the investor sees fit.[33]

PENSION PLANS. Pension plans, or, in U.K. terminology, superannuation funds, saw the real value of their assets increase during the seventies, unlike the other types of institutional investors, because of a steady inflow of new money (table 9), and have been the largest net accumulators of company securities among the various types of institutional investors (table 10). Except in 1973 and 1974, their annual net accumulations of company securities from 1970 through 1977 were more than £1 billion (in 1976 values). The 1974 drop in their net accumulations to £333 million is undoubtedly associated with the weak market of that year and possibly with the perception that other financial instruments offered more attractive returns. The net amount of new money these funds had available for investments in 1974 did not show a similar drop (see table 13).

Although some of the details of the U.K. pension schemes differ from those in the United States, the broad outlines are similar. Both public and private U.K. corporations that provide occupational pension plans to their employees generally use defined-benefit plans in which the amount of the pension is based upon years of services and some final average salary calculations.[34] Like sinking funds that guarantee the repayment of a long-term debt issue, these pension funds are set up to guarantee the payment of their liabilities.[35]

33. Insurance companies can currently issue policies with some variability in premiums, but the amount of variability is greatly restricted. The most binding constraint is that no annual premium can be more than one-eighth of the total premiums payable over a ten-year period.

34. A few groups in the United States, such as some employees of nonprofit institutions, are frequently covered by defined-contribution plans in which an employer makes a current contribution to an investment fund and the amount of the pension is based upon the performance of the fund itself rather than final average salary. In this type of plan the employee bears the risk and rewards of abnormal performance. And many employees covered by defined-benefit plans in the United States also participate in profit sharing or defined-contribution plans.

35. The facts that the repayment schedule for debt is usually fixed in nominal terms and that the liabilities of a pension fund are often linked to wage levels do not alter the basic similarity of a sinking fund to a pension fund.

The three main funding plans in the United Kingdom are insured plans,[36] internally managed trusts, and externally managed trusts. According to figures reported for 1975, 50 percent of all plans were managed internally, and the incidence of this type of management increased with size.[37] Only 18 percent of the plans were externally managed, in sharp contrast to the situation in the United States, where even the largest companies make extensive use of external managers. As in the United States, insured plans were used primarily by smaller firms and represented 31 percent of all plans.

If this preference on the part of the large firms for internal management persists as pension funds continue to grow, there would seem to be no need in the United Kingdom for concern about a concentration of power in the hands of a few financial institutions (a fear sometimes expressed in the United States). Instead, a more pressing potential problem for Britain may be self-dealings or conflicts of interest between a corporate management and the pension plans for its employees. In the United States, one seldom hears allegations of self-dealings involving large corporate pension plans and the sponsor corporations. Such is not the case in Britain.[38] The management structure of pension funds in the United Kingdom may be more conducive to conflicts of interest between corporate management and its employees than in the United States, but without a careful study it is not possible to assess scientifically how prevalent and serious these potential conflicts of interest are.

Individuals

According to the national accounts, the savings rate of individuals in the United Kingdom was 8.9 percent in 1970 and 8.5 percent in 1971. By 1975 the rate had almost doubled to 15.4 percent. With the possible exception of Japan, this jump in the level of individual savings rates in the

36. Such a plan, issued as a rule by an insurance company, usually promises a fixed nominal sum at a specified time in the future. This sum may or may not be sufficient to cover the promised benefits.

37. "A Survey of British Pension Plans," *For Your Benefit,* no. 29 (prepared by George B. Buck Consulting Actuaries, New York, April 1976).

38. See *The Economist,* November 4, 1978, pp. 109–15. The Occupational Pensions Board is charged with the responsibility of preventing such potential self-dealings.

Table 11. *Personal Savings as a Percentage of Net Disposable Income, Selected Countries, 1970–77*

Country	1970	1971	1972	1973	1974	1975	1976	1977a
France	17.1	17.0	16.7	17.8	17.2	17.4	15.7	15.3
West Germany	16.6	15.2	15.2	14.1	14.6	15.8	14.3	13.8
Japan	20.0	20.7	21.7	24.9	26.7	24.9	24.4	24.5
United Kingdom	8.9	8.5	10.5	11.7	14.1	15.4	14.9	14.5
United States	8.1	9.2	6.6	8.2	7.9	7.9	5.8	5.0

Source: Peter Falush, "The Changing Pattern of Savings," *National Westminster Bank Quarterly Review*, August 1978, p. 47.

a. 1977 data partly estimated.

United Kingdom was not matched in other industrial countries (table 11) and has puzzled many students of saving behavior. Various explanations have been proposed, but none of them has been satisfactorily tested.

In 1978 the Central Statistical Office prepared balance sheets of the personal sector exclusive of nonprofit bodies.[39] These balance sheets would correspond roughly to those of individuals or households and, in conformity with the national income accounting conventions, include the assets of pension, or superannuation, funds.

From the point of view of explaining individual saving behavior, however, it is questionable whether superannuation funds or employer contributions to these funds should be included in the personal sector. In an occupational pension plan an employee is promised certain defined benefits under certain conditions. Failure to meet these conditions or even the bankruptcy of the corporation itself can cause these benefits to evaporate overnight. Moreover, changes in the law can vastly change an employee's potential and actual benefits. For example, the United Kingdom in 1978 began to switch to a mandated two-tier, index-linked structure in which each employee will receive a fixed benefit and an income-related benefit. Under this law employers will probably have to increase their contributions to their funded plans. Such an increase would lead to an increase in the personal savings rate as it is calculated. But the plan will only be phased in gradually over the next twenty years, and there is no guarantee that in the interim it will not be substantially changed.

In sum, individuals may not regard employers' contributions as direct

39. *Economic Trends,* no. 291 (January 1978).

Table 12. *Value of Broad Categories of Personal Assets, United Kingdom, 1966–76*
Billions of 1976 pounds

Date	Physical assets			Financial assets						Liabilities	Net worth
	Land and buildings	Other	Total	Liquid	U.K. company and overseas issue	U.K. and local debt securities	Equity in life insurance and superannuation funds	Other	Total		
1966	107.5	38.6	146.1	62.2	56.2	13.7	37.8	11.9	181.9	37.1	291.0
1967	112.8	40.3	153.1	65.9	66.9	13.4	40.9	11.1	198.1	39.1	312.0
1968	119.0	41.6	160.6	66.5	79.3	12.0	43.6	10.4	211.8	39.5	332.7
1969	121.4	42.8	164.2	66.1	66.1	11.7	43.0	9.6	196.4	39.3	321.2
1970	123.1	44.5	167.6	67.8	58.7	9.7	43.9	9.3	189.3	40.7	316.2
1971	131.1	45.4	176.5	69.2	71.6	11.6	47.8	9.0	209.2	41.9	343.7
1972	167.4	48.8	216.1	74.1	80.5	9.0	51.5	8.2	223.3	49.5	389.9
1973	217.6	53.4	271.0	78.0	52.9	8.6	47.2	8.7	195.4	52.9	413.6
1974	193.1	56.5	249.6	75.2	25.3	6.5	36.5	9.0	152.5	49.2	353.0
1975	164.3	54.5	218.7	66.8	35.0	8.9	37.6	8.2	156.4	43.7	331.1
1976	165.8	54.8	220.6	63.5	29.3	9.1	37.1	7.9	146.9	42.2	325.3

Source: Derived from Central Statistical Office, "Personal Sector Balance Sheets," *Economic Trends*, no. 291 (January 1978), p. 103. Figures are rounded.

substitutes for other types of savings.[40] However, the removal of super-annuation funds from the personal sector would have to be based upon some tenuous assumptions that would subject the resulting figures to a wide margin error. Consequently, though I recognize the limitations, the following analysis includes superannuation funds in the personal sector.[41]

INDIVIDUAL BALANCE SHEETS. Reexpressed in 1976 pounds and including superannuation funds, the net worth of individuals more than doubled from £171 billion in 1956 to £414 billion in 1973 and then decreased steadily to £325 billion in 1976—a decrease of 21.5 percent despite the big increase in the savings rate from 1974 on.

Through 1972 the value of financial assets in individual portfolios exceeded the value of physical assets (table 12). In 1973 the value of physical assets jumped dramatically, while the value of financial assets showed a modest drop. The net result was that in 1973 the value of physical assets was 39 percent greater than the value of financial assets. The value of physical assets then continued to surpass the value of financial assets—64 percent greater in 1974, 40 percent greater in 1975, 50 percent greater in 1976.

In terms of consumer purchasing power, the real value of physical assets held by individuals increased slowly but steadily through the end of 1971, somewhat in step with the net capital formation of the individual sector (table 13). In 1972 the value of physical assets held by individuals increased £39.6 billion in real terms (1976 pounds), and in 1973 there was a further increase of £54.9 billion (table 12). Most of this increase represented a reevaluation of land and buildings during this period rather

40. Threadgold reached the tentative conclusion that individuals do not consider employer contributions to pension plans in formulating their savings plans, so that, with wages held constant, employer contributions increase, pound for pound, the level of personal savings in the national accounts. In the longer run, however, there may be some substitution between wages and employer contributions. Threadgold concluded that higher employee contributions increase personal sector savings by about half the amount of the contributions, so that here there may be some substitutability. One might think that for plans with employee contributions the benefits are such that an employee is more certain of receiving them, but this explanation is just a speculation. A. R. Threadgold, "Personal Savings: The Impact of Life Assurance and Pension Funds," Discussion Paper 1 (Bank of England, October 1978).

41. Since there was a slight upward trend in the ratio of the net increase in life insurance and pension funds to personal disposable income during the 1967–76 period, the figures in the text may slightly overstate the proportion held by individuals of those assets that are preferred by superannuation funds, with the overstatement increasing over time.

Table 13. *Value of Individual Savings in the United Kingdom, by Type of Asset, 1966–77*
Millions of 1976 pounds

			Net acquisition of financial assets								
Date	Total saving	Capital formation	Total	Government debt	National savings	Currency and deposits	Life insurance and super-annuation	Unit trusts	Company and overseas securities	Loans and mortgages	Other and residual
1966	6,307	3,358	2,949	562	−479	3,379	3,187	272	−1,319	−1,829	−824
1967	5,994	3,624	2,370	−146	−86	5,197	3,430	212	−1,565	−2,844	−1,827
1968	5,688	4,161	1,527	−212	−89	3,684	3,619	622	−1,831	−2,720	−1,544
1969	5,878	4,106	1,772	729	−537	3,160	3,429	425	−1,223	−2,124	−2,087
1970	6,624	3,991	2,633	−630	−108	5,598	3,698	191	−1,893	−3,076	−1,147
1971	6,453	4,912	1,542	468	777	6,442	4,143	90	−2,629	−4,920	−2,830
1972	8,576	5,883	2,693	−192	827	8,213	5,381	372	−2,702	−8,877	−328
1973	10,087	5,491	4,597	1,848	20	10,173	5,660	272	−3,789	−7,206	−2,382
1974	12,307	4,757	7,551	2,003	−139	7,833	5,107	36	−1,774	−3,741	−1,774
1975	13,385	4,665	8,719	935	475	6,729	5,465	132	−1,516	−3,732	232
1976	12,597	4,475	8,122	2,115	593	5,086	5,713	79	−1,263	−4,777	576
1977	11,934	4,390	7,544	699	1,211	6,543	5,287	−1,580		−5,003	387

Sources: For years up through 1976, figures are derived from *United Kingdom Flow of Funds Accounts: 1963–1976*, pp. 46–47; 1977 data are from Central Statistical Office, *Financial Statistics* (April 1979), p. 117; consumer price indexes are from IMF, *International Financial Statistics*, vol. 31 (May 1978).

than new capital formation. Even though there was new net capital formation every year since 1973, the real value of physical assets in 1976 dropped back to the level of 1972.

The real value of financial assets reached a peak of £223.3 billion in 1972 and then dropped to £146.9 billion in 1976. The real value of liquid assets increased slowly from £62.2 billion in 1966 to £78 billion in 1973 and then slid back to £63.5 billion in 1976. From 1966 through 1972 the real value of individuals' investments in U.K. and overseas company securities increased from £56.2 billion to £80.5 billion (table 12). Since they were, on balance, net sellers of these types of securities over this period (table 13), their real returns must have been positive. The same type of phenomenon has been observed in the United States over roughly this same period.[42] By 1976 individual holdings of these types of securities in the United Kingdom had fallen to £29.3 billion, a drop that was due not only to their net sales over this period, but also to the general decline in market prices (table 12).

Even though individuals acquired substantial financial assets through life insurance and superannuation funds every year over the 1966–76 period, the real value of their holdings through these two types of institutions declined to £37.1 billion in 1976 from its peak of £51.5 billion in 1972. The liabilities of households, again in real terms, increased by £11 billion between 1971 and 1973, from the £40 billion or so of previous years. They remained at this new level through 1974 but by 1976 retreated to slightly over £40 billion. This trend is consistent with the large number of new mortgages issued during the early seventies and the concurrent increase in the value of physical assets.

EXPLANATIONS OF SAVING BEHAVIOR. There is no generally accepted theory that explains why the savings rate in the United Kingdom increased so dramatically in the mid-seventies. One theory that has been proposed and widely circulated in the United Kingdom assumes that households use past experience to extrapolate into the future what they consider to be fair prices of commodities.[43] When households are faced with an increase in the price of a specific commodity due to unanticipated inflation, their

---

42. *Institutional Investor Study Report of the Securities and Exchange Commission,* supplementary vol. 1: *A Report of the National Bureau of Economic Research on Institutional Investors and Corporate Stock—A Background Study,* H. Doc. 92-64, pt. 6, 92 Cong. 1 sess. (GPO, 1971).

43. Angus Deaton, "Involuntary Saving through Unanticipated Inflation," *American Economic Review,* vol. 67 (December 1977), pp. 899–910.

first impulse is to postpone consumption and go to another store to obtain the fair price. Eventually, they revise their assessments of what are fair prices, but in the process their savings increase temporarily. This theory may be able to explain a temporary increase in savings, but it does not seem capable of explaining the sustained high savings rate through 1976, particularly in 1976, when the inflation rate fell off dramatically from its peak in 1975. In the spirit of this theory, one could even argue that households would dissave in 1975 to purchase and stockpile what might appear to be real bargains.[44] Moreover, this theory would seem unable to explain the recent period in the United States when inflation rates increased, probably unexpectedly, but savings rates decreased.

Another theory assumes that individuals require a given amount of liquid assets to support a given level of income—essentially a transaction cost argument. In 1975 Forsythe published some empirical evidence in support of this theory, which has also received wide circulation and prominence in the United Kingdom.[45]

More generally, even if there were no transaction costs, economic theory as embodied in the "life-cycle" hypothesis of Ando and Modigliani would argue for some type of relationship between savings rates and the ratio of net worth to income.[46] Put roughly, this theory holds that an individual will save during his working years to provide for his retirement. (A bequest motive can also be included as a reason for saving.) Consequently, at each point in his lifetime, he will have a desired wealth level based upon his current and prospective income.[47] In a steady-state world there will be a desired level of aggregate wealth for each level of aggregate income.[48] When wealth is above the desired level, individuals will reduce their savings; when below, they will increase their savings. On the assumption that the desired ratio of wealth to income does not vary

44. This argument assumes that at least some portion of the drop in inflation in 1975 was unanticipated.

45. John Forsythe, "Saving, Inflation and Recession," *Morgan Grenfell Economic Review*, September 9, 1975.

46. Albert Ando and Franco Modigliani, "The Life Cycle Hypothesis of Saving," *American Economic Review*, vol. 53 (March 1963), pp. 55–84.

47. In an uncertain world one must carefully distinguish between expected levels of income and transitory deviations from these levels.

48. By a steady-state world is meant a society that, among other things, has a population with a stationary distribution of age and a stationary distribution of income and wealth.

with the level of income, there should be a negative relationship between actual wealth–income ratios and saving rates.[49]

To distinguish between the transaction argument of Forsythe and the life-cycle hypothesis, various ratios were calculated: two variations of the ratio of liquid assets to disposable income, the ratio of net worth to disposable income, and the ratio of financial wealth to disposable income, which, if there were measurement errors in the valuation of physical assets, might measure more accurately the ratio of net worth to disposable income. The two measures of liquid assets were gross liquid assets and gross liquid assets less bank advances, or net liquid assets. In his article Forsythe used net liquid assets; however, one could take the position that the use of gross liquid assets is more in the spirit of a transaction cost argument.

Each of these four ratios appears to be negatively related to savings rates (table 14). A statistical analysis of these relationships, details of which are given in appendix A, indicates that the ratio of financial wealth to disposable income and the ratio of net liquid assets to disposable income have about the same explanatory power and either one explains a great proportion of the variability in savings rates over time. If one makes allowance for the difficulty of correctly measuring physical assets, a component of net worth, it is possible that the ratio of net worth to disposable income would have at least as much explanatory power as either the financial wealth ratio or the net liquid asset ratio. The explanatory power of the ratio of gross liquid assets to disposable income is clearly inferior to that of any of the other three ratios. Since gross liquid assets are probably more closely associated with those assets that are available for transaction purposes than with net liquid assets, it might be argued that the statistical explanatory power of the ratio of net liquid assets to disposable income may be due more to a wealth motive than to a transaction motive.

Thus the high savings rates of the recent past could be explained by the attempt of individuals to maintain a desired ratio of net worth to income as their actual net worth decreased relative to their income. Another explanation, but a related one, is that individuals saw the decrease in their

49. Savings rates might also be affected by the level of uncertainty associated with future income, including wage income, but the direction of this effect cannot be ascertained without further specification of an individual's aversion to risk as embodied in his utility function.

Table 14. *Individual Savings Rates and Ratios of Various Components of Wealth to Disposable Income, United Kingdom, 1966–76*

			Ratios		
Year	Savings rate (percent)	Net worth to disposable income	Financial wealth to disposable income	Gross liquid assets to disposable income	Gross liquid assets less bank advances to disposable income
1966	9.1	4.22	2.64	0.90	0.84
1967	8.5	4.44	2.82	0.94	0.88
1968	7.9	4.64	2.95	0.93	0.87
1969	8.1	4.44	2.71	0.91	0.87
1970	8.9	4.23	2.53	0.99	0.85
1971	8.5	4.52	2.75	0.91	0.85
1972	10.5	4.77	2.73	0.91	0.80
1973	11.7	4.81	2.27	0.91	0.79
1974	14.1	4.03	1.74	0.86	0.76
1975	15.3	3.79	1.79	0.76	0.69
1976	14.6	3.77	1.70	0.74	0.66

Source: Author's calculations.

wealth through inflation as a tax by the government and rationally adjusted, at least to some extent, their spending patterns to compensate for this hidden tax.

The trend in the savings rates for the entire U.K. economy is much closer to that of other nations than the trend in individual savings rates and does give some support to this type of rational expectation hypothesis (table 15). Although the U.K. individual savings rate was usually increasing in the 1970–76 period, the overall savings rate was constant, or slightly decreasing, over the same period,[50] a phenomenon that would be consistent with the hypothesis that individuals adjusted their savings rates to offset the hidden tax associated with inflation.

50. In sum, the high individual savings rates in the United Kingdom may well be associated with wealth effects, but given the available time-series data, it is difficult to ascertain the exact nature of these effects. Consequently, it would be desirable to undertake an analysis of a cross section of households or even a time series of cross sections.

Table 15. *National Savings Ratios,*[a] *Selected Countries, 1966–77*

Percent

Date	United Kingdom	United States	Japan	France	West Germany	Nether-lands	Italy	Belgium
1966	19.7	20.6	35.0	27.3	27.9	26.5	20.1	23.1
1967	19.3	19.1	37.3	27.2	26.4	26.9	20.7	23.7
1968	19.7	18.7	38.9	26.9	28.2	27.8	21.6	22.8
1969	20.8	18.9	39.2	28.6	28.9	27.1	22.5	24.3
1970	21.0	17.6	40.4	26.5	29.9	26.7	22.7	26.9
1971	20.7	18.0	39.3	26.0	29.0	26.9	21.2	25.8
1972	18.9	18.4	38.9	26.4	28.5	27.5	20.3	25.6
1973	20.5	19.8	39.9	26.8	28.4	28.6	21.1	25.3
1974	17.9	18.1	37.2	25.4	26.9	27.9	20.4	25.9
1975	17.3	16.3	32.3	23.4	23.3	23.4	18.3	22.8
1976	18.9	16.7	32.3	23.3	24.4	24.4	20.2	22.1
1977	20.1	17.6	32.2	n.a.	24.0	23.5	20.2	21.7

Sources: 1966–76 data are from IMF, *International Financial Statistics*, vol. 31 (May 1978); 1977 data are from ibid., vol. 32 (May 1979).

n.a. Not available.

a. Calculated as $\left[\dfrac{GNP - (\text{public} + \text{private consumption})}{GNP} \right] \times 100$

Industrial and Commercial Companies

As in the United States, undistributed income in the United Kingdom represents a major source of funds for industrial and commercial companies, going from 68.4 percent in 1966 to 33.1 percent in 1974 and then to 48.7 percent in 1976 (table 16). Overall, there appears to be a slight decrease in the importance of retained earnings in the late sixties and then very little obvious time trend during the seventies. These percentages differ from those that would be obtained from the official statistics published by the Department of Industry, because those figures, unlike the figures presented here, include stock appreciation. The official figures do not show a similar drop in the importance of undistributed income in the late sixties. In an inflationary environment stock appreciation should probably be netted out, since it is a somewhat "phantom" source of funds that must be used largely to increase the value of stocks, given a particular technology. Thus, by excluding stock appreciation, one can partially miti-

Table 16. *Sources and Uses of Capital Funds of U.K. Industrial and Commercial Companies, 1966–76*

Percent of total source or use

Source and use	1966	1967	1968	1969	1970	1971	1972	1973	1974	1975	1976
Source											
Undistributed income	68.4	65.1	56.4	50.8	44.4	52.9	45.9	41.8	33.1	50.0	48.7
Capital transfers	0.7	6.0	9.1	11.5	9.7	9.4	4.3	2.9	3.4	4.9	3.1
External funds											
Bank borrowing	5.0	8.5	11.4	12.7	20.7	11.6	31.8	34.6	40.9	7.2	19.7
U.K. capital issues	15.3	10.6	9.7	9.8	3.7	5.9	6.5	1.2	-0.1	11.2	6.1
Loans and mortgages	2.8	0.6	2.1	4.0	5.4	3.7	1.7	6.1	0.5	5.2	4.5
Overseas	7.8	9.1	11.4	11.2	16.0	16.5	9.8	13.4	22.2	21.5	17.9
Total (millions of 1976 pounds)	9,748	9,888	12,058	11,937	11,675	12,431	17,244	21,851	15,614	10,609	12,907
Use											
Fixed capital formation	64.4	60.4	52.2	57.9	61.9	54.9	40.4	36.6	54.8	76.8	58.4
Working capital											
Value of net increase in stocks[a]	7.1	5.3	7.1	6.8	8.0	-1.1	-1.3	7.5	11.0	-18.9	-1.9
Bank deposits	0.3	9.8	9.2	-2.7	6.1	17.2	24.4	19.2	0.9	23.8	13.1
Other liquid assets	-2.5	1.5	-1.8	-1.2	-1.3	2.5	0.6	0.5	-0.5	3.1	1.2
Overseas	11.3	11.4	12.9	14.7	12.9	5.6	7.9	16.0	17.7	17.4	20.9
Other and unidentified	19.4	11.7	20.4	24.6	12.5	21.0	28.0	20.2	16.2	-2.2	8.2

Source: Derived from Committee to Review the Functioning of Financial Institutions, *Evidence on the Financing of Industry and Trade*, vol. 5: *Accepting Houses Committee, Committee of London Clearing Banks, Bank of England* (HMSO, 1978), p. 53. Figures are rounded.
a. Book increase net of stock appreciation.

gate inflation-induced effects on the accounting numbers applied to the sources and uses of funds.[51]

Over the 1966–76 period capital funds provided from outside Britain and those used outside Britain have both grown in importance. This phenomenon probably stems from the increasingly international character of world business as well as from the possible effects of exchange controls.

As to external funds, the importance of bank borrowings as a source of funds rose dramatically in 1972 to 31.8 percent of the total sources, rose further in 1973 to 34.6 percent, and then reached a peak of 40.9 percent in 1974. In 1975 and 1976 the percentage of funds raised through bank borrowings declined to a more normal level. Marsh has suggested that the increase in bank borrowings in 1972 and 1973 was due to an easing of credit regulations in 1971 and the opportunity for the corporate sector to engage in arbitrage operations by borrowing from the banks on overdraft privileges and reinvesting these moneys at higher interest rates through time deposits and certificate of deposits.[52] According to Marsh, these arbitrage operations ceased around the end of 1973. The high percentage of bank deposits in the use of funds in 1972 and 1973 is consistent with such operations.

Marsh attributes the high level of bank borrowings in 1974 to the high inflation rate in that year and the commensurate increase in the values of stocks, work in progress, and (although he does not mention it) accounts receivable, all of which are often financed by bank borrowings.[53] The de-

51. If one also makes an allowance for depreciation at replacement costs, the importance of undistributed income in the sources of funds drops even further during the seventies. According to the Department of Industry, after allowing for replacement cost depreciation, undistributed income represented from 54 to 58 percent of total funds over the period 1964–69. This percentage then fell to 28 percent in 1973, −11 percent in 1974, −31 percent in 1975, and 12 percent in 1976 ("Structure of Company Financing," *Trade and Industry,* February 3, 1978, p. 243). Counterbalancing these depreciation effects would be the anticipated decrease in the real value of debt in an inflationary economy. This effect would reduce the depreciation effect and could even eliminate it.

Unanticipated inflation will also reduce the real value of debt in the corporate liability structure, a reduction that may result in a shift of wealth from debt holders to equity holders. To determine the full effect of inflation, both anticipated and unanticipated, some allowance might be made for this potential wealth effect.

52. Paul Marsh, "An Analysis of Equity Rights Issues on the London Stock Exchange" (Ph.D. dissertation, London Graduate School of Business Studies, 1977).

53. For this explanation to be correct, some of these uses must be included in the categories of fixed capital formation and "other and unidentified" as well as in the category of value of the net increase in stocks (see table 16).

pressed state of the equity market would also seem to be a factor. The large use of funds in 1975 for bank deposits and the reduction in the value of stocks may well represent an adjustment of the corporate sector to a more normal balance sheet structure following the liquidity crisis of 1974.

The importance of longer-term U.K. capital issues as a source of funds varies widely over time—from 15.3 percent in 1966 to −0.1 percent in 1974. Although there were virtually no net new capital issues by U.K. industrial and commercial companies in 1974, net new capital issues in 1975 represented 11.2 percent of the funds raised by these companies— the second largest percentage of the decade. Again, the ability of the capital markets in Britain to adapt to widely varying demands over time is clearly evident.

The mix of securities that U.K. companies have issued to the public changed markedly over the 1967–77 period. From 1967 through 1973, fixed-interest long-term debt, sometimes convertible into ordinary shares, provided an important source of new capital and often was more important than ordinary shares (table 17). In 1975 and 1976 issues of ordinary shares dominated fixed-interest obligations to such an extent that some observers of the market alleged that government borrowing, for which the Bank of England acts as an agent, had "crowded out" the private sector.

Before the "crowding out" argument is examined, however, a few more details about the 1972–76 period are in order. In 1974 industrial and commercial corporations issued about as much ordinary equity as their retirements of fixed-interest obligations. Financial institutions, however, did issue, on balance, both ordinary shares and fixed-interest obligations in 1974 but at a relatively low level. Yet even these low aggregate figures obscure the magnitude of the slump. According to statistics compiled by the Midland Bank, one issue accounted for 40 percent of the total value of the net new issues. In 1974 there were only 29 new company issues (16 issues of ordinary shares and 13 issues of debt, of which 4 were convertible),[54] whereas there had been 120 company issues in 1973 and 312 in 1972.[55] Midland Bank recorded 200 company issues for 1975—of

54. "Another Poor Year for New Capital Issues," *Midland Bank Review* (February 1975), p. 10.

55. "Capital Issues Slump in 1973," *Midland Bank Review* (February 1974), pp. 4–5.

Table 17. *Value of Net New Issues of U.K. Company Securities, 1967–77*
Millions of 1976 pounds

	Industrial and commercial companies		Financial institutions	
Date	Ordinary shares	Fixed-interest securities	Ordinary shares	Fixed-interest securities
1967	164	964	66	162
1968	730	561	205	210
1969	418	791	103	210
1970	95	428	103	120
1971	311	590	230	238
1972	612	739	651	247
1973	180	276	94	141
1974	64	−65	120	143
1975	1,258	100	431	126
1976	790	45	383	75
1977	557	−34	143	125

Sources: 1967–76 figures are derived from *United Kingdom Flow of Funds Accounts: 1963–1976*, p. 66; 1977 figures are from data provided by the Bank of England.

which 83.7 percent by value were ordinary shares.[56] This revival of the new issue market and the dominance of ordinary shares continued into 1976, when only 9 new debt issues were made.[57]

CROWDING OUT. The shunning of the long-term debt markets by corporations in recent years has led to the concern on the part of some that the Bank of England has crowded out the private sector.[58] The argument pictures the government, through the Bank of England, as having a highly inelastic demand curve for long-term debt and firms as having relatively elastic demand curves, at least more elastic than the government's. On the assumption that the supply of savings is fixed in the short run, a sufficient shift in the government demand curve will drive interest rates up so high

56. "The Year of the Rights Issue," *Midland Bank Review* (February 1976), p. 19.

57. "After the Rights Issue Boom," *Midland Bank Review* (February 1977), p. 13.

58. Gordon T. Pepper, Robert L. Thomas, and Geoffrey E. Wood, of W. Greenwell and Co., in their submission to the Wilson committee provided a theoretical description of what is meant by crowding out, and the presentation in the text is based upon this submission. *Evidence on Financing*, vol. 7: *Association of Investment Trust Companies, Unit Trust Association, Association of British Chambers of Commerce*.

that the government becomes the only participant in the long-term debt market.

In their written evidence to the Wilson committee (see note 58), Pepper, Thomas, and Wood claim that just such a crowding out occurred in 1976, and as a result firms were forced to increase their short-term borrowings from banks and (though the authors did not explicitly state it) from other sources, such as rights issues. Assuming such a crowding out did occur, the natural question is what effect it would have upon the availability of funds to corporations to finance expansion. From the sources and uses of funds, it is clear that firms increased their bank borrowings or overdrafts. In the United Kingdom, corporations tend to use and banks tend to regard overdrafts as a semipermanent form of financing. Thus this crowding out, if it did occur, forced firms to use a close substitute for long-term debt. Indeed, the owners of a firm should care little about the firm's precise financing (except for taxes and potential bankruptcy costs) as long as they can obtain their desired portfolio structure through purchases and sales of financial instruments—in short, the ability to undo whatever the firm does.

To put this argument in a different light, assume that the government were to finance its deficit using exactly the same mix of financing instruments as firms use. Obviously, this is a hypothetical situation but would be possible if the government issued an instrument linked to the stock market. The initial effect would be to drive up the cost of capital to firms. If individuals recognized that the deficit financing of the government was equivalent to a tax, they would just increase their savings rates to accommodate the increased government debt; there is some evidence that they may have done this.

Thus, as long as short-term debt is a close substitute for long-term debt, the crowding out argument is really more an argument about the impact of government deficit financing on the overall cost of capital to firms. To the extent that investors anticipate that the deficit financing is just a tax and correspondingly increase their savings rates, the deficit financing should have no more effect, except for distributional effects, on the real variables in the economy than if the deficit were financed by taxes.

This hypothetical situation is obviously an extreme position, but so is the crowding out argument. Moreover, according to the *Midland Bank Review*, the leads and lags as between government financing and corporate bank borrowings during 1976 were not consistent with the crowding out thesis in that much of the corporate borrowing preceded the demands of the Bank of England.[59] The *Review* also argues that the downturn of corporate financing in the last quarter of 1976 could be attributed to general economic conditions.

If crowding out is not the explanation for the shunning of long-term debt, is there a plausible explanation? Flemming, Price, and Byers have suggested that when nominal interest rates are high because of an inflationary environment, there may be a great deal of uncertainty about their future levels, in part because of uncertainty about the future levels of inflation.[60] In this situation management may be very reluctant, and quite rationally reluctant from its own perspective, to commit a firm to a fixed-interest payment for an extended period. If nominal interest rates were to fall, perhaps owing to a substantial drop in inflationary expectations, the firm would be burdened with a large financial obligation that its competitors may not have, thus putting it at a competitive disadvantage. In the United States, the callable provisions of long-term corporate bonds mitigate this fear.

Unlike U.S. firms, British firms have access to an overdraft system that provides what amounts to medium- to long-term funds at a floating interest rate with no repayment penalty. This system seems to work well enough to keep firms from trying to develop alternative long-term instruments with a more flexible interest rate structure, such as callable bonds or floating rate issues.

As of the end of 1978, only local authorities and the Agricultural Mortgage Corporation have put out floating rate issues and then only since 1977. In nominal terms £118.3 million of the £396 million of long-term loan stocks sold by local authorities in 1977 were floating rate issues.[61] In 1978 roughly a third of the new short-term bonds and long-term stocks issued by local authorities had floating rates. If good secondary markets for these instruments develop, it would not be surprising to see some corporate floating rate issues in the future.

LEVERAGE OR GEARING RATIOS. Partly as a result of their avoiding the long-term bond market, U.K. corporations tend to have more equity in

59. "After the Rights Issue Boom," *Midland Bank Review* (February 1979), pp. 12–13.

60. J. S. Flemming, L. D. D. Price and Mrs. S. A. Byers, "The Cost of Capital, Finance, and Investment," *Bank of England Quarterly Bulletin*, vol. 16 (June 1976), pp. 193–205.

61. Unpublished data from Midland Bank.

their liability structure than corporations in many other countries. These low leverage or gearing ratios have led some to question whether U.K. firms are using the optimal amount of debt in their capital structure to minimize their cost of capital and thus maximize their investment levels.[62] Miller has argued that the debt–equity ratio of a firm should make no difference to the cost of capital at the firm level, even in the presence of taxes.[63] Taxes would be expected to affect the aggregate level of the debt–equity ratio for the economy as a whole, but individual firms in a competitive environment would be expected to act as if their cost of capital were independent of their particular capital structure.

Assuming for the moment, contrary to theory, that firms could reduce their cost of capital by increasing their debt, the question arises whether financial institutions place effective constraints on the amount of debt, either short term or long term, that a company can obtain. To examine this question, a cross-sectional analysis of 925 listed firms, using data from 1977 was undertaken.[64] In such an analysis the macroeconomic environment is constant, enabling one to examine more easily the effect of structural differences among firms. The actual analysis related the ratio of plant and equipment expenditure to total assets to the proportion of total assets financed by equity as well as to measures of profitability, payout, risk, industry, and firm size.

If firms are constrained in the amount of debt they wish to issue, one would expect that as the proportion of total assets financed by equity dropped, firms would find it more difficult to raise new debt, and thus

62. The Confederation of British Industry addressed this question in its testimony before the Wilson committee. *Evidence on Financing,* vol. 2: *Confederation of British Industry, Trades Union Congress, Association of Independent Businesses.* While the confederation agreed that firms in many other countries have higher leverage ratios than those in the United Kingdom, it argued that the highly developed equity market allows U.K. firms to rely more heavily on equity. But it did suggest that possibly some constraint by lenders may keep firms from issuing as much debt as they wish. Samuels, Groves, and Goddard, in *Company Finance in Europe,* explore this issue in great detail.

63. Merton Miller, "Debt and Taxes," *Journal of Finance,* vol. 32 (May 1977), pp. 261–75. This conclusion requires that the investment strategy of the firm be known in advance, so that one class of owners cannot confiscate wealth from another class by changing the investment strategy. Usually, one of the primary purposes of the protective covenants in debt instruments is to force corporations to follow a predetermined investment strategy.

64. A description of the sample and a detailed summary of the results are given in appendix B.

plant and equipment expenditure as a proportion of assets would tend to decline. This assumes that firms could not just turn to other sources of funds. The empirical analysis of the 925 listed firms gives no support to this hypothesis. Indeed, with profitability, risk, industry, and firm size held constant, the empirical analysis indicates that firms with more equity in their capital structure are investing less than their more levered colleagues.

It is beyond the scope of this paper to explain that result, but it may be consistent with the attitudes expressed in a survey of investment attitudes undertaken for the Wilson committee.[65] Where companies had explicit debt-equity criteria, the survey concluded that

they were generally in terms of a balance sheet gearing limitation. In nearly all these cases the gearing was self-imposed and, where relevant, was well within the limits externally imposed by debenture trust deeds or other covenants to lenders—although it was clear from discussion that the limit set often reflected or was related to the perceived expectation of the market or bankers.[66]

Some family-controlled companies, though not all, stated that they would not undertake additional borrowing to finance profitable projects because, after personal taxes, they would not receive much benefit and that they might even lose control. It is therefore possible that in Britain the proportion of assets financed by equity acts as a measure of a firm's taste for expansion. A similar analysis in the United States found no relationship.[67]

The possibility that some firms may not expand as much as possible does not necessarily mean that the aggregate level of investment would be curtailed. If there were free entry, it would be expected that new firms would come in or some existing firms would expand to take on those projects that some firms choose not to undertake.

My analysis also found no relationship between the plant and equipment expenditure ratio and the total size of the firm, suggesting that the smaller listed firms have tended to expand on a percentage basis as rapidly as the larger firms. In the United States, however, the larger firms appeared to be expanding more rapidly than the smaller ones.[68]

65. Coopers and Lybrand, "Survey of the Investment Attitudes and Financing of Medium-Sized Companies," *Committee to Review the Functioning of Financial Institutions,* Research Report 1 (HMSO, 1977).

66. Ibid., p. 14.

67. These results are shown in appendix B.

68. This grow could be due either to internal expansion or to firm mergers and acquisitions; the analysis did not distinguish between these two sources of growth.

In addition, there appears to be no relationship between the plant and equipment expenditure ratio and dividend payout. If true, this suggests that the level of retained earnings relative to total earnings is not a critical variable in explaining differences in growth among firms. This conclusion, however, should be regarded as tentative. For the United States, as for Britain, no relationship was obtained in 1977, but negative and significant relationships were obtained in similar types of cross-sectional analyses for the years 1968, 1969, 1970, 1973, and 1974. In this study I had access only to U.K. data for 1977 and therefore could not determine whether such a negative relationship might also have been obtained for the United Kingdom in earlier years.

Finally, my cross-sectional analysis provides an estimate of the elasticity of plant and equipment expenditures to the sum of net profits and interest payments. In 1977 the estimate of this elasticity in the United Kingdom was slightly less than 0.4. If taken at face value, a doubling of profits would be expected to generate an initial increase in plant and equipment expenditure of 40 percent, which in turn might later generate further increases in plant and equipment expenditures. Estimates of a similar, but slightly smaller, magnitude were obtained for the United States.

SMALL COMPANIES. The information available on the financing of smaller unlisted issues and the peculiar problems associated with venture capital are very sparse. In its testimony before the Wilson committee, the Association of Independent Businesses pointed to several barriers to the development of small businesses. The most important are (1) the lack of an active market for the stock of small companies, (2) a perceived reluctance on the part of the banks to make as much money available as small firms would like, and (3) a taxation system that favors the accumulation of assets through institutions rather than directly.[69]

An over-the-counter market exists in the United Kingdom, but it is not nearly as well developed as that market is in the United States. The Stock Exchange in Britain, under rule 163(2), now permits brokers to participate in trades of unlisted stocks. However, "permission to transact each bargain must be sought so that a continuous market is not allowed to develop."[70] It is difficult to assess the effect of this type of restrictive prac-

---

69. *Evidence on Financing,* vol. 2, pp. 110–22.
70. Ibid., vol. 3: *Export Credits Guarantee Department, Insurance Company Associations, National Association of Pension Funds, The Stock Exchange,* p. 265.

tice on the development of an active over-the-counter market; it certainly would not aid the development of such a market, but whether it has hindered its development is an open question. The fact that M. J. H. Nightingale and Company, an investment banking firm, has set up an extremely limited over-the-counter market outside the exchange to provide over-the-counter brokerage services is evidence that the services provided through the exchange are not sufficient to satisfy the needs of such a market and that, if the demand were there, an active market could be developed.

In his testimony before the Wilson committee, C. J. Dauris of the Association of Independent Businesses estimated that about 2,400 firms are regularly traded on the over-the-counter market in the United States and that a similar type of market in the United Kingdom could support about 400 or 500 firms.[71] He went on to say that the development of this type of market would fill an important gap in the U.K. equity markets. Currently, a company to be listed on the exchange must have a net worth of about £500,000, which translates into a company with a fairly substantial level of sales and profits.[72] With such an over-the-counter market, an entrepreneur might be able to raise additional capital without as many worries about problems of control as would be the case if the funds came from a single source, such as an institution.

The tax bias against direct savings, which has been discussed extensively earlier, certainly does not facilitate the development of small businesses. To avoid the high marginal tax rates, individuals have great incentives to save through contractual arrangements with institutions. Thus a person who later in life wished to start a small corporation or who wished to fund someone else's corporation may not be able to use his savings to do so without substantial penalties. Moreover, even if he did withdraw the money from an institution, he may face higher tax rates on his future investment income than if he left the money with the institution.

There is very little evidence on the impact of this institutionalization of the saving process on the formation of new small firms. But since individuals have traditionally been the suppliers of equity funds to small businesses, the discrimination against direct savings has probably not helped the formation of small firms and may have introduced a distortion in the investment process.

71. Ibid., vol. 2, p. 140.
72. Ibid., vol. 3, p. 263.

To provide capital for smaller businesses, various specialized institutional investors have emerged. Perhaps the most important is Finance for Industry Limited (FFI), 15 percent of which is owned by the Bank of England and the balance by the clearing banks. On March 31, 1977, FFI, through its subsidiary Industrial and Commercial Finance Corporation Limited (ICFC) had investments of £211 million spread over 2,200 accounts, averaging slightly less than £100,000 per account. Although the ICFC will consider commitments as low as £5,000, the costs of applying for funds do not vary substantially with the amounts advanced. Thus the Association of Independent Businesses suggests that the practical minimum is £30,000.

In their testimony before the Wilson committee, the Association of of small businessmen to give up some control of their companies, which the Small Business Administration guarantees loans as a way of making more loan money available to small companies through traditional sources. The association's apparent preference for loan guarantees over funds provided through intermediaries may well be due to the aversion of small businessmen to give up some control of their companies, which they must frequently do in obtaining funds through the FFI. Whether the need to give up some control hinders the development of small firms in the United Kingdom is an open question.

The institutionalization of the venture capital process in the United Kingdom is substantial and has proceeded much further than in the United States. In comparing the U.S. and U.K. systems, it should be noted that the average returns on investments in small, new firms in the United States over the past thirty or forty years have been less than the average returns on larger seasoned issues, reflecting the often substantial losses associated with investments in small firms.[73] These lower average returns are consistent with the hypothesis that there may have been too much venture capital in the United States over these years. It is not clear, therefore, that the U.S. system is better than the U.K. one. The advantage of the developing U.K. system is that it provides professional advice at an early stage in the development of a new corporation and thus may lead to fewer

---

73. Craig A. Simmons, "Immediate, Short, and Longer Run Performance of New Issues" (Rodney L. White Center for Financial Research, the Wharton School, University of Pennsylvania, n.d.), presents some new evidence on this subject and cites some of the earlier literature.

failures than in the United States. The disadvantage is that it may stifle the truly independent and innovative entrepreneur and curtail the undertaking of highly speculative projects that do not meet normal professional investing standards.

It is too early to assess the impact of this institutionalization on the venture capital market in the United Kingdom. Moreover, the available data are very sparse. In view of the importance of venture capital, it would seem appropriate for some government body to initiate the collection of better data that could reveal potential problems before they became serious.

The Stock Market

In the United Kingdom all organized trading of securities is under the control of "The Stock Exchange."[74] In the United States there are, of course, not only the New York Stock Exchange but also the American Stock Exchange and various regional exchanges. In the United Kingdom, as pointed out above, the over-the-counter market is not well developed; however, The Stock Exchange does permit occasional trades in unlisted securities, and M. J. H. Nightingale and Company does provide an extremely limited market for unlisted stocks outside the exchange.

The Stock Exchange in the United Kingdom might be characterized as a competitive multidealer market. A distinct division exists between the dealers, called stockjobbers, and stockbrokers, who act as agents on behalf of their customers. There is usually more than one dealer in each issue. When a stockbroker wishes to trade an issue on behalf of a client, he will ask the jobbers in that issue for bid prices and ask prices without disclosing whether he wishes to buy or sell. He will then select that jobber or jobbers with the best bid and ask prices from the point of view of his client. The execution is not reported on a central tape as it is in the United States.

The New York Stock Exchange has a specialist system in which each issue is assigned to a single dealer who is charged with maintaining an orderly market. When asked by a member, the specialist is also responsible for executing so-called limit orders, which are standing orders from

---

74. The only exception to this statement appears to be a black box system put together by the merchant bankers.

the public to buy or sell at specific prices. In the United Kingdom, there is no formal mechanism to handle such orders.[75]

TRADING COSTS. Because of the differences in institutional structure, it is difficult to compare the operational efficiency of the U.K. and U.S. systems for trading stock. Yet the cost of trading equities is probably greater in the United Kingdom than in the United States, largely because of a transfer or stamp duty of 2 percent levied on each transaction and to a lesser extent because of commission costs. In the United Kingdom there is now no transfer tax on trades involving nonconvertible debt issues. Commission rates have fixed minimum levels and are almost certainly greater than the competitive rates in the United States. On a £50,000 trade, for instance, the commission would be £320. Under the old fixed-rate schedule in the United States, the commission on a comparable $100,000 trade of a stock priced $50 per share would be $797.36. Assuming that one pound equals two dollars, the current U.K. rate is about 20 percent less than the old U.S. fixed rate. At present, however, some U.S. institutions are obtaining a reduction of more than 60 percent from the old fixed-rate schedule, and a 40 to 60 percent reduction is quite common.[76]

That commission rates in Britain may be higher than those in the United States does not necessarily mean that the U.K. minimum rates are above their competitive level, since the costs of the factors used in the trading of securities could differ between the two countries. However, the U.K. practice of occasionally directing one broker who executes an order to transfer a portion of his commissions to another to compensate the second broker for services unrelated to the execution seems to indicate that the minimum commissions are in excess of their competitive levels.[77]

75. The compilation of these orders is known as the "book" and gives the specialist important information about the future course of the prices of the issues in which he deals. Floor traders can and do trade with the public when their prices are better than those provided by the specialist. Thus the traders do subject the specialist to competitive pressure, somewhat reducing his monopolistic power.

76. Gilbert Beebower and William W. Priest, Jr., "What You See and What You Get (Trading Costs: An Empirical Study)," in Center for Research in Security Prices, *Proceedings of the Seminar on the Analysis of Security Prices* (University of Chicago, Graduate School of Business, November 1978), gave some recent evidence on costs of trading.

77. A writer for *The Economist* (March 3, 1979, pp. 96–98) describes these types of transactions and suggests that the second broker may receive commissions to reward him for research, for the selling of units of a unit trust, or for having deposits made to a merchant bank. Such practices, called "give-ups," were quite common in

On top of this commission, an investor would have to pay a small value-added tax and, of more importance, a stamp tax of 2 percent, or £1,000 on a trade of £50,000. The only significant tax in the United States is the New York State tax, which on this hypothetical $100,000 trade would be a maximum of $125. For non–New York residents, this tax is cut in half and can even be avoided.

The other major cost in trading is related to the bid-ask spread (difference between the buying and selling prices) of the dealer. In January 1978 J. Henry Schroder Wagg & Co. Limited had one of its dealers obtain bid and ask prices for various size trades in the equities in the portfolios under its management on the pretense that it was contemplating such trades, so that the quotes represent real quotes. Because of the jobber system, it obtained both a bid price and an ask price that would presumably represent the best bid and ask prices (perhaps from different jobbers) obtainable through normal brokerage procedures. These bid-ask spreads expressed as a percentage of the average of the bid and the ask are summarized in table 18 by size of the potential trade and the market value of the equity outstanding of the company. For example, of the quotes for potential trades of £250,000 received on thirteen issues with market values in excess of £500 million, the average percentage bid-ask spread was 3.4 percent.

As would be anticipated, the percentage spread tends to increase with the size of the trade and decrease with the market value of the issue itself. Because of the differences in institutional structure, comparable figures are not available for the United States. It might be noted, however, that an estimate of the average percentage bid-ask spread for New York Stock Exchange issues in 1974 was 1.6 percent.[78] This spread would only technically apply to a trade of 100 shares, perhaps a $4,000 trade, but may well apply to a substantially larger trade if the stock is actively traded. A cursory examination of the numbers in table 18 suggests that the percentage bid-ask spreads in the United Kingdom may not be that much

---

the United States before the abolition of minimum rates. With competitive rates, such give-ups have become less usual, and the portion of the commissions subject to the give-ups has been greatly reduced. In my opinion the U.S. brokerage community has not yet fully adapted to a competitive commission market, and with full adjustment there may be a further drop in commission rates from their current level. Even individuals in the United States are now able to trade at substantially reduced rates if they wish.

78. Blume and Friend, *The Changing Role of the Individual Investor*, p. 156.

Table 18. *Average Percentage Bid-Ask Spreads by Size of Potential Trade and Market Value of Company Equity, January 1978*[a]

Percent

Market value of company equity (millions of pounds)	Size of trade					
	£1,000	£10,000	£25,000	£50,000	£100,000	£250,000
0–50	2.202	2.282	3.166	4.426	5.318	9.002
	(22)	(22)	(21)	(15)	(9)	(7)
51–100	1.800	1.800	2.356	3.880	6.746	10.094
	(48)	(48)	(47)	(42)	(24)	(10)
101–200	1.656	1.656	1.974	2.922	4.554	8.080
	(50)	(51)	(50)	(47)	(24)	(19)
201–500	1.440	1.440	1.726	2.034	4.546	5.046
	(39)	(39)	(39)	(36)	(25)	(22)
501 and over	1.208	1.208	1.208	1.418	1.704	3.448
	(17)	(17)	(17)	(17)	(14)	(13)

Source: Derived from basic survey data of J. Henry Schroder Wagg & Co. Limited.
a. Numbers in parentheses indicate number of issues upon which average percentage is based.

different from those in the United States, but any such conclusion would have to be tentative.

TRADING ACTIVITY. Fragmentary evidence in the United States suggests that the level of trading activity in equities is not very sensitive to the costs of trading.[79] Despite the apparently higher costs in the United Kingdom, the turnover figures in that country are not much different from those in the United States. Unit trusts have an average annual turnover rate of about 40 percent; insurance companies and pension funds probably have a turnover rate of about 13 percent.[80] These turnover rates are similar to those observed in the United States.[81] Thus the relatively high trading costs in the United Kingdom, primarily due to the transfer tax,

79. Irwin Friend and Marshall E. Blume, "Competitive Commissions on the New York Stock Exchange," *Journal of Finance,* vol. 28 (September 1973), pp. 795–819; Blume and Friend, *The Changing Role of the Individual Investor;* and numerous publications of investors' opinions by the New York Stock Exchange.

80. *Evidence on Financing,* vol. 7, pp. 42–43.

81. In *Current Statistics* the Securities and Exchange Commission publishes on a quarterly basis turnover statistics by major type of institutional investor.

probably do not harm the efficiency of the market; that is, it provides adequate signals to firms about their cost of capital. Quite apart from efficiency considerations, some people have objected to this transfer or stamp tax for equity reasons.

THE PRIMARY MARKET. In the United Kingdom, The Stock Exchange regulates the new issues market and has established regulations that make it institutionally very difficult to issue new equity except through rights offerings. According to Marsh, there were 150 rights issued in 1975, which raised a total of £1.2 billion, but only 11 nonrights issues, which raised a total of £38 million.[82] In the United States, by contrast, most new equity is raised through nonrights issues. During 1971 and 1972, $10.7 billion of new equity was raised through nonrights issues, while only $2.0 billion was raised through rights issues.[83]

The costs of a rights issue as a percentage of the proceeds is very substantial for a small issue but declines rapidly with increases in the size of the issue (up to a certain point). Marsh estimated that in 1975 the cost of raising £50,000 was 13 percent, of £100,000 was 8 percent, and of £1 million was 2.9 percent. For £10 million, the cost fell to roughly 2.4 percent and remained at approximately that level with further increases in the size of an issue.[84] The most recently available cost figures in the United States were collected by the Securities and Exchange Commission in December 1974 and cover the 1971–72 period. There were sixteen rights issues of over $20 million during these years, with an average percentage cost of 3.8 percent.[85] Although the time difference between the U.K. and U.S. figures prevents exact comparisons, it seems safe to conclude that the costs in the United Kingdom are not greater than those in the United States.

Of perhaps more critical importance is the conclusion of the 1974 Security and Exchange Commission study that rights issues in the United States are considerably cheaper than nonrights issues—averaging 1 to 5 percentage points less. This analysis suggests that the U.K. system of raising equity through rights issues may be less costly than the U.S. system,

82. Paul Marsh, "An Analysis of Equity Rights Issues on the London Stock Exchange," p. 40.
83. U.S. Securities and Exchange Commission, *Cost of Flotation Registered Issues 1971–1972* (GPO, December 1974), p. 3.
84. Marsh, "An Analysis of Equity Rights Issues," p. 72.
85. U.S. Securities and Exchange Commission, *Cost of Flotation Registered Issues,* p. 21.

which relies on nonrights issues. Moreover, it appears that the U.K. market is able to absorb these rights offerings with no discernible adverse effect upon the share prices of the issuing companies[86]—in conformity with the belief that the relevant market for a new issue is the entire market of financial claims and not the more narrowly defined market for the specific issue.[87]

Conclusions and Recommendations

One must be impressed with the ability of the financial markets in the United Kingdom to respond to the major economic shocks that the country experienced during the seventies. The markets were able to channel large sums among the different sectors of the economy in nontraditional ways. In 1974, when equities were selling at low values, substantial sums were transferred through the banking system. With the recovery of equity prices in 1975 and 1976, substantial sums were raised through new equity issues.

It seems safe to conclude that the financial institutions in the United Kingdom are working well enough to enable any clearly profitable project to be readily financed. Thus these institutions do not appear to be restricting the growth of the U.K. economy. It therefore follows that any radical change to the structure of U.K. financial institutions would have little stimulative effect on the economy. And one can easily conceive of situations in which a radical change could be detrimental.

As this paper showed, however, there are some areas where improve-

86. Paul Marsh, "Equity Rights Issues and the Efficiency of the UK Stock Market," *Journal of Finance,* vol. 34 (September 1979), pp. 839–62.

87. If rights offerings of equity are preferable from the point of view of costs, the question naturally arises why they are not used more often in the United States. One possible reason is that there exists in the United States no institutional mechanism to protect stockholders who do not exercise or sell their rights, so that with any rights issue some stockholders, particularly the smaller ones, may forfeit the value of their rights through inaction. In Britain, however, unexercised rights are sold automatically at the expiration date and the proceeds distributed to the owner. Other reasons have also been given for the relative sparsity of rights issues in the United States, including the desire of underwriters for greater fees and the perception of management that stockholders would not understand the dilution effects of a rights offering. For whatever reason, however, the predominant use of rights issues in the United Kingdom may make it less costly to raise new equity there than in the United States.

ment may be possible or where a problem may ultimately develop. The investing process has become increasingly institutionalized in the United Kingdom, even more so than in the United States. Nevertheless, it should be kept in mind that individuals in Britain are still important investors in their own right and may be the dominant investors in some types of investments, such as small enterprises.

The tax structure in the United Kingdom makes it very attractive for individuals to save through institutions rather than directly. For example, by saving through a unit-linked life insurance plan, an investor can obtain an initial tax credit and a reduced tax on the subsequent investment income.[88] One might thus expect a large proportion of new savings by individuals to be channeled through institutions.

If in the future, as would appear plausible, individuals were to invest the bulk of their financial savings through institutions, institutional investments would ultimately become very much more important than direct investments. This possible tying up of individual funds in institutions could well reduce the supply of seed capital for starting new small ventures. Traditionally, such capital has been provided by the entrepreneur himself or personal friends, and it is doubtful that intermediaries could ever fulfill this function.

It is, of course, the high marginal tax rates that give individuals the incentive to save through institutions; a reduction in those rates, with a corresponding broadening of the tax base (as recommended by Pechman in the preceding paper), would help to reduce this incentive. If such an overall reform is not politically feasible, an alternative would be to change

88. One of the commentators on an earlier version of this paper pointed out the even greater tax savings associated with pension plans. In the national accounts employer contributions to funded pension plans and the associated income are attributed to individuals. The apparent inference is that these tax savings give individuals an even greater incentive to save through pension plans.

The treatment of pension plans in the national accounts, however, obscures what is really happening. An employee is promised a pension, the amount of which is usually determined as a function of average wages. An asset is thus created for the employee and a liability for the employer. If the employer had an extremely high credit rating, the existence or nonexistence of a pension fund would be expected to have little impact on the individual's saving behavior. In other cases, an individual may perceive a pension fund as affecting the probability of a firm's honoring its commitment; a pension plan is then very similar to a sinking fund for a bond. Hence tax concessions to pension funds are probably less important in explaining individual direct savings than in explaining the distribution of wage income as between current and deferred compensation.

the tax laws so as to give the same tax advantages to income on direct savings as are now given to income on indirect savings through life insurance companies. One way to accomplish this goal would be to make it easy for individuals to create their own personal tax-sheltered investment trusts. While receiving the same favorable tax treatment as currently enjoyed by life insurance companies, an individual would be able to control the investment policy of such a trust and invest in his own company or in whatever else he wished.[89]

Finally, there are three items that probably do not lead to any global misallocation of resources but may cause inequities. First, the U.K. tax system effectively precludes fixed-income unit trusts. This provision, which probably works to the detriment of the smaller investor who does not have sufficient funds to invest directly in the bond market, should be changed. Second, the cancellation penalties associated with unit-linked life insurance policies should be examined carefully. If the U.S. experience with contractual mutual fund plans is applicable to these very similar plans, the losses to small investors may be substantial. Third, the costs of trading equities in the secondary market seems comparatively high because of a stamp tax and a fixed commission rate schedule that appears to exceed the competitive levels. Abolishing the fixed-rate schedule would probably lead to a reduction in commission rates and, extrapolating from the U.S. experience, have no detrimental effect on the functioning of the financial markets.

In sum, radical changes to the structure of financial institutions do not seem to be warranted at this time, although in some areas fine tuning may be appropriate. Furthermore, no evidence was found that institutions, at their present levels of ownership, have adversely affected the efficiency of the capital markets in any significant way.

Appendix A: Savings Regression

To examine the relationship between savings rates and the ratios of net worth, of financial wealth, of gross liquid assets, and of net liquid assets to disposable income, a regression analysis was performed (table 19).

89. Creating such a further distortion in the tax code is obviously a "second best" solution, but it would help to eliminate the discrimination against direct savings implicit in the current tax system.

Table 19. *Summary of Regressions of Savings Rates on the Ratios
of Four Forms of Wealth to Disposable Income*[a]

Independent variable	Intercept	Slope	Regression statistic		
			$\bar{R}^2$	Standard error	Durbin-Watson
Basic data					
Net worth/disposable income	33.20 (3.94)	−5.20 (−2.68)	0.38	2.21	0.43
Financial wealth/disposable income	24.61 (17.70)	−5.76 (−10.21)	0.91	0.84	1.94
Gross liquid assets/disposable income	38.92 (6.59)	−31.85 (−4.80)	0.69	1.57	1.50
Net liquid assets/disposable income	39.68 (13.67)	−36.68 (−10.04)	0.91	0.85	1.43
First differences					
Net worth/disposable income	0.46 (1.46)	−1.99 (−1.98)	0.25	0.99	1.23
Financial wealth/disposable income	0.29 (0.91)	−2.80 (−2.34)	0.33	0.93	2.06
Gross liquid assets/disposable income	0.51 (1.28)	−2.54 (−0.34)	0.00	1.19	1.49
Net liquid assets/disposable income	0.15 (0.41)	−22.31 (−2.07)	0.27	0.97	1.38

Source: Calculations performed at the Rodney L. White Center for Financial Research, the Wharton School, University of Pennsylvania.
a. The numbers in parentheses are t-statistics.

In the regressions of these savings rates on each of the four ratios, the maximum coefficient of determination of 0.91 occurs when either the ratio of financial wealth to disposable income or the ratio of net liquid assets to disposable income is used as the independent variable.[90] Even so, the standard errors of estimates for each of these two regressions, 0.84 percent for financial wealth and 0.85 percent for net liquid assets, indicate that there is still substantial variability in the savings rates that is not explained by these ratios.[91]

90. According to the Durbin-Watson statistic, the specification of the regression with financial wealth is somewhat better than that with net liquid assets.
91. If one were to use as a predictor of the next year's savings rate the past savings rate plus 0.55 (the average yearly increase over the 1966–76 period), the standard error would be 1.14, which can be regarded as the standard error of a naive forecast and can be compared with those in table 19.

To check the specification of the regressions, they were run in first differences. In first differences the ratio of financial wealth to disposable income appears to be slightly better as an explanatory variable than the ratio of net liquid assets to disposable income.

According to the standard error of estimates, the worst explanatory variable in the regressions using the basic data is the ratio of net worth to disposable income, which is the theoretically correct variable under the life-cycle hypothesis. However, the Durbin-Watson statistic suggests that the specification of this regression is poor. In first differences, the specification improves and the standard error drops considerably—almost to that using net liquid assets. Because of the difficulties in measuring the value of physical assets, there is probably more measurement error in the ratio of total net worth to disposable income than in the ratio of financial wealth to disposable income. If one were able to eliminate measurement error and improve the specification, it is not inconceivable that the regression using total net worth to disposable income would produce the best fit. In the first difference form, the ratio of gross liquid assets to disposable income has virtually no explanatory power.

Appendix B: Cross-Sectional Regressions of Plant and Equipment Expenditures

To examine the relationship of plant and equipment expenditures to specific characteristics of firms, a cross section of U.K. firms was studied. This cross section consisted of 954 firms—the largest industrial firms by market capitalization in the DataStream data base as of the end of June 1978. Of these firms 29 were discarded because of missing data, and 24 more were discarded because of negative profit figures, leaving a total of 901 firms. The technical reason for discarding firms with negative profit figures was the impossibility of taking logarithmic transformations, but one could possibly argue on economic grounds that the earnings of these firms may contain substantial negative transitory elements, making their reported earnings poor estimates of their more permanent level of earnings. Moreover, in preliminary work, regressions were run without logarithmic transformations, thus enabling the inclusion of 925 firms (the maximum number with complete data), and the conclusions were not much different.

Table 20. *Cross-Sectional Regressions of the Logarithm of the Ratio of Plant and Equipment Expenditures to Total Assets on Firm Variables Measured in Logarithmic Form and Dummy Industry Variables for U.K. DataStream Companies, 1977*

	Coefficients on independent variables[a]						
Specifi-cation	Gross return on assets	Net return on assets	Ratio of equity to assets	Total assets	Payout ratio	Beta	R^2
1	0.279 (4.52)	...	−0.458 (−3.78)	−0.024 (−1.31)	−0.027 (−0.75)	0.132 (2.72)	0.17
2	...	0.379 (5.72)	−0.505 (−4.18)	−0.023 (−1.27)	0.008 (0.21)	0.115 (2.38)	0.18
3	0.317 (5.83)	...	−0.442 (−3.83)	...	...	...	0.16
4	...	0.395 (6.96)	−0.487 (−4.22)	...	...	...	0.18

Source: Calculations performed at the Rodney L. White Center for Financial Research, the Wharton School.

a. See appendix text for further explanation of variables. The numbers in parentheses are t-statistics.

The financial data on these 925 firms came from the latest available annual reports and thus would generally be 1977 data. The specific variables used in the regressions were:

—the plant and equipment expenditure ratio defined as the ratio of plant and equipment expenditure from the sources and uses of funds to total assets;

—gross return on assets defined as the ratio of the sum of pretax profits and interest payments to total assets;

—net return on assets defined as the ratio of the sum of aftertax profits and interest payments to total assets;

—the ratio of equity to total assets;

—total assets;

—the payout ratio; and

—the equity beta coefficient as calculated by DataStream.

When market values were lacking, the values of equity and total assets were measured by their book values. There were twenty-seven industries. In an attempt to hold industry effects constant, twenty-six dummy variables, one for each of the first twenty-six industries, were included in the regressions; however, the coefficients are not reported here for reasons of space.

Table 20 summarizes the basic regressions that were run in logarithmic form. The coefficients of determination adjusted for degrees of freedom are of a respectable level for this type of cross-sectional regression. The

Table 21. *Cross-Sectional Regressions of the Logarithm of the Ratio of Plant and Equipment Expenditures to Total Assets on Firm Variables Measured in Logarithmic Form and Dummy Industry Variables for U.S. Compustat Companies, 1968–77*[a]

Date	*Net return on assets*	*Ratio of equity to assets*	*Total assets*	*Payout ratio*	R^2	*Number of observations*
		Coefficients on independent variables[b]				
1968	0.201	−0.041	0.069	−0.095	0.28	1,316
	(3.70)	(−0.67)	(5.21)	(−2.90)		
1969	0.201	−0.115	0.082	−0.132	0.29	1,339
	(3.78)	(−2.06)	(6.62)	(−5.28)		
1970	0.216	0.005	0.089	−0.082	0.32	1,309
	(4.31)	(0.08)	(6.90)	(−2.91)		
1971	0.191	−0.028	0.098	−0.043	0.40	1,300
	(3.84)	(−0.47)	(7.53)	(−1.65)		
1972	0.212	0.039	0.077	−0.047	0.40	1,364
	(4.03)	(0.66)	(6.04)	(−1.77)		
1973	0.352	−0.025	0.075	−0.046	0.37	1,454
	(6.71)	(−0.52)	(6.30)	(−2.04)		
1974	0.307	0.040	0.124	−0.056	0.41	1,475
	(6.09)	(0.75)	(10.60)	(−2.46)		
1975	0.339	0.016	0.115	−0.024	0.40	1,500
	(6.88)	(0.32)	(9.82)	(−1.03)		
1976	0.410	−0.056	0.073	0.031	0.43	1,624
	(7.79)	(−0.89)	(5.91)	(1.17)		
1977	0.323	−0.048	0.073	−0.027	0.41	1,531
	(6.20)	(−0.83)	(5.90)	(−0.99)		

Source: Calculations performed at the Rodney L. White Center for Financial Research, the Wharton School.

a. A dummy variable was included for each two-digit Compustat industry, less one industry. For instance, in 1968 there were sixty dummy variables in the regression to control for industry effects. These variables are not shown in the table.

b. See appendix text for further description of variables. The numbers in parentheses are *t*-statistics.

coefficient on the logarithm of beta appears to be of the wrong sign. One would expect that, holding constant profitability and risk as measured by industry, plant and equipment expenditures would increase with decreases in beta.

One possible explanation for this theoretically incorrect sign on beta is a statistical one. It is well known that for inactively traded stocks beta coefficients as would be estimated by DataStream would be downward biased. If the less aggressive firms are the less actively traded, one could argue that the beta coefficient is acting as a measure of managerial attitude and thus rationalize the positive sign on this variable in the cross-sectional regressions. Regardless of the reason for the sign on the beta coefficient, it should be noted that the coefficients on profitability and leverage are roughly the same whether or not this variable is included.

For comparison purposes, similar cross-sectional regressions for the United States were run for each of the last twenty years on all the companies included on the Compustat Industrial Annual File, with the required data. Dummy variables were included for each two-digit Compustat industry, less one. Table 21 contains the regression results for one specification for each of the last ten years to give a flavor of the types of results obtained. Beta coefficients were not included in the U.S. analysis, since they were not readily available.

Comments by Richard A. Brealey

ALTHOUGH in recent years it has become fashionable to blame the United Kingdom's slow industrial growth on the inadequacies of the British financial system, Marshall Blume, like most financial economists, finds no evidence for that view. Thus it is tempting to believe that Britain's financial system has consistently approximated some competitive ideal. But such does not appear to be the case. In his paper Blume lists several important deficiencies in the organization of the U.K. capital markets.

Blume's analysis, therefore, raises the question whether it is likely that one would *ever* observe a strong relation between a country's financial system and its rate of growth. Such widely disparate structures as the bank-based systems of West Germany and Japan and the market-based systems of the Anglo-Saxon world are in fact capable of serving very similar functions. Differences in market structure can encourage or discourage saving only to the extent that they affect the liquidity of savings or the ability of investors to achieve a "fair" rate of return. An active secondary market for securities, such as exists in the United Kingdom and the United States, provides the investor with a considerable measure of liquidity. If he needs funds for consumption, he can simply sell his securities in the secondary market. But an equally efficient source of liquidity is provided in other countries by borrowing. Indeed, even in market-based financial systems it is often more convenient for individuals to take out mortgages, buy on hire purchase, take out policy loans, and the like, rather than liquidate their investment portfolios. Similarly, in the United Kingdom and the United States considerable emphasis tends to be laid on the efficiency of the securities markets. As long as security prices impound all available information, any person can expect neither more nor less than an equilibrium rate of return. But informational efficiency is not necessary for this result. What matters is that savers are able to adopt naive strategies that avoid the risk of inferior performance.

The point I wish to make is that financial systems of very different kinds have an incentive to supply the services that savers need and are also capable of doing so.[92] In any reasonably competitive economy it is, therefore, unlikely that changes in the institutional structure of the capital markets could have a perceptible effect on industrial growth. And moreover, because so many other important variables affect growth, it is almost inconceivable that the effect of changes in the organization of the capital markets could be measured. Hence I believe that U.K. government policy toward capital markets should be principally concerned with the welfare effects of the financial system and its international competitiveness, not with its structure. In this respect Blume's paper contains some important messages.

The paper highlights a number of significant developments in the British financial system. Rather than comment on matters of detail in Blume's analysis, I consider five of these developments in Britain's financial markets and draw attention to the influential role played by government regulation and tax policy.

The Growth of Financial Institutions

In both the United Kingdom and the United States there has been a substantial growth in intermediation, which, as Blume points out, has been stimulated by the tax advantages to saving through intermediaries. It is no coincidence that the growth has been principally in insurance companies and pension funds; investment trusts and unit trusts sold directly to the public have not grown. Similarly, within the insurance industry companies have found it much easier to sell investment-type policies rather than traditional insurance.

It is somewhat ironic that the government both provides substantial tax incentives to saving through an intermediary and anguishes about the consequences of these actions. For example, Blume draws attention to the widespread concern over the growth of shareholder power. Since it

92. Similarly, differences between the financial systems of developed countries are unlikely to have an appreciable effect on the allocation of savings.

seems only recently that we in Britain were being asked to worry about the failure of shareholders to make their voices heard, I think that we have to reconcile ourselves to a state of perpetual worry. It is also frequently asserted that the growth of institutional share-ownership has increased market volatility. In fact, there is little evidence of any long-term upward trend in market volatility as opposed to periodic market shocks. Volatility increased substantially after the 1973 oil embargo, but by 1977 it was no greater than it had been for much of the previous half-century.[93] The growth of intermediaries has increased concentration within the industry. Although any such increase is likely to reduce the informational efficiency of the securities markets, I share Blume's conclusion that such effects are likely to be very small. By most standards the level of concentration is low and the degree of competition high.

I do not wish to imply that we should not be concerned about tax incentives to particular forms of saving. The tax treatment of financial institutions induces individuals to enter into long-term contractual arrangements that provide a specific set of contingent payments. The resultant welfare loss is rather similar to the loss that would occur if greengrocers sold oranges only if the customer also agreed to take out a long-term contract to buy lemons.

The Banking System

One aspect of government policy to which Blume does not refer is the treatment of clearing banks and building societies. Building societies enjoy certain advantages over the clearing banks in competing for retail deposits: they are not obliged to maintain balances with the Bank of England and have not been subject to any statutory limit on the interest that they can pay on small deposits. Partly for these reasons many of the functions of retail banking are being assumed by the building societies. At the other end of the spectrum the British clearers are facing increasingly strong competition from the U.S. banks, which are not encumbered with large branch networks.

I do not wish to imply that I disapprove of competition in banking services, but I would like to believe that the encouragement to building

93. See, for example, R. A. Brealey, J. Byrne, and E. Dimson "The Variability of Market Returns" *The Investment Analyst,* vol. 52 (December 1978), pp. 19–23.

societies to provide many of the services of branch banking represents a conscious policy.

The Change in Financing Methods

One of the intriguing developments of the 1970s has been the demise of the corporate long-term debt market. I share Blume's view that this may be in part due to the increased uncertainty about the rate of inflation. As the variance of the inflation rate increases, the incentive grows for *both* borrower *and* lender to avoid the risk of long-term nominal commitments.[94] Thus it is no coincidence that the decline in the use of long-term debt has been matched by a switch from fixed-rate to variable-rate term loans.

But an equally important explanation of this shift in financing has been the tax system. Merton Miller's presidential address at the 1976 annual meeting of the American Finance Association would lead one to expect a decline in corporate gearing if (a) there is an increase in the rate of tax on investment income, (b) there is a reduction in corporate taxes, and (c) there is an increase in the supply of taxable government bonds.[95] In the United Kingdom we have experienced all three conditions.

As more industrial companies have ceased to pay mainstream tax, debt issues have become less attractive. For these companies leasing has become a preferable alternative, and by value more than half of these leases have been variable rate. A shift has also occurred in the supply of corporate debt funds. Higher rates of tax have reduced the attraction of taxable investment income, and the government has absorbed a higher proportion of the funds that are available for debt.

The government has "crowded out" the corporate sector to the extent that it has attracted investors who have an incentive to hold debt. In doing so it has induced the corporate sector to seek other sources of finance. In some respects, which investor chooses to appeal to which clientele is a matter of secondary interest. But I think the government's decision to issue default-free bonds in order to invest in the equity of some very risky enterprises has serious consequences. The risks do not go away because

94. See Richard Brealey and Stephen Schaefer, "Term Structure with Uncertain Inflation," *Journal of Finance,* vol. 2 (May 1977), pp. 277–89.

95. See Merton H. Miller, "Debt and Taxes," *Journal of Finance,* vol. 2 (May 1977), pp. 261–75.

of government ownership. Either they are passed on to the consumer or taxpayer or they are borne by the bondholder in the form of increased uncertainty about the rates of inflation.[96]

Blume's analysis of British company gearing indicates a relationship between financing method and level of new investment. With profitability, risk, industry, and firm size held constant, his empirical results show that firms with more equity in their capital structure are investing less than their more geared colleagues. Since this result is liable to be seized upon by those who believe that our low rate of investment is a consequence of low gearing, it is worth stressing that Blume's result is exactly what one would expect if companies have a pecking order for sources of finance. Since firms use retained earnings before external finance, those firms with few investment opportunities will tend to finance them with equity rather than debt.

Foreign Investments

Blume provides some interesting ideas on overseas portfolio investment. The case for quota restrictions on portfolio investment is, I believe, very weak.

The effect of a limited pool of investment currency is to cause U.K. investors to hold fewer overseas securities and more domestic securities than they otherwise would. Since it is possible to reduce risk by diversifying internationally, the effect of the investment currency pool is to increase the risk of investment by U.K. nationals.

If U.K. investors are compelled to hold *more* U.K. securities than they otherwise would, foreign investors must be prepared to hold *fewer* U.K. securities. This will occur if the equilibrium return to foreigners on U.K. securities is lower than it would be in a free market. Thus the investment premium works only because it leads to a low real rate of return in the United Kingdom. If the amount of foreign investment that British investors would *like* to undertake is small relative to the world market, then the reduction in the rate of return on domestic securities will also be small.

Clearly, if the government were to remove the limitation on the pool of

96. See, for example, R. A. Brealey, "Inflation and the Real Value of Government Assets," *Financial Analysts Journal* (January–February 1979), pp. 18–21. As Blume points out, "crowding out" occurs in a wider sense whenever the government absorbs savings, whether those savings are provided by borrowing or by taxing.

investment currency, there would be an increase in foreign investment by U.K. residents. But every security has to be held by someone. Therefore, if the supply of securities is held constant, any increase in foreign investment by U.K. residents would have to be exactly counterbalanced by an increase in investment by foreigners in the United Kingdom.

The case for controls on overseas investment, therefore, must rest on the belief that the reduction in the real rate of interest in the United Kingdom has a beneficial effect on direct investment and that this benefit more than compensates for the costs of imperfect portfolio diversification.

The Stock Market

Blume's analysis of the U.K. stock market raised at least two important issues. One, which is of very topical concern, centers on the extent to which development of an over-the-counter market in the United Kingdom could assist small business. It is tempting to think of The Stock Exchange in London as somehow akin to the New York Stock Exchange and Nightingale's over-the-counter market as akin to the American over-the-counter market. In fact, for good or ill the listing requirements of The Stock Exchange are substantially less stringent than those of its New York counterpart. Thus, despite the relatively small size of the U.K. economy, many more stocks are listed in London than in New York. Many of these firms are very small (one-third of the shares have a market capitalization of less than £2 million) and the stocks are rarely traded. It is difficult to believe that relaxing the listing requirements still further would serve any useful purpose. Because The Stock Exchange provides many of the services provided by the U.S. over-the-counter market, it is not surprising that we have not had a similar growth in over-the-counter trading. Nightingale makes a market in fifteen companies, whereas several thousand firms are regularly traded over the counter in the States. The important issues here are whether an auction market or a negotiated market is a more efficient method of trading small company shares and the extent to which The Stock Exchange can in practice provide a negotiated market.

The second issue that Blume considers is the operational efficiency of the British stock market and the cost of trading. It is understandable that one's first concern should be with the existence of minimum commission schedules. I think the interesting thing here is that the fixed commission on ordinary shares in London is very close to the negotiated rate in New

York. The direct effects of changing to negotiated rates in London are, therefore, likely to be small compared with the indirect effects.

The most striking difference between the British and the American securities markets is the very rapid innovation in the States. Many of these changes have been thrust upon the industry by hard times and government action. Many have not been in the interests of the securities firms, and a few have not been in the interests of the public. But in addition to these structural changes, the American market has also been more innovative in its products. Two obvious cases are the development of the traded options markets and the development of the futures markets in currencies and securities. The corresponding lack of innovation in the United Kingdom is in part the fault of the securities industry, but the government and the Bank of England can scarcely be said to have encouraged innovations.[97] I would like to see the Bank encourage, for example, a currency futures market, including a futures market in investment currency. Such a market would provide firms with an opportunity to hedge their currency risk without any impact on external flows. The U.K. financial system has always thrived on its flexibility and imagination. My concern is that we cherish and preserve these qualities.

Conclusion

The British and American financial system are remarkably similar in structure, and many of the issues that we face are identical to those that Americans have encountered. It is Blume's familiarity with the same problems in a different setting that makes his discussion of our financial markets so stimulating.

97. The major exception was the stimulus given to the development of the Euro-dollar market in London by the U.S. interest equalization tax and voluntary restraint program.

HENDRIK S. HOUTHAKKER

The Use and Management of North Sea Oil

THE MOST favorable development in the British economy during the last decade was the discovery of oil reserves in the North Sea large enough to make Britain self-sufficient for the remainder of the century.[1] Not only has Britain become by far the largest oil producer in Western Europe, but in terms of proved reserves it now ranks about number ten in the world, ahead of such long-established exporters as Venezuela and Indonesia. The search for oil continues, though at a slower pace, and may yet lead to further major discoveries. It is also worth noting that the British, so often castigated for their slothful ways, managed—with considerable help from U.S. and other foreign companies—to bring their oil into production with remarkable speed, well in advance of the Alaskan oil that had been discovered a few years earlier, but apparently without incurring

I am indebted to Roger Luscombe for surveying the literature and providing other assistance, and to several persons in the British public and private sectors for helpful discussions, especially to Charles Goodhart for his suggestions about the focus of the paper. Comments on the first draft from participants in the Ditchley conference have been incorporated in the present version without attribution.

1. Although the words *North Sea* and *oil* are generally used together in this paper, this usage is not meant to be restrictive. Promising discoveries have been made onshore near the south coast of England and offshore west of the Shetland Islands. In fact, these recent finds remote from the central oil zone along the British-Norwegian demarcation line are a major reason for optimism about the ultimate size of U.K. oil resources.

the waste of resources that has often accompanied hasty development in the past.

Much has been written about the impact of North Sea oil on the British economy, and particularly on the balance of payments. This paper does not deal primarily with that issue, although it is not overlooked. My main purpose is to discuss depletion policy, that is, the rate at which North Sea oil is to be produced. The central role of the problem of depletion has been widely recognized, but it does not appear that any consensus on this subject has yet emerged. Though not of course the final word on the depletion problem, this paper may be useful in bringing together most of the considerations that would seem to have a bearing on it. These include the economic characteristics of oil production, the prospects for the world price of oil, the effect of North Sea oil on the rest of the British economy, and the methods by which the British government could influence the exploitation of the resource.

Before these matters are discussed, a few words should be said, particularly for the benefit of non-British readers, about the orders of magnitude involved. According to present plans, production from fields that are already operating or under active development will be close to 2.5 million barrels a day in the early 1980s, say, 1982; it was about three-quarters of that level in the middle of 1979 and rising rapidly. Assuming 900 million barrels for 1982 and a world price of £12 a barrel,[2] the contribution to gross domestic product, after allowing for operating cost, would be roughly £10 billion, or between 3 and 4 percent of the nominal gross domestic product likely to prevail in that year. To put this figure into further perspective, British merchandise trade (either imports or exports), extrapolating from recent trends, should then be between £50 billion and £60 billion. Oil production, including service and construction activities, probably employs about 50,000 persons, less than ¼ of 1 percent of the British labor force.[3] However, the oil industry is a large user of capital; in 1977 and 1978 investment in petroleum and natural gas amounted to about 8 percent of total gross domestic fixed capital formation, somewhat

2. An exchange rate of two dollars to one pound is used for convenience throughout this paper; it is not intended as a forecast. Data originally expressed in metric tons ("tonnes") have been converted to barrels at a rate of 7 to 1.

3. Maxwell Gaskin, *The Changing Prospect: North Sea Oil and Scotland* (Edinburgh: Royal Bank of Scotland, 1977), p. 12.

less than 2 percent of GDP in that year.[4] The percentage may be somewhat lower in 1982, depending on the future course of exploration. Finally, North Sea oil will be an important contributor to government revenue, with royalties and petroleum revenue tax accounting for between 8 and 10 percent of the current receipts of the central government by 1982; in addition, there will be sizable revenues from profit taxes.

What this preliminary assessment shows is that North Sea oil will make a significant contribution to the British economy, but not one so large as to completely transform the nonoil part of the economy. For the most part, therefore, I assume here that the nonoil economy stays on its own course, whatever that may be, and concentrate on the oil aspects. It is only in respect to the balance of payments that this partial equilibrium approach needs to be modified.[5]

Economic Characteristics of Minerals

This section first discusses *proved reserves,* a concept much used in public discussions of mineral policy but often misunderstood. Then follow some observations on the optimal rate of extraction and on exploration.

Proved Reserves

It is commonly argued that if proved reserves in the North Sea are 15 billion barrels and production is at an average rate of 750 million barrels a year, then these reserves will be exhausted in twenty years. Though

4. Great Britain Central Statistical Office, *Economic Trends,* no. 306 (London: Her Majesty's Stationery Office, 1979), pp. 78, 98.
5. The North Sea is rich not only in oil but in natural gas. Large gas fields were discovered in the southern part of the North Sea in the middle 1960s, and they are now in full production. The oil fields in the northern and central parts of the North Sea also contain large amounts of associated gas, some of which is already reaching Britain through pipelines; and Britain imports gas from fields in the Norwegian sector.

These gas supplies have already had an important impact on the British economy, particularly by reducing the demand for imported oil even before the domestic oil came into production. Nevertheless, this paper does not deal with natural gas, because most of the important policy decisions have already been taken and the remaining ones are rather similar to those encountered in oil.

arithmetically unassailable, this calculation is quite misleading. To see why, it is necessary to go through a few formal definitions.

In general, reserves, as distinct from resources, may be defined as "identified deposits of mineral known to be recoverable with current technology under present economic conditions."[6] Among the economic conditions is the price of output; consequently reserves are a function of the prevailing price. Reserves are customarily divided into three categories.

1. *Proved,* or *measured, reserves* are those "whose location, quality, and quantity are known from geologic evidence supported by engineering evidence." Engineering evidence can be obtained only by exploratory and development drilling, followed by a detailed analysis of oil flow, gas pressure, and other indicators.

2. *Probable,* or *indicated, reserves* are "based partly on specific measurements, samples or production data, and partly on projections for a reasonable distance on geological evidence." Here again some drilling (perhaps only exploratory) is required, but any subsequent analysis is less conclusive than for proved reserves.

3. *Possible,* or *inferred, reserves* are "based on broad geologic knowledge for which quantitative measurements are not available."

The concept of *resources* is much broader, including not only reserves but also "minerals that have been identified but cannot now be extracted because of economic or technological limitations, as well as economic or sub-economic materials that have not as yet been discovered." Some of these resources will become reserves when the price goes up, technology is improved, or exploration is successful.

The three kinds of reserves and the remaining resources may all occur in the same field. However, most of the possible reserves and remaining resources are likely to be in areas that either have not yet been fully explored, or have not been explored at all but are considered prospective from a geological point of view. Estimates of such resources are necessarily speculative; it will be argued below that contemporary geologists lean to underestimation. For the world as a whole the history of most minerals (including oil), therefore, is marked more by pleasant surprises than by widespread disappointment, though this is not true for particular areas. At present, worldwide oil resources are usually put between 1,500

6. This definition and the following ones are taken from Walter Dupree and others, *Energy Perspectives 2,* U.S. Department of the Interior (Government Printing Office, 1976), p. 223.

billion and 2,000 billion barrels,[7] compared with proved reserves of about 645 billion barrels.[8]

A less precise but nonetheless useful concept in the analysis of particular oil fields is *oil in place,* by which is meant (or should be meant) the total amount of oil remaining in a field regardless of the cost of extracting it. It is generally a much larger figure than resources, because experience suggests that not all the oil can be profitably recovered.[9] Strictly speaking, therefore, oil in place is the absolute upper limit to the oil recoverable from a field. So defined, the concept would be useful precisely because, unlike most of the other concepts mentioned, it does not depend on implicit economic judgments about what will be profitable in the future. It appears, however, that such judgments do sometimes enter into estimates of oil in place when geologists are unwilling to contemplate prices vastly higher than those prevailing at the time the estimates are made. In analyses of oil fields the "original" oil in place (at discovery) is used to obtain the remaining oil in place by subtracting cumulative production. A related but less exact concept is *ultimate recovery,* which also appears to depend on implicit price assumptions.

Enough has been said to show that proved reserves do not tell us a great deal about the potential of a field, a petroleum province like the North Sea, or the world as a whole.[10] Since proved reserves are in effect a

7. See, for example, Richard Nehring, *Giant Oil Fields and World Oil Resources,* prepared for the Central Intelligence Agency, R-2284-CIA (Rand Corporation, 1978); and Pierre Desprairies, "Worldwide Petroleum Supply Limits," in *World Energy Resources, 1985–2020* (Guildford, England: IPC Science and Technology Press for The World Energy Conference, 1978), pp. 1–47. Much larger estimates are given by Bernardo F. Grossling, *In Search of a Statistical Probability Model for Petroleum-Resource Assessment,* U.S. Geological Survey Circular 724 (GPO, 1975), and by some of the experts whose views were collected by Desprairies.

8. *International Petroleum Encyclopedia, 1978* (Tulsa, Oklahoma: Petroleum Publishing, 1978), p. 270.

9. This statement is correct as long as conventional production techniques (drilling and pumping) are considered. In principle, recovery close to 100 percent could be obtained by mining, that is, by bringing the oil-bearing materials to the surface for further processing. This is the technique used in the Canadian tar sands; it has also been used occasionally in very shallow oil fields, but in the present state of the art it is presumably impractical for offshore deposits.

10. An example from actual experience is the Wasson field in Texas, which in 1977 was the second largest producer in the United States (after Prudhoe Bay, which had just come on-stream). In 1968 proved reserves had been estimated at 148 million barrels and production was 30 million barrels, suggesting that the field, discovered in 1936, was close to exhaustion. Yet between 1968 and 1977 it produced a total of

lower limit (assuming prices will not fall), it may seem prudent to confine attention to them rather than go into the more speculative concepts.
Although prudence is an admirable virtue, it should not be allowed to
lead to wrong decisions. Rationality requires consideration of alternatives,
and policies based on "prudent" estimates for oil may imply imprudent
decisions about such other energy sources as nuclear power. Moreover,
proved reserves are themselves a policy parameter, depending as they do
on future rates of exploration and development that are subject to government control.

The Microeconomics of Oil Production

Despite the recent mushrooming of interest in energy problems, the
economic analysis of oil production (including exploration) is still far
from being definitive.[11] Since an understanding of the economics of oil
production is vital to the analysis of depletion, the optimal rate of exploitation of an already discovered oil deposit must first be considered.

The most obvious characteristic of a mineral deposit, of course, is that

---

644 million barrels—83 million in 1977 alone—and presumably had sizable proved
reserves left (this figure is not available at present but Nehring, *Giant Oil Fields*,
p. 105, put it at 808 million barrels at the end of 1975). Between 1968 and 1977, of
course, the price of crude had risen sharply, explaining the new lease on life. Another
interesting case in point is the Kern River field in California, which was discovered
toward the end of the nineteenth century (sources differ as to the exact year). From
1969 through 1977 it not only produced more than proved reserves in 1968 but more
than half its cumulative output in the first seventy or eighty years of its productive
existence. Kern River also shows that the widespread belief in a normal oil field
life of twenty years is without foundation. In fact, nearly all large producing fields
in the United States are now more than forty years old, yet most of them yielded
more in 1977 than in 1968. *International Petroleum Encyclopedia 1978,* pp. 201–02,
and *International Petroleum Encyclopedia, 1970* (Petroleum Publishing, 1969), p.
254.

11. Most of the literature deals with minerals in general and pays only incident 1
attention to oil. An interesting programming model of oil production, emphasiz ng
the concept of rate dependence, was presented by Robert G. Kuller and Ronalo G.
Cummings, "An Economic Model of Production and Investment for Petroleum
Reservoirs," *American Economic Review,* vol. 64 (March 1974), pp. 66–79. Several
theoretical papers on the general equilibrium analysis of mineral production appeared in Symposium on the Economics of Exhaustible Resources, *Review of Economic Studies* (special issue, 1974), but they do not go into the specifics of particular
minerals.

it is exhaustible, or more precisely, nonrenewable.[12] It can be viewed as a stock whose components can be brought to the surface at a rate determined by the owner. It is natural to assume that the owner will attempt to maximize the discounted cash flow from the deposit; mathematically this means that the problem is one in the calculus of variations, or its modern offshoots, dynamic programming and control theory. These techniques make it possible, under a variety of assumptions, to determine the optimal path of extraction from both a private and social viewpoint, but the empirical basis for choosing among those assumptions is still quite weak.

In this theoretical approach two parameters are of particular importance: the rate of interest, which is necessary for discounting cash flow, and the rate at which the price of the product increases or decreases. Clearly, a higher rate of interest will tend to accelerate extraction, whereas a higher rate of price increase will tend to retard it, at least initially.

Unfortunately, a correct understanding of the influence of these two factors has been hampered by a proposition attributed to Hotelling, according to which the rate of interest must be equal to the rate at which the "net" price (the difference between the gross price and the cost of extraction) increases.[13] Actually, there appears to be no compelling theo-

12. The term *nonrenewable* is preferable to *exhaustible* because literal exhaustion is in general unlikely. In any mineral deposit some portions can be more cheaply extracted than others, and it will normally be prohibitively expensive to extract *all* the minerals. The usual end of a mineral deposit, therefore, is abandonment, which will occur when the marginal cost of extraction is equal to the price. After abandonment some—in many cases most—of the mineral will remain in the ground and be available for extraction if the price rises. See also note 10.

13. Since this proposition is often regarded as the cornerstone of mineral economics, it should be pointed out that Harold Hotelling stated it only casually and virtually without proof. ("The Economics of Exhaustible Resources," *Journal of Political Economy*, vol. 39 [April 1931], p. 140.) The entire argument is in one sentence: "Since it is a matter of indifference to the owner of a mine whether he receives for a unit of his product a price p_0 now or a price of $p_0 e^{\gamma t}$ after time t, it is not unreasonable to expect that price p will be a function of the time of the form of $p = p_0 e^{\gamma t}$." He then goes on to say that this holds only under competitive conditions and that the price should be interpreted as a net price. Hotelling did not say what will happen if this price changes at a rate different from the rate of interest, yet without such a discussion his proposition is merely an assertion. Empirical studies of mineral prices have found little or no support for Hotelling's proposition. (See, for example, Harold J. Barnett and Chandler Morse, *Scarcity and Growth: The Economics of Natural Resource Availability* [Johns Hopkins Press for Resources for the Future, 1963]; and Gerhard Anders, W. Philip Graham, and S. Charles Maurice, *Does Resource Conservation Pay?* Original Paper 14 [Los Angeles: International Institute for Economic Research, 1978].) This failure is usually attributed to technological

retical reason why the two should be equal except if the extraction cost is constant over time. The empirical evidence suggests, rather, that for a wide range of minerals net prices have remained constant in real terms when averaged over long periods of time, and this observation has presumably not escaped the owners of mineral deposits. It is true that if the price were to rise more rapidly than the rate of interest, then it would pay to leave the minerals in the ground; but if the price were to rise less rapidly or to fall, a positive profit could still be made by extracting some or all of the mineral according to some appropriate schedule.[14]

An example illustrating this argument is given in appendix A. The key to the determination of the optimal rate of extraction is the production function, and especially the dependence of the cost of extraction on the remaining stock and on the rate of extraction. It may be assumed that extraction cost per unit of output is an increasing function not only of the stock remaining in the ground but also of the rate of extraction. If the unit cost were independent of the rate of extraction, it would pay to remove all the minerals at once unless the net price were expected to rise at the rate of interest.

Aside from the theoretical possibility of immediate exhaustion, the rate of extraction is important because the value of a field can be increased by controlling the reservoir pressure through reinjection of gas or water. Until recently, the use of these techniques was confined mostly to old fields, but higher oil prices have apparently made them economic even in newly discovered ones, including several in the North Sea.[15]

---

change, a factor recognized by Hotelling later in his article, but that is not the only explanation. The flaw in Hotelling's analysis is that he implicitly assumed extraction had to extend over time but did not consider the resulting dependence of extraction cost on the rate of extraction. Hotelling was also inconsistent in his use of the net price, making demand a function of that price rather than of the gross price; this has led some authors to assert that the *gross* price of a mineral must rise at the rate of interest. The latter statement would be true only if extraction cost were zero.

14. David Levhari and Nissan Liviatan, "Notes on Hotelling's Economics of Exhaustible Resources," *Canadian Journal of Economics,* vol. 10 (May 1977), pp. 177–92.

15. Another relevant consideration is increasing opposition to the "flaring" of associated gas. Long considered an unobjectionable (not to say picturesque) concomitant of oil production, flaring has come to be frowned upon as a waste of energy resources and has been made subject (especially in the North Sea) to government permits. If gas cannot be flared and if there is not enough of it to warrant a pipeline, it has to be reinjected, and the rate at which this can be done becomes a constraint on the timing of oil production.

Since the example in appendix A is not based on empirical evidence, it is obviously not conclusive. But it does suggest the following propositions.

First, the rate of interest has little or no effect on the cumulative output from a field, but strongly influences the value of the oil in place and also the timing of production (as indicated by the initial rate of production) when the price increases at a substantial rate.

Second, the rate of price change has a nonlinear effect on the duration of production, on the cumulative output, and on the value of a field. Specifically, a negative rate of change implies early abandonment, but the duration of production (theoretically infinite for a constant price) is shorter as the rate of price increase becomes larger. Cumulative output is relatively small when the rate of price increase is negative or zero, but equal to oil in place whenever it is positive. A higher rate of price increase always reduces initial production and increases the initial royalty.

Third, a higher initial price usually shortens the life of a field. It has no effect on cumulative output if the price increases over time but does increase recovery when the price declines over time or stays constant. Needless to say, the initial price strongly influences the value of the oil in place and the initial royalty. A higher initial price always means high initial production.

The implications of these propositions for the management of North Sea oil are more fully developed in a later section, but some of them are also relevant to exploration.

Exploration

The decision to explore may be viewed as a choice among highly uncertain investment prospects.[16] The prospects themselves arise from geological observations and theories modified by drilling experience. An oil company may be assumed to have a large list of prospects and to pursue those for which the expected return, properly discounted for uncertainty, exceeds the cost of capital. Conceptually, exploration decisions are inde-

16. C. Jackson Grayson, Jr., *Decisions Under Uncertainty: Drilling Decisions by Oil and Gas Operators* (Harvard Graduate School of Business Administration, Division of Research, 1960); and Gordon M. Kaufman, *Statistical Decision and Related Techniques in Oil and Gas Exploration* (Prentice-Hall, 1963).

pendent of production decisions, even though in reality the discoverers of oil fields usually go on to exploit them.[17]

This separability means that the exploration decision depends only on the expected value of the oil in place as determined by potential operators (including the discoverer). Such field characteristics as cumulative output or the optimal timing of production are relevant only to the extent they are reflected in the value of the field. According to the three propositions stated above, this value reflects a rather complicated interaction of the initial price, the rate of price change, and the rate of interest. As long as the rate of price change is zero (which is usually assumed in this context), or a fortiori negative, the value of the oil in place is determined almost entirely by the initial price. In that case the supply function of exploration is as simple as it could be.

When the rate of price change is positive, however, its magnitude has a strong influence on the value of a field, and so does the rate of interest (table 3 in the appendix). Because of the widespread conviction that oil prices will rise in real terms, the rate of interest needs to be considered when discussing government policy on North Sea oil (see below).

To conclude these brief remarks on exploration, something must be said about petroleum geology, the science on whose practitioners oil companies and governments rely in selecting and evaluating prospects. Although obviously important as a general guide in these matters, petroleum geology is far from being an exact science—no closer, it appears to a lay observer, than economics. The oil industry adage "oil is where you find it" recognizes this.

More specifically, the brief history of North Sea oil raises serious questions about the predictive power of petroleum geology. To begin with, it is odd that the North Sea, on whose shores two of the largest oil companies (Royal Dutch Shell and British Petroleum) have their headquarters, was not seriously considered as a potential petroleum province until the 1960s. These companies went to the far corners of the earth to look for oil but apparently were not advised that they might find it in their own backyard.[18] When oil was found—the crucial discovery being that

17. Although sales of entire fields appear to be infrequent, after a discovery there are often rearrangements in the joint ventures among companies formed for a particular exploration project.

18. It is true that the technology for exploration in the deep waters and turbulent environment of the North Sea may not have been available, but it could presumably have been developed earlier, since it appears to differ mostly in scale from the tech-

of the large Ekofisk field in 1969—most official and private experts were at pains to minimize its significance. They published estimates of the North Sea oil potential that in retrospect appear unreasonably low even with the limited evidence then available. Fortunately most oil companies did not take these discouraging estimates seriously, and proceeded to discover a number of giant fields in both the British and the Norwegian sectors. In fact, exploration in the North Sea during the first half of the 1970s was unusually successful, but it was left to geographers to give the first realistic estimate of the total potential.[19] This estimate appears to have been confirmed by exploratory experience to date, considering that large prospective areas have not yet been opened to exploration.

These critical observations are made not to disparage the petroleum geologists, without whom the North Sea oil would probably never have been found at all, but to suggest that their projections may be more helpful on the microlevel than on the aggregate level. Given the apparent conservatism of geologists' aggregate projections, they should perhaps be regarded as lower bounds rather than as best estimates.[20] Until geologists calculate meaningful upper bounds, economists have to use their own devices, fallible though they may be.

The Outlook for Oil Prices

The preceding discussion has made it clear that the future course of oil prices is an important consideration in decisions about exploration and production. At present, it is thought almost universally that the world

niques long used in other offshore provinces. Moreover, some of the North Sea fields, such as the Southern gas fields and the Beatrice field near Inverness, are in shallow water quite close to the coast.

19. Peter R. Odell and Kenneth E. Rosing, *The North Sea Oil Province: An Attempt to Simulate Its Development and Exploitation, 1969–2029* (London: Kogan Page, 1975).

20. This conservatism, which is not of long standing, may be an overreaction to an earlier tendency toward undue optimism. Thus in 1969–70 the U.S. Cabinet Task Force on Oil Import Control, on which I served, was much influenced by sanguine projections of American oil potential presented by the U.S. Geological Survey. These projections, which turned out to be farfetched, were made by estimating the volume of sediments in an area and multiplying it by an average number of barrels per unit of volume. When this technique came under severe criticism, it was abandoned for one that extrapolates from already discovered fields—a method that would appear to have an inevitable downward bias.

price of oil must go up in real terms over the foreseeable future. Indeed, many (particularly among those with limited understanding of the price mechanism) believe that there will be "shortages" of oil before the end of the century, if not sooner.

The United Kingdom has wisely not tried to insulate its oil industry from the rest of the world, though it has reserved the power to do so in the future. Consequently, the world price of crude is relevant to its policies, and this price will now be discussed. Strictly speaking, of course, there is not one world price because of transport costs. However, in recent years a combination of high oil prices and a persistent surplus of tankers has reduced the relative importance of those costs. Although freight charges will not be overlooked, as a first approximation it is legitimate to speak of *the* world price of oil.

The Structure of the World Oil Market

Table 1 shows oil output data for some recent years, starting with 1973, the year before the Organization of Petroleum Exporting Countries quadrupled the price. From then through 1978 world output increased 8 percent, but most of the increase occurred in the Communist countries, whose net trade with the outside world is relatively small. Production in the non-Communist world increased less than 2 percent in the five-year period, reflecting weak demand rather than lack of capacity.

Within this slowly rising total, the market share of OPEC declined about three percentage points from 1973 to 1978, despite a fall in U.S. and Canadian production. Non-OPEC production rose strongly in Western Europe (chiefly Britain) and in Latin America (chiefly Mexico). The declining overall share of OPEC, however, resulted from conflicting developments inside the cartel. On balance, Saudi Arabia increased its share considerably, mostly at the expense of Venezuela and Kuwait. Iraq, the United Arab Emirates, and Indonesia also increased their market share.[21]

It is clear from this redistribution that OPEC is not a tightly run cartel. In fact, some observers consider it an oligopoly rather than a cartel, but

21. U.S. Central Intelligence Agency, National Foreign Assessment Center, *International Energy Statistical Review,* September 5, 1979, pp. 1–2 (available from National Technical Information Service, Springfield, Virginia). Preliminary figures indicate that OPEC's market share fell further in 1979 and that the Saudi share rose again.

Table 1. *World Crude Oil Production, 1973, 1977, and 1978*[a]

Amounts in millions of barrels a day

Area	1973	1977	1978	1978 as percent of 1973
World	58.6	62.7	63.1	107.7
Non-Communist countries	48.4	49.4	49.2	101.7
OPEC[b]	31.3	31.9	30.3	96.8
	(64.7)	(64.6)	(61.6)	...
Saudi Arabia[c]	7.7	9.4	8.5	110.4
	(24.6)	(29.5)	(28.1)	...
Iran	5.9	5.7	5.2	88.1
Other	17.7	16.8	16.6	93.8
Non-OPEC[b]	17.1	17.6	18.8	109.9
	(35.3)	(35.6)	(38.2)	...
United States and Canada	13.1	11.4	11.8	90.1
Western Europe	0.4	1.4	1.8	450.0
Other	3.6	4.8	5.1	141.7
Communist countries[d]	10.1	13.2	13.9	137.6

Source: U.S. National Foreign Assessment Center, *International Energy Statistical Review*, September 5, 1979, pp. 1–2 (available from National Technical Information Service, Springfield, Virginia). Figures are rounded.

a. Includes natural gas liquids unless otherwise indicated.

b. Figures in parentheses are percentages of non-Communist total.

c. Includes the share of Neutral Zone production. Figures in parentheses are percentages of OPEC total.

d. Excludes People's Republic of China natural gas liquids.

this is not a helpful way of looking at it.[22] Unlike full-fledged cartels, OPEC has no formal mechanism for allocating output, relying instead on members' reluctance to produce a glut that would undermine the price. In practice, there appears to be an informal understanding among the members about output shares, reinforced by an explicit agreement not to sell below the cartel price as modified by certain differentials. Table 1, incidentally, does not bear out the common belief that Saudi Arabia acts as a residual supplier while the others produce as much as they can; the Saudis produced less in 1978 than in 1977, but still much more than in 1973.

An interesting light was shed on the relations among the members of OPEC by their response to the Iranian crisis. In the first half of 1978 the world oil market had been so weak that such countries as Iraq, Nigeria,

22. See Hendrik S. Houthakker, "International Aspects of U.S. Energy Policy," *Materials and Society*, vol. 2, nos. 1–2 (1978), pp. 95–101.

and Venezuela (as well as Saudi Arabia) had to reduce output significantly, although others (Indonesia, Algeria) continued to produce at capacity. The fall in Iranian output, accompanied by efforts to rebuild inventories, led to a tighter world market. The initial reactions of most OPEC members was to bring production much closer to capacity. Compared with the first half of 1978, crude output in November 1978 was up 32 percent in Saudi Arabia, 41 percent in Kuwait, 46 percent in Iraq, 37 percent in Nigeria, and 13 percent in Venezuela, but virtually unchanged in the United Arab Emirates and actually lower in Indonesia.[23] When the outlook for Iranian petroleum production deteriorated further in December, however, some of these countries reduced production, presumably to pave the way for subsequent price increases. What all this suggests is that the members of OPEC, loosely organized as they are, keep their respective outputs fairly well in line with one another. OPEC has also been able to accommodate sharp differences in opinion about prices, if only by an agreement to disagree.

Any threat to OPEC, then, must come from the outside. Like any cartel, OPEC has to cope with a fringe of nonmembers who benefit from the high price without assuming the responsibilities of membership. In the case of OPEC, these responsibilities are not onerous, since there are no production quotas, but the advantages of formal membership are not large either—mainly some voice in OPEC price policy. There has been no crowd at OPEC's door clamoring for admission.[24]

As for outsiders, OPEC has had little need to worry about the United States or Canada, whose domestic energy policies (particularly their artificially low oil prices) have until recently played straight into the cartel's hands by increasing the demand for imported oil. Although there are encouraging signs of a return to sanity and North American oil imports have leveled off, it will clearly be several years before the vast oil potential of Canada and the United States at present world prices is fully realized. Nor need OPEC be greatly concerned about the Soviet Union or China, where any growth of production will be readily absorbed by domestic consumption; in fact there is some evidence that Soviet oil output may have peaked.

The remaining non-OPEC producers, chiefly around the North Sea

23. *International Energy Statistical Review,* March 7, 1979, p. 1.
24. Actually, OPEC has fairly strict criteria for membership, intended to limit it to countries that depend predominantly on oil exports. The idea of British or Norwegian membership is fanciful; even Mexico would have difficulty qualifying. It is argued below that formal membership makes little difference in any case.

and in the developing countries, constitute a cloud as yet no bigger than a man's hand. As table 1 shows, this group has had the most rapid growth of any represented there, but the actual volume in 1978 was still less than that of Saudi Arabia alone.

In this group one can detect two patterns of behavior, depending on the relation of domestic production to domestic consumption. Oil-importing countries tend to develop their oil potential with as much diligence as their technical and financial resources permit. Brazil, Denmark, and India are typical examples; so was Britain until about 1974, when it became apparent that self-sufficiency was within reach.

Potential oil exporters, on the other hand, have been much more circumspect. Thus Norway, having discovered Ekofisk at an early stage, realized that it had oil beyond its domestic needs and has exercised marked restraint toward exploration and development. Much the same can be said about the United Kingdom in the 1974–79 period. Similarly Mexico, whose long-established oil production was at a low ebb in the early 1970s, made a major and highly successful effort to find new reserves but has announced export targets that are modest in relation to the new potential. With considerable qualification, this pattern can also be seen in Canada, where exploration has been encouraged by tax incentives, even though exports remain subject to strict limitations.

It is hard to explain in strictly economic terms why the point of self-sufficiency should be so important for oil policy; presumably, a marginal reduction in imports is worth as much as a marginal addition to exports. Psychologically, however, the reason is clear: oil-importing countries experienced the 1974 price increase as a severe shock to which they would rather not be exposed again. Those countries that have succeeded in attaining self-sufficiency, or are close to attaining it, apparently feel that they can now afford to worry about the future use of their mineral resources, and they become reluctant to "give away their national heritage" to foreigners.[25] Rationally, of course, a country should consider its balance of payments and the timing of its mineral production simultaneously rather than sequentially, but policymakers often find it easier to deal with one problem at a time.

Where does all this leave OPEC? The conclusion of the preceding analysis is that in the short run or middle run the cartel is more likely to see its export markets impaired by the attempts at self-sufficiency of net

25. This naive argument, along with more serious ones, can also be heard in U.S. discussions about oil exports from Alaska to Japan.

importers than to find vigorous outside competitors in its remaining markets. The net exporters outside the cartel, in effect, tend to behave as if they were members. Whether Britain, Norway, and Mexico are formal members of OPEC or not is of little importance as long as they share the concerns of the major exporters, most of whom give much thought to the allocation of their resources over time.[26]

In the longer run, however, outsiders do pose a threat to the cartel. Mexico, for instance, may be sincere in its announced intention to limit oil exports to 1 million barrels a day, but if it is at all successful in its industrialization plans it will need further large inflows of foreign capital. It is already heavily in debt and at some point may well decide that exporting additional oil has advantages over an ever-increasing interest burden. Canada is a somewhat different case. It has increased its reserves (especially of natural gas) considerably and now must decide what to do with them; presumably the owners of the new reserves are not prepared to leave them in the ground indefinitely. Whether similar considerations apply to the United Kingdom is the main subject of this paper.

The fact that OPEC is for the time being fairly invulnerable to threats from the outside, and has managed to overcome various internal disagreements, is due in part to its relatively cautious choice of objectives. The quadrupling of prices in early 1974, although inevitably something of a gamble, was justified from the members' point of view by the even higher prices paid for spot cargoes during the preceding embargo as well as by OPEC's remarkably shrewd analysis of supply and demand responses. The price of oil has remained fairly stable in real terms since then.[27] While OPEC lost some of its share in the world market as a result, it did not lose enough to jeopardize its internal cohesion. Indeed, one of the two major constraints on OPEC is that the total demand for its oil should not be so small that some members are tempted to break away.[28] If de-

26. Some cartel members are strongly influenced by balance-of-payments considerations because their imports have outrun their exports. Indonesia and Nigeria are cases in point.

27. In dollar terms real oil prices were raised in June 1979, but in terms of most European currencies they are still close to the 1974 level.

28. In Hendrik S. Houthakker, *The World Price of Oil: A Medium-Term Analysis* (Washington, D.C.: American Enterprise Institute for Public Policy Research, 1976), this minimum was tentatively identified with total output of twenty million barrels a day in the Middle East and Africa. This still appears plausible as a minimum, but the disruption of Iranian production makes it less likely that the minimum will be tested in the 1980s.

mand were to fall to that level, the cartel could lower the price, although doing so would impair its credibility.

The other constraint, on the upside, is more or less symmetric. If demand were so high that some members had difficulty in delivering their normal share, the price would no doubt go up. This is approximately what happened in late 1978 and early 1979 after the Iranian events; although the spot price of crude oil rose temporarily above the cartel price, the net effect was to strengthen the cartel in the longer run.

OPEC has not had control of the world oil price long enough for econometric estimation of the two constraints or of OPEC's price response function. In the following discussion a more informal approach has to be followed.

Long-Run Projections

For more definite, though not necessarily more definitive, ideas about the future price of oil it is desirable to use an explicit model—not because such models are necessarily very realistic, but because the world energy markets are closely interrelated and present more complexities than can be handled informally. In a mathematical model it is also easier to consider alternative "scenarios" and other changes in parameters.

A new version of the World Energy Model is used here.[29] More fully summarized in appendix B, it is a dynamic equilibrium model involving six regions and six energy commodities in which supply, demand, and price are all endogenous; the principal exogenous variables are the growth rates of GNP and population in each region and the "OPEC tax," representing the cartel's price policy. Some of the theoretical considerations reviewed earlier in this paper, in particular the dependence of extraction cost on cumulative output, are incorporated. The model is large enough to provide relevant detail, yet small enough to permit many runs to be made quickly and fairly cheaply. This flexibility is important because the econometric basis of the model is weak—many of the parameters are no more than informed guesses—and the plausibility of the results has to be evaluated by sensitivity analysis (runs with alternative sets of parameters).

29. Hendrik S. Houthakker and Michael Kennedy, "Long-Range Energy Prospects," *Journal of Energy and Development,* vol. 4 (Autumn 1978), pp. 1–28; and Houthakker and Kennedy, "A Long-Run Model of World Energy Demand, Supplies and Prices," in Behram Kursunoglu and Arnold Perlmutter, eds., *Directions in Energy Policy: A Comprehensive Approach to Energy Resource Decision-Making* (Ballinger, 1980), pp. 167–82.

The central question to be answered by the model is whether the real price of oil is likely to rise, fall, or stay constant over the next twenty or thirty years. Since OPEC policy is exogenous to the model, this question can be answered only indirectly—by specifying different paths for the OPEC tax (in effect, a duty on oil exports from the Middle East and Africa, where the bulk of OPEC's production originates). It appears that a small number of alternative scenarios provide enough information for a tentative answer; to ask for more than that would put undue strains on a model that has no claim to precision.

As it happens, just two scenarios suffice to narrow down the problem. In the first of these (scenario A, table 2) the OPEC tax remains constant in real terms, at the level of $10 (1972 dollars) that prevailed approximately from 1974 through 1978.[30] This means that the price of crude in the Persian Gulf rises slightly between 1985 and 1995, then more steeply to $13 in 2005. Worldwide output (excluding Communist countries) rises from 18.3 billion barrels in 1985 (50 million barrels a day, slightly more than in 1978) to 32.2 billion barrels in 2005, but exports from the Middle East and Africa grow at a higher rate, from 8.9 billion barrels in 1985 to 19.9 billion barrels in 2005. In fact, the share of this region in total non-Communist oil production rises from about one-half in 1985 to about two-thirds in 2005. The region's cumulative output (including local consumption), starting in 1972, amounts to 456 billion barrels, a figure roughly equal to present proved reserves; as was argued above, however, this comparison is not very relevant, since the price does not stay constant.

In scenario B the OPEC tax rises linearly from $10 in 1985 to $20 in 2005, corresponding to a price rise from $10.25 to $21.51. This implies a considerably different pattern of output. Non-Communist world production goes up to 27.7 billion barrels in 2005, while exports from the Middle East and Africa fall from 8.9 billion barrels in 1985 to 7.8 billion barrels twenty years later. The region's cumulative output through 2005 is substantially lower than in scenario A, although the output is still well above the presumed threshold for OPEC cohesion.[31] Scenario B also pro-

---

30. Between 1972 and early 1979 the general price level in the United States (as measured by the GNP deflator) rose by about 55 percent, implying a current OPEC tax of $15.50, very close to the value at the end of 1978. The *price* of crude in the Middle East and Africa consists of the tax plus extraction cost, small now but significant in later years. In the World Energy Model all money values are expressed in 1972 dollars; the version used here takes no account of variations in exchange rates. Appendix B lists the GNP growth assumptions underlying the present analysis.

31. See note 28.

Table 2. *Two Scenarios for World Oil Production, Using Alternative OPEC Taxes, 1985, 1995, and 2005*[a]

Item	Scenario A[b]			Scenario B[c]		
	1985	1995	2005	1985	1995	2005
Price of crude (dollars per barrel)[d]	10.25	10.28	13.00	10.25	15.26	21.51
World output (billions of barrels a year)[e]	18.3	24.5	32.2	18.3	22.3	27.7
Exports, Middle East and Africa (billions of barrels a year)	8.9	14.0	19.9	8.9	7.8	7.8
OPEC tax revenue (billions of dollars)[f]	89	140	199	89	117	156
Cumulative output, Middle East and Africa, from 1972 (billions of barrels)	123	256	456	123	224	329

Source: Author's calculations.
a. Dollar figures are in 1972 dollars.
b. OPEC tax constant at $10.
c. OPEC tax $10 in 1985, $15 in 1995, $20 in 2005.
d. F.o.b. Persian Gulf.
e. Excludes Communist countries.
f. Product of OPEC tax and exports from Middle East and Africa.

duces much less OPEC tax revenue than scenario A (in 1995, $117 billion versus $140 billion; in 2005, $156 billion versus $199 billion). This tax revenue is what OPEC is presumably trying to maximize (though that may not be the only consideration).[32] Moreover, OPEC has often said that it wants to keep the real price of oil constant.

32. It might be thought that, since the first tax projection produces more revenue than the second, even more revenue could be obtained by going to tax rates lower than $10 a barrel. Additional runs of the model indicate, however, that a constant real tax rate of $10 comes very close to maximizing revenue through 2005, although a projection with $10 in 1985, $11 in 1995, and $12 in 2005 produces slightly more revenue; the corresponding price in 2005 is $14.70. These runs also show that the maximum is relatively "flat." Small departures (say within $1) from the maximizing tax rate projection affect revenue hardly at all. In other words, the absolute value of the elasticity of demand for OPEC oil happens to be one for prices near $10, less than one for prices below $10, and greater than one for prices well above $10. This particular demand elasticity, incidentally, is *not* a parameter of the model but results from the interaction of a great many supply and demand elasticities for particular regions and energy sources, and other parameters. The own-price long-run elasticity of oil demand specified for the present exercise is −0.45, and there are cross elasticities with the prices of other fuels (see also appendix B).

The main conclusion to be drawn from this analysis is that a major rise (such as a doubling in twenty years) in the real price of oil is not very likely to be sustainable in the long run. Although the real OPEC tax will probably not go up more than $2 or $3 a barrel, the real price itself will rise more than that because of increased extraction costs in the Middle East and Africa. In fact the best guess for the price in 2005 appears to be around $15 (1972 dollars), equivalent to a rate of increase in real terms of less than 1 percent a year.[33] This conclusion needs to be checked by sensitivity analysis, which is done in appendix B. There it is shown that the conclusion fails to hold only if *both* the demand and the supply elasticities are much smaller than assumed so far; if so, the OPEC tax may well go up to $20 a barrel and the world price even higher. In all other cases investigated in appendix B the conclusion is confirmed.

The Macroeconomic Consequences of Increased Oil Production

The preceding argument implies that, *if only the oil sector is considered,* there was little reason for the Labour government to slow down the exploration, development, and exploitation of its oil reserves (nor, for that matter, to speed up those activities artificially).[34] There would be reason

33. This prognosis may appear wildly optimistic in light of the upheavals in the world oil market that followed the 1978–79 revolution in Iran. The spot price went to unprecedented heights, though incomplete data suggest that this was due mostly to precautionary and speculative accumulation of inventories rather than to a short-fall in current production with respect to current demand. At the time this paper went to press, the spot price had fallen well below its peak. No doubt OPEC will try to keep the price up, but this will be difficult as more non-OPEC oil is offered. The events of 1979 illustrate the short-term instability of the market but do not materially change the long-term outlook.

34. The evidence that a deliberate slowdown occurred between 1974 and 1979 is circumstantial rather than conclusive. Thus there were five licensing rounds from 1964 through 1977, in the first four of which an average of 664 blocks were offered and 216 licensed; in the fifth round, five years after the fourth, only 71 blocks were offered and 44 licensed. (U.K. Department of Energy, *Development of the Oil and Gas Resources of the United Kingdom, 1978,* A Report to Parliament by the Secretary of State for Energy [HMSO, 1978], p. 50.) This deceleration does not appear to be entirely explained either by the government's strategy of having smaller but more frequent rounds (p. 20) or by any shortage of blocks to offer; most of the offshore area, including some highly prospective blocks, is still unlicensed. In official documents issued by the Labour government, moreover, one finds frequent references to

for going slow if the outlook were for much higher real oil prices—and if that was the view of the Labour government, it had plenty of company.

Actually, the very prevalence of this view is itself a good occasion for questioning it. The long-term prospects for oil prices are inherently uncertain. Models like the one used above can narrow the range of uncertainty to some extent but are obviously not the last word, even if they were in agreement among themselves. The main justification for their use is that nothing better appears to be in sight, and that is by itself an indication of how little confidence can be placed in any projections of oil prices in the distant future.

If countries such as Canada and Norway try to keep their oil in the ground because they expect the price of oil to rise more than the rate of interest, they are in effect speculating. While speculation can be socially useful, excessive unanimity among speculators tends to be destabilizing, since any disappointment in their price projections leads them to take corrective action more or less simultaneously. Concretely, if the world oil price fails to rise appreciably in real terms, countries that have counted on a price rise may suddenly decide they are missing the boat and put their supplies on the market. Countries that let market developments take their course, on the other hand, may forgo some additional returns if the price does go up sharply, but they are also less vulnerable to disappointment.

In the face of these uncertainties the prudent policy is to decentralize decisions as much as possible. A centralized decision may turn out to be largely mistaken; decentralized decisions, although no more likely to be correct individually, can cancel one another out (provided they are reasonably independent), thus reducing aggregate risk. If politicians and bureaucrats possessed special insights into oil prices a generation from now, there would be a case for a firm policy on exploration and depletion. As it is, the relevant decisions had better be left to those who stand to gain or lose most by them, namely, the oil companies. The proper functions of

---

the possible need for government-imposed depletion controls but few, if any, to the benefits of timely development. Finally, measures to increase the petroleum revenue tax and to require participation by the British National Oil Corporation, whatever their other merits, were presumably not expected to encourage exploration. The net result of these measures was a sharp fall in exploration and the departure of many drilling rigs from the North Sea. Upon taking office in 1979 the Conservative government, confirming that a slowdown had been brought about, took steps to reverse it.

the government are to make leases and permits available as needed, to see that the public is adequately paid for these leases and permits, and more generally to maintain competition.

This argument for a market-oriented policy takes no account of the effects of alternative oil policies on the rest of the economy, a matter that is clearly of concern to the government. As was shown earlier, in an economy as large and diversified as Britain's these effects are not likely to be overwhelming. It is true that the oil sector accounts for a sizable part— somewhat less than 10 percent—of total investment and government revenue, but the first is likely to be largely of foreign origin and the second can be offset by reductions in other taxes.

The effect on the balance of payments can also be easily exaggerated. An expansion of British oil exports from the currently envisaged 600,000 barrels a day[35] to, say, 1 million barrels a day might yield between £1 billion and £2 billion after allowing for the foreign exchange cost of inputs and profits remitted abroad. In macroeconomic terms this amount is not very significant, particularly since most of the additional revenue will go to the government through taxes and royalties.

Most of the concern about large oil exports appears to derive from fear that they would either replace nonoil exports or expose home products to increased competition from imports. Both these effects would operate through an appreciation of sterling relative to other currencies. However, three points need to be considered: (1) increased oil exports would not necessarily drive up the exchange rate, and (2) even if they did, this would not necessarily be undesirable; moreover (3) North Sea oil is not something that will disappear as quickly as it came.

As to the first point, everything depends on how the export proceeds are used. If the British authorities kept the current account close to balance, as they have in the last few years, there would indeed be some appreciation of sterling and a consequent reduction in competitiveness (assuming that domestic prices were unaffected). But it would also be possible to use the oil export proceeds for debt reduction or the accumulation of foreign assets; to accomplish that would require keeping British interest rates below what they would be at current account equilibrium. This al-

35. This figure is a rough average for the 1980s that appears to be consistent with official output projections (ibid., pp. 3–4) in conjunction with estimated demand of about 1.8 million barrels during that decade. A more permissive oil policy would actually affect output only in the late 1980s and especially in the 1990s, but this does not change the argument.

ternative policy is attractive if real returns on capital are lower in the United Kingdom than abroad, which they may well be.[36]

The second point, whether an appreciation of sterling is undesirable, brings up the deeper problems of the British economy, to which other papers in this book are devoted. Those who consider these problems hopeless fear that a higher value of sterling would merely create unemployment because internal adjustment is so difficult. On the other hand, those (the present Conservative government among them) who detect life in the old dog welcome the invigorating effect of competition on British industry. Furthermore, appreciation would help the fight against inflation, which is not merely a symptom but also a cause of Britain's unsatisfactory economic performance. The resulting improvement in the terms of trade would enable the population at large to share in the benefits of North Sea oil in other ways than through reduced direct taxation. On balance, the favorable effects of appreciation would seem to prevail.

Finally, the scenario that would have Britain dismantle its traditional export industries through excessive reliance on oil, then to find there is no export potential when the wells run dry, is highly implausible. Even if the oil does run down ultimately, it will do so gradually over many years, providing ample time for readjustment. By that time the international determinants of comparative advantage will probably have changed drastically, so there is no case for preserving existing industries merely as a standby for the remote future.

To sum up, the exchange rate could be held down, but there were and are good reasons for allowing it to rise. Macroeconomic considerations do not invalidate the case for primary reliance on market forces in decisions about North Sea oil. There will no doubt be adjustment problems in particular industries, but any assistance they may require should be forward-looking rather than aimed at maintaining the status quo.

36. Regardless of the merits of this policy, the point that large energy exports do not necessarily affect the exchange rate has a bearing on the frequent references in British writings to the "Dutch disease" as something the United Kingdom should avoid. By this somewhat loaded term is meant the result of the Netherlands' use of export and tax revenues from natural gas exports for consumption, a use stimulated by expanded government transfer payments. This policy apparently had some adverse effect on traditional exports. The question whether the Netherlands made the right choice is outside the scope of this paper, but that country's recent economic performance, though not exemplary, compares favorably with Britain's: the Netherlands has rather consistently had more real growth and less inflation than Britain. Even if there were a case for avoiding the Dutch disease, this could be done without postponing the further development of the North Sea.

Managing Britain's Oil Resources

What are the roles of government and the private sector in the development of North Sea oil? That the government has a vital role is taken for granted, not only because it is concerned about safety, pollution, and the like, but because it is the legal owner of the mineral resources under the sea in its territory. It is equally clear that the private sector, specifically the major and minor oil companies, has been and will be indispensable to the efficient utilization of these resources.[37] What is more difficult is to define the proper relation of government and the private sector in terms of the public interest.

The most important aspect of this relation in a relatively free economy is taxation. Unfortunately that subject cannot be taken up here,[38] because the additional research required—particularly the incorporation of various taxes in a model of the kind presented in appendix A—remains to be done.[39] The following discussion deals with resource management in a narrower sense.

As the owner of the undeveloped resources, the government is necessarily involved in the exploration process. The main questions here are:
—at what rate blocks should be offered for exploration;
—how the exploring and producing companies are to be selected; and
—according to what formula the government is to be paid.

37. Apart from the Soviet Union, the only country that has been successful in relying exclusively on a state-owned organization for the development of its hydrocarbons is Mexico. Even in that country it appears that the recent spectacular discoveries, most of them in areas that were already productive, could have been made earlier had it not been for the extended disruption caused by the 1938 nationalization. Most other countries with national oil monopolies have had to call on foreign private companies for help, particularly in exploration.

38. A good discussion can be found in Colin Robinson and Jon Morgan, *North Sea Oil in the Future: Economic Analysis and Government Policy* (London: Macmillan, 1978), chaps. 4 and 5. I did not have access to this book when writing the first draft of my paper.

39. One area of taxation may be mentioned in passing, however. A tariff on imported oil, levied jointly by the industrial countries (for example, through the International Energy Agency), would serve to transfer to the consuming countries some of the monopoly profits now realized by OPEC. It would be of special benefit to Britain as the largest potential oil exporter in the group, not only by increasing export proceeds but also by providing a measure of protection in the (unlikely) event that the cartel breaks down. For some calculations on the effect of a tariff, see Houthakker, *World Price of Oil*.

The first question is one that has already been answered, at least by implication, in this paper. Given the great uncertainty surrounding future oil prices, there is no reason why the government should attempt to influence the speed of exploration one way or another. To facilitate industry planning it would be best to announce a schedule of offerings extending over several years, though some flexibility may be needed in case particular areas turn out to be especially promising or unpromising. The schedule should not be so full that companies tend to forgo new opportunities because they are still too occupied with earlier ones, though the large number of companies in the worldwide industry makes this constraint unlikely to be binding. There may also be some advantage in adopting the "checkerboard" patterns of some U.S. lease sales, in which the initial offering leaves out about half the fields in an area. The remaining fields can then be offered in a "drainage sale" if the fields explored first turn out to be productive.[40]

The principal qualification to the preceding recommendations has to do with interest rates. The analysis in appendix A shows that the value of an oil field is very sensitive to the rate of interest. When it is high, therefore, companies are not likely to offer much for the right to explore. In such periods the government, concerned as it should be with public revenues, would be justified in postponing lease sales.

The second question, the selection of companies, raises the problem of how much reliance to place on bidding as opposed to negotiation. Provided there is enough competition, it would seem that bidding is more likely to yield maximum returns to the public. The U.S. experience with bidding has been generally favorable in this respect.[41] The main difficulty is to prevent collusion, which is facilitated by the common practice of forming joint ventures, although little or no evidence of actual collusion has come to light. In the United States the largest companies can no longer participate in joint ventures with one another, though they can join smaller firms.

In the United Kingdom, on the contrary, negotiation has been more

40. The map in appendix 14 of U.K. Department of Energy, *Development of Oil and Gas Resources, 1978,* shows that many segments of highly prospective areas were not yet under license at the end of the fifth round, but no checkerboard pattern is apparent.

41. Edward W. Erickson and Robert M. Spann, "The US Petroleum Industry," in *The Energy Question: An International Failure of Policy,* vol. 2: *North America* (University of Toronto Press, 1974), pp. 5–24.

important than bidding, and there are several joint ventures among major companies, those among Shell and Esso (divisions of the two largest oil companies in the world) being conspicuous. In the early days, when the potential of the North Sea was unknown and oil prices were much lower, negotiation may have been more flexible than bidding. Similarly, the relatively high fixed investment required for offshore exploration may have provided some initial justification for joint ventures among large companies. But now that the area's oil potential is better understood and prices are much higher, the time has come for more formal licensing procedures along American lines.

In the meantime, however, another obstacle to effective competition has emerged: the British National Oil Corporation. Motivated in part by fears that in negotiations with large and knowledgeable private companies the government may be at a disadvantage, BNOC was set up not only to collect revenue through mandatory participation but also to provide the government with expert advice. Perhaps an ideological aversion to private enterprise also played a part in the founding of BNOC. To the extent that BNOC is given preferential treatment in licensing, its existence must be considered an impediment to effective competition. Unfortunately the history of the last thirty years suggests that it is easier to establish publicly owned corporations than to liquidate them, but the present British government has taken steps to reduce the role of BNOC.

The desirability of competitive involvement by the private sector is reinforced by the great uncertainty about future oil prices. When investment decisions have to be made on the basis of very little knowledge, it is best to spread the inevitable risk over many participants, each of whom follows his own judgment. The principal argument sometimes advanced on the other side is that private firms may use higher interest rates in their calculations than is socially optimal; this bias can be overcome by appropriate tax provisions.

Finally, the form that payments to the government will take is evidently related to the problem of taxation (which is not covered here). There are essentially two approaches to the issue. One tries to secure the full rent for the public by letting the companies bid against one another for licenses but then taxes these companies at the same rates as firms in other industries. Within this approach it is possible to vary the relative share of bonuses paid in advance, royalties fixed in money or in oil, annual lease payments, and the like. The other method is to issue licenses on a negotiated basis, subject to such conditions as mandatory participation by BNOC, and then to recoup any rent that may be left by a special tax, such as the petroleum revenue tax now in force.

The first of these alternatives has the considerable advantage of keeping government intervention at a minimum. Once a company has obtained a license it knows where it stands with the authorities and can make its plans accordingly. The second alternative compounds the difficulty of negotiating satisfactory initial settlements with the uncertainties and possible inequities of subsequent corrective taxation.[42] Unless pursued with a combination of expertise, integrity, and flexibility that is not invariably found in governments, this approach could as easily stifle the local expansion of a multinational industry as it could expose political leaders to the charge of selling the national patrimony for a song. It also means that private management talent, most useful in finding and producing oil, is diverted into anticipating and outwitting the government.

Although there is not much to be said for the second approach, the first is not without its difficulties either. Preserving effective competition is one of them; ensuring that the public receives its share even when circumstances change is another. The basic presumption that the oil industry is taxed like other industries can easily be eroded by special provisions, such as the percentage depletion in the United States. Such violations of fiscal neutrality make the first approach more like the second, with all its problems. The price of economic efficiency is eternal vigilance over special interests.

In sum, the public interest is likely to benefit if the government confines its management to those matters for which it has an inescapable responsibility, particularly in the leasing of tracts for exploration. Otherwise there is no obvious need for government management or for publicly owned oil companies provided the oil industry is adequately competitive and subjected to effective and nondiscriminatory taxation.[43]

Conclusion

The discovery of oil and gas in the North Sea has provided the United Kingdom with considerable opportunities that can and should be ex-

42. The process is further complicated by dividing the government's share into a part that is received directly through taxation and another part that accrues indirectly through a national oil company.

43. Robinson and Morgan, in *North Sea Oil in the Future*, p. 207, come to a similar conclusion.

ploited vigorously. Not much time should be spent worrying about what happens when the oil runs out; abundant experience suggests that major oil fields usually have a long life—certainly longer than the twenty years often mentioned. On the other hand, there is little reason for the government to hold back on development in the hope that the oil will be worth much more later on; such speculations should be left to the oil companies. Though subject to great uncertainty, projections for the world price of oil do not point to a very sharp rise in real terms over the long run—if only because too many countries are already speculating on that possibility.

The macroeconomic consequences of North Sea oil appear to have been exaggerated. It will neither transform nor ruin the British economy, but if efficiently managed—which means limiting government involvement to essentials—can make an important contribution to the well-being of the British people and, indeed, of the whole Western world.

Appendix A: An Illustrative Model of an Oil Field

The purpose of this appendix is to amplify statements in the main text about the time pattern of production as it is affected by the rate of interest and the rate of change of the price of output. The central idea is that the cost of extraction from an oil field depends both on the remaining amount of oil and on the rate of extraction. The following model is simple enough to permit (almost) explicit solution, but its realism has not been verified; it should therefore be considered as no more than illustrative of certain general principles invoked in this paper.

Let the total cost of extraction from an oil field be

$$(1) \qquad z[q(t), s(t)] = \beta^{-1} q(t)[\gamma + \delta s(t) + \tfrac{1}{2} q(t)],$$

where

$q(t)$ = the rate of extraction at time t
$s(t)$ = the oil in place remaining in the field at time t
$\beta > 0, \gamma > 0, \delta < 0.$

Under competitive conditions the current rate of total profit from extraction is then

$$(2) \qquad f(t) = p(t)q(t) - z[q(t), s(t)],$$

where $p(t)$ is the (gross) price per barrel at time t. The owner of the field chooses an output schedule to maximize the present value of the oil in place:

(3) $$F[q] = \int_0^\infty e^{-\rho t} f(t)\, dt,$$

subject to

$$q(t) \geq 0,\ s(t) \geq 0,\ q(t) = -\dot{s}(t),$$

where ρ is the rate of interest. If the inequalities are disregarded for the moment, this problem can be solved by the classical calculus of variations. Euler's equation reads (omitting the argument t)

(4) $$\ddot{s} - \rho\dot{s} + \rho\delta s = \beta\rho p - \beta\dot{p} - \rho\gamma.$$

This equation can be interpreted in terms of the royalty, defined as the value to the owner of an additional barrel of oil. It can be shown that if the lower limit is t instead of 0, the derivative of the integral in equation 3 with respect to $s(t)$ equals

(5) $$r(t) = p(t) - \beta^{-1}[\gamma + q(t) + \delta s(t)],$$

and that $r(t)$ is also the derivative of profit $f(t)$ with respect to the rate of output; in fact the last term in 5 is simply marginal cost. Therefore $r(t)$ may be identified with the royalty at time t. Furthermore,

(6) $$\dot{r} = \dot{p} + \beta^{-1}\ddot{s} - \beta^{-1}\delta\dot{s}.$$

Substituting this into 4 yields, after some manipulation,

(7) $$\dot{r} = \rho r + \beta^{-1}\delta q,$$

which describes the behavior of the royalty over time. Since $\beta > 0$, $\delta < 0$, the last term is negative and the royalty increases at a rate *less* than the rate of interest ρ, contrary to Hotelling.[44] Indeed $\dot{r}$ may be negative if q is large enough. The difference with Hotelling, of course, results from the assumed dependence of extraction cost on the rate of extraction.

Suppose now that the price of output increases or decreases at a constant rate σ:

(8) $$p(t) = p_0 e^{\sigma t}.$$

44. *Economics of Exhaustible Resources.* The necessary correction to Hotelling's formula was pointed out by Levhari and Liviatan in "Notes on Hotelling's Economics of Exhaustible Resources."

Then the solution of 4 is

(9) $$s(t) = C_0 e^{\sigma t} - \gamma/\delta + C_1 e^{\lambda_1 t} - C_2 e^{\lambda_2 t},$$

where

(10) $$C_0 = \frac{\beta \rho_0 (\rho - \sigma)}{\sigma^2 - \rho \sigma + \rho \delta}$$

(11a) $$\lambda_1 = \rho + \sqrt{\rho^2 - 4\delta\rho}$$

(11b) $$\lambda_2 = \rho - \sqrt{\rho^2 - 4\delta\rho},$$

and where C_1 and C_2 are constants to be calculated so as to satisfy the inequality constraints in 3. It follows that

(12) $$q(t) = -C_0 \sigma e^{\sigma t} - C_1 \lambda_1 e^{\lambda_1 t} + C_2 \lambda_2 e^{\lambda_2 t}.$$

Since $\rho > 0$ and $\delta < 0$, the parameters λ_1 and λ_2 are respectively positive and negative; indeed $\gamma_1 > \rho$. C_0 is negative because $\rho > \sigma$; otherwise it would be more profitable to leave the minerals in the ground.

At $t = 0$ the stock $s(t)$ has its initial value s_0:

(13) $$C_0 - \gamma/\delta + C_1 - C_2 = s_0.$$

There are three possibilities for the duration of extraction.

1. *Complete exhaustion:* $s(T) = 0$ for some $T < \infty$.

2. *Abandonment:* $q(T) = 0$ for some $T < \infty$ at which $s(T) > 0$; this will happen when the marginal cost of extraction equals the price of output.

3. *Perpetual use:* $\sigma(t) > 0$ and $q(t) > 0$ for all t; this exceptional case can only occur with a constant $p(t)$.

There are also three possibilities for the start of extraction.

1. *Immediate:* extraction begins at $t = 0$. This happens when p_0 exceeds initial marginal cost (at zero output) except when the resulting $q(0)$ is negative.

2. *Postponed:* extraction begins at some $t > 0$. This will happen if $\sigma > 0$ but p_0 is less than initial marginal cost.

3. *Never:* the deposit is not taken into production at all when the initial marginal cost falls short of p_0 and $\sigma \leq 0$.

The detailed development of this model must be left to another occasion, but an example can be given. Consider an oil field with 300 million barrels of oil in place. At $t = 0$ the marginal cost of extracting the first barrel is $2, but at that time the marginal cost rises to $4 a barrel when the rate of production is 10 million barrels a year. When the oil in place is exhausted (at time T, with $s(T) = 0$), the marginal cost is $62 for the last barrel.

These three assumptions suffice to determine the parameters β, γ, and δ; the cost function (equation 1) becomes

$$(14) \qquad z[q(t), s(t)] = \frac{q(t)}{5} \left[310 - s(t) + \frac{1}{2} q(t) \right]$$

with the initial condition $s_0 = 300$. The time pattern of production implied by 14 depends on the rate of interest and the rate of price increase. For $\sigma > 0$ the pattern is usually large production in the beginning, followed first by a gradual decrease, then by a gradual increase,[45] and finally a steep decline to zero. However, if σ is close to ρ, production will start at zero and have only a single peak. If $\sigma \leq 0$, output declines more or less exponentially from its initial peak. Although for $\sigma = 0$ production goes on indefinitely—as is true of tin mining in Cornwall, known since prehistoric times—it actually becomes insignificant fairly rapidly.

It should be pointed out that the model does not allow for the drilling of development wells, an important factor in offshore fields, where the discovery well is often abandoned; this is one of several ways in which the model needs to be made more realistic.

Solutions of equation 14 for a variety of assumptions are summarized in table 3, which combines two initial prices with three rates of interest and four rates of price increase.

According to this table, the duration of production implied by equations 3 and 14 is highly sensitive to the rate of price change.[46] At an interest rate of 4 percent and an initial price of $10, a field will be in production for about six years if the price declines 3 percent a year, but for more than one hundred years if the price increases at that rate. Moreover only 10 percent of the oil in place will be recovered in the first case, as against 100 percent in the second. Both the duration of production and the cumulative output are influenced by the rate of interest and the initial price, but they are much less sensitive to those factors than to the rate

45. This would correspond to the "new lease on life" described in note 10 above. It appears that this second production peak is always lower than the first.

46. More accurately, the "expected" rate of price change. The model does not take uncertainty into account.

Table 3. *Solutions of Illustrative Oil Field Model*[a]

Rate of price increase, σ (percent)	Initial price, p_0 (dollars), and rate of interest, ρ (percent)					
	$p_0 = 10$			$p_0 = 20$		
	$\rho = 0.04$	$\rho = 0.07$	$\rho = 0.10$	$\rho = 0.04$	$\rho = 0.07$	$\rho = 0.10$
	End of production (years)					
−0.03	6.45	6.23	6.06	6.87	6.62	6.41
0.00	∞	∞	∞	∞	∞	∞
0.03	112.14	83.53	76.22	89.04	60.42	41.22
0.06	...	66.68[b]	49.02	...	55.12	37.47
	Cumulative output (millions of barrels)					
−0.03	31.20	31.47	31.69	71.37	72.00	72.51
0.00	40.00	40.00	40.00	90.00	90.00	90.00
0.03	300.00	300.00	300.00	300.00	300.00	300.00
0.06	...	300.00	300.00	...	300.00	300.00
	Initial value of oil in place (millions of dollars)					
−0.03	107.4	103.8	100.5	552.8	533.4	516.2
0.00	131.0	122.9	116.8	663.4	622.2	591.2
0.03	1,069.3	300.9	188.4	2,680.6	1,182.0	865.4
0.06	...	1,596.3	592.7	...	3,582.4	1,796.5
	Initial rate of output (millions of barrels a year)					
−0.03	11.17	12.31	13.30	24.33	27.04	29.36
0.00	7.24	9.28	10.81	16.29	20.87	24.31
0.03	0.81	5.04	7.59	3.43	12.39	17.88
0.06	...	0.00	3.75	...	1.82	10.20
	Initial royalty (dollars per barrel)					
−0.03	5.77	5.54	5.34	13.13	12.59	12.13
0.00	6.55	6.16	5.84	14.74	13.83	13.14
0.03	7.84	6.99	6.48	17.31	15.52	14.42
0.06	...	9.22	7.25	...	17.64	15.96

Source: Author's calculations; solutions are to equation 14 in appendix text.

a. Field in model has 300 million barrels of oil in place; production starts immediately unless otherwise indicated.

b. Production starts after 1.91 years.

of price change. In fact, when σ is positive, the cumulative output does not depend on ρ and p_0 at all, and for σ = 0 it depends only on p_0.[47]

For the value of the oil in place the pattern of dependence is more complicated. When σ ≤ 0 this value is little affected by variations in the rate of interest and in the rate of price change, though it depends strongly on the initial price. For positive σ, all three factors have a marked effect. At σ = 0.03 and p_0 = 10, for instance, the field is worth nearly six times as much at ρ = 0.04 as it is at ρ = 0.10.

The pattern of initial output is rather similar (though with opposite sign

47. The cumulative output for σ = 0 may be interpreted, in accordance with the earlier definition, as proved reserves. In this example, the elasticity of proved reserves with respect to the initial price is slightly above unity. Incidentally, it is puzzling that for σ < 0, cumulative output is larger at higher rates of interest.

for the rate of interest) to the one just described. In particular, at a high rate of interest with $\sigma > 0$ the initial rate of production is much higher than at a low rate of interest. The initial royalty, on the other hand, depends mostly on the initial price. (More general conclusions from this table are stated in the main text.)

The above example of a hypothetical field with 300 million barrels of oil in place can be generalized to fields of any size by multiplying the parameters β and γ in proportion to oil in place. Thus for a 600 million barrel field β and γ are simply multiplied by 2, with δ remaining unchanged. Output at any time is then also multiplied by 2, so the relative timing of production remains the same. The parameters β, γ, and δ also depend on the geological characteristics of the field, which need not be independent of scale.

Appendix B: Sensitivity Analysis of the World Energy Model

The most convenient introduction to the World Energy Model is through printouts of results, one of which forms the basis of table 4. Listed in the left-hand column are six countries or regions (the United States, Canada, Latin America, Europe, the Middle East and Africa, and Asia and the Pacific) and a total called World, which does not include the Communist countries. Under each of those seven designations, six energy commodities are listed: crude oil (including natural gas liquids), natural gas, coal, natural uranium oxide, electricity, and "fissile." This last commodity, which was not included in earlier reports,[48] stands for the fissile component (U^{235}) of natural uranium and serves to distinguish nuclear reactors using enriched uranium (light-water reactors and breeder reactors) from those using natural uranium (the Canadian heavy-water reactors). A seventh commodity, "breeder," is listed twice and refers to the liquid-metal fast breeder reactor currently used (for other than research) only in Europe.

The headings of the other columns are the quantities projected by the model for all the commodities. These are price, (primary) supply (annual

48. Houthakker and Kennedy, "Long-Range Energy Prospects," and Houthakker and Kennedy, "A Long-Run Model of World Energy Demand."

Table 4. *Projections from World Energy Model, 1985*[a]

Billions of units unless otherwise indicated

Country or region and commodity	Price per unit (1972 dollars)	Supply	Imports	Demand	Uranium enrichment	Input	Percent electricity	Cumulative production
United States								
Oil	11.75	2.889	3.237	−5.706	0.000	−0.420	7.18	39.66
Natural gas	1.77	14.727	3.156	−15.107	0.000	−2.776	8.19	238.86
Coal	13.81	0.700	−0.015	−0.154	0.000	−0.531	44.77	8.08
Uranium	30.95	0.068	0.000	−0.000	−0.068	0.000	0.00	0.61
Electricity	18.72	0.380	0.000	−3.044	−0.039	2.702	12.32	...
Fissile	36.27	0.000	0.000	−0.000	0.107	−0.107	27.53	...
Canada								
Oil	11.90	0.590	0.034	−0.615	0.000	−0.009	1.13	7.99
Natural gas	1.47	3.960	−2.421	−1.428	0.000	−0.111	2.42	42.13
Coal	16.93	0.028	0.000	−0.009	0.000	−0.018	11.48	0.29
Uranium	29.23	0.022	0.000	−0.000	−0.007	−0.015	8.42	0.20
Electricity	19.42	0.320	0.000	−0.414	−0.004	0.098	76.57	...
Fissile	35.43	0.000	−0.010	−0.000	0.010	0.000	0.00	...
Latin America								
Oil	11.40	2.218	−0.583	−1.340	0.000	−0.296	34.13	26.66
Natural gas	1.09	3.112	−0.735	−2.377	0.000	0.000	0.00	28.93
Coal	18.18	0.017	0.015	−0.016	0.000	−0.017	9.40	0.18
Uranium	30.59	0.005	0.000	−0.000	−0.001	−0.004	1.88	0.03
Electricity	20.35	0.224	0.000	−0.456	−0.001	0.233	49.00	...
Fissile	36.63	0.000	0.002	−0.000	0.002	−0.003	5.59	...
Europe								
Oil	11.25	1.503	3.302	−4.240	0.000	−0.565	14.96	10.73
Natural gas	1.32	4.832	0.000	−4.151	0.000	−0.681	3.11	61.29

Coal	21.68	0.356	0.000	−0.176	0.000	−0.180	23.49	4.52
Uranium	31.58	0.014	0.044	−0.000	−0.058	0.000	0.00	0.12
Electricity	17.17	0.417	0.000	−1.959	−0.033	1.575	20.92	...
Fissile	36.11	0.000	0.000	−0.000	0.092	−0.092	35.60	...
Breeder	...	...	...	...	...	...	1.92	...
Middle East and Africa								
Oil	10.25	10.227	−8.862	−1.143	0.000	−0.222	32.56	123.35
Natural gas	0.96	2.554	0.000	−2.040	0.000	−0.514	13.01	26.22
Coal	21.57	0.093	0.000	−0.077	0.000	−0.017	11.95	1.07
Uranium	28.58	0.036	−0.022	−0.000	−0.015	0.000	0.00	0.30
Electricity	21.24	0.089	0.000	−0.351	−0.008	0.270	24.72	...
Fissile	35.68	0.000	−0.015	−0.000	0.023	−0.008	17.76	...
Asia and Pacific								
Oil	10.75	0.841	2.871	−3.059	0.000	−0.653	28.25	9.97
Natural gas	1.25	1.431	0.000	−1.098	0.000	−0.333	2.48	13.95
Coal	26.88	0.287	0.000	−0.188	0.000	−0.099	21.08	3.07
Uranium	28.08	0.027	−0.022	−0.000	0.000	−0.005	0.98	0.18
Electricity	25.98	0.389	0.000	−1.219	0.000	0.830	31.89	...
Fissile	36.85	0.000	0.024	−0.000	0.000	−0.024	15.31	...
World								
Oil	...	18.269	...	−16.104	0.000	−2.165	15.16	218.36
Natural gas	...	30.616	...	−26.201	0.000	−4.415	5.33	411.39
Coal	...	1.482	...	−0.621	0.000	−0.861	29.74	17.22
Uranium	...	0.172	...	−0.000	−0.148	−0.024	0.74	1.45
Electricity	...	1.818	...	−7.442	−0.084	5.709	24.15	...
Fissile	...	0.001	...	−0.001	0.234	−0.234	24.36	...
Breeder	...	...	...	...	...	...	0.51	...

Source: Author's calculations.

a. OPEC tax constant at $10; see the text of appendix B for growth assumptions, definitions and units.

production), imports (with a minus sign for exports), demand (or final consumption), supply and demand related to uranium enrichment, input (that is, into electricity generation), percentage of electricity generated from each energy source, and cumulative production starting in 1972 (the base year of the model). The signs given to supply, imports, demand, enrichment, and input are such that they represent availability and add up to zero. For electricity, primary production is only from hydrothermal, geothermal, and solar energy; the quantities generated from other sources appear with a positive sign under "input," while the figures under "percent electricity" refer to primary production. Total electricity generation does not appear explicitly but is the sum of "supply" and "input" (or the sum of "demand" and "uranium enrichment," with sign reversed); there is no interregional trade in electricity.

As to dimensions, except for prices and percentages everything is in billions of units and on an annual basis unless noted below. The units themselves are barrels of oil, thousands of cubic feet of natural gas, short tons of coal, pounds of uranium oxide, thousands of kilowatt-hours of electricity, and grams of enriched uranium ("fissile"). All money figures are in 1972 U.S. dollars. Thus, for example, the first line of table 4 says that in 1985 the price of crude oil in the United States is $11.75 a barrel, annual production 2.889 billion barrels, imports 3.237 billion barrels, final consumption 5.706 billion barrels, and input into electricity 420 million barrels, accounting for 7.18 percent of all electricity generated. Cumulative production, which is not on an annual basis, is 39.66 billion barrels since 1972 (this figure is a linear approximation, since the model is not solved for each year but only for 1985 and at ten-year intervals thereafter).

The program produces additional projections of energy trade balances, total energy produced and consumed, investment requirements, and other related items. Since these numbers are not relevant to the present paper they have been omitted from table 4.

The assumptions about each run of the model are incorporated in several hundred parameters describing supply (including depletion), demand, technology, transport cost, and taxes. In the program these parameters usually assume "default values" unless they are reset, which in most cases can be done without reprogramming. As far as this paper is concerned, the most important parameters, apart from the OPEC tax already discussed in the main text, are those referring to supply and demand and those specifying GNP and population growth. As to growth, the assumptions maintained throughout this paper are as follows: [49]

Country or region	Growth rate (percent a year)	
	GNP per capita	Population
United States	1.5	1.0
Canada	1.5	1.5
Latin America	2.5	3.0
Europe	1.5	0.5
Middle East and Africa	3.0	3.5
Asia and Pacific	2.5	2.5

Perhaps the most controversial parameters in the model are those describing the influence of prices on supply and demand. Instead of arguing the empirical merits of the "default" values of these parameters in the model,[50] it may be more useful to see what happens to the solution when they are modified. The results of this sensitivity analysis are reported in table 5.

It should be explained first that in the World Energy Model supply and demand are not treated symmetrically. In the case of oil, gas, and uranium the treatment of supply is based on an explicit distinction between the short run and the long run and also differs to some extent by region. In the Middle East and Africa, a region that effectively sets the world price, the short-run oil supply elasticity is very large and the long-run supply function serves only to determine extraction costs from the remaining oil in place. In the other regions (and for gas in all regions), the short-run supply elasticity is less than the long-run elasticity. In all these cases the supply functions are linear in price, so the elasticities are not constant.[51] For the sensitivity analysis the slopes of these linear functions for oil and gas were reduced or increased by substantial amounts.[52] The other supply functions were left the same.

49. These growth rates are somewhat lower than the "base case" in Houthakker and Kennedy, "Long-Range Energy Prospects," where a brief discussion of the effect of changes in growth can be found.

50. These are the same as in ibid., p. 6.

51. For coal and hydroelectricity, constant-elasticity supply functions are used; the treatment of uranium resembles that of gas.

52. In terms of figure 2 in Houthakker and Kennedy, "A Long-Run Model of World Energy Demand," the magnitude of future resources at a given price (R_1) was either reduced or increased by 20 percent, leaving the initial reserves R_0 the same. The effect of this change on the slope depends on cumulative production.

Table 5. Sensitivity of Oil Projections from the World Energy Model to Variations in Supply and Demand Elasticities

Item	Year	Elasticity[a]						
		Low demand, low supply	Low demand, base supply	Base demand, low supply	Base demand, base supply	Base demand, high supply	High demand, base supply	High demand, high supply
		Scenario A[b]						
Price of crude (1972 dollars per barrel)[c]	1985	10.26	10.25	10.25	10.25	10.25	10.25	10.25
	1995	10.82	10.48	10.57	10.28	10.27	10.28	10.27
	2005	14.26	13.15	14.07	13.00	12.31	12.88	12.22
World output (billions of barrels a year)[d]	1985	19.0	19.0	18.3	18.3	18.3	17.6	17.5
	1995	24.9	24.9	24.5	24.5	24.5	24.0	23.9
	2005	32.8	33.1	31.6	32.2	32.6	31.3	31.8
Exports, Middle East and Africa (billions of barrels a year)	1985	10.4	9.6	9.6	8.9	8.1	8.1	7.3
	1995	15.4	14.4	15.0	14.0	12.8	13.4	12.1
	2005	21.2	20.9	20.0	19.9	19.5	18.9	18.6
		Scenario B[e]						
Price of crude (1972 dollars per barrel)[c]	1985	10.26	10.25	10.25	10.25	10.25	10.25	10.25
	1995	15.81	15.46	15.55	15.26	15.26	15.26	15.26
	2005	22.93	21.89	22.46	21.51	20.96	21.21	20.77
World output (billions of barrels a year)[d]	1985	19.0	19.0	18.3	18.3	18.3	17.6	17.5
	1995	23.7	23.8	22.3	22.3	22.3	21.0	21.1
	2005	30.4	30.7	27.4	27.7	28.1	25.4	25.6
Exports, Middle East and Africa (billions of barrels a year)	1985	10.4	9.6	9.6	8.9	8.1	8.1	7.3
	1995	10.9	9.1	9.6	7.8	6.0	6.4	4.9
	2005	12.4	10.3	9.9	7.8	6.1	6.1	3.9

Source: Author's caculations.
a. Low, −0.225; base, −0.45; high, −0.9.
b. OPEC tax constant at $10 per barrel (1972 dollars).
c. F.o.b. Persian Gulf.
d. Excludes Communist countries.
e. OPEC tax rising by $5 per barrel per decade (1972 dollars).

The demand functions[53] in the model are all assumed to be long term, since the ten-year interval between solution years was considered long enough for short-run effects to vanish. These functions are all of the constant-elasticity type with respect to the own price and to certain other prices. In the sensitivity analysis all these elasticities were reduced or increased by 50 percent. Thus the own-price long-run elasticity of oil demand was -0.225 in the "low" case and -0.675 in the "high" case.

Table 5 gives the price of oil (f.o.b. Persian Gulf), world oil output (excluding Communist countries), and oil exports from the Middle East and Africa for seven combinations of supply and demand parameters and for the two scenarios for oil production shown in table 2. The default parameters used in the main text are labeled "base."

For scenario A (a constant $10 OPEC tax) the sensitivity analysis shows that the projections in table 2 are not much affected by changes in the supply and demand parameters. The largest discrepancies, as one would expect, are between the low demand, low supply column and the high demand, high supply column, particularly for price and exports in 2005, but even these are not worrisome.

More significant sensitivities are found in scenario B, especially in oil exports from the Middle East and Africa. For the year 2005, for instance, exports range from 3.9 billion barrels when supply and demand responses are both high to 12.4 billion barrels when both responses are low; somewhat narrower ranges occur in 1985 and 1995 exports. The low exports at high elasticities, needless to say, only reinforce the conclusions in the main text that OPEC is not likely to raise its tax in real terms.[54] The high exports at low elasticities are a more serious matter. Comparing the low demand, low supply columns of the two scenarios, one sees that OPEC tax revenues in 1995 are $154 billion for scenario A and $164 billion for scenario B; for 2005 these figures are $212 billion and $248 billion. This

53. These functions apply only to final demand. The intermediate demand for electricity generation is determined by the existing inventory of generating equipment (assumed to be incapable of being switched from one fuel to another, but subject to depreciation) and by the fuel selected for new electric capacity to minimize total cost (including capital cost, which varies by fuel). At present and foreseeable prices, oil turns out to be too expensive to be chosen for new electricity generation, and the price elasticity of intermediate oil demand is consequently zero.

54. For the sake of curiosity it may be mentioned that in this case there are no exports from the Middle East and Africa to the United States; U.S. imports are small and covered entirely by Canada and Latin America. As a result, the Persian Gulf price is no longer the basis for other regional prices, as it is elsewhere in table 5.

is the only one of the seven combinations in which scenario B would yield more revenue than scenario A. Since this combination reflects rather extreme assumptions, it should perhaps not be given much weight, but in the absence of firm empirical estimates it cannot be ruled out entirely.

Comments by Geoffrey W. Maynard

HENDRIK HOUTHAKKER devotes little analysis to the macroeconomic impact of North Sea oil on the U.K. economy, probably because he does not believe that it will be a major one. Some people in the United Kingdom are less sanguine about the impact (there seems to be no shortage of people in Britain who, having seen the silver lining, feel compelled to look for the cloud), so that it may be appropriate for me to expand on this aspect of the problem if only to provide a basis for further discussion. In particular, it should be asked whether the United Kingdom is likely to go down with the dreaded "Dutch disease"—if such a disease exists (which Houthakker understandably seems to doubt).

The North Sea oil resources have three principal economic characteristics.

1. They provide what is really a gratuitous increment of real income to the United Kingdom, which by 1985 will amount to about £ 8.5 billion a year in 1977 prices (£ 13 billion in current prices),[55] say 5 percent of 1978 real GDP.

2. This income is received initially as a "traded" (as distinct from "nontraded") good and is in immediate foreign exchange form; by 1985 there will be an equivalent favorable impact on the balance of payments.

3. A large part of the increment of income (eventually as much as 70 percent) accrues initially to the government in the form of royalties and taxes (by 1985 this revenue could amount to about £ 6 billion a year in 1977 prices, say £ 9 billion in current prices).

In principle, this increment of real income can be absorbed by the U.K. economy in three different ways: first, in increased domestic absorption (consumption and investment, both government and private); second, in

---

55. U.K. gross domestic product increases by somewhat more than this, but part of the increase has to be remitted abroad in interest and dividends. Since these comments were prepared, oil prices have risen substantially, so that all the estimates included here are on the low side.

the acquisition of *net* foreign assets; and third, by the displacement of domestic nonoil production (that is, domestically produced real income). Nonoil imports rise to offset a fall in the net oil imports in the first and third cases but not necessarily in the second case. Some people fear, however, that the increment of real income will be largely consumed and not invested—hence "wasted." It is also feared that domestic production will be displaced in the short run (leading to more unemployment) and manufacturing capacity will go down in the long run, owing to a real appreciation of the exchange rate, caused by the favorable impact of oil on the United Kingdom's balance of payments. Although these undesirable effects can be avoided if the increment of real income is used to acquire assets abroad, such action would imply that North Sea oil was being used to build up productive capacity, and therefore employment opportunities, overseas rather than in the United Kingdom.

The following table, in which the sum of domestic expenditure and exports equals the sum of domestic production and imports, all in real terms, indicates possible ways of absorption (assuming an increment of oil output of 100):

	Case				
	1	*2*	*2a*	*3*	*4*
Domestic expenditure	0	0	0	100	300
Exports (nonoil)	0	0	−50	0	0
Domestic production					
Nonoil	0	−100	−100	0	200
Oil	100	100	100	100	100
Imports					
Nonoil	0	100	50	100	100
Oil (net)	−100	−100	−100	−100	−100
Balance of trade					
(exports less imports)	100	0	0	0	0

It is obvious, of course, that the more domestic expenditure is allowed to rise, the less likely it is that North Sea oil output will have a favorable impact on the balance of trade and therefore the less likely that the real exchange rate will appreciate and contribute to a displacement of domestic production in favor of imports. In case 4 domestic expenditure and domestic production both rise, the latter by a multiple (determined by the marginal ratio of imports to domestic expenditure) of the increase in nonoil imports made possible by a decline in oil imports, leaving the trade balance unchanged. In case 3 domestic expenditure rises just enough to absorb the rise in nonoil imports, leaving domestic production and the balance of trade unchanged. Unless by chance or by design the marginal import propensity of an increase in domestic expenditure were just equal to unity, case 3 would probably involve some appreciation of the exchange rate. In the other three cases, in which domestic expenditure does not increase, an appreciation of the exchange rate and a fall in domestic production can be avoided only if the increment of oil income is used to acquire net overseas assets (case 1). If that use is not permitted (cases 2 and 2a), exchange rate appreciation displaces domestic production (either import substitutes or nonoil exports), and the Dutch disease occurs.

Thus the manner in which North Sea oil can be taken advantage of depends on the nature of the constraints operating on U.K. domestic expenditure and output at the time when oil production becomes significant, and also on potential rates of return on investment at home and overseas. It is hard to envisage a significant constraint on domestic *expenditure,* for even if investment at home is considered unattractive, there can be no difficulty in expanding consumption. In practice, therefore, the constraints on domestic *production* and the relative rates of return on investment are the subjects of concern.

If, as at least one influential school of thought seems to believe, U.K. domestic production is constrained solely by a deficiency of aggregate demand imposed by the government largely because of a *pre-oil* balance-of-payments constraint, then the policy response seems clear: domestic expenditure and domestic production can be expanded to absorb the net saving in oil imports. If this were the situation, then, given a marginal ratio of imports to final expenditure of about 0.25, an oil-induced improvement in the balance of payments of £8.5 billion could enable final expenditure on goods and services to be increased by around £34 billion (all in 1977 prices). Other things equal, nonoil domestic production could be higher by about £25.5 billion, that is, about 15 percent of 1979 GDP. This would be a welcome and significant increase even if only fully attained at the end of five years. Nevertheless, without further change in the economy, it would probably not be large enough to bring about a return to full employment. But the absorption of the oil-induced improvement in the balance of payments through an expansion of domestic demand would remove the danger of an appreciation of real exchange rates and of the U.K. economy being affected by the Dutch disease. Moreover, because domestic resources that would otherwise remain unemployed could then be brought into production, the *social* return on investment at home would probably exceed the *social* return on investment overseas. The major problem would be to ensure that at least some of the domestic absorption took the form of investment (capital formation) rather than consumption.

Such a favorable outcome is possible because it was assumed that U.K. output is initially constrained by, and only by, the balance of payments. But the failure of U.K. domestic production in recent years to respond significantly to increasing aggregate monetary demand for goods and services without accelerating inflation—in particular, its failure to respond adequately to the rapid, though short-lived, rise in consumer real income and purchasing power in 1978—does not suggest that U.K. domestic production has been held back solely, or even mainly, by a deficiency of demand imposed by a balance-of-payments constraint. If, as other schools of thought contend, U.K. domestic production is now being held back by indigenous supply constraints—for example, poor industrial relations, a level of real wages too high for entrepreneurs to combine profitably available labor with existing capital equipment, and a rate of profit on capital too low to induce necessary investment[56]—then the opportunity to expand domestic absorption is restricted. (Cases 1–3 of the preceding table are relevant.) But even if domestic production were rigidly constrained by the factors listed above (which seems unlikely), *in theory,* domestic expenditure could be expanded just enough to absorb the improvement in the current balance of payments made possible by domestic oil production, without an appreciation of the real exchange rate being necessary. *In practice,* the less readily domestic output can respond to an expansion of domestic demand, the more likely that the U.K. authorities will have to choose between some appreciation of the exchange rate and some net investment overseas. The retardation of oil depletion is also a possibility, but for the reasons given by Houthakker probably not a sensible course of action to pursue, since the real return on investment overseas could well exceed the return on keeping oil in the ground. Indeed, insofar as the balance of payments imposes any constraint at all on the expansion of domestic output, the argument can be made that oil today is worth more than oil tomorrow.

The case for significant real exchange rate appreciation is not an easy one to make. Exchange rate appreciation at the present time would un-

56. See G. W. Maynard "Keynes and Unemployment Today," *Three Banks Review,* no. 120 (December 1978), pp. 3–20.

doubtedly contribute to slowing down inflation. But without a substantial increase in real domestic expenditure, which, as indicated earlier, the threat of inflation and other domestic constraints may prevent, exchange rate appreciation would lead to further unemployment and to a decline in profitability of investment in manufacturing industry, at least in the short run. Thus if domestic expenditure can be increased only moderately because of domestic supply constraints or the fear of exacerbating inflation or both, investment overseas should perhaps be encouraged. The return on such investment, which would be in foreign exchange form, would make a welcome contribution to Britain's balance of payments when North Sea oil runs dry.

Nevertheless, the fact that North Sea oil is likely to keep the real exchange rate stronger than it would otherwise be is not necessarily to the disadvantage of the U.K. economy. Although U.K. manufacturing industry is clearly suffering from a severe decline relative to that of other countries, its long-run prospects are not apt to benefit from a deliberate policy (however achieved) aimed at keeping the real exchange rate low. In fact, without a significant rise in productivity, any attempt to bring about a real depreciation could be achieved only if the U.K. labor force agreed to accept declining real wages—which clearly it is not prepared to do. Improved competitiveness at stable or rising real wages can be achieved in the long run only by measures, such as changes in work habits, that will raise productivity or by measures that will increase U.K. nonprice competitiveness. Neither of these results would be much favored by a policy that aimed at keeping real exchange rates and real wages low (or, it might be said, by a policy that protected British manufacturing industry from foreign competition). North Sea oil may or may not lead to an improvement in the U.K. industrial prospects; it seems more likely to do so if government is able to run the economy at a higher level of demand and a higher real exchange rate, with balance-of-payments equilibrium, than would otherwise be the case.

Although the direct and indirect contribution of North Sea oil to U.K. GDP is likely to be only a moderate one, it could make a substantial contribution to an expansion of U.K. industrial capacity if a significant part is devoted to investment.[57] How then to ensure that this is brought about?

57. Gross domestic fixed capital formation in U.K. manufacturing industry in 1978 amounted to £6 billion, as against projected oil income in 1985 of over £8 billion.

Since most North Sea oil revenue accrues initially to the public sector, government policy is crucial. What are the alternatives open to government? In principle, government can (1) increase public expenditure on public consumption or investment, or (2) reduce taxes or increase subsidies generally or for particular purposes, or (3) reduce public sector borrowing. It can also abolish or relax foreign exchange control to encourage investment overseas.

Clearly, increased public expenditure on social consumption and general tax cuts would be apt to favor consumption rather than investment, at least in the short run. Government expenditure aimed at real investment could be undertaken directly, for example, through the nationalized industries or through institutions like the National Enterprise Board. Subsidies could be used to channel private sector expenditure into desirable enterprises, such as energy conservation projects or installations. Reduced government borrowing would tend to lower interest rates, which could favor investment, though personal consumption would also tend to rise. However, making funds available to the private sector will not necessarily induce more investment if the return on investment is low.

The state of the economy will largely dictate the amounts and the manner in which North Sea oil income can be channeled back into the economy. Because U.K. manufacturing output is now being held back, at least to some extent, by supply constraints while inflation remains high, it might seem that a reduction in government borrowing and some relaxation of exchange control on investment overseas should have immediate priority. But some tax cuts are also essential if only to moderate real wage demands in British industry. As domestic supply constraints are relaxed, general measures to stimulate domestic demand become possible. As for direct expenditure, the government should perhaps confine itself to financing or participating in large-scale projects—in the energy field, for example—that the private sector could not easily handle by itself. Investment in the manufacturing sector should probably be left to the private sector, since the government can have no particular expertise in identifying those industries that are likely to be economically viable when North Sea oil runs out.

In sum, North Sea oil resources are not large enough to have more than a moderate impact on the nonoil sector of the British economy, although they could make a quantitatively significant contribution to investment in British industry and therefore to long-run performance. At present, domestic supply constraints in U.K. industry prevent domestic expenditure from being expanded quickly enough or fully enough to absorb North Sea oil real income without a rise in the real exchange rate. But the rise is not necessarily a disadvantage for the long-run prospects of U.K. industry, and in any case the strength of the exchange rate can be held in check by relaxing foreign exchange control.[58]

Comments by Michael V. Posner

HOUTHAKKER is concerned with the decisions about depletion in the North Sea. It is conventional wisdom, arising historically in the literature from an article by Harold Hotelling,[59] and rediscovered in imperfect form by various other writers over the last few decades, that this type of depletion depends on the expectation of the increase in price of the natural resource and the rate of interest. In its naive formulation the doctrine asserts that at any given time there is an expected future price of the natural resource by, say, the end of the decade. This expected future price *level* implies a rate of *increase* in the price of the resource from today on. If this expected price increase is above the rate of interest, then today's production will fall, today's spot price will rise, and therefore the expected rate of increase in that spot price will fall. By this means, the expected future price and today's output levels interact so as to determine today's output and price levels.

Two qualifications need to be made to this analysis. First, it is not the "price" of the resource that is important but the excess of price over costs —the rent. This qualification is well understood in most of the modern literature, although it was omitted in my own early formulation of the point.[60]

Second, the level of costs at any given time is not independent of the rate of production—short-term increasing costs are characteristic of most mines and wells. Houthakker wishes to stress this qualification, which he suggests is destructive of most of the simpleminded modern inferences

58. Since these comments were prepared, foreign exchange control in the United Kingdom has been abolished.

59. "Economics of Renewable Resources."

60. M. V. Posner, "The Rate of Depletion of Gas Fields," *Economic Journal*, vol. 82, supplement (March 1972), pp. 429–41.

from Hotelling's work. If the rate of interest is 10 percent and the expected price increase of oil is 5 percent, it still may be irrational for the Saudi Arabians to increase output substantially at the present time, because they will run into increasing costs. If nature is allowed to take its course, in the way intended by both Almighty Providence and the reservoir engineers who installed the original well equipment, then in a decade the costs of extraction of today's marginal barrel may be only two or three dollars. But if the Saudis rushed to produce that barrel today, they would need extra equipment, and its costs might be very much higher.

I think this second qualification is better recognized than Houthakker suggests—for instance, I did not ignore it in my own informal article cited above, and it is a commonplace in the oral tradition among energy experts. But I think Houthakker is to be congratulated for making the point explicit, because it destroys some of the more naive predictions about OPEC behavior in the coming months.

Houthakker then engages in his own piece of futurology and joins those who expect the oil price to remain roughly constant until the end of the century, with, as an upper bound, the possibility that it might double in that period. Here he is at the lower end of the spectrum of possibilities normally considered by European economists. Establishment doctrine in the United Kingdom has regarded the doubling of the price of oil by the end of the century (from the levels ruling in the early winter of 1978–79) as a near certainty, and I myself have gone on record as expecting a three-fold or fourfold increase. This of course does not mean that Houthakker is wrong, nor that his view merits less weight than those of others. But at the very least, I think it necessary when one is making policy recommendations to consider the full range of received opinion, and I would wish to see Houthakker expand his analysis in that way.

Houthakker goes on to make his own estimate of the likely time pattern of production from the North Sea province, disdaining the official expectations, very current in the United Kingdom, that peak production of about 125 million metric tons a year will continue only for seven or eight years and that the 1990s will see a rapid decline. On this point Houthakker may well be right; he is certainly right in suggesting that other oil and gas provinces have not seen such a decline. However, U.K. experience with the southern basis gas has been the reverse of what he would suggest— if anything the projections are now lower than they were twelve years ago. The fact that a lot of North Sea exploration has been preceded by very full seismological investigations, unlike true "wildcatting," also tells against him. Nevertheless, Houthakker's question is fair and does have some important policy implications—for many economists it is the expected early demise of the North Sea bonanza, or at least the slowing down of the rate of increase in oil revenues, that carries a threat for the future.

Of course Houthakker is right in pouring scorn on the naive "shortage" school of natural resource experts. There will go on being a lot of oil available well into the middle of the next century, all over the world, but it will probably be rather expensive to get—from difficult terrain and at great depths. Sensible economists prefer to interpret this as a "rise in the price of energy" rather than as an absolute shortage of oil or anything else, and here everyone would agree heartily with Houthakker's way of putting things.

Taking all these factual assumptions, Houthakker then applies his improved Hotelling arithmetic and comes to the conclusion that there is no overriding reason for government interference with the rate of depletion from the British part of the North Sea. It might possibly be profitable, but this is the sort of decision better left to the free play of the market and to the oil companies.

That is Houthakker's major conclusion of a positive sort, and on the whole I agree with it, although my arithmetic and assumptions would be different. Successive British governments have, I think, also come to this conclusion, although, with the caution for which British governments are famed, they have preferred, and rightly so, to keep in place an apparatus of potential control. One reason for this control (which was suggested to me by George Soros) was that the discount rate used by the oil companies would be systematically greater than that of a rational public authority.

Houthakker is not very satisfied with the way the British have handled the North Sea; he seems to prefer a system of licensed auctioning like that used in parts of the federal territory in the United States. I am fairly sure that such an approach is wrong; I believe that the British system of the petroleum revenue tax, not dissimilar to the Norwegian system, will turn out to be a useful way of extracting rent from the companies. It is not, I believe, an optimal tax, for all sorts of reasons, but it works reasonably well and has been accepted by the companies.[61] My own taste

61. The United Kingdom has a very different way of extracting rent for natural gas, as explained in M. V. Posner, *Fuel Policy: A Study in Applied Economics* (London: Macmillan, 1973).

for competition in the energy market is as great as Houthakker's, but because I share to a certain extent the skepticism of the U.S. Congress about the degree to which the oil companies are truly competitive, I have no objection to some sort of state participation in the North Sea, either through the British Gas Corporation, or the British National Oil Corporation, or in the various ways managed by the Norwegian authorities.

Apart from these specific conclusions, Houthakker rebuts the proposition that North Sea oil matters very much. He is, I believe, quite right in calculating the potential effect on the GDP—about a 3 to 5 percent contribution to GDP throughout the whole of the 1980s is the right figure to have in mind. But he seems not to consider that the main impact of this improvement will be on the balance of payments and on government tax revenue. A contribution of 5 percent of the GDP to the balance-of-payments surplus is a rather large sum, and even for Britain's swollen Treasury budget the impact is far from negligible. It is precisely for these reasons that so many British economists have written so much about possible ways to spend the "betterment" from the North Sea, and, even more important, about the way to make sure that the North Sea represents a net addition to U.K. resources. These matters are discussed by Geoffrey Maynard in his comments, on which I offer two observations.

First, I believe Maynard's analysis would be substantially accepted by all schools of economists now writing on this topic in the United Kingdom. It is very much like the more informal treatment that I offered in my recent paper to the Manchester Statistical Society,[62] and many other writers have contributed similarly.

Second, although the analysis may be generally acceptable, some of the factual assumptions and policy conclusions are open to question. Maynard draws attention to the difference of opinion about the capacity of the home economy to increase output—obviously differences on this matter of fact lead to very different recommendations. I myself would stress another issue, relating to government policy. Is it possible for Britain to refuse to absorb the extra 3 or 5 percent of GDP? Surely not, says Maynard. But this can happen, I believe, if the real exchange rate (and therefore the real efficiency wage cost of potential British output) is forced up by the contribution of North Sea oil to the balance of payments. That possibility, combined with and reinforced by an unduly restrictive monetary policy at home (in particular a policy that refuses to finance the

62. "Using North Sea Oil and Gas," paper delivered to the Manchester Statistical Society, March 13, 1979 (Manchester: MSS, forthcoming).

extra 5 percent of transactions) might mean that North Sea revenues merely displace the revenues from other types of economic activity and produce the outcome known as the Dutch disease: hydrocarbon revenue up, home absorption constant, home output of nonoil sectors down. That this sad outcome is possible cannot to my mind be denied, and it must be an aim of policy to avoid it.

Conference Participants

with their affiliations at the time of the conference

Anthony B. Atkinson *University College*

Frank T. Blackaby *National Institute of Economic and Social Research*

Marshall E. Blume *University of Pennsylvania*

Richard A. Brealey *London Graduate School of Business Studies*

Sir Henry Phelps Brown *London School of Economics (Emeritus)*

Alan Budd *London Graduate School of Business Studies*

Ian Byatt *H.M. Treasury*

Sir Alec Cairncross *Oxford University (Emeritus)*

Richard E. Caves *Harvard University*

Rudiger Dornbusch *Massachusetts Institute of Technology*

Stanley Fischer *Massachusetts Institute of Technology*

John S. Flemming *Oxford University*

Hon. Wynne A. H. Godley *Cambridge University*

Hendrik S. Houthakker *Harvard University*

Mervyn A. King *University of Birmingham*

Lawrence B. Krause *Brookings Institution*

David Lea *Trades Union Congress*

Robert G. Livingston *German Marshall Fund of the United States*

Sir Donald MacDougall *Confederation of British Industry*

Bruce K. MacLaury *Brookings Institution*

Christopher W. MacMahon *Bank of England*

R. C. O. Matthews *Cambridge University*

Geoffrey W. Maynard *Chase Manhattan Bank*

Joseph A. Pechman *Brookings Institution*

Michael V. Posner *Social Science Research Council*

S. J. Prais *National Institute of Economic and Social Research*

Derek Robinson *Oxford University*

Lord Roll *S. G. Warburg and Co. Limited*

David C. Smith *Queen's University*

George Soros *Soros Fund Management, Inc.*

David Walker *Bank of England*

G. D. N. Worswick *National Institute of Economic and Social Research*

Index